The Problem of Jobs

*Liberalism, Race, and
Deindustrialization in Philadelphia*

GUIAN A. MCKEE

THE UNIVERSITY OF CHICAGO PRESS   CHICAGO AND LONDON

GUIAN MCKEE is associate professor at the Miller Center of Public Affairs at the University of Virginia.

The University of Chicago Press, Chicago 60637
The University of Chicago Press, Ltd., London
© 2008 by The University of Chicago
All rights reserved. Published 2008
Printed in the United States of America
17 16 15 14 13 12 11 10 09 08   1 2 3 4 5

ISBN-13: 978-0-226-56012-0 (cloth)
ISBN-10: 0-226-56012-0 (cloth)

Portions of chapters 1 and 2 were previously published as Guian McKee, "Urban Deindustrialization and Local Public Policy: Industrial Renewal in Philadelphia, 1953–1976," *Journal of Policy History* 16:1 (2004), and is reproduced by permission of the Pennsylvania State Universiy Press.

Library of Congress Cataloging-in-Publication Data
McKee, Guian A.
    The problem of jobs : liberalism, race, and deindustrialization in Philadelphia / Guian A. McKee.
       p.   cm.
Includes bibliographical references and index.
    ISBN-13: 978-0-226-56012-0 (cloth : alk. paper)
    ISBN-10: 0-226-56012-0 (cloth : alk. paper)   1. Manpower policy—Pennsylvania—Philadelphia—History—20th century.   2. Job creation—Pennsylvania—Philadelphia—History—20th century.   3. Philadelphia (pa.)—Politics and government—1865-   I. Title.
    HD5726.P5M35   2008
    331.109748′11—dc22

                                                                2008015837

⊗ The paper used in this publication meets the minimum requirements of the American National Standard for Information Sciences—Permanence of Paper for Printed Library Materials, ANSI Z39.48-1992.

Contents

Acknowledgments

U pon publication, this project will have been part of my life for more than a decade, and I owe a great deal to the many friends, colleagues, and family members who have helped me to reach this point. My greatest intellectual debt is to my advisor and good friend, Robin Einhorn of the University of California, Berkeley. Robin enthusiastically encouraged my early interest in the historical study of urban political economy, and her incisive perspective has been the primary influence on my approach to history. Robin's passion and commitment to the rigorous study of American history has been a continual source of inspiration. Her readings of drafts of the project offered challenging observations and suggestions that pushed me toward new insights. Above all, her friendship, advice, and steady belief in this project have been among my most important sources of support.

Other friends and mentors at Berkeley provided crucial aid and assistance, academic and otherwise. I am indebted to Margaret Anderson, Jan de Vries, David Hollinger, and especially to Margaret Weir and Mary Ryan, all of whom offered intellectual guidance and consistent generosity. A special thanks to the late James Kettner; I am one of many who benefited greatly from his generosity and kindness. Mable Lee made the infamous UC bureaucracy painless to navigate, and the friendship of Healan Gaston, Andy Jewett, Gina Ottoboni, Charles Postel, Louise Nelson Dyble, Phil Soffer, Paul Sabin, Jennifer Gold, Gabrielle Tenaglia, and Mary Ann Sung all helped shape my years in Berkeley as well. Jason Scott Smith read multiple chapters and provided incisive advice as well as consistent encouragement and optimism.

Few historians thank high school teachers upon publication of their books, but I owe a great deal to Victor Brutout and William Baker for the manner in which they introduced me to the critical, engaged study of history. Marjorie Murphy and Robert Weinberg of Swarthmore College provided my introduction to historical research and writing; I could not have asked for better undergraduate mentors. In Chapel Hill, Peter Coclanis and Alison Isenberg generously made the resources of the University of North Carolina and its History Department available to me. I am grateful also for the friendship of Bruce Baker and James Hemingway as we worked and conversed in a coffee shop on Franklin Street, and for my "biology" friends Cindy Hogan, Amy Skypala, Will Mackin, Amy Mackin, Jeremy Hyman, Barbara Ballentine, Brendan Boyle, Jordan Price, and Liz Weaver. And a special thanks to my Swat-XC compatriots, who provided regular reminders of the value of friendship and of activities beyond academia.

For the last six years, my professional home has been the University of Virginia's Miller Center of Public Affairs, where I have benefited from the friendship of colleagues Marc Selverstone, David Shreve, Taylor Fain, Erin Mahan, Ken Hughes, Patricia Dunn, Paul Martin, Russell Riley, Stephen Knott, James Sterling Young, William Miller, Ashley High, Ethan Sribnick, Karl Bon Tempo, and Derek Hoff. Particular thanks to David Coleman and Timothy Naftali, whose administrative leadership allowed me to preserve the space needed for this project, and to Kent Germany, from whom I learned much about the civil rights movement, the War on Poverty, and Lyndon Johnson. Brian Balogh and Sidney Milkis's colloquia series for the Miller Center's Governing America in a Global Era program provided a crucial source of intellectual growth and challenge. I would also like to thank Governor Gerald Baliles and Mike Mullen at the Miller Center for providing crucial backing and leadership that has enhanced the environment for intellectual productivity and creativity at the center.

This project has also benefited from the generosity of Gareth Davies, Tom Jackson, Mark Rose, Thomas Sugrue, Walter Licht, Kevin Kruse, John Bauman, and Leonard Moore, all of whom commented on sections of the book or conference papers. Lisa Levenstein and Wendell Pritchett read the entire manuscript and offered valuable commentary and advice at critical moments during the revision process. At the Philadelphia City Archives, Ward Childs and Jefferson Moak expertly guided me through the archives' incredible holdings on the political and policy history of Philadelphia. At the Temple University Urban Archives, Margaret Jerrido, Brenda Galloway-Wright, John Pettit, and George Brightbill all provided invaluable research assistance and created a wonderful environment in which to work. A special thanks to Brenda and John for their tireless help and inexhaustible patience as I chose photographs for the book from afar. Both of these institutions are of unmatched historical value for the city of Philadelphia, both for their holdings and for the expertise of the people who work there.

I have been fortunate to find a truly wonderful publisher in the University of Chicago Press. My editor Robert Devens brought this project to the press and throughout the process has been a consistent source of advice, encouragement, and insight. Emilie Sandoz provided crucial help as I finalized the manuscript, and Mara Naselli wonderfully sharpened my prose. I owe a tremendous debt to Alice O'Connor and Jefferson Cowie for their insightful reviews of multiple drafts of the manuscript for the press. As editor for the Historical Studies of Urban America series, Becky Nicolaides offered a close reading of a late draft that pushed me to reconsider key aspects of the manuscript at a time when I might otherwise have been willing to bring the project to a close. Her efforts have produced a far stronger book. All remaining faults, of course, remain mine alone.

Finally, my family has offered consistent support, perspective, and an unwavering belief that this book would someday be finished. Thanks and much love to my mother, Linda Jones McKee, and Richard Carey; to my father, Michael McKee, and Carmen McKee. My parents sparked my early interest in history with numerous visits to Civil War battlefields and other historic sites; their commitment and love gave me the opportunity to pursue this passion. Thanks also to my brother Colin McKee and Lucinda Fleurant (and Mason and Ben), and to my grandparents, Betty and Edward McKee and, especially, Adalyn and Edmund Jones, who provided a place to stay and good company during my many research trips to Philadelphia.

My wife, Joanna Vondrasek, may be the only person who is more relieved than I am to see this book completed, as she has lived with it and its effects on our lives while also pursuing her own teaching and research. The years in which I worked to complete this book coincided with the births of our sons, Reece and Nathaniel, and it will always remind me of their arrival and of all that they have added to their parents' lives. Joanna has little use for sentimentality, and in any case there are no words that I can offer to match the value of the love that she has given me. Nonetheless, this book is dedicated to her, to Reece, and to Nathaniel, for so many reasons.

Liberals, Race, and Jobs in Postwar Philadelphia

On a sunny morning in early April 1960, the candy manufacturer Stephen F. Whitman and Son held a groundbreaking ceremony for a new chocolate factory. Only a few months before, the 118-year-old company had been on the verge of moving production of its familiar chocolate sampler boxes from an existing plant in Center City Philadelphia to a suburban location in New Jersey. Whitman and Son had decided instead to remain in the city after the Philadelphia Industrial Development Corporation (PIDC), the city's two-year old quasi-public industrial development authority, organized a transaction that helped the company build a new 400,000-square-foot facility in Philadelphia's Far Northeast section. Although new tract homes, shopping centers, and factories had been developed in the area since World War II, the Far Northeast in 1960 still retained areas of low woods and farms interspersed along the mostly flat plain northwest of the Delaware River. The new Whitman and Son factory was the first plant in what PIDC officials hoped would become a large, planned industrial park on 800 acres of open, city-owned land that surrounded the Northeast Philadelphia Airport. Whitman and Son exemplified the kind of specialty manufacturer that had long formed the core of Philadelphia's industrial base, and the retention of such companies in new city industrial parks was one of PIDC's central goals. At the groundbreaking, city commerce director Frederic R. Mann explained that

FIGURE 1. Stephen F. Whitman and Son Chocolate factory at 4th and Race streets in central Philadelphia, July 5, 1950. The building's multistory design was typical of many older, inner city factories. Traffic is backed up approaching the Benjamin Franklin Bridge over the Delaware River. After Whitman and Son moved to a new building in PIDC's Philadelphia Industrial Park in 1960, PIDC helped the Pincus Brothers–Maxwell apparel firm relocate to this factory. Photo courtesy of Temple University Libraries, Urban Archives, Philadelphia, Pennsylvania.

the Whitman plant was "the beginning of a tremendous development of clean garden-type plants in an area where new homes are being built."[1]

As Mann suggested, the new Whitman factory would rise in a section of Philadelphia that had more in common with nearby suburbs than with much of the inner-city. PIDC, however, was also involved with industrial projects in older, central areas of Philadelphia. Five months to the day after the Whitman groundbreaking, a similar group of local notables attended a second ceremony, this time for the West Wholesale Drug Company. This firm, with PIDC help, planned to build its new facility in a smaller, inner-city industrial park on the site of an abandoned public hospital in the Feltonville area of North Philadelphia. This densely developed urban neighborhood—a motley mix of modern industrial areas and older factories, railroad lines, and brick row houses—had been an

FIGURE 2. West Wholesale Drug Company's new facility in PIDC's Front Street–Luzerne Avenue Industrial District in North Philadelphia, August 8, 1961. This small, inner city industrial park offered modern, one-story facilities typical of postwar suburban development. Photo courtesy of Temple University Libraries, Urban Archives, Philadelphia, Pennsylvania.

important manufacturing center in Philadelphia since the early twentieth century. Although the largely white Feltonville area had not yet experienced racial turnover, it lay barely a mile from the edge of the expanding African American neighborhoods of North Philadelphia. PIDC's success in attracting investment capital to this area—and in building new factories and warehouses there—reflected its extraordinary commitment to solving the economic problems of Philadelphia's aging inner-city neighborhoods.

The "groundbreaking" for West Wholesale Drug, however, was held not at the actual site of the new plant, as the Whitman and Sons ceremony had been, but at the Bellevue-Stratford Hotel in Center City. Instead of traveling to the gritty inner city industrial site, the dignitaries attended a luncheon at the hotel, where they received West Wholesale medicine bottles that had been filled with soil from the construction site and labeled: "This is good medicine for Philadelphia."[2] The figurative distance between these bottles and the actual neighborhood of West Wholesale's new plant symbolized both the boldness and the limitations of Philadelphia's response to deindustrialization: a series of inventive liberal policy strategies brought direct and unexpectedly successful public interventions in the private marketplace, but divisions of race undercut the city's efforts to reshape the process of urban economic transformation.

The contrast between the groundbreaking ceremonies for Whitman and West Wholesale delineated the innovative quality of local liberalism in the postwar United States as well as the constraints that racialized spatial *and* policy boundaries placed on that liberalism. Both companies benefited from strong local interventions in the economy, showing how strands of local governance and state building fundamentally shaped public policy in the postwar United States, and that liberalism in fact deeply influenced multiple levels of the American state. Each case suggests how city officials, business organizations, and community activists in the city drew on American liberalism's rich legacy of policy ideas and experiments to develop a series of local industrial and employment policies that sought to arrest the decline of the city's manufacturing sector.

These local policy initiatives engaged with and, in some cases, relied on the resources and incentives provided by federal programs, but they remained projects of the local state—of liberal policymakers and activists who constructed public, private, and community-based institutions that sought to address the city's loss of industrial jobs. This local state-building project generated significant policy innovation and allowed Philadelphia's postwar liberals to maintain, update, and even expand the engagement with structural economic questions that had typified the most ambitious strands of New Deal and World War II–era liberalism, even as national liberalism moved in significantly different directions.[3] Yet for all of its innovation, Philadelphia's postwar liberalism suffered from a critical flaw. Its core economic strategy bifurcated along racial lines. The resulting division, into parallel, racially defined tracks of industrial and employment policy, ultimately limited the city's ability to respond effectively to the challenges of economic transformation during the post–World War II period.

Postwar Liberalism and Philadelphia

Why does Philadelphia's postwar local liberalism matter? Why is this account of politics and public policy in Philadelphia something more than what anthropologist Clifford Geertz referred to as "another country heard from"?[4] It matters because Philadelphia developed a postwar urban liberalism that differed in crucial ways from national forms of liberalism. In particular, liberals in Philadelphia recognized the problem of deindustrialization at a very early date and used the resources they had available to shape activist, public solutions to crucial economic problems. While they did not always succeed, the vibrancy and creativity of this local liberal response invites a reassessment of the role of urban political actors during this period, and of liberalism generally in the postwar United States.

Philadelphia's local liberalism, of course, evolved within the rich and complex historical context of American liberalism. By the early 1950s—when this study begins—liberalism had followed a varied and shifting course in the United States. Its roots as a political philosophy lay in the seventeenth- and eighteenth-century political and intellectual revolts that rejected the hereditary authority of church and monarchy in favor of constitutional rule and individual liberty in all its forms—property rights, freedom of religious conscience, and political self-determination. By the close of the nineteenth century, the laissez faire tradition of classical liberalism had become dominant in the United States. This version placed almost exclusive emphasis on the rights of private property and individual economic autonomy, including, and even privileging, the rights of corporations. During the first half of the twentieth century, however, the interventions of Progressivism and, most crucially, the New Deal modified classical liberalism almost beyond recognition. While still exhibiting great internal variation, liberalism moved gradually and unevenly toward an acceptance of governmental regulatory intervention in the private sector. It did so on the grounds that in an age of corporate-dominated industrial capitalism, the meaningful preservation of individual social and economic liberty—ideals that lay at the core of classical liberalism—required public constraint of business and provision of at least a limited welfare state, financed primarily through taxation.[5]

By the end of World War II, and for at least two decades afterwards, liberalism attained a position of preeminence as the nation's leading political philosophy. This dominance was buttressed by the Democratic Party coalition of union members, big-city political organizations, racial and ethnic minorities, intellectuals, and Southerners that had built the New Deal. A number of distinctive features characterized this postwar liberalism—some of which Philadelphia's local liberalism shared, and some of which it did not—and set it off from its conservative and radical counter-parts. Liberalism's first characteristic consisted of a philosophical and practical commitment to pragmatism, with its emphasis on the importance of empiricism and scientific inquiry in establishing contingent but useful truth claims; this in turn produced an approach to governance that focused on policy experimentation and practical results.[6] The second principle, a staunch endorsement of anti-communism in both foreign and domestic pol-icy, played a far greater role in liberalism nationally than in Philadelphia.[7]

Postwar liberalism's third and fourth characteristics, a reliance on uni-versalist appeals to the common good and a sometimes hesitant engage-ment in civil rights issues, interacted in powerful and increasingly unsta-ble ways over the postwar decades. Because it is central to my account of postwar Philadelphia, this tension merits elaboration. Postwar liberal-ism deployed a universalist language that drew on the ethos of the New Deal, which had emphasized the reciprocal obligations of citizens. These obligations included both the duty to aid one another through the mediat-ing, socially ameliorative institutions of government *and* the responsibility of individuals to contribute, primarily through work, to the greater good of society. While partly reflecting solidarity borne of the Depression, this universalism also had an element of opportunism in its tendency to suborn the justice claims of particular groups—especially African Americans—to the Democratic party's need to maintain the political support of its south-ern wing. Postwar critics increasingly challenged the failures and exclu-sions of such liberal appeals to the common good and sought redress for those left out of the New Deal paradigm—and particularly, for its racial exclusions. They focused not on the theoretical ideal of reciprocity, but on community empowerment, grassroots democratization, and attainment of rights for racially marginalized groups.[8]

Increasingly, these insurgencies played out in the context of the civil rights movement. While liberals had maneuvered the Democratic Party into support for civil rights during the 1948 presidential campaign, at the cost of temporarily splitting the party, their actual responsiveness to civil-rights demands remained tepid and slow-moving, particularly for issues where race intersected with economics. The wide embrace of Gunnar Myrdal's sweeping study *An American Dilemma* facilitated this cautious approach to racial problems, as Myrdal explained American racism as a fundamentally cultural and psychological problem, rooted in the hearts and minds of whites and thus amenable to education, positive example, and appeals to morality and fairness. This generated a racial liberalism that viewed discrimination as a problem of the individual and that divorced issues of economic inequality from the structural interplay of race and economics. At times, these ideas shaped key aspects of national civil rights strategies, such as the NAACP Legal Defense Fund's successful effort to challenge the separate but equal doctrine in *Brown v. Board of Education*.[9] Yet at the local level, in Philadelphia and around the nation, civil rights activists continued to assert the centrality of economic issues in the movement *throughout* the postwar period. In cities such as New York during the 1940s, civil rights activists formed alliances with trade unions and, until the Red Scare, communists to fight for both economic and racial gains. By the 1960s, economic concerns emerged as a key focus of the 1963 March on Washington For Jobs and Freedom, as the core of A. Philip Randolph, Bayard Rustin, and Leon Keyserling's 1966 *Freedom Budget for All Americans*, and as the center of much of Martin Luther King Jr.'s work long before he turned north to Chicago in 1966. Meanwhile, from New Orleans to Oakland, from Durham to Brooklyn, and from Las Vegas to Philadelphia, both moderate and radical activists challenged both discriminatory employment practices and, increasingly, economic inequality itself.[10]

The persistence of economic concerns in the civil rights movement suggests the continuing salience of the fifth principle of postwar liberalism—belief in the value of state engagement in the economy. This principle of public economic intervention joins civil rights and liberal universalism as core concerns of this study. Liberals in the early postwar years agreed on the general proposition of such intervention, but the exact policy structures remained the subject of much debate. While most liberals by 1945 had accepted the general principles of Keynesianism, and still shared the New Deal goal of broad economic security, disagreements persisted for decades about whether policy should focus on social spending, such as public investments in job and welfare programs and the redevelopment of depressed areas, or on macroeconomic fiscal policy measures such as tax cuts. "Social Keynesians," who favored the more activist social spending course, suffered two key setbacks during and immediately after the war. The first defeat came in 1943 when congressional conservatives defunded the National Resources Planning Board (NRPB), the body that in a variety of New Deal iterations had developed plans for expansive public works, natural resources development, social welfare, and jobs programs. Many of these would have been managed through new cooperative, intergovernmental economic planning bodies that would have given significant authority to state and local governments. Such decentralized structures offered a model for a "liberal federalism," a thoroughly Americanized vision of how the state might play a more active role in the economy. The social Keynesians' second defeat came when Congress eviscerated the Full Employment Act of 1945, which would have formally committed the federal government to maintaining full employment through the implementation of job and public works projects.[11]

After these setbacks, modified versions of social Keynesianism such as area-redevelopment policy, job training, and even full employment remained on the agenda of many liberals. But by the mid-1960s a policy framework of tax cut–based "commercial Keynesianism" became the dominant strain of liberal economic policy. This approach emphasized the use of fiscal policy to achieve overall economic growth, while rejecting any public intervention in the structure of the economy. President Lyndon Johnson, for example, pursued a significant cut in personal and corporate income taxes, followed by a War on Poverty that emphasized community political empowerment, reorganization of social services, and the creation of individual connections to existing economic opportunity, but included no significant efforts at structural economic reform or job creation.[12] Throughout this period, however, Philadelphia's local liberals continued to pursue policies associated with the social Keynesian conception of how government should engage the wider economy.

The historical meaning of these postwar economic policy developments, both in Philadelphia and the United States, depends in large part on interpretation of the New Deal and its postwar legacy. In recent decades, historians of New Deal policy have largely divided into two broad groups. The first group argued that while the New Deal actually did possess transformative potential as a step toward American social democracy, a series of compromises with Southern Democrats and corporate business interests undermined this promise. Collectively, adherents of this "end-of-reform" perspective maintain that the New Deal, and by extension postwar liberalism, abandoned any serious effort to address problems of economic structure.[13]

In recent years, other historians have begun to challenge the end-of-reform view of liberalism. New studies have questioned whether the New Deal *ever* possessed truly transformative, social democratic potential, even as they demonstrated that it undertook and accomplished significant *liberal* reform projects. Such work has shown the centrality of public-works programs to the New Deal, not only as immediate employment projects but also and more fundamentally as projects aimed at spurring long-term economic development as a state purpose. Although subject to greater constraint, such efforts continued in the postwar period, with significant public investments in highway construction, urban renewal, and the development of scientific and health care infrastructure.[14] Another strand of argument places a consumer-driven "pocketbook politics" at the center of the New Deal. This regime, which operated through such agencies as the National Recovery Administration's Consumer Advisory Board and the wartime Office of Price Administration, sought to protect purchasing power through policies that promoted low prices and high wages. Although some scholars find a decline in such consumerist liberalism shortly after the war, others see the 1950s and 1960s as its heyday.[15] Another group of studies takes issue with the postwar solidity of the New Deal coalition itself, contending that as early as the late 1940s, it had already begun to splinter on racial lines around issues of access to housing and jobs, especially in the urban North and West.[16] Building on this recognition of early discontent within the New Deal coalition, historians have more recently traced the rise of a powerful new movement conservatism in the 1960s and 1970s, a conservatism rooted in Sunbelt suburbs as well as in white ethnic urban neighborhoods.[17]

Despite these challenges, the end-of-reform thesis continues to shape most accounts of postwar history. Postwar liberalism emerges as intellectually and ideologically enervated even at the moment of its greatest political influence. Unwilling to alter basic economic structures, unable to address noncultural causes of poverty and inequality, and uncertain in challenging systematic dimensions of racism, liberals during the 1940s, 1950s, and early 1960s restricted political life to pluralist bargaining among interest groups, economic policy to a commercial Keynesian focus on overall growth, and antipoverty efforts to remedies for the cultural and behavioral characteristics of the poor themselves. Further, at the local level, liberalism appears to have fractured from within around the issue of race. Most scholarship on the role of localism in the postwar history of liberalism has focused on the frequently bitter narrative of how racial division and violence among the urban working class, along with the rapid growth of segregated suburbs, undermined efforts to achieve residential integration, progressive public housing, and, more broadly, class-based social movements.[18] With liberals seemingly so lacking in imagination and ambition, radicals and conservatives become the only dynamic historical actors, especially at the local level. My difficulty with such accounts lies less with their accuracy in their own field of view, where they offer vitally important insights, but with their failure to account for what I see as the full policy agenda of postwar-urban liberalism, taken on its own terms.

This book tells a different story. It finds not enervation, but a vibrant liberal activism alive and well in the American city. This was a liberalism that adapted the New Deal and wartime tradition of economic engagement for postwar conditions and that focused the power of the state on questions of economic structure and employment. Yet it also moved beyond such 1930s roots. Local liberals in Philadelphia, both in and out of government, developed new mechanisms of state intervention in the economy and shaped civil rights strategies that challenged employment discrimination and demanded economic opportunity for the marginalized. Perhaps most notably, African American activists emphasized a strand of liberal ideology that most critics have missed: an embrace of self-reliance, self-help, and responsibility as core values that liberal policy could and should promote. The state, in this view, had a responsibility to make real resources available to citizens who had none, but those citizens too had a responsibility to then improve themselves and their communities. Philadelphia's local liberalism thus relied on an amalgam of pragmatic approaches: a readiness to experiment, a belief in state activism, a commitment to civil rights, and an incorporation of "mainstream values" that rendered its efforts readily acceptable to a wide and diverse public. This was a relevant and bold American liberalism that has been widely overlooked in histories that emphasize only a national story of pro-growth Keynesianism, group-based rights claims, and anti-communism.

For all its innovation, Philadelphia's postwar local liberalism was not without serious faults. Some liberal initiatives achieved only modest success, some faced significant political obstacles, and others simply failed. More typical, though, was a nuanced pattern in which liberal initiatives worked well in certain key areas, yet left others unaddressed: building new factories in the inner city, for example, but failing to link such projects to job training programs that targeted the city's most needy residents. Above all, divisions of race bifurcated the economic policy initiatives that Philadelphia's postwar liberalism undertook and constrained the results that they achieved. Innovative planning proposals that sought to draw the resulting parallel tracks of liberal policy together failed to achieve implementation. Meanwhile, the wider restructuring of the U.S. economy away from manufacturing and toward services placed increasing pressure on Philadelphia policymakers and activists as the promise of the 1960s faded into the bleakness of the 1970s. Still, liberal activists accomplished much in postwar Philadelphia. Political, business, and community leaders fought back against deindustrialization through local industrial and employment policies that were deeply rooted in the employment-focused liberalism of the New Deal–World War II period, but that took on their own shape as the postwar era unfolded.[19] Most of this story has been lost. When restored, it forces reassessments both of the nature of postwar liberalism in the United States and of the political and social history of American cities.

Clifford Geertz ultimately concluded that detailed studies of the local case mattered because they offered an intellectual path through which "the mega-concepts with which contemporary social science is afflicted... can be given the sort of sensible actuality that makes it possible to think not only realistically and concretely *about* them, but, what is more important, creatively and imaginatively *with* them."[20] So it is with the mega-concept of liberalism and the case of Philadelphia. For all its reach, all its power, all its centralization, liberalism for most Americans in the postwar years actually wore a local face. It was in communities across the country that people interacted with their government on a daily basis and that liberalism took on concrete meaning. In cities like Philadelphia, liberalism became lived reality.

The Problem of Jobs

The loss of manufacturing jobs, first as threat and then as reality, posed a fundamental quandary not just for Philadelphia but for American urbanism generally. For centuries, cities in America had offered the promise of plentiful and rewarding work and with it, the prospect of a better life. Generations of migrants and immigrants had left farms and villages to pursue this urban promise. Since the advent of industrialization, this pull had originated with the factory, with manufacturing jobs that offered more regular and higher income than anything available in rural occupations. Reality, of course, had not always matched the ideal of the bountiful city workplace. Many manufacturing jobs had always been dangerous, repetitive, and low-paying. For skilled workers, though, the urban factory often did meet expectations, and after the rise of mass industrial unionism with the CIO (Congress of Industrial Organizations) organizing drives of the 1930s, even unskilled workers achieved improved working conditions, higher salaries, and benefits such as retirement pensions and health insurance. Regardless of actual factory conditions, however, mass movements of people continued to flow toward the city through the middle of the twentieth century. For most migrants, the implicit promise of work drove their decisions. Industrial work and both its lure and limitations became ingrained in the process of urbanization itself.

This long-standing association of the city with good job opportunities began to unravel after World War II. The loss of industry in Philadelphia and similar cities created a dramatic "problem of jobs" that consisted of the imbalance between the availability of employment, for both men and women, that paid wages sufficient to meet workers' basic economic needs and the size, spatial distribution, and skills of the city's working-age population. Along with the material deprivation that it wrought, this problem of jobs jeopardized a key element of the social and political identity of working people. For many, it even threatened the very basis of citizenship itself, as work had defined the autonomous and independent status that for much of U.S. history had been a prerequisite for full membership in the polity, albeit often along distinct racial and gender lines.[21]

The problem of jobs affected nearly all of the urban working class, but it struck Northern, urban African Americans with particular ferocity. Since the 1890s, but particularly during World War II, African Americans had left the violence and desperate poverty of the Jim Crow South for the lure of industrial jobs in the urban North. With the limited exception of the war years, when huge labor demands opened previously closed manufacturing jobs to blacks, the reality of life in the North had often proved disappointing. Overt racial discrimination in hiring, as well more subtle discriminatory structures such as closed union hiring and apprenticeship systems, combined to limit blacks to the lowest-paying, dirtiest, and most dangerous jobs. For African American women, at least in peacetime, few openings existed outside of domestic service.[22]

Deindustrialization made such problems dramatically worse, as the pool of manufacturing jobs that had pulled many African Americans north gradually began to shrink. Metropolitan housing discrimination exacerbated the problem still further. White workers, at least those who could save for a down payment or qualify for assistance from the GI bill or other federally assisted home ownership programs, could always follow the jobs to the suburbs (at least when companies remained in business and in the region). Trapped by the "white noose" that excluded them from most

FIGURE 3. The Problem of Jobs. Residents line up to apply for municipal jobs at a city "job mobile," August 1968. Photo courtesy of Temple University Libraries, Urban Archives, Philadelphia, Pennsylvania.

new suburban developments around Philadelphia, African Americans, with limited exceptions, could not make such moves.[23] This interplay of racial, economic, and spatial structures meant that the problem of jobs proved particularly devastating for Philadelphia's African Americans. Yet it also generated a range of innovative efforts to solve the problem from within the African American community, efforts that built on the resources of blacks and their institutions but also drew on and sometimes worked with the liberal state. Much of this study focuses on the interaction of Philadelphia's African American liberals with the state, with their white liberal counterparts and sometime partners, and with the city's wider African American community in seeking solutions to the problem of jobs. What they and others found in Philadelphia suggests that devastating as the problem of jobs may have been, potential paths to its resolution did exist. Those paths lay within the field of mid-century U.S. liberalism; yet barriers that would ultimately block those paths lay within liberalism too.

Local Liberalism

The vibrancy, and even the viability, of local liberalism depended on the circumstances. In Philadelphia, such conditions emerged in 1951 when a group of reform-oriented liberals came to power with the support of an often tenuous coalition of civic and political organizations, labor unions, African Americans, Democratic ward organizations, and business groups. This coalition neatly mirrored the national New Deal coalition, with the exceptions that business held a position of greater influence in Philadelphia and that no parallel to the Southern Democrats existed. Originating in the mayor's office under mayors Joseph Clark and Richardson Dilworth but continuing after the reform mayors left office and extending into the sphere of community activism—particularly African American activism—these Philadelphia liberals pursued policy goals that seemed obsolete to many by the 1950s and 1960s.[24]

Acting in the tradition of pragmatic liberalism that had characterized much of the New Deal, Philadelphia liberals between the 1950s and the 1970s engaged in a series of evolving experiments that infused old approaches with new meanings and possibilities, with the goal of meeting the demands of an altered situation.[25] These liberal policymakers and activists only occasionally linked their efforts to New Deal–wartime liberalism in an explicit way; more often, such ties were demonstrated through policy assumptions, ideological orientations, and intellectual affinities. While liberal leaders and activists drew on the past in their commitment to state intervention in the economy, their reliance on state-sponsored economic development, and their repeatedly frustrated efforts to implement an economic planning agenda, they pushed local liberalism in new directions quite different from its national counterparts.

Such differences emerged especially in three critical policy areas. First, public intervention in private realms of the marketplace moved from bitter controversy to routine administrative procedure in just a few years, as city government entered and transformed the operation of the local industrial real estate market. It did so in a way that sought to maximize the retention of good jobs as well as tax revenue (which supported the reformers' social service agenda). More broadly, it pursued the old reform liberal goal of creating economic order in a key private market. As implemented by the Philadelphia Industrial Development Corporation, Philadelphia's industrial renewal program used federal tax incentives to provide low-cost plant financing for small- and medium-sized firms that made up a large percentage of Philadelphia's industrial base. This strategy, which is examined in chapters 1 and 2, reversed the usual pattern of federal subsidy of suburban development and achieved a surprising degree of success, even in the city's aging industrial core.

Second, African American liberals during the 1960s built on the civil rights movement's long-standing engagement with economic concerns even as they reappropriated traditional discourses of self-help and community uplift for liberal purposes. This approach intertwined challenges to racial discrimination with attention to issues of economic structure and class. In the 1960s, a group of black Philadelphia ministers deployed the public resources provided by the War on Poverty to build one of the nation's largest job training and business development programs, the community-controlled Opportunities Industrialization Centers (OIC) and the affiliated Progress Movement. As chapter 3 explains, federal anti-poverty warriors of the period assumed that in a high-growth macroeconomic environment, job training could reduce poverty by improving individual skills and changing behavioral characteristics without addressing the structure of the economy. Faced with the harsh realities of discrimination and limited African American control of capital in the city, OIC soon rejected this central premise of postwar "manpower policy" and expanded its reach to include questions of economic structure and security. Drawing on a well-established base of community support, as well as federal minority contract set-asides and private philanthropy, OIC developed a series of community-owned manufacturing enterprises and commercial businesses. At its core, this effort sought to restructure American capitalism around a model of community control and social responsibility as well as the profit motive. For more than a decade, these efforts succeeded. Explored in chapters 4, 5, and 6, this on-the-ground evolution of the War on Poverty in Philadelphia indicates that federal inattention to economic structure and employment policy did not preclude a local focus on such issues; careful attention to local policy history thus demonstrates how local actors reshaped federal policy and determined its actual, on-the-ground operation.

Division of these policies along lines of race, however, would prove crucial in determining the effectiveness of Philadelphia's postwar local liberalism at devising solutions to the problem of jobs. Despite the innovations of its local industrial and employment policies, Philadelphia failed to form effective links between publicly funded but community-based programs such as OIC and public-private initiatives such as PIDC. As a result, PIDC and OIC existed as parallel, racially bifurcated tracks of policy in the city. While each track included elements of an effective response to deindustrialization, this racial divide meant that neither could grapple effectively with all aspects of Philadelphia's economic problems.

A third area of liberal activism offered the promise that this racial divide in Philadelphia's industrial and employment policies could be closed. Throughout the 1960s, economic planning remained an ongoing subject of debate among Philadelphia liberals in both the public and private sectors. This local planning discourse, which I assess in chapters 3 and 8, transcended the typical physical design concerns of postwar city planning and led to the creation of protean forms of the local planning bodies that had once been called for by the New Deal's National Resources Planning Board.[26] Eventually, these planning efforts forged tentative new ties across the city's racially divided industrial and employment policies. Meanwhile, chapter 7 shows how other inter-racial initiatives during the late 1960s and early 1970s supported both the development of autonomous African American construction contractors and the implementation of the federal "Philadelphia Plan" for integration of the local construction industry—an immediate precursor of affirmative action. This effort not only opened a crucial source of employment in the city to African Americans, but also provided a new source of unity for black and white liberals in Philadelphia. But with these improvements came setbacks. Inter-racial initiatives alienated much of the local labor movement during a period in which the local liberal coalition had come under increasing strain.

Ultimately, this study argues for the continued relevance of localism and place in post–World War II political history. Despite the growth of the federal state during the twentieth century and the attendant, if partial, centralization of state authority, local governments, policymakers, and community activists continued to exert extensive and often defining influence over the implementation and on-the-ground operation of American public policy. This persistent localist strand had both negative and positive characteristics for American governance. Along with the important and well-documented limitations that local racial boundaries and entrenched political cultures placed on federal policy, this study shows that under specific place-based circumstances, local institutions could be sites of significant policy innovation and creative liberal activism. Although often obscured by reactionary qualities of the local state and limited by powerful forces of national and global political economy, this local liberalism is an important but underemphasized piece of recent American political history, the neglect of which impoverishes the sense of political possibility for historians and for Americans generally.

Economic Crisis and Local Liberalism

O n election night 1951, liberals danced in the streets of Philadelphia. As news spread of Joseph Clark and Richardson Dilworth's victories in the mayoral and district attorney elections, supporters of the two reform candidates spilled out of Democratic headquarters at the Bellevue Hotel in Center City Philadelphia. Trolleys, buses, and cars slowed to a crawl as "thousands danced and screamed" and "a few wept." A voice from a sound truck adorned with large Clark and Dilworth campaign banners proclaimed "I'm telling you folks—we're happy, yes sir, very happy. Whether you're Democrats or Republicans you helped us and we're gonna do our best to give you a good government." Another truck, joined by a "makeshift band," led the celebrating throng on a raucous parade up Broad Street. As they passed the Union League building, with its windows darkened and an iron grate closed across its wooden doors, many of the marchers booed; the Union League served as the political and social clubhouse of elite Philadelphian Republicanism. Turning onto Chestnut Street, the marchers cheered the combined headquarters of the Independent and maverick Republican Committees for Clark and Dilworth. Someone in the crowd lit green and red flares that "turned the impromptu parade into an old-fashioned torchlight procession." A block later, the parade reached the campaign headquarters of Daniel Poling, the defeated Republican mayoral candidate, where the revelers brought out brooms and celebrated their "sweep" of key races by sweeping the sidewalk outside the nearly deserted building. Meanwhile, other Democratic sound trucks circled the massive granite bulk of City Hall, with its looming tower capped by a statue of William Penn. Loudspeakers on the trucks cast jeers and taunts about pending unemployment for any Republican officeholders who happened to still be inside.[1]

This night of joy and triumph in Philadelphia marked the culmination of decades of work by liberal activists and started a period of profound change in the city's governance. With only brief interruptions, the local Republican Party had dominated Philadelphia politics since the Civil War. For much of that time, the Democratic Party existed as little more than a subsidiary of the Republican organization, trotted out at election time to provide token opposition. At times the Republicans even paid the rent for Democratic headquarters to maintain the veneer of legitimacy provided by an opposition party. During the Great Depression, however, brick manufacturer John B. Kelly and building contractor Matthew McCloskey revitalized the Democratic Party organization and began to challenge Republican control. Kelly might even have won the 1935 mayoral election if not for creative vote counting by the Republican-dominated Board of Elections. Following World War II, elite, reform-oriented liberal activists affiliated with such organizations as Americans for Democratic Action and the Citizens' Council on City Planning directly attacked the Republican machine. In 1947, reform leaders Dilworth and Clark secured the support of the city Democratic organization and ran serious but ultimately unsuccessful campaigns for mayor and district attorney, respectively. Two years later, after a series of corruption scandals led to the suicides of several city officials and the indictment of others, Dilworth captured the post of city treasurer, Clark won city controller, and the state legislature authorized a new Home Rule Charter that would reorganize city government.[2]

During this period, top executives of Philadelphia's major corporations, law firms, and financial institutions, most of whom had long supported the Republican Party, concluded that the city's combination of political scandal and physical deterioration had begun to harm Philadelphia's national reputation and their own business interests. They formed an organization known as the Greater Philadelphia Movement to pursue the reorganization of city government and, not incidentally, the redevelopment of Center City. Although most of its members remained Republican, the new business group allied with the reform Democrats in support of the charter campaign. In April 1951, following a second round of graft

FIGURE 4. Joseph S. Clark and Richardson H. Dilworth in front of Philadelphia City Hall, c. 1950s. Clark and Dilworth served as leaders of the liberal reform movement in the late 1940s and 1950s. Clark served as mayor from 1952–56, and Dilworth served as mayor from 1956–62. Photo courtesy of Temple University Libraries, Urban Archives, Philadelphia, Pennsylvania.

revelations and suicides by prominent Republican officeholders, voters approved a new city charter that established a strong mayoral form of government, limited the role of City Council, expanded the civil service system, and enhanced the power of the City Planning Commission. In November, Clark won the mayoral election, Dilworth won the district attorney race, and reform candidates captured every major city government office. The reformers' victory rested on their successful construction of a coalition of business leaders, union members, African Americans, Democratic Party ward leaders, and intellectuals. With the exception that it lacked a regional component (that is, an equivalent of the Southern Democrats who played a crucial but constraining role in the New Deal), this alliance neatly mirrored the New Deal coalition that had defined Democratic politics since the 1930s.[3]

Clark and Dilworth also exemplified a national trend toward reform in urban politics during the 1950s. This political shift had brought John B. Hynes to the Boston mayor's office in 1949 and would continue in 1953 with the election of Robert F. Wagner Jr. in New York, Raymond Tucker in St. Louis, and Anthony Celebrezze in Cleveland. Like the Philadelphia reformers, all of the "new" mayors promised municipal housekeeping and the physical rebuilding of their cities.[4]

Despite the resurgence of such urban reform movements, the anti-communist political rhetoric and tactics of the McCarthy-era weakened progressive organizations and political coalitions around the country. In cities such as New York, Los Angeles, and Detroit, anti-communism undermined public housing initiatives, campaigns for racial integration, and economic reform efforts.[5] Philadelphia did not completely escape the anti-communist scare, but it avoided its worst excesses. Although the national Americans for Democratic Action organization became emblematic of liberal anti-communism, the organization's local chapter focused not on anti-communism but on municipal issues and played a central role in the reform movement. Meanwhile, the city government hired public officials who had been forced from positions in other cities by red-baiting tactics. Examples included City Planning Commission director Edmund Bacon, who returned to Philadelphia from Flint, Michigan, and Commission on Human Relations director George Schermer, who came from Detroit. This relative tolerance extended to the private sector as well. When the FBI arrested a group of local communists under Smith Act charges of advocating overthrow of the U.S. government in 1957, prominent attorneys from the city's leading law firms organized a successful defense. In another case, the Philadelphia Board of Education fired a group of public school teachers for their membership in the communist party, but the teachers succeeded in overturning their dismissal in the courts. The absence of anti-communist hysteria in Philadelphia may be partially explained by the city's lack of a large and vibrant local communist movement. Nonetheless, the comparative calm created a policymaking environment more amenable to liberal experimentation than that of many other cities during the period.[6]

Some analysts have argued that the 1951 reform victory simply represented the arrival, half a century late, of progressivism in Philadelphia.[7] While the reformers' emphasis on efficiency, professional expertise, and structural change in city government does offer parallels to progressive era efforts, other aspects of the reform movement indicate that it was an essentially different political phenomenon. The primary influences on the reformers' approach to government and urban problems had been the New Deal and World War II. Unlike their progressive predecessors, they assumed that once in power they would implement an activist policy package formed in direct partnership with the federal government. With the examples of public housing and assertive planning principles already articulated at the national level, the reformers envisioned bold new public interventions in the marketplace. More generally, they adopted an activist, trial-and-error approach to governance that echoed the policy style of the New Deal and, at a deeper level, the pragmatic, Deweyan foundations of twentieth-century American liberalism. As one official in the reform city government later wrote, "although nobody knew what should or could be done (any more than the New Deal had known it) it was the [New Deal's] national example of pragmatism and experimentation that showed Philadelphia the method of approaching the many newly recognized problems."[8]

This political transformation, however, took place in a context of increasing economic disruption. Although in popular perception the 1950s are remembered as a decade of prosperity—and in terms of aggregate national growth it was—the U.S. economy actually experienced serious downturns during both 1953–54 and 1957–58. These recessions had an especially harsh effect on older industrial cities in the Northeast and Midwest. Some local analysts had warned as early as 1949 that obsolete infrastructure and competition from other regions would place Philadelphia in an increasingly precarious economic position, and the first recession exposed these weaknesses in Philadelphia's economy.[9] It also created the impetus for the city's industrial renewal program.

After slowly reaching a plateau in early 1953, factory employment in the city began to fall in late spring. The decline continued throughout the remainder of the year and accelerated in early 1954, dropping 3 percent between December 1953 and January 1954 alone.[10] By May 1954, Philadelphia manufacturing employment had fallen by more than 13 percent since the start of 1953. The weekly average of unemployment claims in the city increased from 22,263 in 1953 to 38,160 in 1954, and the count of city residents who had exhausted their unemployment benefits rose from 1,039 in March 1953 to 2,666 in May 1954. Meanwhile, regional unemployment shot from 2.7 percent to nearly 7 percent. A less conventional measure of economic distress reflected the recession's manifestation for workers: during the 1953–54 period, the monthly average of help-wanted ads in leading Philadelphia newspapers fell from 396,100 to 182,700. Further, such key local industries as textiles, transportation equipment, electrical machinery, and apparel bore the brunt of the slowdown, accounting for 53,900 of Philadelphia's 78,600 lost manufacturing jobs.[11] In June 1954, with the local unemployment rate still well over 6 percent, the federal government acknowledged the seriousness of the problem by declaring the Philadelphia region a surplus labor market area.[12] Three years later, Philadelphia experienced the worst of yet another downturn. More importantly, most of the industrial jobs lost in the two recessions were not quickly recovered. With the exception of a small uptick in 1959, manufacturing employment in Philadelphia fell each year from 1954 to 1964, with a cumulative loss of 101, 400 jobs, or nearly 29 percent of the city's manufacturing employment base.[13]

Philadelphia's economic problems meant that the reformers faced a complex challenge as they attempted to shape new policy initiatives. Without a sufficient employment and tax base, Philadelphia would lack the municipal revenue necessary to pursue the reform liberals' agenda of housing, health care, education, and transportation. Despite the expansion of the national state during the New Deal and World War II, the federal government during the 1950s still provided only limited assistance to American cities. Although the Housing Act of 1949 offered federal funding for urban redevelopment and public housing construction, any possibility that public housing would serve as the opening wedge for fully realized, labor-based social democracy in the postwar United States had been obliterated by the evisceration of the Full Employment Act of 1945 and the passage of the Taft-Hartley Act, as well as the Red Scare. These events delineated the point at which social democratic policy initiatives vanished from the national political agenda, a development that drastically limited the impact of federal urban policy.[14]

Unable to change the incentives of federal policies, city officials in Philadelphia faced the future prospect of an impoverished, racially segregated population and an increasingly inadequate tax base. Although the reform liberals initially pursued a progressive public housing policy, housing alone could not resolve these problems. In such an environment, the decision to pursue job development through local industrial policy was one of the few immediate prospects for assuring the city's social and fiscal stability. Without an adequate employment base, little else would be possible. This was the dilemma posed by the problem of jobs after World War II, and industrial renewal was the solution developed by Philadelphia's postwar liberals.

FIGURE 5. Philadelphia City Economist Kirk R. Petshek, undated. Petshek served as Philadelphia's official economist from 1954–62. His studies and reports highlighted the issue of deindustrialization at an early stage and provided the impetus for an industrial renewal program. Photo courtesy of Temple University Libraries, Urban Archives, Philadelphia, Pennsylvania.

Experts and the Crisis of Industrial Philadelphia

Scholars have long noted that industrial cities hemorrhaged manufacturing jobs during the postwar decades. What has not been recognized is that as early as the mid-1950s, Philadelphia's reform mayoral administrations realized that such job losses signified something far more serious than cyclical downturns. The nature of the local economy was changing. As a result, the Clark and Dilworth administrations developed policy strategies to manage and even reshape the impending process of local economic change.

Mayor Joseph S. Clark's decision to fill administrative staff positions with policy experts rather than political appointees played a key part in recognizing this economic decline. In a tacit challenge to the Democratic Party organization, which hoped to reap patronage spoils from the reform victory, Clark recruited social scientists from around the United States for key policy and administrative posts. Among them was Kirk Petshek, a Harvard-trained economist who had previously served as director of post-war economic aid to Yugoslavia. In 1954, Petshek came to Philadelphia to serve in the newly created position of city economist in the city's Commerce Department. There, he proved to be the most perceptive early analyst of Philadelphia's industrial decline. During the first two years of the Clark administration, Petshek compiled data that differentiated employment and economic trends within the city from those of the metropolitan area, the state, and the nation. Such information had never before been systematically collected.[15]

Petshek's studies showed a city undergoing wrenching, long-term economic change. In his July 1955 report, for example, Petshek observed that Philadelphia's recovery from the 1953–54 recession lagged so far behind that of the region, state, and nation that it could hardly be said to constitute an improvement. Racial discrimination, he added, led to an "incidence of unemployment among Negro workers ... at least twice as high as among whites," and concluded that "this can only partially be explained by qualifications, and indicates still existing discriminatory practices in spite of this Administration's efforts."[16]

Initially, Petshek thought that the cause of Philadelphia's slow recovery lay in the unequal distribution of defense contract cutbacks after the Korean War. By November 1955, with city employment figures still showing only seasonal improvements, he concluded that Philadelphia's economy "is obviously suffering from a chronic illness which goes deeper than merely lagging behind the national recovery." Although service and retail employment had increased nationally since the war, Philadelphia's shift from manufacturing to services had far outpaced the rest of the country. Capital expenditures in the Philadelphia region as a whole were in decline and bank deposits had dropped sharply. Along with the fall in defense contracts, Petshek pointed to a series of structural factors that helped explain these trends: the rapid suburbanization of economic activity and the movement of hosiery and textile firms to other regions with cheap, non-union labor. The immediate challenge, however, remained one of awareness: "the central point of the entire problem is the fact ... that our citizens have yet not recognized the seriousness of the problem. The problem, to repeat, is one particularly of an Eastern metropolitan center, but in some respects uniquely our own." Unless Philadelphia addressed these economic changes in a systematic and aggressive manner, the economist warned, it faced the prospect of continually falling farther behind. If this happened, the city's most vulnerable citizens would suffer the most.[17]

Petshek's analysis demonstrated that Philadelphia's manufacturing sector had entered a period of extended decline, and highlighted the basic outlines of the problem of jobs that would face the city in the following decades. Although Petshek would not have used this language, the trends that he identified deeply threatened the economic citizenship of working-class Philadelphians by eroding their status as both producers and consumers. African Americans and other, less prominent minority groups, such as the city's small but growing Puerto Rican community, were most vulnerable to such change. More immediately, the economist's work convinced city commerce director Walter M. Phillips to pursue an industrial renewal program that would attempt to maintain viable components of Philadelphia's manufacturing base.

When he entered public office in 1952 for the first and only time, Walter Phillips embodied much of the character and ideals of Philadelphia's liberal reform movement. A graduate of Princeton and, like Mayor Clark, a member of an old and prominent Philadelphia family, Phillips abandoned his ancestral Republicanism during the Great Depression and joined the nascent reform network that had emerged amidst John Kelly's rebuilding of the local Democratic Party. An active member of the progressive Philadelphia Housing Association, Phillips was a founder of both the local Americans for Democratic Action (ADA) chapter and the reform-oriented Committee on City Policy (later the Citizens' Council on City Planning). After World War II, these relatively elite activist groups seized the reform initiative from Democratic Party powers such as Kelly and Matthew McCloskey and provided a crucial institutional base for both the charter campaign and the Clark-Dilworth challenge to Republican control of city government. Through these organizations, Phillips played a crucial behind-the-scenes role in reform politics as an organizer and strategist. In particular, he maintained vital connections across the reform movement's disparate constituencies. Phillips served on the board of the business-dominated Greater Philadelphia Movement, worked closely in the ADA with liberal labor leaders like Joseph Schwartz of the Knit Goods Workers and William Rafsky of the Hosiery Workers (later a key reform policymaker), and, through his work as a trustee of the historically black Lincoln University in nearby Chester County, gained the trust of key African American ministers.[18]

FIGURE 6. Walter M. Phillips campaigning in Center City Philadelphia as a reform candidate for the 1963 Democratic mayoral nomination, May 15, 1963. During the 1940s and 1950s, Phillips played a key role in the liberal reform movement that culminated with the passage of a new City Charter and the election of Joseph S. Clark as mayor in 1951. As city commerce director under Clark, Phillips developed the first proposals for a municipal industrial renewal program. In 1963, he would lose the mayoral nomination to incumbent James H. J. Tate. Photo courtesy of Temple University Libraries, Urban Archives, Philadelphia, Pennsylvania.

When Joseph Clark became mayor, he appointed Phillips to the joint position of commerce director and city representative. The cabinet-level Commerce Department had a charter-defined mission to "promote and develop the City's commerce and industry and encourage the increased use of the Ports and Airports of Philadelphia."[19] This vague charge might easily have led to little more than boosterish promotion efforts, but Phillips instead used it to provide a starting point and a legal justification for an unprecedented public intervention in the local economy.

Jarred into action by Petshek's warnings about the city's loss of manufacturing jobs, Phillips formulated specific ideas about how a local industrial policy might be structured. In particular, he called for collaboration between city government and the local business community to develop new factories on city-owned land and modernize existing industrial facilities

on private land. In these proposals, Phillips focused on a single factor
in the city's loss of manufacturing: the need for physical space to build
single-story factories in park-like settings.[20]

This emphasis on one-story plants reflected changes in industrial ar-
chitecture, production processes, and transportation technology that favored suburban areas over central cities. In 1949, the Philadelphia City
Planning Commission had observed that "it is possible for auto trucks as
well as belt railroads to service outlying industrial districts where one-
story factories, spread out over cheaper land, permit all factory processes
to be conducted on one-floor level without any break in the flow of manufacturing at each floor level."[21] Such one-story plants, relying on industrial electric motors perfected during the first half of the twentieth century, stood in stark contrast to the multistory loft factories common in
the dense urban manufacturing districts of older cities. Phillips pointed
out that industry's apparent preference for the new plant facilities did not
bode well for Philadelphia: "Much of the City's industrial housing is old
and obsolete.... Everywhere the trend is away from loft buildings and toward one-story facilities with convenient access, off street truck loading
and unloading, and ample space for employee parking. Such plants take
up three to four times as much land as before. If Philadelphia industry
cannot renew itself within the City of Philadelphia it will go elsewhere,
confronting the City with growing decay and a shrinking tax base."[22]

Just as the new suburbs drew white, middle-class residents away from
the cities, the lure of suburban and rural industrial sites affected cities
across the United States after World War II. Different cities adopted a variety of approaches to the problem: some undertook extensive industrial
planning programs, others did nothing at all. In Oakland, the powerful
Chamber of Commerce and its government allies envisioned the city, and
especially its downtown office district, as the heart of a regional "industrial garden" that would mix modern industries with pleasant residential
areas of single-family homes throughout the East Bay. Oakland pursued
this goal through a cooperative program with the surrounding suburban
communities that sought to recruit industry from other parts of the country. Although the factories came to the East Bay's suburban towns and
small cities, they ultimately brought few gains to Oakland itself, which
had no way to benefit from the property taxes generated by the new industries; furthermore, its growing minority population had little access
to the jobs the plants provided. Policymakers in St. Louis also recognized
the threat of industrial decentralization and developed a regional strategy

that included inner-city industrial redevelopment. They did so, however, through a program of widespread slum clearance that destroyed African American neighborhoods. Yet industrial renewal in St. Louis quickly assumed a secondary place in a regional strategy: redevelopment was focused on the city's riverfront and central business district as a hub of tourism, and placed manufacturing in new industrial parks on the suburban fringe. In Detroit, a conservative city government made little effort to stem the movement of the auto industry and its suppliers into the suburbs and beyond. During the 1950s, Detroit built only one small industrial park on cleared land that took years to develop. Throughout the country, cities and suburbs engaged in competition for industry, with the suburbs nearly always gaining the upper hand.[23]

In Philadelphia, Walter Phillips and his staff argued that this problem of industrial "suburbanitis" could be solved by assembling tracts of vacant, city-owned land into an "industrial land bank" and gradually transforming them into planned industrial districts offering single-story, continuous-flow factories. Unlike Oakland, St. Louis, Detroit, and most older cities, Philadelphia possessed hundreds of acres of such land in undeveloped areas around Northeast Philadelphia Airport and in the Penrose and Eastwick sections of southwest Philadelphia near the city's growing International Airport. Phillips also suggested that a nonprofit corporation be organized to develop and market new factories in these districts. Proceeds from such sales would be held in a "revolving fund" that would in turn be used to acquire additional private land for the industrial land bank. As explained by Phillips, the purpose of such a program would be to reverse, or at least contain, the flight of industry that threatened to deliver "two serious blows to the city: first, the loss of the best source of local tax revenue, and second, the loss of job opportunities where they are needed most."[24] For the next fifteen years, the twin goals of securing the tax base and preserving manufacturing jobs would provide the underlying rationale for Philadelphia's local industrial policy.

Even with its solitary focus on the relatively neutral factor of industrial space, Phillips's proposals for a city industrial program met determined opposition throughout 1954 and 1955. City Planning Commission executive director Edmund Bacon fought the idea on the grounds that it violated a city charter provision requiring open competitive bidding for the sale of all city-owned land, and less explicitly, because the creation of a separate industrial authority would undermine his control over land-use planning.[25] From the private sector, local real estate magnate Albert

FIGURE 7. Northeast Philadelphia Airport, Philadelphia, PA, February 23, 1952. Undeveloped woods and farm fields surrounded the airport, all within the Philadelphia city limits. A suburban housing tract is visible in the upper left; on the lower right is Northeast Village, a low-cost housing project built for war workers during World War II and later converted into temporary public housing. The presence of such open space made the construction of modern, suburban style industrial parks by PIDC possible during the 1960s. PIDC would build its largest facility, the Philadelphia Industrial Park, around the Northeast airport. Photo courtesy of Temple University Libraries, Urban Archives, Philadelphia, Pennsylvania.

M. Greenfield endorsed Bacon's position on competitive bidding even as he sought to secure the prime tracts of city land for development by his own real estate firm. A Ukrainian-born Jewish immigrant, Greenfield had built a real estate and department store empire in Philadelphia and New York and, according to one possibly apocryphal account, "owned, or brokered . . . half of Philadelphia" during his career. A member of the Democratic National Committee and a primary financier of the local Democratic Party, Greenfield exerted significant influence in city politics, despite his status as an outsider estranged from the city's Protestant business and social elite. Greenfield barely bothered to hide his real interests in the industrial issue: he sent representatives to Phillips's office with an offer to purchase the surplus land at Northeast Philadelphia Airport from the city. Already engaged in running battles with Greenfield over a new wholesale food distribution center, redevelopment of the historic Society Hill neighborhood, and the Penn Center office complex in Center City, few in the Clark administration wanted to cross the local power broker in support of Phillips. Greenfield's opposition also split the Chamber of Commerce, the city's most likely partner in a quasi-public industrial project (and in which Greenfield played a leading role), and it contributed to a City Council vote against rezoning a portion of the airport site for industry at the close of Mayor Clark's term.[26]

Mayor Clark's priorities posed another problem for Phillips. Rather than industrial decline, Clark preferred to focus on administrative reorganization, creation of a civil service system, social service provision, and urban redevelopment. Clark was interested in the broad implications of policy, to the point of holding daily discussion sessions with key advisors "to intellectualize the problems." He emphasized programs to expand public housing, create new recreation areas, build modern city-run health centers, and eradicate tuberculosis. In urban redevelopment, the mayor focused on housing and on shaping the broader nonresidential renewal program made possible by the 1954 amendments to the U.S. Housing Act.[27]

Industrial development, in contrast, held less interest for Clark. Commenting on a draft of Clark's 1955 budget message, Phillips chided the mayor for his inattention to the issue: "the unemployment problem of the City is still so acute that I recommend you give it more emphasis in your budget message than you seemed to have in mind yesterday when you discussed the subject at the Cabinet meeting. I think it deserves separate treatment, rather than being tagged on to transportation, housing and redevelopment."[28] In 1964, Phillips recalled that as mayor, Clark "didn't have too much feeling for the economic or, for that matter, the physical. He had an abstract mind, was interested in administration, and didn't concern himself with freeways and industrial land and things of that nature."[29] In combination with Phillips's inability to build a coalition either among Philadelphia's business and civic leadership or within the city government, the mayor's focus on other issues made it highly unlikely that the administration would undertake a program as ambitious, and untested, as the industrial renewal concept. When Phillips left office after Clark's 1955 election to the U.S. Senate and Richardson Dilworth's ascension to the mayor's office, the proposal for a local industrial policy remained unfulfilled.[30]

Urban Renewal or Industrial Renewal?

Phillips's ideas about industrial renewal had not gained immediate political support because they required a significant departure from traditional business and development practices, as well as revisions of existing policy structures and priorities. Following Richardson Dilworth's election as mayor, however, the prospects for initiating an industrial program improved. Unlike Clark, Dilworth made industrial renewal one of the three core issues on his policy agenda, along with urban renewal and mass transit. Although his origins were just as elite as Clark's, Dilworth came from Pittsburgh and thus lacked his predecessor's connections to elite Philadelphia society. He had served in both world wars and been wounded in each; in the early post–World War II years, Dilworth had been the preeminent reform leader and had run unsuccessfully for governor in 1950. Although he could have been the mayoral nominee in 1951, he passed the chance to Clark in hopes of running for governor again in 1954. More pragmatic than his predecessor, and more inclined to reach deals with the Democratic party organization, Dilworth also preferred the practical details of policy to the administrative issues that preoccupied Clark. City solicitor David Berger later explained that "contrary to Clark who was the reformer and the theorist, Dilworth was the activist and was interested in things he could see and feel. He wanted to get going with the program rather than do the theoretically necessary things like civil service." Berger credited Frederic Mann, who replaced Walter Phillips as commerce director, with convincing Dilworth that the proposed industrial program represented a significant opportunity.[31] In his first weekly report to the mayor in January 1956, Mann described "the present disturbing trend toward deterioration of the City's economic base" as "undoubtedly the most serious single problem confronting the Director of Commerce at the present time (and, because of its direct effect on municipal revenues and the level of employment throughout Philadelphia, one of the most serious problems facing the entire City government)."[32] Mann's background in manufacturing made him sensitive to the problems of Philadelphia's industrial firms, and he immediately adopted almost all of Phillips's ideas for industrial renewal, often claiming credit for them as his own. Unlike Phillips, Mann had little interest in the daily details of the Commerce Department's operation, which he left to his staff, and his irregular attendance at Dilworth's cabinet meetings became well known. Nonetheless, Mann's knowledge of the local business community and his capacity to prioritize his efforts around a limited number of specific issues made him more effective than his predecessor at advancing the industrial renewal concept.[33]

Meanwhile, Philadelphia's increasing experience with other economic development strategies created new openings for policy innovations such as the industrial program. None of the standard public or private practices in the field seemed to offer appropriate tools for confronting the problem of jobs generally or the difficulties of the manufacturing sector specifically. Two prominent cases demonstrated these limitations. First, the privately developed Penn Center office tower project indicated that the city would have great difficulty protecting the public interest in development projects generated by private investment. Serious planning for Penn Center began in early 1952 when the Pennsylvania Railroad announced that it would demolish and redevelop Broad Street Station and the surrounding elevated tracks, which crossed the Schuylkill River at Pennsylvania Boulevard and continued east for ten blocks to the station atop an imposing edifice of smoke-blackened stone and brick. Most observers believed that construction of the Penn Center complex on the site would determine the future physical, social, and economic character of Center City. Mayor Clark and Planning Commission director Edmund Bacon struggled to control the design of Penn Center through a series of official plans, public oversight bodies, and, occasionally, efforts to intimidate private developers with threats that the city might deploy its eminent domain powers. But Clark and Bacon's efforts proved insufficient. Because the city was unable to finance a seizure of the land, it lacked a financial stake in the project. Penn Center thus proved to be economically successful but aesthetically mediocre. The city's troublesome early experience with Penn Center offered Philadelphia planners and policymakers a vivid lesson in the limitations inherent in relying on the private sector as a mechanism for redevelopment: planners lacked the political, legal, and financial tools necessary to control urban redevelopment projects implemented solely by private actors.[34]

While Penn Center showed the inadequacy of relying on private development, the massive 3,000-acre Eastwick urban renewal project along the city's semi-rural southwestern boundary highlighted problems with the federal urban renewal program. As the largest urban renewal project in the United States, the $78 million Eastwick plan projected a self-contained "city-within-a-city." It proposed an interrelated mixture of housing, industrial and commercial areas, and community facilities that would provide 20,000 jobs and homes for as many as 60,000 people—and it would be racially integrated. By the 1980s, the Eastwick project would attain many of its original goals, if on a significantly smaller scale; in the mid- and late-1950s, however, the project slowed nearly to a halt, as the federal government repeatedly rejected the city's plans and grant applications on technical grounds. Meanwhile, the determined opposition of Eastwick's existing inter-racial, working-class community to the clearance of homes and the displacement of 8,636 people further delayed the project and embarrassed city officials. The Eastwick neighborhood resistance movement suggested the sort of social conflict that would be generated if the city used urban renewal as a primary instrument of local industrial policy.[35]

Although Eastwick offered a particularly dramatic illustration of the problems with using urban renewal as a vehicle for industrial redevelopment, planners encountered other difficulties with urban renewal in the heavily industrial Franklin and Callowhill areas, and in a single-company project with the Abbott's Dairies company.[36] Local and federal bureaucratic channels through which urban renewal projects moved simply took far more time than the average industrial firm was willing to wait for a new plant. From start to finish, the process of planning, approval, condemnation, relocation, and site preparation for an urban renewal project could take as long as five years. In addition, until the early 1960s, urban renewal programs remained partially constrained by the authorizing legislation's requirement that projects be "primarily residential" in character. Successive revisions of the federal housing act in 1954, 1959, and 1961 increased the percentage of funds that could be used for nonresidential projects, but as in Eastwick, the residential restriction required cities to link industrial projects, at least nominally, to housing. This complicated the use of federal urban renewal grants for either the redevelopment of obsolete factories or the establishment of free-standing industrial parks on open ground.[37] Cities such as St. Louis, Cincinnati, Buffalo, and Cleveland attempted, with only limited success, to use urban renewal for large industrial projects during this period. Philadelphia officials, in contrast, concluded that these problems made the federal program unattractive as an instrument for implementing economic development plans in areas other than downtown commercial and office districts.[38]

The Penn Center and Eastwick projects also took place within a broader context of significant change in Philadelphia's urban renewal and housing policy, change that would both advance Phillips's agenda and bring the need for a new policy instrument to the forefront of discussion among local policymakers. Since the early months of the Clark administration, leading figures from local public and private planning organizations had participated in a comprehensive review of the progress and future priorities of the city's urban renewal program. After more than two years of work, they released the Central Urban Renewal Area (CURA) study in March 1956 (shortly after Dilworth had succeeded Clark as mayor).[39] The study's conclusions reflected growing dissatisfaction with urban renewal. Contrary to the planners' expectations, the Redevelopment Authority's strategy of targeted clearance, which sought to create "islands of good" by clearing large swathes of "blighted" structures and replacing them with new residential, commercial, or institutional facilities, had in practice failed to eliminate the most acute deterioration. In most cases, the replacement of slums with "spores" of "good" public housing or other new structures had not only failed to exert improving influences on nearby areas, but instead, had actually made them worse. As in many other cities, slum clearance displaced residents at a rate that outpaced new housing construction. This produced overcrowding and further deterioration in adjoining neighborhoods. Little or no new private investment could be attracted to such areas, whether cleared or not. Meanwhile, public housing in Philadelphia had remained almost entirely segregated, as efforts to build integrated projects in white areas met determined resistance from residents and City Council members.[40]

The CURA study proposed a new approach. It divided the central city into categories designated as either A, B, or C in descending order from most blighted to conservable. Most of the C areas lay outside the central core, while the A and B areas generally lay in centrally located neighborhoods either already occupied by African Americans or undergoing racial transition. The CURA study estimated that if the city continued with its existing strategy, total costs of clearance in the A and B areas would rise to as much as $1 billion, an amount far beyond what Philadelphia could finance through its own resources or the federal urban renewal program. Even if such funds could somehow be found, large areas of marginal housing in B and even C areas would deteriorate into new slums before redevelopment in the A areas could be completed.[41]

The Dilworth administration spent the following year coming to grips with the CURA study. In March 1957 Development Coordinator William Rafsky (the former Hosiery Workers official) announced a major reorientation of the urban renewal program. Based on the CURA study's recommendations, the new city policy focused on the "conservable" and mostly white C areas, where it would employ urban renewal funds to clear limited bad spots and use rehabilitation and code enforcement to conserve the remainder. Public housing would be built in these areas, but "in small scattered clusters" instead of large projects. The city would complete the large A and B area projects already underway, along with Eastwick. Thereafter, however, it would delay all clearance in the A and B sections until a later date when new funds might become available. In the interim, aggressive code enforcement would be used to arrest further deterioration, and tax delinquent properties would be seized and demolished to create open spaces such as parking lots or playgrounds. The largely minority neighborhoods in the A and B areas would thus get relatively little from CURA. But this was not altogether a bad thing. Previous urban renewal clearance efforts in these areas had brought only limited benefits for residents and had caused widespread displacement of people while offering at best uncertain prospects for adequate rehousing. While in one way an abandonment of such neighborhoods, CURA in another sense offered a measure of relief from what in practice had often been an inhumane policy.[42]

Further, Dilworth and Rafsky tried to address these neighborhoods' problems through another measure: an attack on patterns of racial segregation in the wider region. As he described the new CURA policy, Rafsky argued that "no program of urban renewal can succeed within a housing market that is discriminatory and restrictive .... programs designed to lift the discriminatory restrictions now prevalent in the housing market are an essential adjunct of this program." As a result, the city campaigned for a statewide open-occupancy housing law to break what Mayor Dilworth described, in an early use of what would soon become a common discourse about suburban segregation, as the "white noose" of the region's suburbs. Still, both the city's advocacy of a state-wide housing law and its new focus on conservation in the CURA C areas were explicitly intended to slow or halt racial turnover in city neighborhoods. Unless those neighborhoods could be stabilized, Dilworth argued, Philadelphia would continue to lose financially better-off residents, with devastating consequences for its tax base.[43] Under CURA, racial integration became a secondary goal behind the city's interest in fiscal self-preservation.

Housing, however, was only one part of the CURA plan. A second component reflected the 1954 federal Housing Act's reformulation of the original urban redevelopment program into a broader "urban renewal" program that allowed some federal funds to be used for nonresidential projects. This provision meant that CURA's "triage" residential strategy would be accompanied by a three-pronged economic development program: the first prong consisted of efforts to develop "a strong downtown keystone" through projects in and near Center City; the second involved assisting the expansion of the city's universities and other large institutions, a process that soon became one of the defining characteristics of Philadelphia's urban renewal efforts; and the third entailed the adoption of a program of industrial clearance and renewal. Although only partially formulated at the time of Rafsky's announcement, the industrial renewal goal soon became a key part of the CURA program. It would focus, however, on rehabilitation and new "green-field" construction rather than on the neighborhood-erasing clearance approach often associated with urban renewal.[44]

Phillips and other Commerce Department officials had earlier concluded that in formulating a specific local industrial policy that would fit in the forthcoming CURA strategy, Philadelphia would have to develop a new policy mechanism that provided public control without sacrificing the flexibility necessary to meet the needs of manufacturing firms. Fortuitously, a simultaneous effort to replace Philadelphia's aging wholesale food market on the edge of Center City with a modern food distribution center in South Philadelphia provided a model for such a policy device. This structure, the nonprofit quasi-public corporation, not only prevented a repetition of the problems of Penn Center and Eastwick, but also provided an institutional template for the implementation of local industrial policy in Philadelphia. Incorporated in early 1955, the Food Distribution Center Corporation included representatives from both the city and the Greater Philadelphia Movement on its board, specified that all revenues above operating costs would be transferred to the city, and established that the facility itself would become the property of the city once the corporation had amortized its debt. Despite the opposition of Albert Greenfield, City Council approved the final plan for the center in late 1955; shortly thereafter, the city acquired the land and worked with the corporation to begin preliminary construction work. The Food Distribution Center (FDC) thus provided an operating example of a quasi-public, nonprofit corporation engaged in an industrially oriented development project. Petshek later noted that "the FDC endeavor had moved a step beyond the Penn Center Development, which had often left the government powerless to influence decisions affecting what it considered to be in the public interest. By contrast, the public was directly involved in the FDC, not merely as an observer, although not yet as a partner."[45] The food center experience suggested that nonprofit, public-private corporations could be an effective administrative instrument for the city's effort to address the problem of jobs through industrial development. With the new CURA policy just coming into effect, it suddenly seemed possible that Walter Phillips's ideas might at last become public policy.[46]

Toward an Industrial Renewal Program

By 1958, the political calculus on industrial renewal had been transformed: the new CURA policy was in place, Mayor Dilworth had neutralized Albert Greenfield by ensconcing him in the City Planning Commission chairmanship, the state government had established a program of matching funds for municipal industrial development projects, and the University of Pennsylvania's Institute for Urban Studies had completed a study of the industrial space problem that provided detailed social scientific support for the position that Walter Phillips had taken earlier in the decade.[47] In addition, Dilworth himself became alarmed about Philadelphia's ongoing job losses and made industrial renewal a priority. After an intricate series of negotiations, the mayor reached an agreement with the Chamber of Commerce for joint sponsorship of a nonprofit, quasi-public authority known as the Philadelphia Industrial Development Corporation (PIDC) that would implement the industrial renewal concept.[48]

The new corporation's board of directors included representatives from city government, the Chamber of Commerce, and Philadelphia's major labor unions. The board, however, made no provision for participation by either neighborhood-based community organizations or groups that represented Philadelphia's African American community.[49] Thus the structure of the PIDC made it possible for it to ignore the city's racial problems. It also insured that the program would be broadly oriented toward the interests of business and, secondarily, organized labor. Yet it was the very acceptance of these limitations that made it possible for Philadelphia's local liberals to address an important aspect of deindustrialization through public intervention in the industrial real estate market.

The Chamber of Commerce's position on racial issues delineated the political constraints that forced such choices. In 1963, the city's Commission on Human Relations issued a directive that required Philadelphia employers to keep comprehensive records of recruitment processes and hiring decisions in order to document employment discrimination. The Chamber blasted the requirement as a "high-handed outrage" that would impose burdensome costs on employers. Unwilling to risk further conflict, the commission rescinded the order, "agreed to a course of persuasion and education rather than one of persecution or prosecution," and granted official recognition to a new Chamber-sponsored employers' committee. As one of its first acts, this committee undercut a similar anti-discrimination program run by the state of Pennsylvania.[50] Along with its positions on civil rights, the traditionally Republican Chamber had maintained a stance of hard-line ideological opposition to the Clark and Dilworth administrations. The industrial renewal program marked the first case of Chamber cooperation with the city, but it rested on a tremendously tenuous accommodation. As late as 1957, a member of the Chamber's board informed the business organization's new chief operating officer that "the most important job at hand was to prevent city hall from getting political dominance of industrial development."[51]

Under more moderate leadership in the mid- and late-1960s, the Chamber would significantly moderate these positions. At the time that PIDC was organized, however, any city effort to link industrial renewal with civil rights or labor issues would have combined with the Chamber's distrust of the reform administrations, and of activist government generally, to eliminate the possibility of public-private cooperation in the project. Why, then, did Dilworth involve the Chamber at all? While the city could have proceeded with a purely public initiative, the Chamber's participation provided PIDC with a crucial source of political support and legitimization within the Philadelphia business community. In 1964, a PIDC official commented on the functional importance of such credibility: "If business didn't believe [us, we] could always send them to well respected people like [William F.] Kelly, president of the [First] Pennsylvania [Banking and Trust] Company, who was president of PIDC, or Gangware of the Pennsylvania Railroad."[52] The formation of PIDC depended on a pragmatic liberal compromise, as the reformers deliberately ignored causal elements of urban deindustrialization in order to gain a flawed but useful partner in a viable industrial renewal program. Without such participation, the business community would have been much less willing to accept PIDC as a legitimate actor in the local industrial development process.

The nonprofit, quasi-public corporation, as proposed by Walter Phillips, as demonstrated by the food center project, and as ultimately implemented in full form by PIDC, would emerge during the 1960s as the preferred method for implementing public projects in Philadelphia. This structure provided public control over economic development, efficiency in responding to the private sector, and significant, if not particularly democratic, insulation against popular pressures regarding development policy. Establishing the industrial program had been difficult because of the magnitude of the departure that it represented from past practices and ideological assumptions, and also as a result of the contentious nature of underlying questions about the cause of the city's loss of manufacturing firms. Resolution of such conflicts depended in part on the formation of an acceptable balance between the public and private roles in the project, and even more on the construction of a socially neutral explanation of urban economic change. By emphasizing manufacturers' need for adequate space to accommodate one-story plants and modern transportation systems, the advocates of industrial renewal deliberately ignored more problematic causes of urban industrial decline such as racial change and labor costs. This discursive strategy would shape Philadelphia's local industrial policy in definitive and sometimes constraining ways. Had the supporters of industrial renewal pursued any other strategy, however, they would have had great difficulty in gaining the cooperation of the business community. Without that cooperation, the program would have been nearly impossible to implement. While such compromises reflected the very real limitations of postwar Philadelphia's pragmatic liberalism, PIDC's accomplishments would provide a clear demonstration that this liberalism nonetheless retained the capacity to make meaningful interventions in the city's economic life.

CHAPTER TWO

Good Medicine for Philadelphia? Local Industrial Policy and the Problem of Jobs

The Penn El Service Company never counted among Philadelphia's industrial giants. Occupying a worn, two-story building on North Street in the Fairmount section of Lower North Philadelphia, the company employed at most twelve people and in the mid-1960s had annual revenues of just $2 million. Penn El Service, however, typified a crucial sector of Philadelphia's industrial economy: small, highly-specialized companies that performed a particular, often highly technical, niche function for a specific group of customers. Collectively, these small manufacturers and wholesalers made up a huge proportion of the city's industrial base. In the case of Penn El Service, a wholesaler, this function consisted of providing electrical components for ships, with a specialization in "'stuffing tubes' which carry wires and cables through watertight bulkheads and compartments." Few other companies in the world—perhaps none—provided this service. As a 1967 profile of the company noted, "Who ever heard of Penn El Service Company? Nobody except a few thousand guys who build and repair ships in ports in every part of the world." Penn El Service's owner, a sixty-year-old, white businessman named Sam Reiver, had purchased the company in 1943. As the business expanded, Reiver struggled with conditions in the surrounding neighborhood. With a mix of aging row houses, factories, and warehouses, interspersed with vacant lots, the neighborhood had become primarily African American and Puerto Rican, and among the poorest in the city. Many of the area's larger businesses left, as did most middle class residents. By the mid-1960s, Penn El Service sat across the street from an abandoned carpet factory and a few doors away from a brothel. Crime rose, and Reiver suffered a half-dozen break-ins and many more attempts. Thefts ranged from office staplers to window air conditioners to the metal in a backyard fence. The company bore the costs of new security measures, as well as increases in city wage and mercantile taxes. By 1967, a frustrated Reiver acquired a 10,000-square-foot building in suburban Conshohocken and left Philadelphia. Whether or not they were accurate, or fair, or free of racial connotations, Reiver's perceptions of his neighborhood and city paralleled those of thousands of other business owners in inner city Philadelphia during the postwar decades.[1]

PIDC failed to prevent the loss of Penn El Service, but it did prevent the departure from Philadelphia of many other similar companies. Such actions emerged as a core component of the quasi-public agency's mission. PIDC's first executive vice president (the operational head of the agency) shaped this focus. Richard Graves came to PIDC from California, where he had directed the California League of Cities for nineteen years before running unsuccessfully as the Democratic nominee for governor in 1954.[2] Although Mayor Dilworth and the Chamber of Commerce had intense private debates over the distribution of power within PIDC, Graves soon centralized planning and decision making around his own technical staff. In most cases, the PIDC board simply approved the executive vice president's decisions.

Graves implemented Walter Phillips's plan for transforming vacant city land into industrial parks, but also added innovations of his own. Shortly after arriving in Philadelphia in 1958, Graves recognized a crucial characteristic of the local economy: the core of Philadelphia's manufacturing base lay less in large, integrated corporations than in small- and medium-sized specialty and batch manufacturing and wholesaling firms that occupied specific production niches. These firms were often family-owned, and in many cases, were undercapitalized. Many struggled with obsolete facilities and neighborhood problems such as those that plagued Reiver.[3] As a result, even when these companies had good credit ratings, they lacked the equity necessary to finance either the modernization of existing plants or the construction of new facilities. In some cases, such firms left Philadelphia for cheaper land, financing, and labor in the suburbs or the southern United States, encouraged by federal tax deductions such as accelerated depreciation for new industrial construction. In more marginal cases, firms stagnated or went out of business. Either way, such companies would be lost to Philadelphia.[4]

Graves concluded that if PIDC could provide low-cost financing for these companies, it might be able to maintain this segment of Philadelphia's industrial base. This policy reflected Graves's decision to emphasize the retention of existing firms rather than the attraction of outside companies.[5] With urban renewal effectively rejected as a policy instrument for the program, Graves had to find an alternative financing mechanism. Drawing on his experience in California, he developed one. Since the 1930s, many states and localities, especially in the South, had provided low-cost industrial financing through the use of industrial revenue bonds. Although Pennsylvania state law prohibited this practice, Graves realized that because of its status as an agent of the city government, PIDC could accomplish the same thing by acting as an intermediary between lenders and firms in the industrial mortgage market.[6]

The key to this strategy lay in the federal tax status of municipal debt instruments. Interest payments on the debt obligations of cities and municipal authorities had a long-standing exemption from federal income tax, and Graves recognized that if PIDC assumed the actual mortgage on a new or renovated industrial facility, the federal tax exemption would apply to PIDC's mortgage interest payments just as it did to payments made on industrial revenue bonds in competing states. Because PIDC's payments were tax-free, lenders would offer lower interest rates and require less equity from participating manufacturing firms. The strategy became a viable option in 1959 when the IRS declared PIDC a "municipal instrumentality" and ruled its debt obligations tax-exempt.[7] Under this system, PIDC took on the mortgage for the facility, secured a reduced interest rate, and entered an installment sale agreement with the private firm that would use the plant. The firm would then make payments equal to PIDC's mortgage obligations plus all project costs except non-assessable municipal infrastructure improvements. Once the mortgage had been fully amortized, the property title would be transferred from PIDC to the firm. This use of industrial mortgages became the basis of PIDC's operations throughout the 1960s.[8]

By acting as the borrower in industrial transactions, PIDC thus used its federal tax exemption to lower the cost of financing new or renovated industrial facilities, within the city limits, for undercapitalized Philadelphia manufacturing firms.[9] Relying on the federal tax exemption allowed PIDC to avoid local subsidies or tax abatements that would have damaged

the city's revenue base and placed the burden of industrial renewal on local taxpayers. Instead, PIDC shifted much of the program's cost to the
federal government. This meant that in at least one case in the postwar
United States, the federal government subsidized urban rather than suburban industrial development. In effect, PIDC implemented a local industrial policy that employed federal tax structures to reorganize the spatial geography of industrial production and preserve viable elements of
Philadelphia's manufacturing base.[10] This form of postwar local liberalism thus demonstrated that the local state could undertake productive
interventions in the urban economy and pursue the creation of a more
ordered economic world. The very existence of such an industrial policy
suggests that in one major American urban center, postwar liberalism engaged the problem of jobs through direct policy action. PIDC's strategy
had only one drawback: the entire program rested on the 1959 IRS ruling,
which could be revoked at any time.

The establishment of a viable financing mechanism resolved important
problems for the new nonprofit corporation, but other questions remained.
PIDC faced a pressing need to define its specific goals and establish exact
development standards. In part, such issues became contentious because
of two early PIDC projects that reflected an opportunistic rather than
systematic approach to industrial development. Richard Graves characterized these two projects—a $3.5 million distribution center for the Sun
Ray drug store chain and a storage facility for Gulf Oil, both in the Penrose area of Southwest Philadelphia—as a "BB gun holding action." More
broadly, PIDC spent its first year of operation responding to immediate
crises involving the possible departure of companies from the city and
did not formulate a clear set of policies and priorities. This pattern worried city officials who advocated a more careful industrial policy grounded
in social-scientific theory regarding regional development and industrial
location. City economist Kirk Petshek emerged as the leading advocate
of this technocratic, planned approach to industrial renewal, which he
sought to advance through the Mayor's Economic Advisory Committee
that Dilworth had formed in the spring of 1958 to bring together leading local economists and planners from the public, private, and academic
sectors.[11]

Petshek and the advisory committee argued that PIDC should focus on
industries that would provide the greatest economic gains, and seek the
most efficient possible allocation of firms through the city and even the
region. They also criticized the city's failure either to clarify its economic

development goals or to formulate a "coherent policy" for industrial land development. In the committee's view, the City Planning Commission's recently completed Comprehensive Plan had failed to address these issues. PIDC's early projects only reinforced these concerns. Solutions, the economists argued, should be pursued within a broad framework in which "policymakers, both public and private, might have the opportunity to coordinate their objectives and seek to achieve common goals."[12] This planning-oriented approach could be traced to Walter Phillips's tenure as city commerce director during the first reform administration, and it rested on the assumption that social science could generate government solutions to public problems.[13] This view did have some influence within PIDC. Paul Wilhelm, who had served as Phillips's assistant director of commerce and later joined PIDC as an industrial development planner, recalled that "Kirk had imbued me with his ideas about linkage use and the type of growth and guessing who was going to be good and that had a lot of influence on me.... In three years I sat in on almost every meeting that Graves had and I was able to inject Kirk's approach." Nonetheless, among Petshek's band of economists, PIDC's initial transactions provoked specific, immediate concerns. Responding to a suggestion that PIDC emphasize firms outside the city, Petshek noted "that he was more disturbed by some of the industries that PIDC had retained."[14] In particular, Petshek believed that neither the Sun Ray nor Gulf transactions was a sufficiently labor-intensive use of the city-owned Penrose land; in both cases he thought PIDC had simply seized available development opportunities without adequate planning or evaluation.[15]

Graves and his staff at PIDC had no objection to the establishment of development standards, which they saw as potentially helpful. They believed, however, that they could not delay the industrial program while the complicated studies proposed by the Mayor's Economic Advisory Committee were completed. PIDC officials also discounted the social scientists' concerns about providing assistance to the wrong kind of firms. PIDC projects chief Harold Wise told the Mayor's Economic Advisory Committee in September 1960 that such "'undesirables' are a very small portion of [PIDC's] problem."[16] While PIDC officials wanted better, more explicit criteria for using specific land tracts, they refused to reject possible transactions so that land could be held in reserve for a hypothetical ideal user. Instead, Graves and the staff preferred an opportunistic approach under which PIDC would accept a wide range of firms, subject only to the financial capacity of the participating company and the best available use of the tract. In part, this position reflected the large number of Philadelphia firms that had already requested PIDC assistance. By the end of 1960, the new agency had made contact with 687 firms, and Graves felt compelled to assist as many as possible.[17]

Although the Mayor's Economic Advisory Committee did formulate development standards for specific industrial tracts in the Franklin and Eastwick Urban Renewal areas, Graves's approach predominated because the studies needed to establish the comprehensive criteria envisioned by the committee proved to be prohibitively complex and costly.[18] Nonetheless, the underlying issues in this debate of pragmatism versus planning suddenly became very real when PIDC brought in a private developer for the city-owned land at Northeast Airport. Beginning in late 1959, PIDC entered discussions with the New York–based Tishman Realty and Construction Company; eighteen months later Tishman became the exclusive developer for three of the four tracts of industrial land at Northeast Airport upon which the new Philadelphia Industrial Park would be built.[19]

Graves pushed the Tishman deal for two reasons. First, Tishman provided a dependable source of added financing and access to traditional lenders for the low net worth companies that Graves hoped to serve through the PIDC program. Second, as a national real estate developer, Tishman brought promotional resources that PIDC could not match on its own.[20] Such rationales failed to convince Petshek and the Mayor's Economic Advisory Committee. Shortly after PIDC announced a tentative agreement with Tishman, the committee challenged core aspects of the arrangement. In an October 1960 memo to Rafsky, the city development coordinator, Petshek questioned several of these: the propriety of the rate-of-return that Tishman stood to earn on its investment, the impact of Tishman's profits on the industrial revolving fund, the developer's true ability to recruit an increased number of firms, the capacity of PIDC to control Tishman's costs without competitive bidding, the proposed balance between local and out-of-town companies in the park, and Tishman's willingness to accept city criteria governing development of the park.[21]

Recognizing the apparent inevitability of the Tishman contract, however, the Economic Advisory Committee formulated a list of development criteria for the airport land and argued that these standards should be applied before the PIDC board approved the deal. Along with such general, project-wide standards as cyclical stability, minimum employment density, high growth potential, and overall complementarity of firms, the criteria included specific recommendations that firms should offer skilled and semi-skilled jobs, that 50 percent of the land should be reserved for firms "new to the city," and that 25 percent should be held for Philadelphia companies that either suffered from low credit ratings or had been displaced by urban renewal or highway projects. Finally, the committee suggested that preference be given to companies with a high percentage of workers "residing in the city." This final item was the most important of the proposed standards because it recognized Philadelphia's growing problem of jobs and the need to link development of the industrial park to city residents' need for employment.[22] This concern lay at the core of the economists' effort to promote economic planning as a central PIDC function. More broadly, the committee's development criteria outlined the kind of locally-based economic and industrial planning that the National Resources Planning Board (NRPB) had advocated during the New Deal (see the introduction). No equivalent existed, of course, for the kind of comprehensive national coordinating function that the NRPB itself would have supplied in such a system.[23]

Despite their efforts, Petshek and the Economic Advisory Committee failed to gain the support of the Dilworth administration, let alone the Chamber, for the imposition of such strict development standards. As a result, the final version of the contract contained only a series of nonbinding provisions in which Tishman acknowledged the city's interest in attracting low net worth firms and providing jobs, as well as a clause specifying that the facilities be offered at "more favorable rentals" than those available in competing suburban parks.[24]

The dispute over the Tishman contract marked the effective conclusion of the debate over whether PIDC would employ rigorous planning standards in its selection of firms, and the episode demonstrated the economists' inability to build political support for a social scientific, planned approach to industrial development. Instead, Graves's pragmatic strategy shaped Philadelphia's program. On June 2, 1961, PIDC signed the development contract with Tishman, and on June 20, at a luncheon at Philadelphia's Bellevue-Stratford Hotel attended by Governor David Lawrence and Mayor Dilworth, publicly presented the plans for Philadelphia Industrial Park.[25]

As the industrial program gained momentum over the following years, the PIDC board did apply a number of very broad standards in evaluating proposed transactions. For the most part, however, it simply relied on staff judgments regarding the advisability of each project. Petshek remained unhappy about the policy direction and resigned as city economist in 1962. Despite Petshek's resignation and the inability of the Economic Advisory Committee to influence the PIDC program, the episode marked only the start of what would become a wider effort among liberal Philadelphia planners to develop technocratic, social scientific standards for comprehensive local planning and economic policy. Pursued most rigorously within the planning frameworks required by the federal Area Redevelopment, Community Renewal, and Model Cities programs, this project represented postwar Philadelphia's most direct expression of technocratic, reform liberalism, in effect an updated and adapted version of ideas developed by the NRPB during the 1930s.

PIDC in Operation

In practice, manufacturing firms came to PIDC through a number of routes. PIDC itself engaged in extensive outreach, as staff members called on companies around the city, and both staff and board members spoke to business and community groups and made television and radio appearances. PIDC also advertised in local and national newspapers and magazines, engaged in direct mail promotions, and set up displays in bank offices; all of these tactics yielded contacts and direct inquiries from firms. Along with such direct techniques, PIDC received referrals from the Chamber of Commerce, the city Commerce Department, and even the Philadelphia Electric Company. Finally, the city's industrial real estate brokers emerged as a crucial source of PIDC clients. Initially wary of PIDC's quasi-governmental nature, the brokers soon realized that the agency's activities would increase their own business and voluntarily brought firms to PIDC.[26]

Meanwhile, debates over formal planning aside, PIDC's staff developed practical criteria for selecting companies that would receive assistance. As basic conditions, firms had to be engaged in manufacturing or closely related activities, and they had to be financially sound enough to meet the debt obligations that the transaction would create.[27] PIDC had no interest in propping up companies that would be likely to fail. The agency next assessed whether the company truly needed assistance. Although PIDC did take a few "grade A" clients when a company would otherwise be lost (or when the company's presence would bolster one of PIDC's industrial parks), the agency prioritized the strong but undercapitalized small- and medium-sized firms at the core of Philadelphia's industrial base. The final, central qualification, however, consisted of the transaction's potential to serve PIDC's basic purposes of maintaining (or ideally, improving) the city's tax base and supply of good jobs.[28] While future growth potential entered into each assessment, the agency lacked the sort of systematic, overall industry projections for which Kirk Petshek had unsuccessfully lobbied.

While most companies that came to PIDC received assistance, some met with rejection. On May 7, 1963, the PIDC board's executive committee considered an application from a company known as Air Products and Chemicals to build an acetylene manufacturing plant in a PIDC industrial park. The committee rejected the project on the grounds that the plant would create hazardous conditions and "that on the five acres created, there would be only about 40 jobs and a rather inexpensive plant which would not create a substantial tax ratable." Later in the year, the same committee rejected a proposal from a furniture company for a new warehouse because the "transaction involved a company engaged primarily in retailing and represented no increase in job opportunities and tax ratables."[29] But occasionally, the board reconsidered. In 1965, the Bethlehem Steel Company requested PIDC's help in building a new facility for its wire rope distribution division in the Philadelphia Industrial Park; the proposal was rejected because the facility would only employ five people. Two weeks later, Bethlehem Steel clarified that moving the wire rope division would free space at its existing North Philadelphia facility for an expansion of its reinforcing bar division, adding between 20 and 35 employees to an existing workforce of 300. With this new information, PIDC accepted the project.[30]

With its administrative organization and operational methods established, PIDC's program went into operation. During the 1960s, the corporation completed transactions in almost every part of Philadelphia. These projects can be classified on a geographic basis according to whether they took place in peripheral, intermediate, or central areas of the city.[31] Within each of these zones, PIDC's work involved a mix of new and rehabilitated facilities, and these different project types and locations had varying consequences for the program and for the economic future of Philadelphia.

In peripheral sections of the city, almost all of PIDC's transactions involved new buildings in "green-field" industrial parks modeled on the fully planned suburban industrial developments of the period. The 650-acre

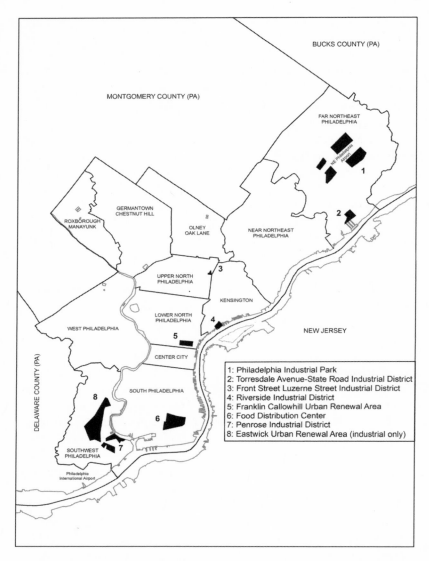

FIGURE 8. Philadelphia planning analysis sections and PIDC industrial parks, 1959–70. Map prepared by the author, using ESRI ArcMap 9.2.

Philadelphia Industrial Park at Northeast Philadelphia Airport (figure 8) was by far the largest and most prominent of the peripheral parks. By the spring of 1966, development in the park outpaced that in competing suburban industrial parks, and in 1968, PIDC reported that the park constituted the largest such facility "within any large city in the nation." Two years later, Philadelphia Industrial Park had sixty-seven plants, and only forty-five acres remained to be developed. During the 1970s and 1980s, PIDC built three additional industrial parks on undeveloped land in the area, and by 1980, the Far Northeast section had a higher level of combined manufacturing and wholesaling employment than any other area of Philadelphia.[32] The other major peripheral area of industrial development lay in southwest Philadelphia near the International Airport, where PIDC oversaw the development of both the 167-acre Penrose Industrial District and the industrial sections of the massive Eastwick urban renewal area.[33]

PIDC's industrial parks attracted a wide diversity of companies in terms of both size and industry. Examples of this breadth at the Philadelphia Industrial Park included the chocolate manufacturer Stephen F. Whitman, which after an expansion operated in a 500,870-square-foot plant and employed 1,650 workers, and the E. F. Hauserman Company, a Cleveland-based manufacturer of movable partition systems, which acquired a 23,154 square foot facility and employed only 10 workers. Most firms in the park, however, had between 100 and 300 employees. The Crescent Box Corporation, which made folding cartons and specialized cardboard shipping containers, operated a 68,800-square-foot plant on Erie Avenue in North Philadelphia for thirty years. By the early 1960s, Crescent Box needed to expand, and spent three years evaluating sites in both suburban Pennsylvania and New Jersey as well as in Philadelphia. Finally, in 1965, the company accepted a $900,000 installment sale agreement for a new, 100,000-square-foot facility on nine acres of land in Philadelphia Industrial Park. Company president Jack Swope explained that the company "decided that we didn't want to be in a cow pasture, far away from the things our business needs." Key selling points included the ready supply of skilled labor and the site's proximity to the North Philadelphia Airport, which allowed the company to bring customers directly to the plant and gave its executives access to branch plants in other areas of Pennsylvania.[34]

Crescent Box's decision suggests the important effect of the nation's rapidly developing passenger and freight air services on the spatial location of industry in the postwar period. Companies around the country made similar decisions because of their need to be near distribution networks and travel services, and industrial and office parks became common features of the landscape surrounding both large and small airports. As unremarkable as such facilities may have appeared, this change quietly transformed the spatial patterns of economic activity in U.S. metropolitan areas.[35] With two airports located within or immediately adjoining the city's boundary, Philadelphia possessed an advantage over other cities whose airports lay in far flung suburbs. Throughout the 1960s and 1970s, PIDC used this accident of geography as a means to preserve parts of the industrial, wholesaling, and distribution sectors of the city's economy.

With their one- and two-story factories, landscaped grounds, and expansive parking lots, Philadelphia Industrial Park and PIDC's other peripheral parks marked an almost total transformation of the traditional urban industrial landscape. As such, they reflected the broad influence of the automobile (as well as the airplane) on the built environment, even suggesting that PIDC sought in part to create a new "urban suburbia." Not all of PIDC's industrial parks, however, lay in these peripheral areas. In an intermediate zone four to six miles from Center City, PIDC developed the Torresdale Avenue-State Road Industrial Park on a seventy-six acre tract near the Delaware River that the city had previously used as the site of Camp Happy, a children's summer camp. Construction of the Delaware Expressway (Interstate 95) placed a cloverleaf exit ramp in the center of the site and rendered it useless as a camp. PIDC, however, determined that the forty acres not taken by the highway could be developed industrially, and in 1959 the city transferred the tract to PIDC's "industrial land bank."

The second company to move into the new park represented a particularly valuable coup for the new industrial development agency. In 1955, the Deruss Machine Products Company had moved to suburban Bucks County after a fire destroyed its Philadelphia plant. Six years later, facing the clearance of its plant for the Bucks County section of the expressway, Deruss returned to the city when it moved into a new facility in PIDC's Torresdale Avenue–State Road Industrial Park. In 1963, PIDC placed the Detroit-based Richard Brothers Punch-American Drill Brushing Company, the first firm from outside the Philadelphia region, in the Torresdale Avenue–State Road district as well. By 1965, PIDC reported that it had developed all fifteen sites in the industrial park. All of the firms that PIDC relocated there were small- or medium-sized, with employment ranging

FIGURE 9. Undated aerial view of North Philadelphia (taken in the vicinity of 2nd Street and Tioga Street), looking south toward Center City, c. 1940s or 1950s. The photo shows the dense mixture of rowhouses and multistory loft factories typical of much of the central city (compare this photo to the aerial photo of Far Northeast Philadelphia in chapter 1). PIDC was very active in this area in the 1960s and 1970s, both in moving firms out and in renovating and modernizing existing factories for reuse. Photo courtesy of Temple University Libraries, Urban Archives, Philadelphia, Pennsylvania.

from 5 workers at Fox Iron Works up to 150 at the Miller North Broad Storage Company. While the Torresdale Avenue–State Road district represented the only formal PIDC industrial park in the intermediate zone of the city, PIDC also completed numerous transactions involving existing buildings in this area.[36]

In inner-city areas less than four miles from City Hall, PIDC also maintained an active presence, in regard to both industrial parks and, even more prominently, existing buildings. This finding is both surprising and significant, as inner-city racial conflict remained an ever-present factor in decisions about industrial movement and location.[37] Despite this obstacle, PIDC managed to achieve a relatively successful record in inner-city Philadelphia, beginning with the thirteen-acre Front Street–Luzerne Avenue

Industrial District. Built on the site of an abandoned hospital in the Feltonville section of North Philadelphia, Front-Luzerne had space for only three firms, which moved into newly built plants between 1960 and 1964 (including West Wholesale Drug, profiled in the introduction).[38] Along the Delaware River, PIDC built four new facilities in the Riverside Industrial Center, a small inner-city industrial park developed on the former site of the William Cramp and Sons Shipyard in the Kensington area.[39] More important than their size, however, the Front-Luzerne and Riverside projects provided an anchor for PIDC's engagement in surrounding neighborhoods. This section of the city contained a substantial number of industrial facilities, many of them relatively new and still attractive to firms seeking space. In 1960, a PIDC consultant evaluated the district to the east of Front-Luzerne as "unquestionably the best industrial area surveyed," and described the district immediately to the south as one of the three best areas in the city. The consultant reported similar findings for the areas adjoining the Riverside Industrial Center. The presence of this high-quality infrastructure meant that PIDC was able to finance a large number of transactions in privately owned buildings throughout the corridor running between the Front-Luzerne and Riverside properties.[40]

In this area, as well as elsewhere in the city's industrial core, PIDC consistently emphasized the reuse of older buildings. In 1965, an internal analysis of the agency's work explained that "the problem of industrial development is not only of simply making land available for new plants— it is equally concerned with providing the fullest utilization, expansion and rehabilitation of existing facilities."[41] One notable example came in the aftermath of the Crescent Box transaction, as PIDC moved the Triangle Container Corporation into Crescent's old Erie Avenue facility and then moved the Standard Paper Company (a distributor) into the plant that Triangle Container had vacated in Lower North Philadelphia. Each firm gained a larger facility. During the 1960s, when these transactions took place, the census tracts where the plants were located experienced declines in white populations of 700 to 900 people and increases in nonwhite populations of 100 to 500 people, placing both on the borderline of neighborhood racial change. As of this writing, a corporate descendant of Triangle Container (purchased in 2002 by a Wisconsin packaging company) continues to produce cardboard packaging and displays at the Erie Avenue plant.[42]

Closer to Center City, in the Independence Mall urban renewal area, PIDC in 1966 helped the Pincus Brothers-Maxwell apparel firm acquire the plant that Whitman's Chocolates had vacated when it moved to the Philadelphia Industrial Park six years before. One of the largest manufacturers of men's clothing in the country, Pincus Brothers-Maxwell moved from a smaller leased facility a few blocks to the east. PIDC's financing allowed the company to acquire and renovate the existing factory and construct an adjoining 42,500-square-foot building. The project nearly collapsed when the Planning Commission refused to approve the construction of a large sign on the building's roof, but PIDC's intervention with the commission secured a reversal of the decision. The company increased its employment from 500 to 750, and it remained at the location until 2001, when it ceased operations. At the time, it was Philadelphia's last remaining apparel firm.[43]

In some cases, PIDC's efforts proved inadequate. During the fall of 1964, the agency worked closely with Mayor James Tate to prevent the closure of E. Hubschman and Sons, a Philadelphia company that "was known internationally for making one of the finest calfskin leathers in the world." Hubschman and Sons, which was actually a subsidiary of the Glen Alden Corporation, employed 466 workers in a plant in the Callowhill area, a largely industrial district located just north of Center City that the Philadelphia Redevelopment Authority (RA) had designated for industrially focused urban renewal (one of the few such projects it undertook). In October, PIDC learned that Glen Alden planned to sell the Hubschman division to the Ohio Leather Company, which in turn planned to close the Philadelphia plant and relocate its operations to Ohio. The plant's primary union, the Amalgamated Meat Cutters and Butchers Workmen, appealed to Mayor Tate to save the company, and over the following weeks PIDC and Tate assisted the son-in-law of Hubschman's president as he formed a partnership with Boston's Allied Kid Company to purchase the plant and retain it in Philadelphia. Using its tax exemption, PIDC took on a low interest, $2.2 million bank loan on Allied Kid's behalf; Allied Kid itself took out a $700,000 loan, and the combined financing allowed the partnership to purchase the building, land, and all equipment from Glen Alden. Unlike its other projects, PIDC never actually took title to the property but instead accepted a loan guarantee from Allied Kid along with a plant mortgage as security. The certainty that the plant would otherwise be closed and that "employment at the site would be virtually eliminated" led PIDC to accept this unconventional arrangement. The project, however, soon unraveled. World prices for raw calfskin— Hubschman's chief input—skyrocketed in 1965, and with little elasticity in the prices for its finished goods, Hubschman took heavy losses that rapidly pushed down Allied Kid's overall earnings. Seeing little prospect for improvement, Allied Kid liquidated the Hubschman plant. Although PIDC had sought to include a provision requiring "that the operating company will remain in Philadelphia for the duration of the transaction," the Hubschman plant closed by mid-1966.[44] This failure demonstrated the costs of Richard Graves's decision to disregard the detailed economic analysis and planning that Kirk Petshek had advocated, as the local leather industry by 1964 had gone into a serious and readily apparent decline.[45]

Such failures aside, PIDC's industrial development effort in inner city areas remains extraordinary. Facilities such as the Front-Luzerne industrial park and Triangle Container's Erie Avenue plant lay in or near neighborhoods that underwent racial turnover during the 1960s. Throughout this period, North Philadelphia struggled with the racial tensions and unrest that typified inner city areas from Watts to Detroit to Newark. In August 1964, African Americans and police clashed through three days of upheaval along Columbia Avenue. In 1965, Philadelphia NAACP President Cecil B. Moore led a bitter, seven-month protest at Girard College, an all-white North Philadelphia orphanage and school. Later in the decade, Police Commissioner Frank Rizzo clashed with the city's nascent Black Power movement and deployed an aggressive, racially charged rhetoric of law and order that culminated in his successful 1971 mayoral campaign. Throughout the postwar decades, residential segregation hardened as white residents abandoned inner city neighborhoods. The fact that PIDC could attract investment capital of any kind into the area is highly surprising, as it ran counter to well-documented patterns of discriminatory residential lending.[46] PIDC's record thus indicates that conclusions about industrial investment cannot be drawn automatically either from the better-known housing experience or from assumptions about inner-city racial tensions.

Race, Urban Space, and Jobs: Implications of Philadelphia's Local Industrial Policy

PIDC's efforts in the inner city suggest that full evaluation of the program requires a comprehensive assessment not only of its new industrial parks, but also of its rehabilitation of existing facilities. Such an analysis provides insights into both PIDC's differential impact on various neighborhoods and its long-run implications for the city as a whole. Between 1959 and 1970, PIDC financed the construction of 196 new industrial and wholesale facilities, along with the renovation or expansion of 244 existing buildings. Total costs exceeded $245 million. The 440 transactions together created more than 25,900 new jobs and retained more than 41,300 existing jobs.[47] Using Philadelphia city records, newspaper real estate listings, PIDC publications, and local industrial directories, information was compiled about 354 of these transactions, involving 333 separate firms.[48] Using these data, four central questions can be addressed. First, what type of firms did PIDC assist, in terms of both size and industry? Second, what were the racial characteristics of the neighborhoods that PIDC-assisted firms left, and of the neighborhoods to which they moved or in which they expanded? Third, how much of PIDC's relocation activity involved firms displaced by urban renewal or highway construction? Fourth, to what extent did PIDC-assisted firms remain in their new or renovated facilities during the following decades?

The answer to the first question reflects Richard Graves's policy of supporting Philadelphia's small- and medium-sized manufacturing firms. Of the 333 PIDC-assisted firms, 135 had fewer than 50 employees, while 289 (86.7 percent) had fewer than 250 employees. Only 22 had 500 or more workers. This indicates that PIDC focused heavily, if not exclusively, on the small- and medium-sized manufacturers and wholesalers that traditionally constituted the largest component of Philadelphia's employment base.[49] Recognizing the significance of PIDC's work in this area, Philadelphia neighborhood activist Edward Schwartz later observed that "throughout the 1960s and '70s, ... [PIDC] was saving jobs by concentrating financial and technical assistance on hundreds of small firms that nobody else took seriously."[50]

The industries most frequently aided by PIDC included wholesalers, food processors and metal fabricators, followed by the fields of nonelectrical machinery, publishing, electrical machinery, apparel, furniture and fixtures, paper and allied products, miscellaneous manufacturing, textiles, chemicals and allied products, primary metal industries, and scientific instruments. Overall, PIDC aided firms in at least thirty-two different industries, across a broad range of sectors that reflected the full breadth of Philadelphia's diverse industrial base.[51] Apparel and textiles were a notable exception, completing PIDC-financed transactions at a lower rate than their prominent position in both overall employment and number of firms would have predicted. This omission reflected ongoing changes in Philadelphia's economy. Textiles had already gone into steep decline in the city, and apparel, although still relatively strong in the 1960s, would lose more jobs between 1963 and 1982 than any other industrial or wholesale sector in Philadelphia. The relative inattention to both industries suggests that despite its unwillingness to follow city economist Kirk Petshek's plans for a carefully targeted industrial program, PIDC still minimized its involvement with sectors that had little future viability.[52] Although it never explicitly articulated the criteria for such choices, PIDC efforts to save firms in dying industries (such as the Hubschman and Sons project) proved the exception rather than the rule.

The second question, regarding the location of PIDC transactions and the racial makeup of surrounding neighborhoods, is even more important than the type of firms assisted. Philadelphia during the 1960s remained largely white and African American, with the "white" category retaining many ethnic subgroups that still reflected earlier periods of European immigration to the city (particularly Italian and Irish). Although the city did experience a rapid increase in Puerto Rican immigration during the 1960s, that group's overall numbers remained relatively small, at approximately 26,700 by 1970. In contrast, the African American population at that date stood at just under 654,000. With notable exceptions in areas such as the Spring Garden neighborhood, where Puerto Ricans concentrated (in slightly smaller numbers than whites or blacks), Philadelphia remained a black and white city.[53]

As previously noted, PIDC's new, suburban-style industrial parks accounted for a significant share of the agency's activity: between 1959 and 1970, 101 of the 354 PIDC-financed transactions involved either a move to a PIDC industrial park or an expansion of facilities already located in one of the parks. As a result of the parks' location in peripheral areas of Philadelphia, this aspect of the industrial renewal program facilitated the decentralization of industry within the city. The maps in figures 10 and 11, which respectively show the location of firms before and after they received PIDC assistance, clearly reflect this relationship, as the firms plotted on figure 11 are notably more dispersed than those in figure 10.[54]

Along with this tendency toward decentralization, the peripheral industrial parks had only limited mass transit connections to inner-city areas of concentrated poverty. Philadelphia's subway, trolley, and commuter rail lines did not serve the industrial parks, and workers from other parts of the city had little choice except to drive or complete a long bus trip with multiple transfers. For many Philadelphia residents, the parks thus proved to be largely inaccessible. The composition of the industrial parks' workforce indicated that this orientation towards automobile transportation reinforced preexisting patterns of employment discrimination. A 1975 survey found that 26 percent of workers in Far Northeast Philadelphia's manufacturing and wholesaling firms came from the suburbs, but that only 12 percent came from North Philadelphia. A mere 14 percent of employees in area firms used mass transit to get to work, and 55 percent of the firms described public transportation as a problem. This relationship between urban space, transportation, and employment had distinct racial implications, as the Far Northeast and its surrounding suburbs remained almost entirely white, while many (although not all) of the city's poorer, centrally-located neighborhoods had primarily minority populations.[55]

Two countervailing observations, however, indicate that the PIDC program cannot simply be viewed as a quasi-public effort to speed up changes already underway in the racial and industrial geography of post-World War II Philadelphia. First, for most of the firms that moved to the industrial parks, the relevant set of choices was not between the PIDC facilities and a centralized urban location. Instead, it was between these peripheral Philadelphia locations and a site in the suburbs or completely outside the region. PIDC's provision of land in Eastwick, Penrose, and the Far Northeast kept such businesses, and the jobs and tax revenue that they generated, within the political boundaries of Philadelphia. In a period of intense urban deindustrialization and rapid change in the spatial organization of American industry, the successful promotion of such industrial parks often constituted the best option available to policymakers in the aging cities of the industrial Northeast and Midwest.[56]

Second, 253 of the 354 traced PIDC transactions involved the construction, renovation, or expansion of plants that were not located in the industrial parks. This component of the program reveals one of the most significant features of PIDC's activity. Although the industrial renewal program did in part facilitate industrial decentralization, it also spurred a surprising amount of reinvestment in older, centrally located industrial areas. In a striking contrast to patterns of housing investment during the period, this activity took place in both African American and racially transitional neighborhoods.[57] PIDC never explicitly directed its efforts at

African American neighborhoods, but instead simply operated in almost every preexisting industrial area in Philadelphia (figures 10 and 11).

Both the original and new locations of PIDC-assisted firms reflected this pattern. Lower North Philadelphia, which experienced the greatest amount of outward, PIDC-financed industrial movement of any section in the city (figures 10 and 11; table 2–1), also had the highest percentage of African American residents.[58] It also had a small but rapidly growing Puerto Rican population. Other areas with large black populations, such as Upper North Philadelphia (which had the second highest concentration of Puerto Ricans), West Philadelphia, and South Philadelphia, also experienced a significant loss of firms from PIDC activity. High levels of firm loss, however, took place in white areas as well. Center City and Kensington, both of which had negligible African American populations, had the second and third highest rate of firm losses from PIDC transactions. Together, these two "white" areas accounted for 93 of the 243 PIDC-assisted moves (38 percent). In contrast, Germantown–Chestnut Hill, Olney–Oak Lane, and Southwest Philadelphia all had substantial African American populations and experienced high rates of racial turnover during the 1960s yet lost a combined total of only eleven firms. The relative level of firm loss due to PIDC activity, in short, depended less on racial composition than on the pre-existing geography of industrial location in Philadelphia. If an area had industry, PIDC helped some of it move, regardless of the racial makeup of the surrounding population.

This was also true of the locations to which PIDC-assisted firms moved or in which they expanded existing facilities (figure 11; table 2–1). Excluding the Far Northeast and its new industrial parks, the all-white, heavily industrial Kensington area experienced the highest total gains during the 1959–70 period, as it had 60 move-ins or expansions despite the loss of more than 15,000 residents during the 1960s. Lower and Upper North Philadelphia, South Philadelphia, and Southwest Philadelphia experienced the next highest level of gain from industrial renewal. By 1970, the African American population in these areas ranged from 30 to 76 percent of total population, and these sections gained a total of 134 move-ins and expansions.[59] Figure 11 reflects this result. While it depicts the dispersal of many firms to the peripheral industrial parks, it also shows a significant concentration of PIDC activity in central areas of Philadelphia. A comparison of this pattern with the map's depiction of Philadelphia's 1954 manufacturing employment density indicates that the pre-existing location of industry determined PIDC's pattern of activity.[60]

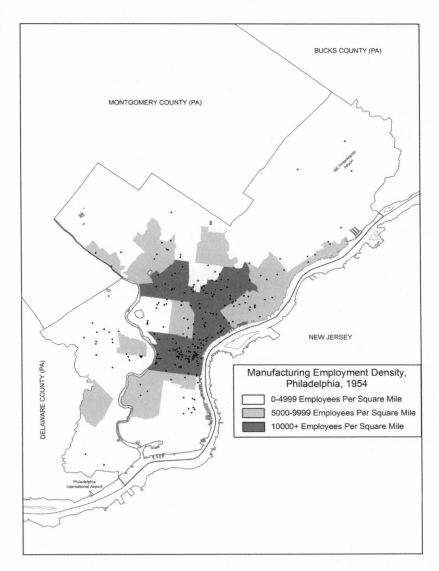

FIGURE 10. Original location of firms moved or expanded by PIDC, 1959–70, versus manufacturing employment density, 1954. Note the concentration of PIDC activity in existing industrial areas of the city. Map prepared by the author, using ESRI ArcMap 9.2.

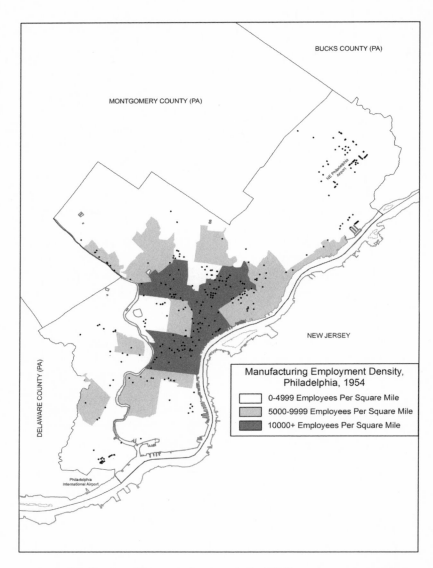

FIGURE 11. New location of firms moved or expanded by PIDC, 1959–70, versus manufacturing employment density, 1954. Note both dispersal of firms to PIDC's peripheral industrial parks and the high level of activity in existing, inner city industrial areas. Map prepared by the author, using ESRI ArcMap 9.2.

TABLE 2.1 **PIDC–Assisted Firm Movement, by Planning Analysis Sections, 1959—70**

Section	Firms lost	Move-ins & expansions	1960 nonwhite (%)	1970 nonwhite (%)
Lower North	60	59	69.0	76.3
Center City	48	9	21.6	10.7
Kensington	45	60	0.6	1.0
Upper North	27	38	19.9	51.7
West	20	16	52.8	68.2
South	15	20	26.0	30.5
Near Northeast	10	17	1.2	2.1
Germantown–Chestnut Hill	6	4	22.5	44.7
Far Northeast	4	94	5.3	2.4
Olney–Oak Lane	3	10	4.2	28.3
Southwest	2	17	11.0	33.0
Roxborough-Manayunk	2	9	2.1	2.5

In some sections, such as the neighborhoods around the Front-Luzerne Industrial District, PIDC was able to attract industrial investment to the inner city because those areas had a significant existing concentration of relatively modern industrial facilities. In other centrally located areas, however, this success rested on the affordability of PIDC-financed facilities that matched the space requirements of individual firms, as well as transportation infrastructure and proximity to suppliers, customers, and employees. For many firms that worked with PIDC, these considerations outweighed racial change, labor relations, city taxes, or federal incentives.

Despite its success in attracting capital to inner-city neighborhoods, PIDC's limitations highlighted the costs of the strategic compromise that had brought it into existence. A firm's decision to locate in African American or racially transitional areas did not mean that it would hire black workers, and throughout the 1960s, civil rights activists repeatedly challenged the discriminatory practices of Philadelphia employers and labor unions. PIDC took no position, publicly or privately, on such issues. It also failed to develop connections with the War on Poverty until 1971, when it took over the economic development components of the city's struggling Model Cities program (chapter 8). Because PIDC's founders had decided to address problems of industrial space alone, PIDC had little capacity, or willingness, to engage racial problems directly. Yet paradoxically, it was this constrained, noncontroversial scope that allowed it to bring industrial capital into older, racially mixed urban neighborhoods at all during the 1960s. Although PIDC's success remained partial, its accomplishment in bringing capital investment to the inner city outstripped the achievements of most other urban policy initiatives during this period.

Federal programs such as urban renewal and highway construction affected industrial firms as well, and the third question is to what extent
these policies forced the relocation of the companies assisted by PIDC.
Superficially, at least, PIDC appeared to facilitate urban renewal in Philadelphia by helping relocate companies displaced by the RA's clearance
projects. During 1959–70, for example, no part of Philadelphia lost more
firms as a result of PIDC-assisted transactions than the area affected by
the city's massive Independence Mall urban renewal project. Funded by
state redevelopment money, Independence Mall had been created during
the 1950s by clearing hundreds of industrial and commercial buildings on
the three city blocks immediately north of Independence Hall. During the
1960s, the federal urban renewal program cleared the blocks ringing the
new mall to facilitate redevelopment of a complex of new private and
governmental office buildings.[61] Between 1959 and 1970, this section of
Center City became an important focus of PIDC activity, as a total of
thirty-two PIDC-aided firms moved out of the two census tracts that encompassed the Independence Mall project and its surrounding area (no other
census tract in the city lost more than seven firms as a result of PIDC-
assisted moves). In contrast to this outward movement, PIDC financed
only two transactions that moved companies into the Independence Mall
area during this period. These patterns emphasize the importance of urban renewal programs in removing manufacturing and wholesaling firms
from urban central business districts.[62]

While there is no question that urban renewal caused significant
amounts of industrial displacement, some caution must be exercised in
assessing the federal program's role in PIDC's operations. The relationship between urban renewal and PIDC-sponsored industrial movement is
not as direct as the Independence Mall case initially suggests. Large sections of the two census tracts included in the analysis above lay outside
of the urban renewal boundaries and were not subject to clearance. Eighteen of the thirty-two PIDC-assisted moves under consideration actually
originated from these nearby, uncleared areas.

Two conclusions may be drawn from this. First, urban renewal had
"spillover" effects in the blocks adjoining project areas. Spillover may have
been related to changes in rents and property taxes induced by an urban
renewal project's influence on the overall neighborhood environment. Second, the result may reflect the quality of industrial facilities in the area. An
independent 1960 evaluation of Philadelphia's industrial facilities found

that Center City was "highly congested, and...has many multistoried structures of varying size" and ranked it as one of the five least desirable industrial locations in the entire city. Quite simply, many of the factories near Independence Mall faced increasing obsolescence. In some cases, this led their occupants to search for more modern quarters regardless of urban renewal. In contrast to the spillover effect, which emphasizes urban renewal as an indirect but causal force, this second interpretation suggests that much of the factory movement in the Independence Mall area would have occurred regardless of urban renewal activity.

Elsewhere in Philadelphia, PIDC relocations indicate that urban renewal was one of a number of factors that determined where the industrial renewal program would be most active. In part, this reflected the federal authorizing legislation's focus on residential and institutional projects (such as Philadelphia's University City and Temple urban renewal areas) rather than on industrial areas. Even in the few urban renewal areas that had significant concentrations of industrial activity, PIDC played a relatively small part in moving firms to other sections of the city. Immediately to the north of the Independence Mall area, for example, the Franklin and Callowhill East projects moved into the clearance stage during the mid- and late-1960s. Although these two project areas involved the removal of more than forty industrial buildings, PIDC helped only six firms move out of Franklin and Callowhill East.[63] Overall, of the 243 surveyed firms that used PIDC aid to move within the city, thirty-five (14.4 percent) had original addresses in urban renewal areas.

Highway construction, especially that of Interstate 95 along the Delaware River, also displaced many Philadelphia manufacturing and wholesaling firms. Once again, PIDC played a role, as it relocated twenty-one firms displaced by the expressway. The American Bag and Paper Corporation, which exemplified Philadelphia's mid-sized, highly specialized manufacturing firms, had 125 employees and made thermoplastic bags for "food products, chemicals, and fertilizers" sold in the United States, Europe, and South Africa. American Bag and Paper's existing, multistory plant in South Philadelphia's Queen Village area had been condemned due to the construction of I-95, leading the company to consider relocation sites in the suburbs, and even to purchase land in New Jersey. A PIDC-financing package, however, lured the company back to the city, and in late 1964 it broke ground on a new one-story, 139,000-square-foot plant on a fifteen-acre site in Philadelphia Industrial Park. The company's

FIGURE 12. American Bag and Paper Corporation's new facility in Philadelphia Industrial Park, Northeast Philadelphia, 1964–65. This low, spread-out plant was typical of facilities in PIDC's leading industrial park, and of new industrial construction around the United States after World War II. Note the parking lot and grassy lawn surrounding the plant, as well as the still undeveloped field in the foreground. Photo courtesy of the Architectural Archives, University of Pennsylvania.

workforce gradually increased to 200, and it remained in the plant until at least the 1980s.[64]

As with urban renewal, highway building played an important part in Philadelphia's loss of industrial firms, and PIDC responded in part to the needs of such firms and in part to the imperatives of city and federal planning. As such, PIDC operated as an informal adjunct of the RA and the federal and state highway agencies on projects that, overall, did more to harm industrial Philadelphia than to preserve it. Together, firms displaced by urban renewal and highway construction accounted for 56 of the 243 PIDC relocations for which original addresses have been identified (23 percent). While the relocation of firms displaced by public projects did not constitute PIDC's primary mission, it did define a significant subset of its activities.

Despite the PIDC program's success in stimulating inner city industrial investment and developing peripheral industrial parks, Philadelphia still lost nearly 5,700 manufacturing and wholesaling firms between 1963 and 1992.[65] This raises the third and final question, about whether the local industrial policy embodied by PIDC had any meaningful long-run effect on the social and economic health of Philadelphia. A cursory answer is no. By 1990, 124 of the 333 identified firms that had been aided by PIDC between 1959 and 1970 remained somewhere in Philadelphia, for a loss rate of 62.9 percent. Citywide, Philadelphia experienced a 62.3 percent decline between 1963 and 1992 in its total number of manufacturing and wholesaling firms (from 9,130 to 3,438), indicating that companies assisted by PIDC did not exhibit an increased likelihood of remaining in the city. This result could lead to the conclusion that for all of PIDC's policy innovations and near-term success, the magnitude of deindustrialization ultimately dwarfed the industrial renewal response.[66]

Two other considerations, however, temper such a dismissal. First, even the relatively limited number of PIDC-assisted firms that stayed in the city provided a substantial share of all remaining industrial employment in Philadelphia. In 1990, these 124 firms employed a total of 23,035 people, or 22.7 percent of the 101,452 wholesaling and manufacturing jobs in the city (1992 data); adding the remaining employment from transactions that could not be identified and from transactions that PIDC completed after 1970 would make this percentage even higher.[67] In sum, an important part of Philadelphia's remaining industrial base in 1990 and beyond could be directly traced to the industrial renewal program. PIDC's efforts thus had far more relevance than simple firm-retention statistics alone would indicate. Second, the eventual departure or closure of a company that had previously worked with PIDC does not indicate that the transaction should be counted as a failure. In the interim between the transaction and the company's disappearance, workers benefited from increased employment and the city gained increased tax revenues. The longer an individual firm remained in place, the greater were these gains relative to the costs of the transaction.

Together, these factors suggest that the most judicious conclusion regarding industrial renewal's long-term effectiveness in Philadelphia is that the program slowed the progress of deindustrialization and moderated its effects. PIDC's version of local industrial policy certainly did not save industrial Philadelphia—regional, national, and global economic and social forces made that impossible—but it did prevent the city's situation from becoming far worse. Although PIDC largely dodged underlying issues of racial change, labor conflict, and taxation, its focus on the physical and technological causes of urban deindustrialization allowed it to preserve some of the most viable segments of Philadelphia's manufacturing economy. Perhaps most significantly, PIDC even found some success in attracting investment capital to Philadelphia's older industrial neighborhoods, including those occupied by African Americans and Puerto Ricans. This pattern confounds conventional assumptions about urban racial change and capital movements. More broadly, the basis of PIDC's relative success lay in its reversal of the usual structure of federal political-economic incentives. While most federal policies both implicitly and explicitly favored suburban, southern, and western areas of the United States, PIDC managed to find an opening in the federal tax code that allowed it to gain a marginal but important advantage over Philadelphia's suburbs. This strategy demonstrated that as late as the 1960s, even relatively minor shifts in structural federal policy incentives could produce a different balance between older cities and their economic competitors.

Local Industrial Policy in Other Cities

In 1972, three planners from the New York City Planning Commission wrote in a professional journal that "Philadelphia's Industrial Development Program . . . has certainly been the most outstanding among older cities."[68] Given New Yorkers' propensity for finding nothing positive about Philadelphia, the comment was high praise indeed. Philadelphia, though, was far from alone in trying to save its industrial base during the 1960s, as other U.S. cities undertook programs aimed at both retaining and attracting manufacturing firms. Most cities, however, chose a path different from that of Philadelphia, as they relied on urban renewal funds rather than municipal debt instruments and on clearance strategies rather than rehabilitation or "green field" construction. Many of these efforts ended in failure, or even, in worst-case scenarios, in the deployment of federal money in ways that subsidized the prosperous at the direct expense of the poor.

Detroit's experience exemplified the difficulties with urban renewal. The motor city faced two key problems that differentiated it from Philadelphia. First, it depended almost entirely on the automobile industry and closely related fields, in contrast to the highly diversified industrial base of Philadelphia. Second, it had few large areas of open land available for industrial uses. Rather than rehabilitate existing factories, or demolish them to make way for new construction, Detroit pursued a strategy of residential clearance. Beginning in the mid-1950s, the city used local funds—because federal urban renewal funds could not be used for an exclusively industrial project—to clear the mostly residential Corktown neighborhood for the 167-acre West Side Industrial Project. Although the West Side district attracted a few industrial firms, its development moved so slowly that a group of warehouse operations dislocated by the city's riverfront Civic Center project moved elsewhere. Much of the district remained empty decades later. A second Detroit industrial project, Milwaukee-Junction, met with even less success and eventually developed just seventeen acres. By the 1960s, high municipal debt levels, lack of federal support, and poor results had led Detroit to abandon its industrial redevelopment efforts. In Detroit, urban renewal proved too slow, too expensive, and too disruptive to effectively serve local industrial policy.[69]

While similar outcomes emerged in Buffalo, Cleveland, and Cincinnati, an egregious example of the abuse of urban renewal occurred in Trenton, New Jersey. An industrial renewal project in the Coalport neighborhood displaced 400 mostly minority residents, even as real estate speculators garnered massive profits from land that had received wildly inflated assessments immediately prior to urban renewal condemnation. Industrial urban renewal followed a more complicated pattern in St. Louis, where a regional business-government partnership implemented the massive Mill Creek Valley project. Mill Creek relied on federal funds to link the construction of new industrial parks to nearby housing and highway construction projects. It also required the clearance of thousands of residential structures in a mostly low-income, minority neighborhood. Although the project eventually attracted some light industry, it received little follow-up. Instead, the regional consortium pushed future industrial projects not to inner city St. Louis, but to outlying suburban areas.[70] Oakland pursued a different strategy, as it used funds from the federal Economic Development Administration (EDA) to undertake a massive expansion and modernization of its port. Although the project succeeded in transforming the Port of Oakland into one of the primary shipping hubs on the West Coast, port management later reneged on commitments it had made to the EDA to hire minority residents of the nearby East Oakland flatlands.[71]

After limited early engagement with the problem of urban industrial decline, New York and Boston eventually adopted policies that more closely resembled PIDC's program. While New York's early urban renewal projects typically replaced factories with housing, office towers, and highways, the city finally established an industrial renewal program in 1965. In some respects, New York's strategy followed that of Philadelphia. It operated through a combination of rehabilitation and expansion projects in existing industrial areas and new plant construction in industrial parks on vacant, city-owned land. In other ways, New York's approach differed from PIDC. The program did not offer low-cost financing, as it did not have the IRS authorization necessary to obtain tax exemptions on its interest payments. The city also retained title to the property and the building at the close of a lease; this increased the engagement of the local state in the process, but also meant that participating companies had to accept such non-ownership terms. New York's program also drew on multiple interested agencies, rather than on a single industrial development agency such as PIDC. Industrial projects in New York thus had to go through at least six different municipal agencies before construction could begin. While this process brought in multiple sets of expertise and allowed much greater public input than in Philadelphia, it also slowed projects, increased their complexity, and raised costs. Finally, New York had no single business organization that spoke for the city's manufacturers in the manner that the Chamber of Commerce did in Philadelphia. As a result, the program lacked a nongovernmental intermediary with the business community. The Flatlands Industrial Park, built on 95 acres of previously vacant land in Brooklyn, was the most prominent component of New York's program. By 1972, companies in Flatlands employed approximately 7,500 workers. Flatlands proved the exception, though, as the city set up only one other industrial park during the late 1960s. Beyond Flatlands, the remainder of the program generated only about 2,500 jobs.[72]

Boston most closely approximated Philadelphia's model. Established in 1971 under Mayor Kevin White, the Boston Economic Development and Industrial Corporation operated much like PIDC as a quasi-public agency offering low-cost financing through the use of tax exempt industrial revenue bonds (and other debt instruments). Like Philadelphia, Boston benefited from an ample supply of open land suitable for industry, including former military installations (the closure of which had contributed to Boston's loss of jobs) and Massachusetts Port Authority holdings. The corporation assembled the land and offered it at favorable terms, attracting more than 200 companies to the largest of the industrial parks alone.

Both as a city and as part of a wider region, Boston also had more success than Philadelphia in attracting high-tech industries and jobs.[73]

Given the relatively greater effectiveness of Philadelphia's industrial program, and later, of Boston's, why did so few cities adopt this model during the 1960s and 1970s? First, the appeal of urban renewal as a strategy to stem industrial decline grew out of the lure and increasing availability of federal money, combined with a persistent belief among politicians and city planners that the solution to urban problems lay in the clearance and rebuilding of "blighted" neighborhoods. For most cities, urban renewal simply represented standard operating practice, the most readily available approach to managing urban change. Philadelphia avoided this because the experts installed by the liberal reform administrations became wary of the dangers of industrial urban renewal and explored other options. While the industrial urban renewal strategies of other cities represented experiments just as PIDC did, policymakers elsewhere found themselves trapped in a position of "path dependence" as it became clear that the urban renewal approach had failed; with large funding commitments to long-term projects, few cities could quickly abandon the urban renewal model in favor of Philadelphia's more deft and effective strategy of new construction (which also depended on land availability) mixed with rehabilitation. Second, as the next section will show, both the IRS and Congress became increasingly hostile to the tax exemption for industrial revenue bonds and mortgage obligations during the mid-1960s. PIDC officials actually visited St. Louis in 1965 to explain their program, but the IRS refused to grant St. Louis an exemption comparable to the one that PIDC had received in Philadelphia.[74] This issue would eventually be resolved, after much damage to PIDC itself, but it demonstrated the central if sometimes subtle role of obscure federal policy determinations in shaping the character of local public policy.

Politics and Strategy

Public policies are always shaped by the political and institutional environment in which they evolve. Despite PIDC's political insularity, its industrial renewal program was no exception. During the 1960s, changes in those environments at both the local and federal levels would have crucial effects in shaping the program's operations and its relationship to other levels of government. At home, the reform movement out of which PIDC had been born began to ebb, while in Washington, federal officials challenged core elements of PIDC's program. Both developments hindered PIDC during the decade, but neither led to the agency's transformation. More significant changes would come in the 1970s.

The first local change came on September 20, 1961, when Richard Graves informed the PIDC board that he planned to resign as PIDC's executive vice president.[75] The board soon unanimously approved city finance director Richard McConnell as Graves's replacement. McConnell brought a distinctly different management style to PIDC. The new executive vice president regularized and refined PIDC operations, worked more closely with the PIDC board, and maintained closer ties to other city agencies. This latter characteristic reflected the mutual trust that McConnell had built up with other officials during his years in city government. In practice, McConnell largely shared Graves's sympathy with the problems facing city businesses, and he maintained his predecessor's policy of accepting all industries provided that they met basic criteria of job creation and tax-revenue generation.[76]

PIDC remained a relatively low profile organization, and Graves's exit received little notice outside of Philadelphia's business and political communities. In February 1962, a more widely noted transition took place when Richardson Dilworth resigned as mayor in order to run, unsuccessfully, for governor. The ascendance of Dilworth's replacement, City Council president James Tate, marked the effective end of reform in Philadelphia. In contrast to Clark and Dilworth's blue-blood backgrounds, Ivy League educations, and good-government ethos, Tate seemed the archetype of the traditional American urban politician. An Irish Catholic (and Philadelphia's first Catholic mayor), Tate had graduated from Strayer's Business College and began his career as a stenographer and business secretary before attending Temple University Law School. During the 1930s and 1940s, he joined in the revival of the local Democratic Party, serving as a committeeman and ward leader in the Hunting Park section of Upper North Philadelphia, and later, as the Democratic City Committee's executive secretary. Through these positions, Tate skillfully constructed an autonomous political base amid the rival party factions, and shifting alliances, of Congressman Bill Green, Party Treasurer Jim Clark, and Party Chairman James Finnegan, as well as the increasingly powerful reform liberals Joseph Clark and Richardson Dilworth. Elected to City Council in 1951, along with other party regulars swept in by that year's reform wave, Tate became council president when Green and Jim Clark forced Finnegan out of the post and into a state government position that exiled him from the local party.[77]

Possessed with an intense attention to detail, Tate suffered from severe migraine headaches and a fear of physical attack that led him to keep bodyguards with him throughout his workday. He was also prone to angry outbursts at subordinates, journalists, and political opponents. At one 1970 press conference, he suddenly declared his staff and cabinet incompetent and publicly fired several top officials. As mayor, Tate lacked the patronage (due to the city charter and Republican control of state government) and popularity among ward leaders necessary to consolidate control over the party in the manner of Chicago's Richard Daley. Still, he managed to win reelection twice despite alienating much of the city's political, intellectual, and business establishment. As early as 1963, reform stalwart Walter Phillips sought to marshal this elite opposition by running against Tate in the Democratic primary (figure 6). He lost badly.[78]

The political base that allowed Tate to overcome such opposition lay in his close ties to Philadelphia African Americans and to the city's still powerful labor unions. Both of these constituencies turned out strongly for Tate in 1963 and 1967. As a result of the labor association, Tate's relations with the business community began on a basis of mutual suspicion and then steadily deteriorated as the mayor raised taxes, gave municipal unions generous contracts, and deployed Great Society social programs as a substitute for the patronage resources he lacked. Nonetheless, Tate supported PIDC as a central component of the development programs with which he still hoped to tie himself to the legacy of Clark and Dilworth. In some cases, Tate demonstrated an almost obsessive concern with the details of PIDC's operation, such as zoning ordinances in Philadelphia Industrial Park.[79]

Gradually, increasing tensions between Tate and the business community affected the mayor's interactions with PIDC. In 1967, the Greater Philadelphia Movement endorsed Republican district attorney Arlen Specter (a former reform Democrat and a future U.S. senator) for mayor. With heavy support from labor and blacks, however, Tate narrowly won reelection. He then immediately severed his ties with the city's business organizations.[80] For PIDC, the problem of city-business relations became acute after McConnell left PIDC in 1968 to become senior vice president of Girard Bank. McConnell's status as a widely respected figure in both business and governmental circles had allowed him to maintain relatively

open communication with city hall and to preserve relationships between
the business and city representatives on the PIDC board.[81]

When McConnell resigned, however, Tate replaced him with Paul Croley, a long-time city official and political ally. Croley served for slightly
more than two years before being replaced by Tate's finance director, Edward Martin. Many of the business participants in PIDC viewed both Croley and Martin as entirely unqualified for the critical executive vice president job and interpreted these appointments as attempts by the mayor
to capture PIDC as a source of patronage. Opposition within the board,
however, blocked Tate's efforts to exert additional control over the program. At the staff level, PIDC appointments remained largely professional rather than political, and included a high representation of technically trained planners and industrial development specialists.[82] Andrew
Young, the PIDC president during this period, later described the situation as "an armed truce" but observed that as far as meaningful city assistance for PIDC, "City Hall was a vacuum."[83] PIDC's relative independence from Tate indicates that even after the last reform mayor left office,
such quasi-public organizations institutionalized the technocratic ethos of
the reform by maintaining expert professional staffs that remained largely
isolated from political pressure.

The breakdown in relations between PIDC and city hall, however, occurred at an inopportune moment. PIDC's reliance on the tax-exempt
status of its mortgage interest payments had always left the industrial renewal program vulnerable to changes in IRS policy. In early 1967, this la-
tent threat became reality. During the mid-1960s, widespread controversy
had emerged regarding municipalities' use of tax-free industrial revenue
bonds, an industrial financing device permitted in thirty-seven states. Critics charged that such bonds abused the tax-free status of municipal debt
obligations, which had traditionally been used only to finance public facilities, by extending the use of such instruments to private sector firms.
This practice, they maintained, shifted finance costs away from individual
companies and onto taxpayers. By mid-1966, more than a dozen bills had
been introduced in Congress proposing modifications to the tax-status of
industrial revenue bonds.[84]

Although PIDC technically employed mortgages, it was quickly caught
up in the debate about bonds.[85] On January 30, 1967, the IRS issued a
new ruling that revoked the tax-exemption not only on industrial revenue

bonds, but also on industrial mortgage interest payments made by any organization other than a formal municipal authority. PIDC's authorizing ordinance designated it as the city's official "instrument for industrial development," but the corporation had never requested a state charter legally recognizing it as a municipal authority. As a result, the IRS determined that PIDC was merely a nonprofit corporation and not a "government instrumentality" and ruled that creditors could no longer receive tax-exemptions on PIDC mortgage interest payments.[86] The city immediately appealed. City solicitor Edward Bauer argued that PIDC constituted a city policy instrument: "the Treasury's position was unsound as a matter of public policy. One of our biggest problems is to bring industry to the ghetto areas in Philadelphia and PIDC had been successful in doing this. Without the tax-exempt feature, PIDC would be out of business and ... the Federal government would have to spend more money in the big cities in attempting to accomplish what PIDC was doing."[87] Bauer, however, erred in his assumption that the federal government shared any particular interest in such goals. By the time of PIDC's tax-exemption crisis, advocates of using the War on Poverty as a tool to create jobs had long since lost out to supporters of job training and community mobilization in the Johnson administration. The IRS rejected Philadelphia's appeal and maintained its stance on the tax-exemption ruling.[88]

PIDC eventually regained the authority to issue tax-free municipal debt obligations, but only after a two-year struggle that involved a rewrite of state law, the creation of two PIDC subsidiaries, and a 1968 revision of the federal tax code.[89] In the interim, PIDC's activity slowed dramatically, albeit temporarily. From 1964 to 1966, PIDC completed between fifty-four and seventy transactions each year. During the period of the tax-exemption crisis, annual transactions fell to thirty in 1967 and nineteen in 1968. Even this level of activity was possible only because PIDC worked with the city's Redevelopment Authority to complete projects on city-owned land. The RA could do nothing, however, to help with transactions involving the renovation of privately held industrial facilities. This meant that PIDC had to suspend the modernization or expansion of existing industrial facilities, which was the bulk of its work in inner city neighborhoods.[90]

In the years that followed the tax-exemption controversy, PIDC gradually returned to pre-1967 levels of activity, as it completed forty-five transactions in 1969 and forty-three in 1970. During this period, city officials and PIDC board members began to consider the long-term role of the corporation in Philadelphia's economy. With the service sector of the economy growing nationally, both city and Chamber of Commerce participants in PIDC began to examine the possibility of expanding the program's scope beyond industrial development alone. The ensuing discussion soon led to the transformation of Philadelphia's quasi-public local industrial policy. In February 1971, PIDC announced that it would expand its range of activities to include commercial, retail, and service industries.[91]

The results of PIDC's shift in focus are assessed in chapter 8, but it is important to note that industrial projects remained the largest share of PIDC's work. Nonetheless, the change in mission did draw the agency closer to the model of the much-maligned pro-growth coalitions that typified urban economic development strategies in the final decades of the twentieth century. Recently, urban scholars and policy analysts have proposed new strategies that challenge this emphasis on corporate services and echo the early industrial renewal concepts of Philadelphia's postwar liberals. They note the large employment multipliers associated with "high-road" manufacturing, as well as the failure of local tax abatements and subsidies to create jobs in service-oriented finance, insurance, and real estate sectors, and argue that the development of specialized, high-quality manufacturing offers a path toward the revitalization and diversification of American urban economies.[92] PIDC in the 1960s did exactly that. With its emphasis on Philadelphia's small- and medium-sized specialty and batch manufacturing firms, PIDC in this period offers a model for such strategies and a historical indicator of their potential viability—and their limitations.

PIDC demonstrates that rather than being powerless to address the problem of deindustrialization, local public policy could have a significant effect on the rate and character of economic change. Even more importantly, PIDC achieved this record within the constraints both of transformational macroeconomic forces and of national urban policies that were at best indifferent and at worst openly hostile to the economic needs of American cities. These observations suggest that an alternative path for urban areas might have existed in the postwar United States. Such an approach would have explicitly linked the creation and retention of urban manufacturing jobs to the social and political initiatives of the War on Poverty, all within a wider framework of planned, urban-oriented industrial policy.

Beyond the Factory: PIDC's Inattention
to Labor and Racial Issues

Despite its surprising "bricks and mortar" success, PIDC's scope remained limited. The program ignored factors in Philadelphia's problem of jobs other than the obsolescence of loft factories and the demand for single-story, continuous-flow industrial plants. Instead, throughout the 1960s, PIDC dodged many of the social problems that vexed the city's economy. Avoidance of such explosive issues as racial discrimination, labor-management conflict, and local taxes had formed a key part of the strategy that allowed political and business leaders to construct a loose consensus around the industrial renewal concept during the late 1950s. Partially out of a desire to avoid controversial actions that might undercut its core mission, but also because its quasi-public form isolated it from the normal pressures of democratic politics, PIDC remained largely disengaged from these social problems long after its founding and initial establishment as a legitimate participant in Philadelphia's economic life.

This stance evolved logically in regard to labor relations. Although Philadelphia remained a strong labor city, the number of strikes in the city dropped throughout the 1960s. Employers still complained about high labor costs and intransigent union bosses, but the Philadelphia labor movement had rarely exhibited the radicalism of its counterparts in New York, Chicago, and Detroit. In part, this relative quiescence could be attributed to the AFL's dominance of Philadelphia unionism, as the high skill levels of the city's work force meant that many workers had long been associated with more conservative AFL craft unions. As a result, the more politically engaged, activist CIO unions—organized across skill levels on an industrial basis—accounted for only one-third of area union members. Further, after a wave of strikes immediately following World War II, local unions had become increasingly complacent and usually followed the lead of the national AFL-CIO in focusing on wages, benefits, and seniority provisions.[93] Reflecting this trend, a 1961 *Harvard Business Review* survey of corporate executives rated Philadelphia's labor costs as the best among the nation's ten largest cities, and only slightly below the average for all other cities; for labor force quality, the city tied for first with Chicago. Such ratings, though, did little to stop the outflow of manufacturers to low-cost, non-union states in the South and West, especially in such mobile, cost sensitive industries as apparel and textiles.[94]

Although PIDC remained a project of the city government and the business community, it took steps to involve labor in the partnership. During the period preceding PIDC's organization, Commerce Department officials sought the support of the local CIO and AFL councils, and one or two labor representatives always sat on PIDC's board of directors. These appointments went to high-ranking local union officials. The initial board included Norman Blumberg, business manager of the AFL Central Union, and Joseph Kelley, president of the Electrical Workers and the CIO Industrial Union Council. Some years later, PIDC added AFL-CIO Philadelphia Council President Edward Toohey to the board. At times, the labor seats even went to some of the city's more confrontational labor leaders, such as the Amalgamated Clothing Workers' Anthony Cortigene, who sat on the PIDC board during the late 1960s. The business presence on the board far outweighed this limited labor block, but the latter at least brought a labor voice into the board meetings.[95]

Generally, however, the labor participants found little reason to object to PIDC's activities. PIDC transactions usually led to improved working conditions, expanded operations, and often, more jobs. Although some of the new plants relied on automated production processes, a 1971 survey of 108 PIDC-assisted firms found that the companies had increased their employment by a total of 3,571 jobs, or an average of thirty-three jobs per company. Expansions associated with most of the projects thus outweighed any technologically-induced job losses.[96] In a reflection of this relationship, Toohey occasionally provided brief, enthusiastic summaries of PIDC activities at meetings of the local AFL-CIO Council, and in no case did he or any other labor leader criticize the program for anti-labor bias.[97]

Labor's largely passive role also reflected internal problems in the Philadelphia labor movement during the 1960s. Philadelphia's CIO Industrial Union Council and AFL Central Labor Union did not form a joint organization until 1960, five years after the national merger between the two unions. Persistent factionalism persisted, however, and in 1965 the former CIO unions broke away from the AFL-CIO Council and formed a new Philadelphia Council of Industrial Organizations. This split persisted until 1970. Even when the AFL-CIO Council was nominally unified, however, it lacked meaningful authority over its constituent unions. As a result, labor's PIDC representatives could in reality speak only for their particular unions, not for the local labor movement as a whole.[98] During the 1960s, local unions also became embroiled in a bitter dispute over racial integration in the skilled building trades. By 1967, the issue remained unresolved and led to the Philadelphia Plan, a federal intervention that would become the basis for affirmative action throughout the United States (chapter 7). The AFL-CIO Council resisted the Philadelphia Plan, as did most of its constituent unions. Throughout the 1960s, these internal and external controversies largely distracted institutional unionism in Philadelphia from any concentrated focus on the problem of deindustrialization. On occasion, however, individual unions did take steps to combat aspects of deindustrialization that threatened their particular interests. In the early 1950s, the Textile Workers Union of America negotiated contract provisions that subjected plant relocation decisions to collective bargaining, and in 1956, the Amalgamated Clothing Workers blocked H. H. Daroff's move of additional production offshore after the company shifted a line of pants to a Puerto Rico plant. Overall, however, preoccupation with internal battles combined with the national prosperity of the postwar decades to mute any sense of crisis among Philadelphia unionists until the 1970s.[99]

For most of the 1960s, PIDC took an even less direct approach to racial problems than it did to labor issues. While PIDC completed a significant number of transactions in African American neighborhoods, it made no systematic effort to engage the racial issues that affected both the location decisions of Philadelphia firms and the residential choices of white workers. PIDC took no steps to make nondiscrimination a requirement for participation in its transactions, and further, it failed even to establish liaisons with such anti-discrimination organizations as the city's Commission on Human Relations, the Fellowship Commission's Council on Equal Job Opportunity, the AFL-CIO's Human Relations Committee, or the NAACP.[100] Linking industrial renewal assistance to active nondiscrimination policies might have constrained PIDC's core purpose of keeping employers in the city, but ties to civil rights groups could have been created with minimal costs and would have allowed PIDC to serve a mediating function between these organizations and the individual companies with which it worked.

Participation in targeted anti-discrimination efforts would have required a significant broadening of PIDC's mission. No such constraints, however, prevented the corporation from working with inner-city economic development and job training programs implemented in Philadelphia during the War on Poverty. PIDC remained almost completely disengaged from such efforts. PIDC's Richard McConnell participated in the city's Community

Renewal Program in the early 1960s and in 1964 served as chair both of a planning committee in an early stage of the city's War on Poverty program and of the city's Overall Economic Development Program committee (chapter 3). Yet McConnell never brought the issues discussed by these committees back to the PIDC board for consideration of their possible relationship to the corporation itself.[101]

At a more program-specific level, PIDC established no connections with such organizations as Opportunities Industrialization Centers (OIC), Leon Sullivan's job training and African American business development program, or the Philadelphia Urban Coalition, a city-sponsored clearinghouse for cooperative efforts to address the city's social and economic problems. OIC could have benefited from PIDC's connections in placing its trainees in job openings and from PIDC's expertise in business planning for its entrepreneurial projects. The Urban Coalition might have provided an appropriate venue for a wider PIDC role, as it brought together government, community, labor, and business groups and worked on projects including economic development and job training. PIDC, however, did not even offer support for an Urban Coalition effort to extend mass transit service from North Philadelphia to the Philadelphia Industrial Park.[102] Similarly, PIDC developed no contact of any kind with Philadelphia's Model Cities Administration until the early 1970s. Although this gap had much to do with the racial and political tensions around the local Model Cities effort, it also represented one of the most significant missed opportunities of the period. In 1973, this changed, and Model Cities became a policy vehicle that allowed PIDC to work on an intense basis within a limited, economically depressed area of the inner city (chapter 8). Such developments might have occurred far earlier with far greater benefits for inner city residents.

Perhaps the most striking example of such avoidance came in August 1968 when PIDC officials actually did meet with leaders of the Greater Philadelphia Enterprises Development Corporation. The GPEDC was a small, under-staffed African American community-based economic development organization that eventually financed the expansion of ten industrial facilities and the construction of a shopping center. Beyond a vague promise of future cooperation, the meeting did not produce an agreement to coordinate efforts or to help the community group take advantage of PIDC's technical and financial resources. Instead, the two entities agreed to stake out separate territory: "PIDC and GPEDC will notify each other in writing as they develop new projects. It is understood that the first party to notify the other of its interest in the project will continue with the project and that the other will not interfere." This mutually defensive agreement, repeated twice elsewhere in the document, put the racial bifurcation of Philadelphia's industrial policy into writing.[103]

Rather than confronting the charged issues of race and employment, PIDC remained narrowly focused on the physical problems of industrial obsolescence in Philadelphia. The agency, of course, had not been created to do anything else. Yet this constrained purpose meant that PIDC could address only one among a number of factors that contributed to the decline of Philadelphia's manufacturing base. Similarly, PIDC made little effort to address labor conflict and cost, or the increasing regional and offshore competition that lay behind many firms' decisions to leave the city or close. PIDC's indirect method of dealing with race, however, had the greatest long-term consequences for both the city's future and the agency's own legacy in confronting deindustrialization and the resulting problem of jobs. By dodging the racial question, PIDC remained almost completely isolated not only from a major cause of the problem that it was trying to resolve, but also from the community most dramatically affected by economic change. Ignored by the city's official industrial development agency, the African American community turned inward and deployed its own resources, as well as those it could attract from sources other than PIDC, to address the increasingly crushing problem of jobs. The result was that by the end of the 1960s, local industrial policy in Philadelphia proceeded on two parallel tracks defined almost entirely by race. These tracks slowly and haltingly converged during the 1970s, but by then, the moment of opportunity provided by the political and macro-economic conditions of the 1960s had already passed.

How, in the end, should Philadelphia's industrial renewal program be evaluated? Ultimately, PIDC proved to be only a moderating check on deindustrialization. Yet this alone represented a significant achievement, as the industrial renewal program preserved jobs and tax revenues without which Philadelphia would have faced even more severe social and fiscal crises in the following decades. Walter D'Alessio, PIDC's executive vice president during the 1970s, summarized the dilemmas implicit to PIDC's work when he noted that despite his agency's best efforts, "we've obviously had a decline over these years but it would be kind of frightening to contemplate what it might have been if those opportunities weren't presented to industry to relocate within the city."[104] By 1990, firms that had engaged in a PIDC financed transaction between 1959 and 1970 accounted for nearly one out of four manufacturing and wholesaling jobs that remained in Philadelphia. Further, PIDC accomplished this with only minimal local costs in terms of either direct subsidies or residential displacement. Given the obstacles the program faced and the limited resources with which it had to work, these aspects of PIDC's record represent an unheralded success of the pragmatic local liberalism that lay behind Philadelphia's local industrial policy in the decades after World War II.

While it remained only a partial solution to urban deindustrialization, PIDC did shift the cost of the spatial reorganization of urban industry to the federal level through its use of the tax-free status of its debt obligations. This strategy reversed the typical postwar pattern of federal subsidization of suburban economic development. Most importantly, PIDC's comparatively simple restructuring of federal tax incentives showed that industrial investment could be attracted to economically depressed and racially isolated inner-city neighborhoods. During the late 1950s and the 1960s, the Philadelphia variant of liberalism thus demonstrated that the local state could productively intervene in private markets. Significant in its local context, yet increasingly isolated on a national stage dominated by social service-oriented anti-poverty programs and soon to be captured by an anti-statist, anti-urban conservatism, Philadelphia's industrial renewal program stood as a vibrant reminder of an earlier American liberalism that had focused on the structural roots of economic and social problems. In the end, PIDC's greatest limitation in the 1960s lay less in its failure at the impossible task of resolving Philadelphia's deindustrialization-induced problem of jobs than in its inability to bridge the gap separating Philadelphia's racially bifurcated, parallel tracks of local industrial and employment policy—parallel tracks that it did much to create.

"Economic development is but a means": The War on Poverty and Local Economic Planning

D uring the same period in which PIDC rejected Kirk Petshek's appeal for rigorous industrial planning, Philadelphia's city government actually began to develop a far broader program of comprehensive economic planning. Liberal experts, still ensconced in key public, quasi-public, and private positions during the post-reform era of Mayor Tate, seized this moment to articulate an ambitious program for coordinating Philadelphia's industrial development, job training, urban renewal, and social service efforts. This program drew on long-running conversations, both in Philadelphia and beyond, about how to fight poverty. Significantly, it also drew on ideas about economic planning and the role of the state developed during and since the New Deal. In particular, it reflected key aspects of proposals for coordinated local and inter-governmental planning that had been developed in the 1930s and early 1940s by President Roosevelt's National Resources Planning Board. The formulation of this local planning program predated the federal War on Poverty, which would soon offer a very different model of postwar liberal activism. In particular, the War on Poverty would place far less emphasis on structural economic issues and planning itself. The Philadelphia planners' program would never be fully realized, but it is a crucial episode in the narrative of Philadelphia's response to the problem of jobs. This "road not taken" adds a new layer of complexity to the story of twentieth century American liberalism. It shows that Philadelphia's local liberals remained concerned with questions of economic structure and even economic justice, rather than solely with macroeconomic growth or the "rights revolution" that is typically identified as the core concern of postwar liberalism. As such, it demonstrates that at the local level, postwar liberalism remained a vibrant ideology that sought to use planning and the power of the state to address the spiraling problems of urban economic life. This story is also crucial in fully comprehending the steps that *were* taken in 1960s Philadelphia, particularly by community activists who soon became deeply engaged in the local implementation of the federal War on Poverty.

This revived planning effort took place within a policy context defined by two comparatively obscure federal initiatives, the U.S. Housing Act of 1959 and the Area Redevelopment Act of 1961. While neither of these measures has been ranked among the leading legislative accomplishments of the post–World War II American state, the conjunction of the two acts led to a new approach to comprehensive planning in Philadelphia that, for a time, offered the potential for a fundamental break from past practices. This unprecedented emphasis on comprehensive planning arose from the statutory requirements of each act. The 1959 Housing Act provided funding for Community Renewal Programs (CRP) that were supposed to relate the housing and economic development aspects of local renewal programs both to one another and to the overall needs of the city.[1] Two years later, the Area Redevelopment Act required that each city prepare an Overall Economic Development Program (OEDP) with much the same content as the CRP.

In late 1961, Mayor James Tate created a task force to plan the city's CRP, and in 1963, he appointed an Economic Development Committee to prepare the area redevelopment program. Despite the mayor's strained relationship with the liberal reformers, the actual membership of both groups consisted of the usual array of city officials, business leaders, and civic groups that had typified such efforts during the reform period. In an important contrast to the leadership of organizations established in the 1950s, such as PIDC or the Food Distribution Center Corporation, both the CRP task force and the Economic Development Committee also included representatives from the Commission on Human Relations, the Urban League, and the Advisory Commission on Civil Rights.[2]

The real work of both initiatives, however, took place at the staff level, and here the CRP and the Economic Development Committee worked closely together. CRP staff economist Elizabeth Deutermann wrote the CRP's technical report on economic development and assisted new city economist John Culp with the preparation of the Economic Development Committee's Overall Economic Development Program.[3] As a result, the two studies offered a consistent vision of Philadelphia's economic future that built on the industrial planning ideas that Petshek and the Mayor's Economic Advisory Committee had advocated during the debate over PIDC's development practices. Both reports offered a now ritualized acknowledgement of the 1950s "Philadelphia Renaissance," but they also observed that such physically oriented projects as Penn Center, Independence Mall, Society Hill, and the Food Distribution Center had failed to produce the expected universal benefits for all city residents. Unemployment and underemployment in Philadelphia remained high, and indicated that the city's job losses during the preceding decade had taken a heavy toll. Between 1952 and 1962, employment in Philadelphia had fallen by 90,000, approximately 8 percent. Further, the manufacturing sector accounted for 70 percent of these lost jobs, far out of proportion to its 33 percent share of total jobs in the city.[4]

The two economists noted that these trends placed a disproportionate burden on older workers, young males, the unskilled and semi-skilled, and especially African Americans, who made up 26 percent of the city labor force yet constituted 43 percent of the unemployed. This racial gap could only partially be explained by low skill levels and the reports emphasized that widespread employment discrimination played a central part in the disproportionate rate of black unemployment. They also projected that by 1970, Philadelphia's labor force would become younger, blacker, and more female. This analysis signaled an important shift away from the universalistic assumptions that had guided the formation of PIDC. It recognized that Philadelphia's problem of jobs had distinct racial and gender components that would not be fully resolved by a generalized industrial policy targeted at the city as a whole.[5]

Culp and Deutermann's most important contribution, however, lay in their recommendations. The economists calculated that to achieve an "interim full-employment" level of 6 percent unemployed, Philadelphia would have to create 21,000 new jobs immediately and another 54,000 by 1970. To attain a true full-employment level of 4 percent unemployment (the national target set by the Council of Economic Advisors) would require as many as 99,000 new jobs. "Current efforts," Deutermann

FIGURE 13. Economist Elizabeth Deutermann. As staff economist for the Philadelphia Community Renewal Program, Deutermann wrote the CRP's technical report on economic development and assisted new city economist John Culp with the preparation of the Economic Development Committee's Overall Economic Development Program. These proposals offered a vision for coordinated economic planning in 1960s Philadelphia—and a way to close the racial gap in the city's industrial and employment policies. Photo courtesy of Temple University Libraries, Urban Archives, Philadelphia, Pennsylvania.

concluded, "are inadequate to the task." The reports suggested new techniques to reach these goals: the federal Area Redevelopment Administration should provide financing for plants and equipment to supplement PIDC's work with undercapitalized firms; it should also create a pilot program that would attempt to rehabilitate empty factories for reuse; existing institutional expansion programs such as those for hospitals, universities, and scientific research facilities in West Philadelphia should be accelerated, as should industrial renewal, center city redevelopment, and port and airport expansion; funding for a nascent Small Business Opportunities Corporation should be made permanent; and financial support should be provided for the development of tourist-based businesses. The City Planning Commission, which had vastly underestimated the effects of land use planning on job opportunities in its 1961 comprehensive plan, should also increase its efforts to balance spatial planning for highways, houses, and park space with "parallel efforts" to combat unemployment and poverty.[6]

Although Deutermann and Culp argued that job creation should be the city's top priority, they recognized that it would not be sufficient to resolve Philadelphia's employment problems. As a result, they also recommended expansion of job training programs. This would require the support of new vocational counseling and job placement services. An estimated 100,000 Philadelphians might require the services of such programs by 1970, but Culp pointed out that the public sector could not achieve these goals alone. For such a massive program to succeed, employers would have to recognize that they too had a "major responsibility" to support local training programs, provide on-going training, and modify their practices "with respect to hiring younger workers, particularly males."[7] This emphasis on training for men reflected assumptions common to job training efforts in the 1960s. In addition to holding conventional views about family structure and gender roles in the workplace, policymakers believed that industries with traditionally male work forces such as manufacturing and mining had gone into decline nationally, while the trade and service fields that employed a higher proportion of women had undergone expansions. Deutermann made a similar point and also connected the need to end racial discrimination with the need for expanded employment in the city: employers, she argued, would more readily eliminate racial barriers in a tight labor market.[8]

Culp noted Philadelphia Reverend Leon Sullivan's recent creation of the Opportunities Industrialization Centers (OIC) job training program, and he outlined the need to tie such community-based efforts into wider systems of economic and physical planning, industrial rehabilitation, and social services. In particular, Culp emphasized that successful urban economic initiatives would require the services of the city's welfare, health, and housing programs. Much of the support for improved local social services, he suggested, might be provided by the anti-poverty legislation then under consideration in Congress. More important, however, was the point that economic planning could not be separated from such services, which met basic short-term needs while also serving "to improve labor force motivation and to raise aspirations of those living in poverty and economic deprivation." Without such aid, demoralization might convert the merely unemployed "into *unemployable* persons" before long-range job training and job creation programs could take full effect. Culp noted the stakes: "these are personal and family tragedies. This is also a community tragedy and represents an economic loss of incalculable proportions. Jobless people cannot be good consumers; nor can they be happy people." This intertwining of Keynesianism, consumerism, and emotional well-being with the planning imperative suggested the interconnected quality of liberal thought during the period. The productive capacity of individuals still mattered, but it had been paired with, and perhaps even become secondary to, imperatives of supporting the consumer economy and performing therapeutic social functions.[9] The broader point, however, represented one of Culp and Deutermann's most important insights: if properly implemented and skillfully coordinated, social services and economic development could be mutually reinforcing rather than mutually exclusive policy goals.

Building on this observation, the core conclusion of the two reports called for the establishment of a structure for coordinated, comprehensive economic planning in Philadelphia. Deutermann noted that "currently, over 45 programs have been identified as operative in the City which have objectives of increasing employment opportunity and/or developing our labor force. . . . no mechanism exists for preparing and carrying out a comprehensive and integrated policy for a frontal attack on unemployment."[10] Although nominally assigned to the Development Coordinator's office in the mayor's cabinet, the resources necessary to accomplish such a complex task had not been allocated. Instead, coordination took place only through an internecine structure of "inter-agency committees and interlocking directorates." In contrast, Culp and Deutermann argued that job creation and training programs had to be planned in relation both to one another and to social, welfare, and urban renewal programs. As Culp put it, Philadelphia had to develop "a vigorous, multi-pronged approach. . . . no narrow approach will suffice." Deutermann characterized the overall process as one of "adaptive planning." The city would need to identify external forces shaping its social and economic structure, understand the opportunities and the dangers that these forces created, and respond with all available policy tools. The success of this new approach, Culp added, would also require "the vigorous elimination of discrimination."[11]

Culp also briefly noted the need for regional development. Efforts to promote cooperation between the city and its suburbs during the reform mayoral administrations had met with success only in mass transit. The suburban counties had resisted all other efforts to adopt a regional approach. More recently, a privately sponsored regional loan fund had been established to provide "working capital and machinery and equipment in risk cases," but it had only one permanent staff member and had no true planning function, let alone governmental authority.[12] As a result, Culp called not for voluntary city-suburb coordination, but for the Area Redevelopment Administration to act as coordinator, with a particular emphasis on allocating federal spending and jobs on an equitable basis through the region. Such coordination of federal spending would provide at least a first step toward regional economic planning.[13]

Regardless of regionalism, Culp maintained that a comprehensive planning strategy for the city had to reflect a fundamental recognition that "social overhead or welfare investment is a requisite for economic development. For economic development is, after all, but a means to achieving social and welfare objectives."[14] With the earlier references to discrimination, these statements summarized the liberal rationale for economic policy in postwar Philadelphia. Rather than a tool for the promotion of capitalist interests (although no planner would have denied that businesses could benefit), development represented a way to increase employment opportunities and secure the local tax base that supported social services. Those services in turn made economic development itself viable by maintaining (or developing) an intact community with high levels of human capital. Social services and development, and in particular employment policy and industrial policy, could not be separated.[15]

The implementation of such a comprehensive strategy would require an administrative mechanism capable of drawing the job creation, training, and social service programs together in a common structure. Culp offered only the vague suggestion that "a comprehensive, day-to-day planning-coordination-action instrumentality is required to carry out the program."[16] Deutermann, however, presented a far more specific, two-part proposal. First, the city would prepare a detailed annual development program relating its short-term budgetary needs and fiscal restraints to its long-term social and economic goals. All fiscally viable alternative approaches would be presented to policymakers, allowing them to make program decisions with full knowledge of the available options and their implications. Ideally, Deutermann maintained, this planning process would orient specific budget decisions around long-range programmatic goals, making it possible to "see the interrelationships among the different programs."[17] Second, a new city agency should be created with the sole purpose of coordinating the annual development program and should be given "pin-pointed authority and responsibility for long-range as well as opportunistic planning and with assigned responsibility for implementation of such plans." The fragmentation of the existing system, Deutermann argued, prevented anything except "opportunistic planning." Without a new agency, the development-programming apparatus would disintegrate into merely an advisory process with little or no authority.[18]

Together, Deutermann and Culp's CRP and ARA proposals called for the creation of a powerful system of coordinated local economic planning. As such, they demonstrate that during the postwar period, a locally based form of urban liberalism rehabilitated and reshaped economic planning ideas that had been proposed for national implementation during the New Deal. Local economic and industrial planning structures had formed a key component of proposals developed by the National Resources Planning Board for coordinated local, state, and federal planning structures. Long after such planning goals had been abandoned nationally, liberal planners in Philadelphia proposed and in part created similar structures, albeit on a city rather than regional basis. Despite their flaws, both the Area Redevelopment Act and the Community Renewal Program provided a preliminary basis of federal support for this endeavor.[19] In their proposals for the two programs, Deutermann and Culp suggested that large-scale economic trends could be rationally assessed and that local economic policy could be structured to derive maximum benefits for the city's residents and the municipal tax base. Most significantly, and in striking contrast to the "pro-growth," downtown-dominated development strategies that typified urban policy after World War II, this form of urban liberalism held that through such planning, economic development and social welfare could be linked in consistent and mutually reinforcing ways.

The War on Poverty and Employment

The completion of Culp and Deutermann's proposals for coordinated economic and social planning coincided with a remarkable rise in concern about poverty in the United States. In his state of the union speech on January 8, 1964, President Lyndon Johnson announced that "this administration today, here and now, declares unconditional war on poverty in

America."[20] Far from supporting the planning ideas outlined by Culp and Deutermann, however, Johnson's new initiative soon undermined comprehensive economic planning in Philadelphia, and with it, the prospects for an urban liberalism fully attuned to the problem of jobs.

The national political, policy, and intellectual currents that produced the War on Poverty first formed during the mid-1950s in response to alarms about the automation of industrial production. As new technology altered the relationship between labor and capital, the possibility that automation would eliminate manufacturing jobs spurred a wave of proposals for public interventions to assist displaced workers. The high unemployment of the 1953–54, 1957–58, and 1960–61 recessions heightened such concerns and brought additional calls for structural interventions in the American labor market.[21]

This analysis produced a "nascent issue network," developed by scholars, activists, and policymakers, that focused on the creation of a coordinated national employment policy. Advocates of such policy, who included John Kenneth Galbraith, Gunnar Myrdal, Eli Ginzburg, and E. Wight Bakke, argued that the root causes of unemployment lay in a combination of automation, regional underdevelopment, labor exploitation, racial discrimination, and mismatch between existing worker skills and the skills demanded in local labor markets. Such problems, they maintained, could be resolved by policies that would reallocate the nation's labor resources, retrain workers in declining industries, improve personal adjustments to the modern workplace, expand public investments and subsidies in "depressed areas," manage public spending to ensure full employment, and provide direct public jobs when other measures failed. Together, these varied strands of labor market policy would moderate the market forces that condemned potentially productive workers to underemployment.[22]

The goal of creating such a national labor market policy formed the core of liberal proposals for targeted responses to the ravages of regional economic change. During the 1950s, Senator Paul Douglas of Illinois sponsored area redevelopment legislation that included extensive redevelopment funds for depressed industrial and mining areas, as well as expanded unemployment assistance and support for the retraining or relocation of workers. After President Eisenhower vetoed two versions of Douglas's bill, President Kennedy finally signed a weak version of the Area Redevelopment Act in 1961. Kennedy also supported Pennsylvania Senator and former Philadelphia Mayor Joseph Clark's 1962 Manpower Development and Training Act (MDTA), which for the first time involved the federal government in large-scale job training programs specifically designed to address unemployment.[23]

Although sometimes criticized as an effort to explain unemployment solely in relation to the deficiencies of individual workers, job training proposals in the late 1950s and early 1960s actually constituted a core strand of this distinctly structural analysis of unemployment. "Manpower theory," as the subset of policies that focused on training became known, offered a promising, if partial, solution to the problems of the labor market. It suggested that older (and, as the gendered term itself implied, mostly male) workers could be retrained to fill new, more technical jobs and that younger workers could master the skills required in growing sectors of the economy. This analysis "operated on the structuralist premise that unemployment was not just a cyclical phenomenon."[24] Planning efforts and public subsidies, however, would still be required to revitalize depressed areas. Manpower theory thus was one part of a proposed policy response to the structural transformation of the post–World War II American economy. As such, it was part of a broader continuation of the structurally oriented liberalism once embodied by the National Resources Planning Board (NRPB) and the postwar Full Employment Act. It also reflected liberal economists' rejection of the idea, central to the emerging neoclassical economic synthesis, that market efficiency prevailed in private labor markets.[25]

Overall, however, the Kennedy administration provided only tepid support for structural labor market policies, as it increasingly emphasized a tax-cut based form of Keynesian, macroeconomic growth management as its primary approach to unemployment reduction. As conceived by early supporters, active labor market policies formed a crucial complement to such Keynesian fiscal policy. Economist John Kenneth Galbraith, for example, advocated a form of "social Keynesianism" that emphasized public spending on social programs and public facilities to achieve both fiscal stimulus *and* gains in overall social welfare. From this perspective, labor market policies such as the manpower act and the ARA were "selective interventions to boost employment," while the government spending that such programs entailed provided Keynesian demand stimulation. Galbraith, however, was excluded from Kennedy's Council of Economic Advisors (CEA). As labor market and Keynesian policies developed during the early years of the administration, the two strategies were posed as counterpoints rather than complements. Where social Keynesians such as

Galbraith emphasized the maintenance of full employment through federal spending on public works and social programs, CEA chairman Walter Heller preferred a policy of fiscal stimulus based almost solely on tax cuts. The economic growth that such cuts created, the CEA maintained, would overwhelm most structural imbalances in the economy.[26]

Despite the determined advocacy of secretary of labor Willard Wirtz, structural theories of unemployment gradually lost influence as the administration adopted a more narrow, "commercial Keynesianism" that rejected public spending and selective labor market intervention in favor of a broad-based tax cut.[27] Although job training persisted as an important policy structure in this new environment, it did so only in a dependent position, lacking the related planning, job placement, economic development, and public employment programs that a broader labor market policy would have encompassed. As implemented, job training programs relied on the premise that macroeconomic growth management could maintain full employment without inflation. That idea would prove problematic because of the persistence of employment discrimination, the inter- and intra-regional imbalances in growth-based job creation, and the challenge of sustaining long-term, low-inflation growth through the commercial and later military Keynesianism that dominated fiscal policy under Kennedy and Johnson. Training programs thus operated without the support of broader structural measures to address the employment consequences of technical change and uneven development in the postwar United States.[28]

At the same time that commercial Keynesianism trumped both social Keynesianism and structural manpower theories, a new and broader focus on poverty, rather than unemployment, moved to the center of liberal policy debates. During the early 1960s, social scientists and journalists such as Oscar Lewis, Michael Harrington, Dwight MacDonald, Richard Cloward, Lloyd Ohlin, Kenneth B. Clark, and others raised new concerns about the persistence of poverty amidst overall postwar prosperity. Rather than explicitly shaping policy, this intellectual ferment contributed to the construction of a broad political context receptive to new anti-poverty initiatives. The distinctiveness of the approach lay in its explanation of poverty. These writers saw poverty as a cultural and even psychological phenomenon that could be separated from both cyclical macroeconomic fluctuations and deep-seated structural economic problems. Particularly in the work of Lewis, this perspective shifted attention toward the social and cultural roots of poverty. It suggested that the deprivations and hardships experienced by the poor transformed behavior, attitudes, and cultural characteristics in ways that reinforced and replicated poverty itself. The result was that a cyclical "culture of poverty" explained the persistence of poverty itself across multiple generations. This idea implicitly downplayed the importance of the structural inequities of market economies, and emphasized instead the characteristics of poor people and their communities. In the late 1950s, the broad culture of poverty thesis produced two specific, often overlapping ideas. One was the concept of community action, which held that the functional "competence" of poor communities could be increased through expert-guided efforts to organize and mobilize the poor to demand redress of basic problems of social order and public service delivery. The other was the closely related concept of opportunity theory, which held that such efforts could remove barriers to opportunity that frustrated the supposedly conventional aspirations of poor youth and forced them into lives of juvenile delinquency followed by adult unemployment and inescapable poverty.[29]

The culture of poverty, community action, and opportunity theory concepts quickly garnered support both in government and among the nation's major philanthropic institutions. Between 1961 and 1963, a series of foundation and governmental demonstration projects, such as the Ford Foundation's Gray Areas Project and the President's Committee on Juvenile Delinquency, explored the implications of the new ideas by organizing poor communities to attack poverty through the coordination, expansion, and reorganization of social services and local political structures. Such strategies, it was hoped, would empower the poor and shatter the cultural patterns that replicated and reinforced poverty. Within the Kennedy administration, the poverty culture thesis indirectly shaped the perspective of the CEA, which in 1962 had been asked by the White House to formulate a new anti-poverty policy. Although CEA chairman Heller avoided the discursive structure of the culture of poverty argument, he nonetheless accepted its premise. Heller concluded that social characteristics, along with racial discrimination, explained most poverty that could not be eliminated through Keynesian fiscal policy. After Lyndon Johnson assumed the presidency in November 1963, an administration task force shaped a poverty program that focused primarily on the resolution of individual, family, and community handicaps rather than on job creation or public employment (which Wirtz advocated but Johnson personally rejected).[30] Job training found a place within the War on Poverty, but only in a subsidiary role that focused on the individual deficiencies of the poor, rather than on concerns with structural unemployment. In Philadelphia, however, job training would become central in defining the War on Poverty. More broadly, Johnson's martial rhetoric in his 1964 state of the union speech vastly overplayed the War on Poverty's program content and funding. Nonetheless, the service- and empowerment-oriented anti-poverty campaign quickly superseded the structural focus of the area redevelopment and manpower acts.[31] As a result, the War on Poverty in Philadelphia undermined the economic planning ideas that had been put forth by Deutermann and Culp. Different dimensions of postwar liberalism came into conflict, and in the area of planning, the national won out over the local.

Philadelphia's War on Poverty and the Defeat of Economic Planning

Less than a week after President Johnson formally initiated the War on Poverty by signing the Economic Opportunity Act in a White House Rose Garden ceremony, Philadelphia's simmering racial tensions erupted into open conflict. In the late summer heat of August 28, 1964, violent clashes broke out in North Philadelphia after a confrontation between police and a black motorist. For four days, North Philadelphians looted stores, set fires, and battled with police in an expression of anger and resentment against multiple layers of discrimination, police brutality, and exploitative business practices by white merchants and landlords. More broadly, the uprising signified a rejection of both official and civil rights liberalism by many African Americans in Philadelphia and around the United States. Many white Philadelphians, in turn, interpreted it as mob violence, and, in some cases, used it to justify their own resentment, anger, and racism.[32]

Although smaller in scale than the cataclysmic uprisings that would follow in Watts, Newark, Detroit, and other cities, the North Philadelphia conflict illuminated the local racial environment in which the War on Poverty would unfold. Earlier in the year, Johnson's war on poverty declaration had set off a scramble for control of any new anti-poverty programs and their anticipated political largess. Following his 1963 reelection and the deaths of both Democratic city chairman (and congressman) Bill Green and party treasurer Jim Clark, Mayor Tate had become embroiled in a bitter power struggle with new Democratic city chairman Francis Smith. Tate quickly determined that his political enemies would not dominate the anti-poverty program.[33] Accordingly, his initial War on Poverty plans established a multilevel structure known as "the Mayor's Program for the Elimination of Poverty." Even its name emphasized the primacy of the mayor. The first level of the program consisted of two committees responsible for reviewing project proposals from community organizations and city departments. One committee, chaired by PIDC's Richard McConnell, consisted of the Economic Development Committee that had overseen John Culp's preparation of the Overall Economic Development Program. It would evaluate all proposals related to economic development, job training, and small business assistance in accord with Culp and Deutermann's plans for economic coordination.[34]

A second committee, under welfare commissioner Randolph Wise, would consider proposals related to the social service and educational dimensions of the anti-poverty campaign. Initially, this Human Service Committee consisted entirely of present or former city officials. Under pressure from both the Ford Foundation's Paul Ylvisaker and federal anti-poverty chief Sargent Shriver, Tate agreed in July 1964 to shift control of the committee to the local branch of the Ford Foundation's Gray Areas project.[35] Known locally as the Philadelphia Council for Community Advancement, this project was staffed by city officials, representatives of public and private social service agencies, and social scientists from Temple University. The Ford Foundation had envisioned the council as a device to improve the delivery of social services to Philadelphia's poor by streamlining the efforts of city and private agencies and promoting social scientific research about poverty. Instead, since its inception in 1960, the council had generated bitter internal contests for control of the program, while also alienating much of Philadelphia's African American community. Throughout the first half of 1963, the new NAACP president, Cecil B. Moore, bitterly attacked the council for the selection of former district attorney (and future Watergate prosecutor) Samuel Dash as the organization's executive director, and called for the appointment instead of an African American. Although Moore's charges actually had as much to do with consolidating his control over the Philadelphia NAACP and the local civil rights movement as they did with the council itself, his critique accurately reflected the project's previous disregard for the African American community and resonated with many black Philadelphians.[36] Although Mayor Tate viewed the council as a tool of the reform wing of the Democratic Party, he hoped to use Ford money to meet local matching fund requirements imposed on the poverty program by Congress. In

addition, the council by mid-1964 had undergone such severe cutbacks
and had been so badly weakened by Moore's attacks that Tate assumed
it could be easily controlled. He thus accepted Ylvisaker's demand, under threat of removal of all Ford funds from the city, that the Council for
Community Advancement be given authority over the poverty program's
Human Services Committee.[37]

Despite this nominal concession to Ford, Tate retained ultimate control. Upon completion of the proposal review process, all acceptable proposals would be submitted to the program's second level, known as the
Mayor's Task Force, which would be chaired by Tate himself. The "May-
or's Program for the Elimination of Poverty," in short, left no doubt about
where control of the War on Poverty would lie in Philadelphia.[38]

Still, this initial Philadelphia interpretation of the War on Poverty had
one positive aspect: it included a specific mechanism for economic planning and coordination in the form of the Economic Development Committee. It also had a serious flaw, as it made no provision for grassroots
"community action," even though the federal Economic Opportunity Act
explicitly required the establishment of local mechanisms to insure the
"maximum feasible participation" of the poor in local anti-poverty programs. In addition, the Council for Community Advancement's tarnished
reputation in the African American community meant that its designation
as the official representative of the poor produced an angry backlash. At
a public meeting held to announce the new arrangement, Cecil B. Moore
denounced the council's participation in the poverty program. CORE, the
local Americans for Democratic Action chapter, the Health and Welfare
Council (a regional social services funding organization), and the city's
newspapers also opposed the plan.[39]

By mid-1964, Mayor Tate had made two critical mistakes in shaping the
poverty program. The first had been to believe that Washington had no real
interest in community participation and that the poverty program would
simply represent "business as usual" between the administration and urban mayors. As a federal anti-poverty official later put it, "no one told
him the rules had been changed." The second had been to assume that he
could gain access to Ford Foundation money without taking on the racial
baggage that the Council for Community Advancement now carried.[40]

These miscalculations led to the quick collapse of Tate's initial plan
for the War on Poverty—including the provisions for comprehensive economic planning. In late 1964, after the Mayor's Task Force gutted or rejected any program proposal that challenged mayoral control, the federal

Office of Economic Opportunity (OEO; the agency charged with implementing much of the Economic Opportunity Act) rejected Philadelphia's entire funding application. OEO justified its decision on the grounds that Philadelphia's anti-poverty plans did not include a meaningful community action component. In the aftermath of the OEO rejection, the Ford Foundation announced that it would provide no additional support for the Council for Community Advancement, which promptly relinquished its position in Philadelphia's anti-poverty program.[41]

Faced with continued local and federal demands for community participation, the Tate administration had no choice but to restructure its program.[42] Although the mayor maintained a defiant public front, blaming the OEO rejection on "the great game of bureaucracy" in Washington, he privately formed a committee to develop a complete reorganization plan. Ideas for a new antipoverty structure came primarily from Samuel Evans, an African American concert promoter who had organized Philadelphia's delegation to the 1963 March on Washington and had emerged as Tate's primary advisor on poverty and racial issues.[43] Evans warned that Tate's tight control over the local anti-poverty structure exposed the mayor to any political liability that might emerge from the experimental program: "the public seems to place full responsibility for a workable Poverty Program on your shoulders. This represents a great danger." Evans urged Tate to shift responsibility for administering the program, and with it the inherent political risks, to "the various organizations involved" in the Human Services Committee. To satisfy OEO's community action requirements, Evans suggested creating neighborhood-based poverty councils, each of which would select a representative to serve on an expanded Human Services Committee. This committee would assume all responsibilities previously held by both the Economic Development Committee and the Mayor's Task Force. These steps, Evans believed, would provide a mechanism for involving the poor while shifting the anti-poverty program's risks away from the mayor's office.[44]

With support from Tate, the reorganization committee endorsed Evans's proposals and presented them to OEO in early February 1965. The revised program eliminated the Mayor's Task Force, the Economic Development Committee, and the Human Services Committee, and replaced them with a twenty-six-member governing body known as the Philadelphia Anti-Poverty Action Committee (PAAC). This new committee, the city claimed, had been explicitly designed "to combine the City's community assets with its established social agencies." This meant, in effect, that the new structure would include civil rights leaders, representatives of business, labor, and social service organizations, enough city officials to insure a strong role for city hall, and a sufficient number of actual poor people to satisfy OEO's demands for community participation. As the city's primary anti-poverty agency, PAAC would be responsible for all facets of program development and administration. The new plan also created six Community Action Councils (based on Evans's idea of neighborhood poverty councils), each of which would choose a delegate to serve on PAAC. OEO deputy director Jack Conway announced that the new Philadelphia program "may well become a model for the organization of programs in other cities." The federal agency, though, still offered only provisional approval of the proposal.[45]

Reflecting the concerns behind this provisional endorsement, OEO suggested that this provisional status would be removed if PAAC were established as a nonprofit corporation (as already implemented in Washington and Pittsburgh) to insure its political independence. The Tate administration, however, preempted this idea by expanding the plan's community action components. In response to community objections that the PAAC board still included too few representatives of the poor, the administration agreed in April to increase the number of neighborhood-based Community Action Councils from six to twelve and proposed that the poor be allowed to select their own representatives for the councils in a special anti-poverty election. Each council would have twelve elected members, who would in turn select a delegate to serve on the citywide PAAC board. As with the broader PAAC concept itself, Evans suggested this compromise. No other city in the country had allowed the poor to choose their own representatives in a direct electoral process. The idea immediately gained the enthusiastic support of OEO, which dropped its call for a nonprofit corporation and recognized PAAC as Philadelphia's official community action agency. This new plan became the basis for the War on Poverty in Philadelphia.[46]

In the years that followed, however, earlier doubts about PAAC's capacity for independent action proved well founded. Despite extensive efforts to mobilize Philadelphia's poor through a series of rallies, parades, and town meetings, the May 26, 1965, election to select Community Action Council representatives drew only 2.6 percent of eligible poverty-area voters. Critics charged that this low turnout reflected "cynicism and apathy among the poor" regarding the poverty program.[47] Following similarly disappointing results in 1966 and 1967 elections (participation rates

FIGURE 14. Children from a "Get Set" pre-school program at Bethlehem Baptist Church parading to build interest in PAAC's 1966 elections. The vote would select members of PAAC's twelve Community Action Councils, which represented Philadelphia's primary official effort to foster the "maximum feasible participation" of the poor in the local War on Poverty. Photo courtesy of Temple University Libraries, Urban Archives, Philadelphia, Pennsylvania.

of 5.4 and 3.5 percent respectively), OEO eliminated any funding for additional elections.[48]

While the low turnouts for PAAC elections undercut the organization's legitimacy, the nature of both the election results and PAAC's ensuing operations limited the War on Poverty's effectiveness in Philadelphia's poor neighborhoods. Although strict income limits meant that all Community Action Council representatives met a technical definition of poverty, many were actually well-established neighborhood activists who ran as part of cooperative election slates organized by influential community groups. The executive director of the North City Congress, for example, later acknowledged that the organization had effectively "controlled" the poverty elections in five of the twelve poverty areas. Still, the PAAC elections helped to institutionalize key African American community groups, provided them with new channels of political and policy access, and also brought African American women into unprecedented positions of political leadership. These were not insignificant accomplishments.[49]

Other, more serious drawbacks, however, also plagued Philadelphia's anti-poverty program. The PAAC elections, as well as the War on Poverty more generally, generated even less interest among the city's low-income whites. Only 10 of the 144 elected representatives on Community Action Councils in 1965–66 were white, even though white families constituted 57 percent of all poor families in the city. As a result, the War on Poverty in Philadelphia developed an image as a black program and thus contributed to the racial fissures that increasingly divided the city's poor and working class population.[50]

In terms of practical politics, the Tate administration quickly gained almost complete control over both PAAC and the Community Action Councils. Soon after its organization, PAAC became a key part of Tate's strategy to counteract an alliance of reform Democrats and ward leaders by maintaining the loyalty of the city's black voters.[51] The first step was the selection of the PAAC executive director, a post that Tate had agreed would go to an African American. This set off a behind-the-scenes battle between black political factions. The NAACP's Moore hoped to use the position to control PAAC by installing his own candidate, NAACP legal counsel Isaiah Crippens, as executive director. Evans countered with his own candidate: Charles Bowser, a well-regarded thirty-four-year-old attorney, had cleared land mines and defused bombs during the Korean War, and had since built a reputation as a favorite of the city's black ministers and as the organizer of a successful campaign to ban blackface in Philadelphia's annual New Year's Day Mummer's Parade. After initially backing a police officer who immediately failed a civil service examination, Tate delayed, avoiding a decision for more than two months and even asking OEO to make the choice for him. OEO declined and simply declared all the candidates qualified. Finally, Tate appointed a selection committee consisting of Evans, Moore, and two representatives of local private welfare organizations. This makeup insured that Bowser would get the position because the welfare agencies would not side with Moore after the Ford Foundation debacle. The committee also offered Crippins a $15,250 a year job as PAAC legal counsel; Crippins, who faced financial pressure because of tax problems, accepted the position against Moore's advice. Although committed to the anti-poverty effort, Bowser understood the political context of his position and worked closely with Evans and Tate.[52]

The second component of the mayor's domination of PAAC consisted of patronage. OEO inadvertently facilitated this when it refused to allow PAAC to pay the Community Action Council representatives. This meant that Tate and Evans could secure the allegiance of many council members by offering them paid jobs elsewhere in the poverty program or city government. By the summer of 1966, 118 of the 144 PAAC council members held such paid positions, as did 78 of their relatives. When OEO later issued a national directive banning representatives of the poor and their immediate families from employment with the poverty program, PAAC had to suspend 500 workers. Meanwhile, Evans used his chairmanship of PAAC's Subcommittee on Community Action Councils to maintain such tight control over PAAC's hiring and activities that one OEO official quipped in 1966 that Philadelphia's poverty program had succeeded in attaining the "maximum feasible participation of Sam Evans."[53] The administration's strategy worked so well that the PAAC board was often divided between a coalition of city officials and Community Action Council representatives on one side and an unlikely alliance between Cecil Moore, CORE, and the private social service agencies on the other.[54]

Tate's efforts produced a handsome reward in the 1967 mayoral election, as he received 66.2 percent of the vote in city wards with primarily African American populations, compared to only 43 percent in white wards. This black support provided the crucial difference in the election, as the mayor defeated district attorney and future U.S. senator Arlen Specter by the smallest margin in Philadelphia history. Before the election, however, Tate attempted to shore up his popularity among ethnic whites by ap-

FIGURE 15. Philadelphia Anti-Poverty Action Committee executive director Charles W. Bowser speaking at a PAAC meeting, June 8, 1965. Samuel Evans, chairman of the Sub-committee on Community Action Councils and a key African American ally of Mayor James H. J. Tate, is on Bowser's left (with his hand on his forehead); committee chairman C. F. Mc-Neil is on Bowser's right. Photo courtesy of Temple University Libraries, Urban Archives, Philadelphia, Pennsylvania.

pointing the controversial Frank Rizzo to the powerful position of police commissioner. An originator of the racially charged "law and order" approach to both policing and urban politics, Rizzo soon emerged as Tate's anointed successor and was elected mayor in 1971.[55]

At a more substantive level, PAAC's Community Action Councils neither seriously challenged the existing political order in Philadelphia nor created new mechanisms for helping the city's poor. In part, this reflected Evans and Bowser's proclivity toward secrecy. PAAC staff frequently neglected to inform board members about decisions, and Evans and Bowser refused to either hold public hearings or allow Community

Action Council members to participate in hearings held by Americans for Democratic Action and the Republican City Committee. Similarly, PAAC acting deputy director Barbara Weems attempted to control news coverage prior to the July 1966 council elections by barring all PAAC workers from speaking to the press. Her memo on the subject was immediately leaked to the *Philadelphia Bulletin*.[56]

More significantly, control over policy development and implementation remained concentrated within the PAAC staff, the agencies of city government, and participating private organizations such as OIC. The elected, neighborhood-based Community Action Councils remained largely shut out of the process. By the end of 1965, the situation produced a rebellion within the PAAC staff that culminated when Bowser fired PAAC program planner David Ericson, who publicly charged that PAAC had ignored proposals developed by the Community Action Councils. Eight months later, in August 1966, a scathing OEO evaluation confirmed Ericson's claims:

> Philadelphia does not have an effective anti-poverty program.... Although there are some individually impressive programs, these have been developed by delegate agencies rather than by PAAC. PAAC gives the impression of being more of a hindrance than a positive force in developing a comprehensive anti-poverty plan for the community. PAAC has prevented the Community Action Councils (CACs) from playing the dynamic role of which they are capable by a combination of inordinate control and the stifling of local initiative. The CACs lack real authority or power. It is felt that the CAC concept will soon wither and die if the CACs are not permitted to assume a more influential role.[57]

Despite the anti-poverty elections, Philadelphia's poor had no more influence over most PAAC programs than they had over the city's traditional system of top-down social service delivery.[58]

In the months that followed, OEO moved to contain the influence that Evans, Bowser, and by extension Tate exerted over the anti-poverty effort. In November 1966, OEO Pennsylvania coordinator Pablo Eisenberg informed Tate that additional OEO funding for PAAC would be contingent on reform. Along with open hearings, hiring controls, and empowerment of the councils, OEO demanded the elimination of Isaiah Crippins's counsel position and the adoption of qualification criteria for the deputy director position that would prevent Barbara Weems from occupying the job on a permanent basis.[59] Weems, an African American Ph.D. candidate at the University of Pennsylvania and a protégé of Evans and Bowser, had been one of PAAC's first administrators; elevated on an interim basis to the second ranking staff position under Bowser, she oversaw the hiring and administrative structures that supported her mentors' control over the program. Although Bowser accused Eisenberg of racism, PAAC eventually forged a compromise with OEO. This agreement actually avoided the substance of the OEO reforms by re-hiring Crippins on a consulting basis and by redefining Weems's job so that it did not fall under the federal criteria for the deputy director position. Cecil Moore nonetheless resigned from PAAC's board in protest of any accommodation to federal demands.[60]

When Bowser resigned from PAAC in early 1967—he would soon join Tate's reelection campaign and later serve as the city's first black deputy mayor—Weems replaced him as executive director, at first temporarily and then permanently. Through a lengthy and intricate process in 1967 and 1968, Tate, Evans, and Weems deflected another OEO reform campaign by transforming PAAC into a nominally independent nonprofit corporation that still gave the mayor authority to appoint all PAAC board members and to shift current staff into the new entity. Congress had facilitated this when it amended the Economic Opportunity Act in 1967 to deemphasize the direct participation of the poor and reassert the control of city governments.[61]

Periodically, opposition emerged to the Tate-Evans domination of PAAC and community action. In some cases, this came from neighborhood-based groups such as the North City Congress, an umbrella association of mostly African American block, civic, and social organizations in North Philadelphia. In 1968, North City Congress director Alvin Echols blasted PAAC for denying blacks "the full range of social, economic and political options which America has always provided for the white community." More radical black groups urged a boycott of the 1966 poverty elections to protest PAAC's political domination. In other cases, opposition came from elite, largely white liberal groups such as Americans for Democratic Action and the Maximum Participation Movement, the latter organized by a University of Pennsylvania sociology professor. This effort led to the election of six "reform" candidates in the 1966 community action council elections (with seven more narrowly losing), but neither the community groups nor the liberal organizations could mobilize enough disaffected "poverty area" residents to counter Evans's patronage network.

Within that network itself, very different views of PAAC prevailed. Philadelphia Urban League director and PAAC board member Andrew Freeman claimed, at an Americans for Democratic Action-sponsored hearing on PAAC, that "there is no political control. If there was, I would refuse to sit on PAAC. What we need is grass-roots political activity to pressure Washington for more money to fight poverty." Less directly, but tellingly, the chairman of the Area C Community Action Council responded to questions about political control by criticizing his neighbors' unwillingness to become involved in civic life and by dismissing suggestions that structures such as PAAC produced such "acute apathy."[62]

These divisions reflected a wider conflict among African Americans about what "community action" specifically and liberalism more generally meant in the struggle to achieve black empowerment in the urban north. For Evans and his allies, it consisted of building a political organization and gaining access to public jobs and resources, with the goal of following the path by which German American, Irish American, and other urban ethnic groups had supposedly achieved social and economic success and influence.[63] This was liberalism as pluralist bargaining over resources. For the reformers and radicals who opposed Evans, community action meant something else: the direct empowerment of poor blacks and other minorities to demand services and benefits that might fundamentally improve their communities. This was liberalism as an attempt to close the gaps and racial exclusions of the New Deal state itself. This strand of liberalism sought to remedy the racial limitations of the state in areas ranging from Social Security to housing policy to the failure of active full employment policy. Such divergence would never be reconciled within PAAC, but in the actual programmatic operation of Philadelphia's War on Poverty, community action would soon take on meanings that transcended questions about patronage or the dominance of city hall. It would be in such functioning programs that the true legacy of the community action concept, the War on Poverty, and postwar urban liberalism itself would be found.

War on Poverty Programs

Although community action in Philadelphia seemed to be a failure as a federally sponsored tool for empowering poor communities, even the August 1966 OEO report acknowledged that PAAC-funded programs such as Head Start and Leon Sullivan's Opportunities Industrialization Centers (OIC) job training program had produced valuable results. Their accomplishments, however, had little to do with the PAAC–Community Action Council structure. Their success indicated instead that PAAC succeeded programmatically when it provided funding for autonomous policy initiatives. Other independent but PAAC-funded programs also had real achievements, primarily in the area of service provision. Conceived as a complement to the federal Head Start program, the Board of Education's "Get-Set" program offered a combination day care and preschool for young children, focusing on nutritional and medical services as well as school-readiness preparation for three- and four-year-olds from high-poverty areas. Operated out of 100 neighborhood churches and community centers, Get Set provided services to more than 5,000 children. Another significant program, which would have a long-lasting legacy in the city, consisted of the development of new and rehabilitated low-income housing though the nonprofit Philadelphia Housing Development Corporation. Beginning with the construction of twenty new row houses in West Philadelphia, this organization provided community groups with technical and legal services, as well as low-cost mortgage assistance. The organization's mission was to pursue the "development of neighborhood leadership and manpower resources into indigenous neighborhood organizations which are or will be incorporated as housing enterprises." Despite early difficulties, the Philadelphia Housing Development Corporation survived the War on Poverty and developed into a permanent institution in Philadelphia. Other key War on Poverty programs included Community Legal Services, which offered legal services to the poor through the Philadelphia Bar Association, the Defenders' Association, and the Legal Aid Society; Medicare-Alert, through which nearly 300 poverty workers went door-to-door to enroll senior citizens in the federal government's new Medicare program, reaching as many as 130,000 people who might not otherwise have known about Medicare benefits. All of these initiatives, however, originated either with federal agencies or local social service agencies (some of them new), rather than with the neighborhood community action councils as OEO had envisioned. While many improved crucial services for poor communities, they did not restructure the city's social service system around a new basis of community empowerment, any more than the PAAC-CAC elections offered true political empowerment. In reporting on its programs, PAAC tellingly offered statistics on grant dollars received, workers employed, and clients served, but offered nothing in the way of measurement of actual effects on poverty levels.[64]

Valuable as many of these services were for recipients, and significant as Samuel Evans's hiring system may have been for those who benefited, neither provided a basis for actually resolving the problem of poverty. This was particularly so in regard to the structural issues that underlay Philadelphia's problem of jobs. Along with OIC (discussed in chapters 4–6), a component of the War on Poverty run by the Small Business Administration (SBA) was a partial exception that built on a pre-existing program. In January 1964, the SBA had formed a partnership with a newly-created Philadelphia community organization known as the Small Business Opportunities Corporation. This organization attempted to facilitate SBA lending in inner-city neighborhoods by publicizing the federal agency's programs, particularly to businesses owned by minorities. It also recruited business owners, guided them through the SBA loan application process, administered the actual loan, and provided limited management training.[65]

The Small Business Opportunities Corporation's partnership with the SBA provided a model for Title IV of the Economic Opportunity Act of 1964, which authorized the establishment of similar small business development centers throughout the country. Title IV thus sought to expand capital access for minority and low-income business owners. This provided the War on Poverty's only true attempt at structural economic reform. Ironically, the advent of the War on Poverty actually brought about a significant decline in the Small Business Opportunities Corporation's effectiveness in Philadelphia. Title IV placed the small business development centers in charge of administering newly created SBA Economic Opportunity Loans, but it imposed maximum income limits on participants. These restrictions eliminated as many as 80 percent of the corporation's loan applicants, and the organization failed to recruit an equivalent number of candidates among low income residents. The Economic Opportunity Loans also could not exceed $25,000, as compared to a maximum of $350,000 for regular SBA loans. Only 9 percent of the 272 loans coordinated by the Small Business Opportunities Corporation between January 1964 and September 1966 occurred in the final twelve months of this period, when the Economic Opportunity Act took full effect; earlier loans had gone mostly to individuals with incomes above the poverty level. In early 1967, amendments to the Economic Opportunity Act relaxed these restrictions, but in another retreat from community participation, the new legislation also shifted administration of the program away from the small business development centers and recentralized it under the SBA itself.[66]

The War on Poverty and the Parallel Policy Tracks

Community Action's wider failure to create either meaningful political empowerment for the poor or truly community-based social service reorganization in Philadelphia is a familiar story. The significance of urban deindustrialization during this period, however, suggests another, less recognized cost of PAAC's emergence as the institutional core of Philadelphia's War on Poverty. By eliminating the Economic Development Committee, the PAAC plan destroyed a potential mechanism for linking economic development and anti-poverty efforts in the manner envisioned by Culp and Deutermann in the OEDP and CRP reports. Specifically, it meant that PIDC's program to provide inner-city factory space for local firms would have no direct relationship to such War on Poverty–funded initiatives as OIC. On February 9, 1965, PIDC's Richard McConnell received a note from Mayor Tate thanking him for his efforts on the recently defunct Economic Development Committee; McConnell responded politely two days later, offering his services at any point that they might prove useful. With this exchange, PIDC's potential relationship with the poverty program ended before it began.[67]

The failure to create such connections hardened the racial bifurcation of industrial and employment policy in Philadelphia. Although the elimination of the Economic Development Committee was intended to empower the poor through participatory community action, it actually had the effect of separating them from many of the resources necessary to make such empowerment meaningful. The resulting structure restricted Philadelphia's capacity to bridge either the emerging gap between the parallel racial tracks of local policy or the separation between the sociocultural and economic dimensions of poverty that the Economic Opportunity Act had enshrined at the federal level.[68]

This outcome indicates that Philadelphia, and perhaps the War on Poverty as a whole, would have been better served if the federal government had simply provided increased funds for the city's most innovative economic plans and programs—both public and private—without stipulations about restructuring urban political relationships. The problem of community power was a significant component of urban poverty after World War II, but the interconnectedness of urban political and institutional relationships meant that federal political intervention was an ineffective and sometimes counterproductive strategy. Although less dramatic, the federal government in contrast played a crucial and more effective role in the urban arena when it provided vital funding for community-based projects, such as OIC's job training program, that effectively addressed discrete problems. Such programs operated outside of existing institutional structures and had resource needs that could never be met through local or philanthropic sources.

Despite the federal focus on political empowerment and service provision, a late and limited addition to the War on Poverty provided a model for such a strategy. Its approach might be described as "liberal federalism" because of its emphasis on direct federal provision of resources to local, community-based initiatives. In 1966, senators Robert Kennedy and Jacob Javits co-sponsored an amendment to the Economic Opportunity Act that created a new Special Impact Program for low-income urban and rural communities. Although the two New York senators specifically sought to provide funding for a community-based economic development project in the Bedford-Stuyvesant section of Brooklyn, the new program also reflected Kennedy's dissatisfaction with the service-based orientation of the War on Poverty. Charged with the intentionally vague task of creating "an appreciable impact—in arresting tendencies toward chronic dependency, chronic unemployment, and rising community tensions," the Special Impact Program (SIP) provided direct OEO grants for community-based business development, job creation, "human resource development," and housing and commercial projects. The program also required the formation of community-business alliances and "coordination with city-wide planning efforts." Along with its unprecedented (for OEO) attention to job creation and structural economic issues, SIP's major innovation lay in its evasion of the War on Poverty's normal bureaucratic and political channels. SIP funding flowed directly from OEO's national Economic Development office to the community organizations that would put it to use. Regional OEO offices, state and local governments, and local Community Action agencies had no input at any stage of the process. Most SIP grants went to locally based community development corporations (CDCs), which began to form in cities around the United States during the mid- and late-1960s.[69]

Unsurprisingly, SIP encountered significant hostility both from OEO officials, who preferred to preserve the agency's existing funding structure and program emphasis, and from the Johnson administration, which feared anything associated with Robert Kennedy. Under the Nixon administration, which sought to remove all remaining vestiges of community control from federal urban policy, SIP faced even greater difficulties. OEO director Donald Rumsfeld, who feared that "Black Panthers" might take over SIP-funded CDCs, imposed new restrictions on SIP at the federal level and attempted, unsuccessfully, to increase the authority of local business groups over community projects.[70] SIP remained only a small part of the overall War on Poverty. Still, between 1968 and 1971, it provided $73.8 million in grants to forty-two urban and rural CDCs. In the aftermath of the PAAC experience, however, SIP provided no funds for Philadelphia. Although the effectiveness of SIP-supported projects varied, the program provided crucial early support for the creation of community development corporations in American inner cities. This strategy emerged as one of the few successful tools for inner-city redevelopment in the final decades of the twentieth century.[71]

The War on Poverty, both in Philadelphia and in the United States, marked in part a moment of lost opportunity for liberalism. Economists John Culp and Elizabeth Deutermann had outlined how comprehensive economic planning could generate a coordinated program for addressing Philadelphia's problem of jobs. At the same time, the federal Great Society promised to make new resources available for addressing urban problems in such a comprehensive fashion. By the end of the decade, these opportunities had been undercut by both local and federal missteps.

First, the federal Economic Opportunity Act and the ensuing War on Poverty placed little emphasis on job creation, comprehensive economic planning, or any other structural dimension of the problem of jobs. Focused on the social and cultural causes of poverty, the War on Poverty dealt with structural economic problems only indirectly, either by addressing the personal characteristics of individual poor people or by offering impoverished areas political empowerment through vaguely defined and inadequately supported community action initiatives. Funding cuts later exacerbated these limitations. Second, in the local context in which the War on Poverty actually operated in Philadelphia, the programs served primarily as an arena for contests over local political power and control of federal funds rather than as tools for addressing urban poverty. Samuel Evans, Charles Bowser, Barbara Weems, and Mayor Tate deftly transformed the Philadelphia Anti-poverty Action Committee into a patronage operation that helped the mayor win reelection. The organization never transcended this initial identity, and never made a serious effort to address the problem of jobs.

Among African American activists interested in forming something more than a black adjunct to Tate's political organization, the mayor's near total capture of PAAC produced deep alienation. As a result, by the time that the Model Cities program shifted the focus of urban policy back to questions of economic planning and coordination, a series of acrimonious, racially based confrontations between activists and the city largely overwhelmed the program and its meager resources. The effective consequence was that during the 1960s, no component of federal anti-poverty policy dealt seriously with the need to bring together Philadelphia's parallel tracks of local industrial and employment policy, represented most clearly by PIDC and OIC, into a single, coordinated strategy for addressing the consequences of the city's transition away from a manufacturing-based economy. Instead, federal programs actually reinforced the existing bifurcation of local policy by facilitating fights over patronage and power that prevented the development of the kind of comprehensive planning strategies proposed by the CRP and OEDP.

Yet redemptive value may still be drawn from Philadelphia's difficult War on Poverty experience. At an immediate level, the program provided valuable political experience for African Americans who would later participate in various levels of citywide politics. At an institutional level, PAAC contracted much of its job training responsibilities to Leon Sullivan's OIC program and served as a crucial conduit of federal funding for that organization. Despite receiving more War on Poverty money than any other organization in Philadelphia, OIC managed to avoid becoming embroiled in the political maelstrom that swirled around PAAC. Instead, it used the resources available from the federal government to construct an innovative job training program that eventually reformulated the local War on Poverty around concerns of race, economic structure, and employment.

CHAPTER FOUR

"We are going to protest *and* prepare": Civil Rights and the Origins of OIC

On the evening of October 11, 1972, audiences in forty-three cities across the United States watched a closed-circuit television broadcast of a benefit show performed simultaneously at the Palladium in Los Angeles and the Waldorf-Astoria Hotel in New York. The show marked the culmination of a national "OIC Day," held to raise funds for the Opportunities Industrialization Centers, the African American–run job training program founded eight years earlier in Philadelphia by Reverend Leon H. Sullivan. Organized around the theme "Everybody Can Be Somebody," the benefit opened with an introduction by Billy Graham and featured appearances by Bob Hope, Dick Gregory, Carroll O'Connor, Sammy Davis Jr., James Brown, Rita Moreno, Nancy Wilson, the Dance Theatre of Harlem, Joe Frazier, Buffy St. Maurie, and other cultural icons of the early 1970s. Davis, who had flown to the Los Angeles benefit between performances at Harrah's Casino in Lake Tahoe, stopped his band midway through "I've Got To Be Me," cleared his throat, and told the audience "I'm not flying all the way in here from Lake Tahoe and not giving these OIC people the best I've got. Take it from the top, boys." The show also included a filmed conversation between Sullivan and Lyndon Johnson, held at the former president's Texas ranch. Johnson closed the tape by turning to the Philadelphia minister and stating "Leon, we shall overcome." Senator Hubert Humphrey spoke about a bill then pending in Congress which, if passed, would appropriate $475 million in federal funds for OIC. Sullivan himself delivered a stirring oration, proclaiming that "I'm 6 foot 5 inches of black power, but OIC is black power, white power, brown power, yellow power all working to create American power!" Ray Charles closed the program with what the *Los Angeles Times* described as "a stirring soul version of 'America.'" Together, OIC Day festivities raised more than $1 million for OIC.[1]

Such attention highlighted the remarkable development of OIC from its origins in an abandoned jail in North Philadelphia, and also demonstrated the program's well-established ties to mainstream political and social power. By 1972, OIC had grown into an international organization with 100 training centers in the United States and additional centers in six countries in the developing world. It had trained more than 100,000 people and placed as many as 72,000 in jobs. It had attracted supporters from across the political spectrum, from the business community, and from the labor movement. It had a total annual budget of more than $47 million.[2]

Beyond such practical accomplishments, OIC represented an important but under-recognized strand of postwar urban, African American liberalism. In its core philosophy, OIC claimed the longstanding American traditions of self-help and self-reliance, blended them with themes of community uplift that had animated northern African American communities since before the Civil War, and placed them in the context of the reciprocal obligations—of the citizen to work and of the state to provide pragmatic assistance when needed—that underlay the commitments of the liberal U.S. state as it had evolved out of the New Deal. OIC spoke of self-help, yet received most of its funding from the federal government's War on Poverty. Crucially, it saw no contradiction between the two. African Americans, Sullivan and other OIC leaders argued, would willingly embrace mainstream ideas of work and self-reliance, but they simply lacked the resources necessary to make such concepts meaningful. Both the state and society at large had failed them and excluded them in the past. Only government, with secondary support from the private sector, could provide the resources to right those wrongs. This was the core of OIC's urban liberalism. As it expanded on the wider postwar civil rights movement's engagement with economic issues, OIC challenged the government and also the business community to meet moral and ethical obligations to African Americans. Through such tactics, OIC created community-based forms of local employment policy and industrial policy that worked to bring the realities of American economic life, and of liberalism itself, into closer accord with deeply held but often only casually observed ideals.

Leon Sullivan, Selective Patronage, and Civil Rights

Throughout the postwar decades, the interaction of job discrimination and industrial decline in Philadelphia had placed African Americans at a severe disadvantage in the local labor market. Although African Americans and other minorities accounted for 22.4 percent of Philadelphia's male labor force in 1960, nonwhite men held a disproportionate share of low-wage, low-skill jobs in the city: 54.8 percent of the city's male unskilled laborers and 78.0 percent of male domestic servants, but only 8.7 percent of male professional and technical jobs, 6.2 percent of managerial and proprietor positions, 14.3 percent of clerical and sales jobs, and 14.4 percent of craftsmen and foremen. Similarly, nonwhite women constituted 28.6 percent of the city's female labor force, but accounted for 45.9 percent of female unskilled laborers and 86.5 percent of female domestics. Yet they held only 18.3 percent of professional and technical jobs, 11.1 percent of managerial and proprietor positions, 11.2 percent of clerical and sales jobs, and 19.9 percent of craftsmen and foremen positions.[3]

African Americans also suffered from disproportionately high rates of both unemployment and underemployment. In 1959, blacks made up 43 percent of the unemployed in Philadelphia, and in 1960, nonwhites had an unemployment rate of 10.7 percent, compared to only 5 percent for whites. Younger African Americans faced even more serious job problems. Fourteen- to nineteen-year-old African Americans had an unemployment rate of 25 percent, more than double the rate for whites of the same age. Along with both direct and indirect discrimination by employers, blacks' limited access to union membership reinforced these economic disadvantages: African Americans accounted for only 12.5 percent of Philadelphia's 200,000 union members in the early 1960s. Three-quarters of these black union members belonged to industrial unions formerly affiliated with the CIO. Craft unions in the city, as in most other northern cities, remained largely closed to African Americans. In the lucrative building trades, for example, only the locals of the low-skill Hod Carriers and Common Laborers had more than "token Negro membership." These employment patterns and union practices had produced marked income disparities between racial groups: in 1959, nonwhite individuals and nonwhite families earned barely two-thirds of the median income for their white counterparts.[4]

Although liberals of all races sought remedies for these problems during the 1950s and early 1960s, no public or private agency found an effective solution. PIDC addressed the spatial and technological dimensions of industrial decline, but made no attempt to resolve deindustrialization's closely related social and racial dimensions. The city's Commission on Human Relations (CHR) pursued aggressive, if generally ineffective, campaigns to promote housing integration, but limited its efforts against employment discrimination to investigations of complaints, occasional public hearings, and interviews with employers and union officials. Further, the CHR had little real authority to enforce its rulings in such cases. The local NAACP branch conducted occasional negotiations with discriminatory employers and pursued behind-the-scenes efforts to encourage CHR investigations, but had few tools beyond political pressure and moral suasion.[5] Both the CHR and the NAACP pursued a gradualist strategy that focused on opening "breakthrough" positions in which blacks, in theory, could slowly eliminate white prejudice through the competence of their performance in previously closed job categories. This approach reflected an analysis, advanced by Gunnar Myrdal and other social scientists, that interpreted racism as an "individual pathology" resolvable through education and counterexample. While such efforts occasionally produced small concessions, they offered no systematic challenge to the racial dimensions of the problem of jobs.[6] Regardless of the CHR's limitations, however, the 1951 city charter produced one crucial improvement in African American employment opportunities: it created a nonpartisan, merit-based civil service system that opened significant numbers of city jobs to black workers. Even this victory was partial, as black public employees remained heavily concentrated in the lowest paying municipal jobs.[7]

With more activist civil rights strategies emerging elsewhere, the marginal gains produced by gradualist approaches seemed increasingly inadequate to many Philadelphia blacks.[8] During the first half of 1960, the Southern lunch counter sit-ins had demonstrated the potential efficacy of direct action civil rights protests. Philadelphia blacks had supported the sit-ins by picketing local Woolworth, Grant, Kress, and Kresge stores. Beginning in the summer of 1960, however, a group of "400" African American ministers brought direct action tactics to Philadelphia itself through a series of "selective patronage" campaigns targeted at discriminatory employers. Rejecting the gradualism of earlier breakthrough strategies, the selective patronage movement sought to open desirable jobs for blacks by mobilizing American African economic power against companies that either did not employ blacks at all or denied them access to positions with the potential for promotion and career advancement. "Selective patronage" marked the first step toward the formation of a black liberalism in Philadelphia that placed employment discrimination not in the context of supposedly correctable pathologies of individual racism but in the far less tractable domain of local and national economic structures. This was the politically dangerous intellectual shift that the white liberals who had conceived of industrial renewal had never been able to contemplate, much less complete.[9] It also brought the Reverend Leon H. Sullivan to citywide prominence.

Born in 1922, Leon Sullivan had grown up in poverty in Charleston, West Virginia. At the age of ten, he staged a series of solo sit-ins at segregated lunch counters, at least one of them successful. Sullivan attended West Virginia State College on a football and basketball scholarship until a knee injury ended his athletic career, though his impressive stature (he stood six feet, five inches tall) would contribute to his charisma as a leader. At that point, he worked the night shift in a steel mill to pay for his education, but also became interested in the ministry and served as pastor for two local churches. He later recounted that he found this calling in the aftermath of his grandmother's command, delivered on her deathbed in the dark bedroom of a rundown house, "Leonie, help your people. And don't let this happen to anyone else."[10] Sullivan made a crucial connection when Adam Clayton Powell, the influential pastor of Harlem's Abyssinian Baptist Church, visited one of Sullivan's churches prior to an appearance at a West Virginia NAACP meeting. With Powell's help, Sullivan gained admission to New York's Union Theological Seminary following his 1943 college graduation. At Union, Sullivan was exposed to the Social Gospel theology that would later undergird much of the civil rights movement. In addition, he served as assistant pastor at Abyssinian Baptist Church and assisted with Powell's first congressional campaign. Sullivan also worked with A. Phillip Randolph and Bayard Rustin in the March on Washington Movement, organized anti-gang and juvenile delinquency programs in Harlem, and recruited African American police officers for precincts in Harlem. Randolph had a particularly significant influence on the young minister, and Sullivan later noted that "it was from him that I learned much of the art of massive community organization, and he taught me the meaning of nonviolent direct action." Concerned, on the prompting of his wife, about "losing my sense of proportion" in Harlem, Sullivan accepted the pastorate of a small church in South Orange, New Jersey in 1945. After serving in South Orange for five years and completing a theology degree at Union and a master's in religion at Columbia University, Sullivan moved to North Philadelphia's Zion Baptist Church in 1950.[11]

At Zion, Sullivan established a reputation as a charismatic minister and again threw himself into community organizing. In the aftermath of a 1953 gang killing, he established the Citizens Committee Against Juvenile Delinquency and Its Causes, an organization of black neighborhood groups. At its peak, according to Sullivan's estimate, the juvenile delinquency committee had 100,000 members. By focusing on such issues as parental supervision of teenagers, neighborhood cleanliness, inadequate recreation facilities, police-community relations, and the proliferation of taprooms in black neighborhoods, the committee sought internal solutions to the problems of the African American community. Although the program drew national recognition, Sullivan grew increasingly frustrated with its limitations. In his autobiography, he noted the constraints that undercut the program's effectiveness: "Citizens' committees do no more than 'dust off' the slums while the forces that created and maintain them remain and expand. . . . unless we do something tangible to remove the depth causes— joblessness, crime, discrimination, and all of their vicious attendants—the slums will remain slums."[12] Seeking to do "something tangible," Sullivan founded the North Philadelphia Youth, Community, and Employment Service (NPYCES) in the basement of Zion Baptist. This program sought to find jobs for black teenagers and young adults. Between 1953 and 1958 it successfully placed thousands in jobs. In 1957, NPYCES earned a citation from the Freedom Foundation "as the most effective privately developed youth employment program in the nation." Still, NPYCES interviewed thousands of additional applicants for whom it could not find positions. Sullivan concluded that the program "was still in many ways a failure" because it did not attack racial discrimination by local employers.[13]

This troubling result forced Sullivan and associates such as Reverend Thomas Ritter, the NPYCES program director, to confront the discrimination issue. Although Sullivan served on the Philadelphia NAACP's executive board as a member of the moderate faction that then dominated the organization, the experience with NPYCES convinced him of the need for a more aggressive approach than the NAACP had been willing to consider.[14] Surveying Philadelphia's employment structure, Sullivan noted that "everywhere you went where the jobs were good, you saw whites, and everywhere you went where the jobs were poor, you saw blacks."[15]

In March 1960, Sullivan met with fifteen of the city's leading African American ministers to discuss shared concerns about employment discrimination. In the aftermath of the meeting, the group rapidly expanded into a loose association known as the "400 Ministers," though Sullivan later acknowledged that "we never really had that many."[16] Influenced by both the "Don't Buy Where You Can't Work" campaigns conducted in Harlem during the Great Depression and World War II and the Southern sit-ins, the 400 Ministers soon arrived at a new strategy: black Philadelphians would refuse to purchase the products of discriminatory companies, thus mobilizing their economic power to pressure employers into integrating their workforces. Concerned about their legal vulnerability to charges of conspiracy in restraint of trade, the ministers described their new tactic not as a boycott, but as a "selective patronage campaign."[17] Whatever the nomenclature, the effort marked a significant break from traditional strategies, as it used the threat of potential damage to company profits to backup negotiations that had previously relied on little more than assumptions of mutual goodwill.

The 400 Ministers expressly avoided establishing a clear organizational structure, selecting permanent officers, or even keeping written records. Instead, they created an informal "priority group" with a rotating interdenominational membership.[18] This priority group selected one company at a time, reviewed available data about the target's employment practices, and determined specific demands both for the immediate hiring of blacks and for long-term changes in the company's personnel procedures. In addition, the priority group nominated a different spokesman for each campaign. It then submitted these recommendations to the remaining members of the 400 Ministers, who had to provide unanimous approval before a campaign could begin. Next, the ministers selected a "visitation team" that would arrange a series of meetings with company executives. After an initial "exploratory" meeting, the ministers scheduled a second interview at which they presented their demands. If, as occasionally happened, the company agreed to make the requested changes, the ministers would announce this result to their congregations and select a new target.

If the target resisted, however, on the following Sunday the ministers would urge their congregations to stop buying the company's products and selective patronage would begin.[19]

While the 400 Ministers thus determined the strategy and provided the public face of the selective patronage movement, actual implementation relied heavily on internal networks within the community. Although Philadelphia's major daily newspapers ignored the movement until the *Philadelphia Evening Bulletin* itself became a target in April 1962, black newspapers such as the *Philadelphia Tribune, Philadelphia Afro-American,* and *Pittsburgh Courier* provided extensive coverage of each campaign. Community organizations, clubs, and social networks also played a role in publicizing the boycotts.[20] Ready access to these networks constituted an important advantage over more formal, elite-dominated civil rights organizations that could not as readily reach the community. The ministers employed more mundane publicity methods as well, such as the mass circulation of handbills in black stores, bars, and other businesses. They were so effective that by May 1962 *Greater Philadelphia Magazine* reported that 60 percent of the black community was aware of a new boycott within twenty-four hours of its commencement, and that "almost complete saturation is achieved in four days."[21]

In each case, the ministers sought to secure desirable positions at the boycotted company. This meant that they sometimes targeted firms that already employed black workers in low-level positions, but not in executive, supervisory, clerical, delivery, and skilled production jobs. The 400 Ministers, in other words, sought "sensitive" jobs with good pay, potential for promotion, and, not least, extensive contact with customers. They also often demanded the integration of cafeterias, changing rooms, and restrooms.[22]

The 400 Ministers' initial targets were a pair of local bakeries with which the NAACP had negotiated unsuccessfully in 1959. The first target, the General Baking Company, immediately met the demands and avoided a boycott. The second target, the Tasty Baking Company, proved more resistant. The ministers responded by launching their first actual selective patronage campaign. In a sermon titled "The Walls of Jericho Must Come Down!" delivered on June 6, 1960, Sullivan implored his congregation not to buy Tasty Baking's products. It was, for the ministers, the most difficult campaign of the movement. This arose, in part, from Tasty Baking's existing relationship with the African American community: the company's popular line of snack cakes and pies, known as "Tastykakes," provided an important source of revenue for many small, black-owned grocery stores. In addition, Tasty Baking already employed many black production workers. To counter these factors, the 400 Ministers obtained an agreement from 150 grocery stores to stop carrying the products and publicly emphasized the company's segregated bathrooms and locker rooms. Their specific demands included the hiring of black employees in Tasty Baking's clerical departments, on its desirable, "fixed-route, salesman-driver" delivery staff, and in specific production departments.[23]

Over the summer, as the black community's initial enthusiasm lagged, Tasty Baking launched a barrage of counter publicity. The company also induced the Chamber of Commerce to request a CHR (Commission on Human Relations) investigation of the situation, hoping that a favorable report would strengthen its position. The CHR, however, concluded that although the company had not violated fair employment laws, it also had not taken positive steps toward full integration. In addition, both the Chamber and the company's own lawyers advised Tasty Baking that the selective patronage campaign's loose organizational structure would make legal action futile and probably counterproductive. Increasingly frustrated, the company initiated new negotiations, and in early August, after eight weeks of the boycott, it hired blacks for two salesmen-driver positions, two clerical positions, and six positions in the previously segregated icing department. It also agreed to desegregate all locker rooms and washrooms. The ministers called off the boycott, and as Sullivan recalled, "black people were walking ten feet tall in the streets of Philadelphia." Ironically, during the 1970s, Tasty Baking became a local leader in corporate responsibility. The company upgraded its North Philadelphia plant and invested more than $400,000 in housing renovations and social programs in the surrounding neighborhood, while also employing local workers.[24]

Over the following three and a half years, the 400 Ministers gradually shifted their focus from industry to industry, starting with the baking and soft drink industries and moving to the oil, dairy, and grocery industries. Shortly after the Tasty Baking settlement, the Friehoffer Baking Company reached an agreement with the ministers without a boycott. In October, Philadelphia's Pepsi-Cola bottlers agreed to the ministers' terms two days after the initiation of selective patronage. In all, the ministers targeted twenty-nine firms, including Gulf Oil, Sun Oil, Mobil Oil, Abbotts Dairies, Breyer's Ice Cream, the *Philadelphia Bulletin,* the *Philadelphia Daily News,* Acme Markets, Food Fair, and A&P Grocery Stores. If the companies argued they already employed blacks, the ministers demanded black employment in specific, desirable positions. Other firms, including Coca-Cola, Seven-Up, the *Philadelphia Inquirer,* Atlantic Richfield, Cities Service Oil, Sinclair Oil, and Esso, followed the example of General Baking and Friehoffer's by cooperating to avoid a boycott.[25] Some companies, however, resisted the campaigns. Sun Oil and Breyer's Ice Cream held out for three and seven months, respectively. Despite threats of legal action and episodes of intimidation, the 400 Ministers never called off a campaign without securing agreement to their demands. Occasionally results reached beyond Philadelphia. When Sun Oil agreed to the ministers' demands, it also announced that it would extend nondiscriminatory hiring to Detroit, Cleveland, Chicago, and thirty Pennsylvania cities.[26]

In part, the 400 Ministers were successful because their demands remained reasonable, making it easier for companies to comply than resist. The ministers called off the Gulf Oil boycott, for example, when the company hired a black accountant, four black office workers, a sales representative, and a number of truck driver–salesmen. The immediate changes involved fewer than ten positions, but they broke Gulf's established hiring practices and included a commitment to "fair job distribution" in future hiring.[27] As Sullivan later explained, these tactics succeeded because "it was not our intention to destroy a business, but only to awaken it and to get it on the right road as far as the employment of black Americans was concerned. . . . we wanted to be sure that no unreasonable hammer was held above the company, pressuring and threatening for unrealistic results and for things it could not do."[28] Sullivan also noted that the ministers carefully studied whatever information they could obtain on company job turnover rates and employment classifications. With these data, the ministers could develop realistic demands that still pushed the target company hard to increase black employment. This included asking for all of the job openings in a particular month. Sullivan added that "if employers protested that . . . this would be unfair to the white workers, our reply would be that the company had been unfair to black workers ever since it began."[29] The ministers extended this principle to questions of internal promotion as well, thus establishing an early model of affirmative action. These tactics occasionally led to clashes with labor unions, which objected to the ministers' disregard for the hiring, promotion, and seniority provisions established in existing contracts. This conflict between union interests and demands for integration remained unresolved and would soon emerge as a key civil rights issue in Philadelphia and around the United

States. Partially as a result of such disagreements, critics of selective patronage often charged that the 400 Ministers favored the establishment of quotas. Sullivan countered that while such a goal might have been justified, as "black people had been 'quota'd' out of the company's employment as long as the company had existed," it was not the ministers' aim; they simply wanted to "break the company's entire pattern of discriminatory hiring practices."[30]

According to one estimate, the selective patronage campaigns opened at least 2,000 skilled jobs for black Philadelphians in the directly affected companies alone. In addition, the 400 Ministers reached an agreement in 1963 with 300 other Philadelphia area firms who agreed to implement nondiscriminatory hiring and promotion procedures, changing at least the official pattern, if not always the reality, of employment policies in the Philadelphia area. Although Sullivan told a Senate Committee in 1966 that "the selective patronage program was the least publicized effort of the civil rights movement ... because it was the least visibly dramatic," the concept actually had a wide national influence.[31] The success of selective patronage in Philadelphia led civil rights groups in New York, Chicago, Boston, Cincinnati, Detroit, Baltimore, Pittsburgh, and Boston to develop similar initiatives. In 1962, Martin Luther King Jr. invited Sullivan to Atlanta to discuss the campaign, and the selective patronage concept soon became a model for the Operation Breadbasket campaign directed by Jesse Jackson.[32]

In the immediate context of Philadelphia, selective patronage demonstrated that blacks could successfully undertake direct civil rights actions without either government or white assistance.[33] The campaigns, however, also led individuals on both sides to other, very different conclusions. The companies' implementation of the integration plans proceeded more smoothly than many business and labor leaders expected, and the ministers made special efforts to insure that the community increased purchases of the previously boycotted products. For many business leaders, the selective patronage movement provided evidence that the black community's demands had to be taken seriously, but it also demonstrated that the black church represented an institution with which business might find shared values and mutual accommodation. For Sullivan himself, the experience demonstrated that the business community included individuals who, under carefully exerted pressure, might provide crucial support for his agenda.[34] This lesson would guide most of his actions for the next three decades as he expanded his efforts into job training and community development. The limitations of this strategy would become apparent only later, as the implications of structural change in Philadelphia's economy and of the racial divide in local industrial and employment policy took full effect.

The Organization of OIC

The relative success of the selective patronage movement revealed that the employment problems of Philadelphia's African American community operated on two levels. The first consisted of the blatant employment discrimination that had prevailed for decades in Philadelphia and that had begun to be addressed through the direct action tactics of selective patronage. The second operated through more subtle channels that reinforced such overt discrimination. As the boycotts proceeded and jobs slowly became available for blacks, employers increasingly complained of difficulties in identifying qualified black applicants to fill the newly opened jobs.[35] The ministers initially viewed such claims with skepticism, but Sullivan and Ritter's experience with the NPYCES job placement program, along with their own investigation, convinced them that the skills issue was a significant problem. A number of factors created this dilemma. First, many employers based their requirements for entry-level jobs on the assumption that an employee would eventually be promoted to more demanding positions. As a result, hiring criteria often required skills that exceeded those actually needed for the initial job. Second, the combination of inadequate educational opportunities and years of discrimination had often made it difficult for black Philadelphians to obtain skills, and even harder to take full advantage of skills that were developed. Lack of access to the apprenticeship systems of the highly discriminatory building trades and other craft unions exacerbated this problem. Sullivan and Ritter concluded that together, these factors meant that many African Americans in Philadelphia lacked the vocational skills necessary to fill the jobs that selective patronage had opened.[36]

This analysis reflected Sullivan and Ritter's pragmatic willingness to engage the on-the-ground dilemmas that faced their community, but it also marked the first of a series of compromises with the city's existing racial and political economic order. It led the ministers to move their efforts off the streets, away from direct protest tactics, and toward more subtle forms of activism and, crucially, institution building.[37] Sullivan described the situation bluntly, contextualizing his choices in relation to the violent unrest that broke out in North Philadelphia during the late summer of 1964: "as important as opening the jobs had been and still would be for a long, long time, I could see that integration without preparation was frustration. . . . if something was not done now . . . we would start tearing our cities down, and most of the blood that would flow then would be our own."[38] Sullivan soon redirected his effort toward the creation of a job training program that would attempt to meet the need for vocational skills. The massive, community-based project that resulted reflected a pragmatic strategy to achieve immediate, concrete gains in employment, community stability, and economic security for Philadelphia African Americans. The project was the second phase of the civil rights–oriented action campaign that had begun with selective patronage, but it also reflected a decision to work for change within the existing employment system rather than to push for more dramatic alterations from outside. This strategy brought significant material benefits and opened real opportunities, but it also tied the resulting program to the shifting structure of mid-century American capitalism. To counter this constraint, Sullivan also created an investment cooperative among the parishioners of Zion Baptist Church to pool capital for the development of black-owned businesses. In 1968, Sullivan offered a blunt summary of the rationale behind the decision to pursue skill training and business development, as well his own perception of the relationship between economic and civil rights activism: "I realized we couldn't integrate the suburbs with relief checks."[39]

While the business project required years of development, the job training program addressed a direct and pressing community need. In the early 1960s, flaws permeated every existing training institution in Philadelphia. The School District of Philadelphia had never provided useful vocational education, and especially not for African Americans. Existing community-based job placement efforts remained understaffed, underfunded, and without any capacity to provide actual job *training*. The new federal programs implemented under the 1962 Manpower Development and Training Act suffered from limited scale, uncertain priorities, and a tendency to select better-prepared candidates who would be easiest to train and place in jobs. Frequently, African Americans were completely excluded.[40] Examining the limited achievements of existing programs, Sullivan concluded that "we had to be just as militant in getting our people ready for the jobs as we were in opening up the jobs for them.... it must be not just another Government program, screening black people out, but a people's program, screening black people in along with anybody else who was underskilled, unskilled, or poor."[41] As the selective patronage campaigns continued during the winter of 1962–63, Sullivan and Ritter formed a research council to study possibilities for community-based job training.[42] Over the following months, this group formulated an ambitious plan for a job training program organized around three key principles. First, the program would provide the specific skills necessary to obtain entry-level jobs with potential for advancement. This emphasis on job-specific instruction would insure that the training remained tightly linked to the skill and job categories in demand within the local economy, and thus, to actual job opportunities. Second, the program would extend "beyond the cure of mere re-employment" by addressing remedial education, personal problems, motivation, and self-confidence. This approach, the ministers believed, would not only prepare students to take full advantage of the training itself, but would increase the likelihood of success in an actual work situation.[43] In the early 1960s, this comprehensive effort had few precedents. Third, the ministers determined that, above all, the new program had to be rooted in the community that it served. This community-based orientation would be reflected in the new program's organizational structure, staffing, and fund-raising techniques. It also created a natural fit with the War on Poverty's emphasis on "community action." This would soon prove advantageous in obtaining federal funding.[44]

Above all, the new program would rely on a philosophy of self-help, self-reliance, and self-improvement through training.[45] Although this philosophy had a historical pedigree among African Americans from Booker T. Washington to Marcus Garvey to A. Phillip Randolph, the program had to place trainees in desirable jobs to maintain its legitimacy, especially in a climate of growing militancy. This meant that even as they moved away from selective patronage, Sullivan and the other ministers maintained and even extended the movement's original, civil rights–based demands for an end to employment discrimination.[46]

In July 1963, the ministers announced the formation of a new, nonprofit organization known as the Opportunities Industrialization Centers (OIC). Ritter became OIC's program administrator, while Sullivan served as board chairman. Five other ministers, five teachers, a law student, and a psychologist joined Sullivan and Ritter on the OIC Board. All but one were African American. Shortly after the announcement of the program,

FIGURE 16. Leon H. Sullivan (white suit) at the announcement ceremony for the Opportunities Industrialization Centers, July 29, 1963. Reverend Thomas H. Ritter, who would serve as director of the Philadelphia OIC center, is at the far left. An early name for the program is written on the chalkboard. Photo courtesy of Temple University Libraries, Urban Archives, Philadelphia, Pennsylvania.

Sullivan held an organizational meeting for volunteer instructors and advisors that attracted more than 100 "craftsmen and technicians familiar with the workings of industry." By early 1964, this group grew to include more than 300 volunteers, drawn from both industry and such progressive unions as the International Ladies Garment Workers Union (ILGWU).[47]

During the second half of 1963, Sullivan and his associates established liaisons with local industry and initiated preliminary fundraising. An important breakthrough came when OIC identified an abandoned police

station at 19th and Oxford streets in North Philadelphia as a possible location for the program. African American city councilman Thomas McIn-
tosh arranged for OIC to lease the building from the city at an annual rent
of $1, but the old police station was so dilapidated that Sullivan described
it as "the worst place in town." OIC determined that it would require more
than $50,000 in renovations.[48] These costs combined with the expenses of
hiring staff, acquiring equipment and supplies, and developing the program's curriculum to place increasing financial pressure on OIC. To meet
these needs, Sullivan and Ritter undertook a fund-raising campaign in the
African American community that raised $102,000 by mid-1964. An "Op-
portunities Women's Drive" conducted by an African American women's
group raised almost half this sum through door-to-door fund-raising. In
addition, OIC secured a major contribution from a local foundation that
had previously supported the NPYCES program. The overall campaign
thus not only addressed OIC's immediate financial needs but also demonstrated the extent of community support for the project. Along with the
donated labor of early trainees and volunteers from the community, these
funds allowed OIC to transform the decrepit jailhouse into a thoroughly
renovated training center.[49]

    During this period, Sullivan also built on the business connections es-
tablished during the selective patronage campaigns. Although selective
patronage had initially generated opposition and resentment among local
businessmen, it slowly produced a grudging respect for the ministers' organizational abilities and reliability. As business leaders became increasingly fearful about inner city unrest, many also concluded that they might
do better to work with, rather than against, the African American ministers. During the spring of 1963, the Congress on Racial Equality and
the NAACP, with the latter then under the leadership of President Cecil
B. Moore, organized protests against union discrimination on public construction projects, generating clashes between protestors, construction
workers, and Philadelphia police. Although the 400 Ministers participated
in the construction protests, Sullivan's tactics of discussion backed up by
possible boycott suddenly seemed comparatively benign. In light of the
construction-industry protests, the prospect of Leon Sullivan directing an
innovative self-help program became immensely attractive to white business leaders. As Sullivan told the *Reporter* magazine, the city's business
leadership "all began to love me because suddenly they were big liberals.
Nothing bad had happened, and we'd helped their public image."[50] This
relationship between black militancy and black liberalism—a connection

that was far more intimate than is often recognized—would prove crucial to OIC's efforts at institution building in Philadelphia.

The increasingly apparent problems with existing job training programs also contributed to the business community's openness to Sullivan's entreaties. By early 1963, the Chamber of Commerce of Greater Philadelphia had grown frustrated with the struggling federal, city, and School District manpower programs and had begun to prepare an application of its own for the next round of MDTA funding.[51] Shortly before the public announcement of the OIC plan in summer 1963, Chamber executive director Keeton Arnett and president Richard Bond visited Sullivan and asked for his assistance in recruiting students for a possible Chamber program. Sullivan listened politely and then offered his assessment: "Gentlemen, I didn't know that white men could be that smart."[52] After learning of Sullivan's own plans, Arnett and Bond proved smart enough to recognize that a job training program based in the black community, with black leadership, had a greater chance of succeeding than anything that the Chamber might create. As a result, they soon offered their organization's full support to OIC. This alliance proved to be extremely valuable for OIC, as it provided legitimacy and direct access to the business community and its associated funding, equipment, expertise, and, most important of all, jobs.[53] The endorsement occurred only a few months after the Chamber had undercut the CHR's order that Philadelphia businesses keep detailed hiring records to document discriminatory employment practices. While the alliance marked the first crack in the Chamber's resistance to employment-oriented civil rights initiatives, it also demonstrated that Sullivan would work with anyone who offered assistance and resources, regardless of their position on related issues.

The critical importance of such support quickly became apparent. With the assistance of the Chamber, OIC received initial donations of $200,000 worth of equipment and $50,000 in cash from such companies as Philco, Pennsalt Chemicals, Bell Telephone, Scott Paper, Smith Kline & French, Sharpless, Jerrold Electronics, Philadelphia Gas Works, Western Union, Budd, Westinghouse, I.B.M., and General Electric.[54] Such contributions could be written off as a tax-deduction, and much of the initial machinery donations proved to be obsolete. At this stage in OIC's development, its largely ministerial leadership lacked the knowledge about industrial technology to recognize the difference. Although Sullivan made a number of critical public comments about this problem, the outdated machinery did provide the means to start the training program.[55] Once OIC demonstrated its effectiveness and gained experience, it secured a higher quality of equipment. As Sullivan later put it, the antiquated machinery "was a beginning for us, and day by day we were learning the game. We would be back for more. The rest that we would get would be new and modern. And it was." This optimistic assessment obscured some continuing difficulties in obtaining adequate equipment for certain training courses, but in general, OIC's problems with obsolete machinery diminished.[56]

Of even greater importance than the equipment donations, local companies also provided assistance with OIC's curriculum planning through Technical Advisory Committees that reviewed the curriculum for each course to assure relevance in the local labor market. Occasionally, such participation extended beyond advice alone. In 1964, the Philadelphia-based institutional food vendor Automatic Retailers of America evaluated OIC's plans for a "restaurant practices" course and "found the layout and equipment about ten years behind the times." The company assisted OIC with the redesign of the facility and donated much of the necessary restaurant and cafeteria equipment. These business connections also provided an all-important source of job placements. For example, after the Budd Company donated equipment for a sheet-metal training course, it hired 200 OIC trainees.[57]

The business community's interest in OIC drew on a number of motivations. First, OIC's self-help philosophy appealed to the ideological predilections of business, as did its origin outside of government. A Smith, Kline, and French executive wrote in 1965 that "we were particularly pleased that the motivating force for the program came from within the community itself; we are convinced that such indigenous effort is almost mandatory for complete success in projects of this type."[58] Second, the combination of the Kennedy-Johnson tax cut and increased spending for the Vietnam War created a sustained period of economic expansion during the mid- and late-1960s. As a result, Philadelphia industries faced shortages in some skilled job categories. OIC promised to meet these needs by providing training for an untapped component of the labor force. De facto full employment policies thus increased employers' willingness to end hiring discrimination.[59] Third, progressive elements of the business community who gained control over the Chamber during the mid-1960s increasingly recognized that urban racial problems required some form of positive social action. OIC provided an accessible and potentially effective mechanism for pursuing such aims.[60] Finally, Sullivan did not hesitate to use fears of urban unrest to build support for OIC by presenting the program as a direct alternative to violence. When asked his opinion of black power, for example, he replied that "some interpret 'black power' with the three B's as 'Burn, baby, burn.' I interpret it as, 'Build, brother, build.' It depends on how you look at it and interpret it. . . . it was initiated during a period of great movement and marching and loud protests, in which of course, I have been involved all my life. But out of it the connotation of violence and destruction became the word of the day."[61] While this combination of factors explained business's initial support for OIC, the results that OIC produced solidified the relationship. By early 1966, a Chamber spokesman observed that "support from the business community has become so great that failure of OIC would mean almost as great disillusionment in the business community as in the Negro community. Therefore, the OIC simply cannot be allowed to fail."[62]

Sullivan acknowledged the mixed nature of such corporate impulses, recognizing them both as evidence of a "new spirit in business" and as a reflection of industry's self-interest. OIC's leadership also realized that such support brought with it the danger of co-optation. In order to insure that it remained, in Sullivan's words, "a program that comes from the folks," OIC did not include any business representatives on its board of directors. This avoided "any appearance of dominance or 'take-over'" by business. Instead, OIC established the Technical Advisory Committees that allowed business to assist OIC but offered no decision-making authority. The arrangement demonstrated the tenuous balance between OIC's need for the resources that business could provide and its equal imperative of maintaining an identity as a community-based organization rooted in the militancy of the civil rights movement.[63]

During the mid-1960s, OIC and its subsidiary organizations would rapidly develop into a black form of quasi-public employment and industrial policy, operating in parallel with the white form of local industrial policy embodied by PIDC. These two tracks remained almost entirely separate in operation, bifurcated along the lines of race by which they had formed. OIC's relationship with Philadelphia's white business community, and particularly with the Chamber of Commerce, might have bridged this divide. The Chamber's participation as the primary private partner in PIDC and as a key local supporter of OIC offered the possibility of collaboration in resolving Philadelphia's problem of jobs. The business organization, however, chose to view the two projects as discrete solutions to unrelated problems: PIDC was seen as addressing the technical and spatial dimension of structural economic transformation while OIC was seen as addressing the supposed skill deficits and cultural maladjustments of low-income urban African Americans. This position, defined by both a particular analysis of urban problems and a cautious calculation about the appropriate extent of local public policy, prevented the Chamber from recognizing possible connections between the two projects. Even as OIC began to explore the relationship between structural economic change, discrimination, and job training, it did not push its allies in the private sector to support a more comprehensive approach that would have merged Philadelphia's parallel, racially defined tracks of policy.

OIC's relations with the labor movement remained far more problematic than its connections with business. Primarily, this reflected the hostility between Philadelphia's African American community and many of the city's conservative craft unions. OIC enjoyed strong ties with racially integrated, former CIO unions like the Amalgamated Clothing Workers Union, the Laundry Workers Union, and in particular, the ILGWU, which provided technical assistance and funding for a power sewing course. In contrast, OIC often faced hostility from the city's highly discriminatory building trades unions. Under attack from the local civil rights movement, the building trades resented OIC's use of trainees and volunteers instead of union craftsmen to renovate its facilities. They also objected to OIC's attempted circumvention of the traditional white-only union apprenticeship systems in its training courses. The relationship gradually improved as building trades officials joined OIC's Technical Advisory Committees and some union apprenticeships eventually accepted OIC trainees. Overall, though, OIC-union relations remained strained.[64]

OIC's First Months of Operation

OIC assembled its core administrative staff by November 1963 and dedicated the newly renovated training center in the old police station on Sunday, January 26, 1964. The project had clearly captured the imagination of the community: the ceremony attracted 8000 people despite zero-degree temperatures, with thousands more stuck in nearby traffic jams. The event also demonstrated the creative tension in OIC's strategy: its roots in direct-action civil rights tactics on the one hand, and its ability to generate support from mainstream leaders on the other. Emphasizing the former, *Ebony* magazine described the event's atmosphere as "strongly reminiscent" of civil rights rallies elsewhere in the United States. The

FIGURE 17. Dedication ceremony for the first OIC, in a renovated jail at 19th and Oxford streets in North Philadelphia, January 26, 1964. Photo courtesy of Temple University Libraries, Urban Archives, Philadelphia, Pennsylvania.

presence of Pennsylvania senators Joseph Clark and Hugh Scott, Mayor Tate, numerous city councilmen, state legislators, and civil rights, labor, and business leaders testified to the latter dimension of OIC's identity.[65]

OIC's motto, "We Help Ourselves," further evoked the program's dual nature. In one sense, the phrase reflected the growing emphasis within the civil rights movement on black autonomy and independence, a tendency that would influence activists ranging from Malcolm X to the Black Panthers to Jesse Jackson. This component of OIC's philosophy would play a crucial role in maintaining the legitimacy of OIC, and Leon Sullivan, within the black community. At the same time, the OIC motto appealed to traditional American ethics of uplift, self-reliance, and independence. As such, it endorsed prevailing liberal cultural discourses about the availability of opportunity, as well as the contemporary focus of poverty analysis on the adjustment of individual characteristics to take advantage of such presumed opportunity. Speaking at the dedication ceremony, Sullivan evoked OIC's link to the protest tactics of the wider civil rights movement, but emphasized even more strongly its character as an agent of uplift: "From this day on, we are saying to our people and to America, that we are adding a new dimension to the civil rights effort. And whereas before, we were just protesting, now we are going to protest *and* prepare! In this center, we shall lift the competencies and the spirits of our children, and we shall prove to the world that genius is colorblind! We shall help our boys and girls to know, that it is not the color of a balloon that determines how high it can fly, but what it has inside of it."[66] The uplift component of OIC's ideology allowed Sullivan to appeal successfully to sources of business, foundation, and government support which would have had little interest in the more radical implications of the OIC motto. The resulting tension between the traditional and transformative elements of its mission proved crucial to OIC's growth and development, but it also created internal and external contradictions that the organization could neither fully transcend nor resolve.

In the weeks after the dedication ceremony, such nuances of philosophy and ideology mattered less than the practical imperatives of implementing an ambitious, community-based job training program. Building on the enthusiasm generated by the center's opening, the staff spent the following months processing applications for the program, and on March 2, the first training classes began in the former jailhouse. On May 18, OIC graduated its first twenty students, all of whom had already found jobs. Most of these graduates were in the power sewing course and found employment in the garment industry.[67] Despite this rapid implementation, OIC's future remained uncertain because of its weak financial position. Organizational, salary, and operational costs exhausted the proceeds of OIC's initial fundraising efforts, and in order to meet new expenses during this period, Sullivan borrowed $40,000 from Zion Baptist Church and took out a mortgage on his house. At one point, OIC faced the prospect of not being able to pay its staff when a donation from a dissolved trust fund arrived and allowed the program to continue. In his memoir, Sullivan recounted that he had prayed for divine assistance immediately before receiving news of the donation. Although possibly apocryphal, the story underlined the strong faith-based sensibility that ran beneath OIC's official secular character.[68]

Still, it became clear that OIC's month-to-month costs exceeded what it could raise from local sources; planned future expansions would only increase these financial requirements. OIC desperately needed autonomous and reliable sources of outside support. The emergence of poverty as a central political issue, in Philadelphia and in the nation, soon provided a solution to this dilemma. Ironically, the immediate source of this support came from the Philadelphia Council for Community Advancement (PCCA), the Ford Foundation Gray Areas project that Cecil Moore had attacked in 1963 for insensitivity to the African American community it purported to serve.

Although Moore soon turned his attention to the campaign against discrimination by the building-trades unions, PCCA's tenuous legitimacy in Philadelphia's African American community had been badly compromised by the controversy.[69] When PCCA appointed a new board, it included fifteen blacks among its forty-eight members, but none came from the most militant elements of the city's African American leadership. Among those who turned down an invitation to serve was Leon Sullivan.[70] Desperate to increase PCCA's legitimacy among African Americans, PCCA administrators began to cast about for "indigenous" community programs in North Philadelphia for which PCCA could provide funds and assistance. OIC was one of two candidates that it identified.[71]

Leon Sullivan had rejected the PCCA board position after correctly assessing the political implications of the appointment, but he had more interest in the prospect of obtaining Ford Foundation money for OIC. Such a relationship satisfied each organization's most crucial need: OIC's for immediate financial support and PCCA's for legitimacy in the African American community. PCCA staff coordinated OIC's application with its own 1964–65 request to Ford, but the application was not submitted until the day before the dedication of the OIC training center in the old police station. Within the Ford Foundation itself, serious doubts had emerged about PCCA's capacity to fulfill its objectives and about the wider desirability of the entire Gray Areas project. As a result, a significant faction within the foundation opposed the OIC request. Gray Areas project director Paul Ylvisaker, though, had previously served as Mayor Clark's executive secretary and knew Philadelphia well. Impressed with the OIC project, Ylvisaker fought for the proposal and secured the full amount that PCCA had requested. On March 2, 1964, the foundation announced that over the following eighteen months, OIC would receive a $200,000 grant.[72] This funding arrived at a crucial moment; without it the complete OIC program could not have been implemented.

In recent years, scholars have correctly criticized the Gray Areas project for its emphasis on the reorganization of social services and its inattention to the structural roots of poverty. In the case of OIC, however, the Ford Foundation successfully identified and funded a black-run, community-based project that challenged prevailing structures of employment discrimination, educational inequity, and eventually, disinvestment in inner city Philadelphia.[73] The foundation's early support of OIC suggests the importance of the long-term, institutional implications of liberal public and philanthropic initiatives during the postwar period. While the Ford Foundation's approach to urban poverty had severe shortcomings, its ultimate legacy is tied as much to programs such as OIC as to its well-documented failures.

The support that OIC received from the Ford Foundation was also indicative of Leon Sullivan's fortuitous timing. The establishment of OIC coincided not only with the crest of the civil rights movement, but also with the emergence of a reinvigorated national commitment to confronting poverty and a new interest in neighborhood-level social and political action. As a result, the community-based, self-help initiatives envisioned by Sullivan and the other ministers soon proved to be immensely attractive to both public and private funding sources. Eventually, they constituted the largest and most successful component of the African American track of employment and industrial policy in Philadelphia. As such, OIC's attempts to confront Philadelphia's problem of jobs produced a set of strengths and weaknesses that formed a nearly perfect inverse of those which characterized PIDC. Where PIDC ignored the social dimensions of the problem of jobs, OIC dealt directly with employment discrimination, the inadequacy of basic educational opportunities, and the African-American community's lack of access to investment capital, among other issues. Despite great effort, however, OIC and its affiliated development initiatives never found an adequate solution to the broader problems of structural and technological change that PIDC did address. The contrasts between OIC and PIDC delineated the consequences of the racial bifurcation of policy, as the inability to cooperate, or even exchange information, across the two racial tracks of local economic policy in Philadelphia limited the ultimate effectiveness of each initiative.

CHAPTER FIVE

"All 200 million of us are going to make it": The Rise of OIC

In the months that followed the January 1964 dedication of its North Philadelphia training center, OIC not only developed an innovative approach to job training but also proved adept at negotiating the treacherous politics of race at both the local and national levels. As political, social, and racial conflict rapidly enveloped Philadelphia's War on Poverty during 1964 and 1965, OIC could easily have become embroiled in the disputes between organization and reform Democrats or radical and liberal African Americans. Instead, the job training program limited its engagement with any faction and focused on using the War on Poverty to gain access to greater programmatic resources.

This strategy succeeded. The federal government soon became OIC's largest source of financial support and the program quickly became a major recipient of federal anti-poverty funds. The first such grants came in 1964, when the Area Redevelopment Administration (ARA) awarded OIC a $50,000 grant. Late in the year, the Department of Labor's Office of Manpower, Automation, and Training provided a more substantial $458,000 demonstration grant for OIC's new pre-training preparation or Feeder Program.[1] Still, OIC did not attain financial stability until June 23, 1965, when the Office of Economic Opportunity (OEO) finally approved grants totaling $5.9 million for Philadelphia's first six community action proposals. While the largest grant, for $2,988,152, went to a nursery school and day care program operated by the Board of Education ("Get Set"),

OIC received a grant of $1,756,163. Over the following six years, PAAC allocated a total of $14,465,832 in federal grants to the Philadelphia branch of OIC alone, an amount far exceeding the War on Poverty grants that had been given to other Philadelphia programs.[2] A combination of policy innovation, demonstrable results, political skill, and fortuitous timing produced this bounty for OIC.

In doing this, OIC reformulated midcentury liberalism by simultaneously embracing both federal support and an ideology of self-reliance. The latter made sense for urban African Americans only if resources were available to make it meaningful, and self-help could work only if the liberal state moved beyond the universalistic claims and exclusionary realities of the New Deal era to accept that the full economic integration of African Americans required state support. Through such a formulation, OIC sought to reconcile traditional American cultural claims about the value of work and individualism with the necessity of an activist state deeply engaged in economic and employment policy.

"OIC's Most Creative and Unique Contribution": The Feeder Program

In its first year of operation, OIC used the support from the Ford Foundation and the federal government to implement courses in electronics, drafting, power sewing, restaurant practices, sheet metal techniques, machine tool operation, laboratory chemistry, and teletype operation. Initially, these programs could accommodate only 300 students. Three months after the training center opened, however, OIC's waiting list contained 6,000 names. Responding to the pressing need to accommodate these applicants, as well as to the results of the initial training courses, OIC officials decided to create a new pre-training program component that would address the intertwined relationships between race, poverty, and unemployment at a more fundamental level than skill-training alone. These classes would address literacy, self-confidence, personal motivation, and knowledge about employer expectations in order to prepare trainees for the demands of both their training courses and, ultimately, the workplace. Sullivan and OIC Executive Director Thomas Ritter conceived of this strategy as part of a comprehensive, "on-going process" approach to training that differed from previous manpower initiatives by attempting to serve the "whole man"—or in reality, the "whole woman," as 57 percent of early OIC trainees were female.[3]

To implement this approach, OIC created the Feeder Program, launched in October 1964 in North Philadelphia's abandoned Adath Jeshurun synagogue. Later described by an OEO consultant as "OIC's most creative and unique contribution to the field of manpower training," the feeder provided critical educational, counseling, and support services before a student began skill-training. This meant that individuals whose past educational deficiencies barred them from other training programs could not only enroll in OIC but could also receive remedial help. The overall purpose of the feeder was "to improve the academic level of the trainee as well as to improve his emotional life."[4] Sullivan believed that life-long experiences of discrimination eroded African Americans' self-respect as well as their ability even to recognize, much less realize, their innate potential. The Feeder Program sought to correct this situation before specific skill training began. As Sullivan explained, "the feeder program is designed to 'unwash the brainwashed minds' of enrollees who have come to OIC with poor opinions of themselves and who have been brainwashed into inferiority."[5] With this optimistic mission, OIC attempted to mix two long-standing traditions of African American thought: the ideology of self-help and uplift that had been advocated by African Americans from free blacks in the antebellum North to Booker T. Washington in the early Jim Crow South to the Nation of Islam in the post–World War II cities, and the philosophy of race pride, community development, and rejection of externally imposed inferiority advocated by W. E. B. DuBois and Marcus Garvey. OIC's philosophy fused these orientations into a pragmatic operational strategy that undergirded the program's success, but also demarcated its ultimate limitations.[6]

All OIC participants enrolled in the feeder, including Sullivan, who symbolically attended for one day. Once in the feeder, students could progress at their own pace (between about two weeks and three months) through the specific course curriculum best suited to their individual needs. Instructors started at whatever level the student required. Recognizing that many students' past educational experiences had been negative, OIC attempted to create a supportive and nontraditional environment in the feeder. Courses took place in brightly painted classrooms designed to create a pleasant, positive atmosphere. Subjects included communication and computational skills, minority history, job search strategies, job holding techniques, and the bluntly titled "grooming and hygiene." The communication and computational skills classes provided instruction in basic literacy and arithmetic skills; OIC's euphemistic nomenclature for these classes reflected its emphasis on building trainees' self-esteem and personal motivation and avoided stigmatizing them as illiterate. As Sullivan explained, "people are not anxious for others to know that they want to learn to read and write and do arithmetic, so we call it 'communication skills' and 'computational arts,' and people by the thousands flock into the classrooms." OIC grouped students in these classes by ability, ranging from basic literacy to remedial instruction to high school equivalency studies.[7]

The literacy courses proved to be among the most critical components of OIC. Inability to read or complete simple mathematics had not only limited the employment opportunities of many who came to OIC, but also frequently had a devastating affect on confidence. An OIC case study of one trainee, identified only as Elma S., noted that "her main problem was in English. She felt the lack of vocabulary and the inability to cope with uncommon words, contributed to her lack of confidence in speaking and writing." With daily work in the feeder, including close attention from instructors, Elma S.'s skills improved and she eventually accepted employment at Sears Roebuck in a better position than any of the "menial" jobs she had previously held. Another student, "Roger M.," came to OIC with the express purpose of improving his poor reading skills. A high school dropout, he explained that "because I was a slow reader, it was terribly frustrating to want to learn without being able to read." Along with his regular feeder course, Roger received individual tutoring from a volunteer assigned to OIC by the War on Poverty's VISTA (Volunteers in Service to America) program. Conceived as a domestic counterpart to the Peace Corps, VISTA placed young people, usually recent college graduates, in public and private service agencies around the country where they would work in poor communities. John S., an OIC trainee who had moved to Philadelphia from Mississippi, also benefited from a VISTA worker's help when he struggled with his initial feeder courses because of his limited educational background. Although critics frequently criticized the War on Poverty for a lack of coordination among programs, cases such as these show that VISTA provided crucial supportive services for War on Poverty–funded organizations like OIC, and more importantly, for individuals such as Roger M. and John S.[8]

OIC also organized feeder classes according to vocational groups. This meant that students entered an ongoing course with trainees of varying skill and ability levels, and that teachers adjusted the level of instruction according to individual needs. As one evaluator observed, the feeder's structure encouraged innovation in lesson plans, but also "represents a difficult teaching situation" that "requires highly skilled teachers whose dedication exceeds the requirements of the job." The report noted that the teaching staff not only met this challenge, but used it to develop a striking camaraderie in and out of the classroom: "The teachers ... almost without exception, possess unusual skill in relating to trainees, involving students in class participation, and in presenting ideas and concepts in meaningful and positive fashion. Because of this teacher skill, students are interested and not fearful of expressing themselves. The student-teacher relationship frequently extends beyond the classroom, e.g., to the less formal setting of the lunchroom and informal after class groups. ... the human quality of mutual respect is clearly evident."[9] The flexibility of this system, however, produced wide variations in course content and provided no fixed structure for the exchange of new teaching ideas and methods.[10]

All feeder courses shared OIC's basic philosophy. The minority history course, in particular, reinforced OIC's underlying messages of self-respect and race pride through the examination of the past achievements of blacks and other minorities. Noting that "traditional American history is an integral part of the color line," the course sought to increase self-confidence by making trainees aware of the history and achievements of minorities and by eliminating any sense of shame about their racial background. One set of course guidelines highlighted scholars who had begun to break down the racism of traditional historiography, including Carter G. Woodson, C. Vann Woodward, Benjamin Quarles, Lawrence Reddick, John Hope Franklin, and Kenneth Stampp. The course not only established that minority groups had played a central part in American history, but also showed that they shared a common history of "exclusion from full participation in the social, political, and economic life of the country."[11]

The minority history course also examined the historical origins of contemporary societal problems, emphasizing pragmatic strategies for advancing social change. Implicitly invoking DuBois, an overview of the course explored this theme: "should we struggle blindly, destructively, and hopelessly? No, we must grasp this history, seek its meaning, and see ourselves in it, and learn to dissolve the color line, until the net no longer entangles us, and the pattern of our history is no longer woven by the threads of racism."[12] The course's emphasis on social issues increased as the program developed. An outline of the course from the late 1960s, for example, featured units on peace movements and militant groups. In addition, the course outline suggested units on ghettos, the Appalachians, and migrants. This interplay of the historical and the topical provided trainees with tools to understand the relationship between their personal situations and broader social structures. For many, the course provided their first exposure to minority history; teaching the subject in a federally funded job training program was a radical innovation in itself in the mid-1960s.[13] One student, identified only as "Miss C.," came to OIC dispirited and depressed from "being broke and unemployed," with "no job, no skill, and no prospect for the future." When she learned about the minority history class during her initial counseling interview, she realized that "she needed just such a course as this to boost her morale."[14]

Other courses, like Job Seeking and Finding, Job Holding and Advancement, and Grooming and Hygiene, aimed to increase trainee confidence by demystifying the workplace for students who lacked experience with its norms. The job-seeking class introduced trainees to the mechanics of finding employment, such as evaluating interests and skills, assessing job requirements, identifying openings, and filling out applications. The grooming and hygiene course discussed the standards of "dress, physical appearance, and behavior" expected by employers, both in job interviews and in the workplace. The job-holding course emphasized punctuality, on-the-job work habits, and personal deportment, and offered guidance on how to handle employer, co-worker, and union relations. In each of these courses, OIC operated on the assumption that "job-oriented social training is an integral part of job success."[15]

From one perspective, this emphasis on self-presentation, appearance, and workplace behavior imposed middle-class norms on the minority poor while reinforcing a prevailing cultural discourse that explained poverty as the result of personal irresponsibility.[16] With its emphasis on "grooming and hygiene," OIC unquestionably demanded changes in behavior and attitude from its trainees. But this critique inadvertently highlights serious social and cultural dilemmas that OIC actively attempted to resolve—or at least defuse. Social and geographic isolation often created cultural barriers that drastically limited inner-city residents' ability to enter the mainstream workforce. Without a fluency in the social norms and expectations of the workplace, minorities and the poor were at a disadvantage in applying for jobs. White employers could easily seize such standards as a convenient justification for hiring decisions that were in reality based on racial prejudice.[17]

FIGURE 18. A "grooming and hygiene" course at the OIC Feeder, July 19, 1965, taught by Maytha Ransom. The photo was taken while the Feeder was housed in a National Guard Armory after a fire destroyed its original building. Photo courtesy of Temple University Libraries, Urban Archives, Philadelphia, Pennsylvania.

OIC fought in practical ways to remove these barriers. One program manual noted that "O.I.C. realized that men differ widely in their social and cultural traits and that no set of these characteristics can be adjudged inherently 'superior' or 'inferior'...yet the world of work does have rules and practices that must be understood by those who would succeed in this realm."[18] Miss C., the student who had been drawn to the minority history class, came to view these courses this way, as she reported that being "taught good grooming, how to speak correctly, Math and other courses she so badly needed.... GAVE HER CONFIDENCE" (emphasis in the original). Miss C. eventually secured a clerk-typist position with Dun and Bradstreet.[19] In practice, OIC's efforts to provide its trainees with needed cultural skills was not so much an act of oppression as it was an attempt to lessen disadvantages and eliminate superficial factors that maintained the racial status quo. By conveying cultural knowledge, OIC not only provided individual African Americans with prerequisites for employment, but also equipped them with the tools to confront the racial stereotypes and prejudices of white employers. In effect, OIC challenged the white business world to live up to its own rhetoric of equality.[20] While perhaps retrospectively naïve in view of the racial polarization and permanent deindustrialization that had begun to unfold in Philadelphia and other cities, this strategy still appeared reasonable during the mid-1960s. The approach also had the very real advantage of making OIC highly attractive as a candidate for federal, corporate, and philanthropic funds. These resources, in turn, made possible a process of African American institution building unmatched by more radical approaches.

Significantly, the Feeder Program also included a course called "Male Orientation," reflecting an explicit assumption that men in OIC's target population faced especially severe challenges in the labor market. The course primarily enrolled young, African American men, many of whom were "alienated from any formal classroom experience." Much of the course content consisted of group sessions aimed at preparing participants simply to return to the classroom. Instructors discussed the trainees' past frustrations with school and work, and attempted to provide "psychological and motivational preparation" for both the OIC program and the workplace. Often, instructors pursued these goals by verbally challenging the men to improve their earning capacities and to assert their masculinity as family breadwinners. As one observer noted, instructors pushed students to take charge, asking tough questions like "'How much do you want this thing?' 'Do you want it bad enough?' or say: 'The good money is there waiting for you, if you can do the job.'" With its mix of therapeutic counseling, group support, and masculinist challenge, the class attempted to "set the stage for developing new insight and self-expectation."[21]

These features of the male orientation course reinforced traditional gender roles in both the home and the workplace. In part, this reflected broader liberal worries about black family structure and gender relations articulated in the 1965 Moynihan Report's claim that "matriarchal" black family structures produced a "tangle of pathology" and contributed to high rates of black male unemployment.[22] But the male orientation class also was a response to the transformative social changes brought on by the reduction in job opportunities for unskilled and semi-skilled men, a problem exacerbated by long-standing patterns of employment discrimination. While many of the jobs available for African American women in the postindustrial urban economy remained largely the same as they had been in the industrial age—low-skill, low-wage domestic and service positions without benefits or opportunities for advancement—many jobs for black men simply disappeared. This decline in male work opportunities benefited neither men nor women. Although traditional in its approach, OIC's male orientation class addressed a serious problem that had a particularly deleterious effect on young men with limited skills and opportunities.

Regardless of gender issues, OIC's feeder instructors emphasized the importance of personal motivation of all students as a condition of workplace success. OIC tried to convince its trainees that by accepting the program's self-help philosophy, they could transcend past failures and dramatically improve their future prospects. Beginning with the earliest intake interviews and continuing with classroom content, this message was constantly reinforced, as was OIC's insistence that a direct relationship existed between training, employment, and self-respect. Even the nontraditional style of classroom instruction, which emphasized student participation and leadership, supported this message as it "encourages self-expression and creativity...[and] independent thinking....in line with the OIC philosophy of self-help."[23] Feeder instructors decorated the bright walls of their classrooms with uplifting slogans like "Integration without Preparation Is Frustration," "Genius Is Colorblind," "OIC is 75% Attitude—25% Skill," and "There Is No Need for OIC if *Training* Is All We Do." Reinforced by Sullivan's own penchant for such rhetorical flourishes, the repetition of these and other slogans established what one observer described as "a motivational paternoster" that helped to create a sense of common mission at OIC.[24] Such feelings led Stanley McBride, a 1966 graduate, to compose an OIC song, the final verse of which celebrated the organization's basic premise:

> No more jobs of unskilled labor,
> Now our hearts are filled with glee,
> And as we shout and cheer
> We want the whole world to hear,
> We got our start here at OIC,
> We got our start at OIC.[25]

McBride's song captured the enthusiastic optimism of the program's early years: the inner-city poor would use self-help to transcend the constraints of low-wage work and take their rightful place in American Society. In its celebration of this ideology, OIC engaged African American traditions of community and individual uplift that dated to the nineteenth century and before.[26]

OIC's staff and instructors understood the program from this perspective, but also thought of OIC as part of the civil rights movement. A 1972 summary of the Feeder Program explained this orientation: "O.I.C., it should be realized, is also the outgrowth of the civil rights movement;...there probably would have been no O.I.C. without this struggle for human dignity and equal opportunity. Thus O.I.C. is also viewed as a positive, constructive and tangible phase of the rights movement." Reflecting OIC's close relationship to national liberalism, the promotional materials also asserted that the organization "considers itself part of the war on poverty."[27] OIC reasserted the civil rights movement's commitment to economic as well as racial justice, and to the Great Society's focus on increasing access to opportunity among the poor; yet it transcended both in its direct connection of such issues to the African American uplift tradition and to the wider American cultural focus on self-reliance and responsibility. OIC generated a new definition of "self-help" liberalism when it combined self-reliance and uplift with a call for resources from the federal state to make those concepts meaningful. This became one of OIC's signal contributions to liberal thought and activism during this period. This strand of postwar urban liberalism has not been recognized in histories that focus only on liberalism nationally. Its importance lay in the way that it integrated "mainstream" values, commonly associated with conservatism, into a powerful and compelling form of grassroots social and economic activism.

The motivational and uplift dimensions of the feeder extended beyond rhetorical exhortation, though, as OIC also established an extensive counseling program. Counselors met with trainees as often as four times a month, and, in keeping with OIC's "whole man" philosophy, attempted to address issues "encompassing educational, vocational, social, psychological, economical, and personal factors" that might limit a student's progress. Counselors' intimate knowledge of their trainees' personal situations sometimes made it possible to intervene in personal crises and devise solutions that allowed students to remain in the program. In one case, a trainee's husband fell ill and lost his job while she was part-way through her training, but a counselor arranged a "temporary Public Assistance Grant" that provided the family with a source of support and allowed the woman to complete her course.[28] Nonetheless, significant problems still emerged, mostly as a result of the counselors' broad responsibilities. In particular, counselors often failed to provide detailed information about possible career paths, which in some cases led to poor vocational choices as well as to enrollment imbalances between different training programs.[29] One such case was "Mrs. Trease Y.," a single mother of three, who had received welfare for twelve years before coming to the program "with a mind full of doubts...feeling shy and insecure." Placed in the electronics assembly course, she did not make adequate progress and eventually had to switch over to the power sewing class. After being reassigned, however, she completed the program and secured a job at the Philadelphia Quartermaster Corps.[30]

OIC's dependence on federal funds meant that despite its origin in the African American church, the ministerial presence among its leadership, and its quasi-moralistic invocation of self-help, the program never relied directly on religion as a specific part of its philosophy or curriculum. This secular character raises questions about whether OIC should be seen as an antecedent of the faith-based social policy initiatives that rose to national prominence at the turn of the twenty-first century.[31] In a strict sense, it was not, as no part of the OIC program imparted religious instruction. An explicitly religious program in the 1960s would have faced difficulty in securing federal funding, as OEO's repeated rejection of a youth program proposed by the Archdiocese of Philadelphia made clear. OIC's secular character is thus further evidence of the elemental pragmatism that guided the organization.[32]

Still, religious motivations and a sense of Christian social ethics drove OIC's leaders, and despite its secular qualities, the program remained rooted in the church. As Sullivan wrote in his autobiography, "one thing must be made crystal clear:...the Selective Patronage Program and the Opportunities Industrialization Center Program are essentially the work of the Christian Church. They represent for me the translation of my ministry into concrete living terms." Elsewhere, Sullivan made this even more explicit: "The program was born in a colored church and community.... those of us who are intimately involved in this self-help program look upon it as a program of religious faith. We know that it was born in prayer and that, through hard work, what we call 'calculated faith'...the program has succeeded."[33] One early analyst of OIC observed that Sullivan's "ability to mix the social gospel with more traditional religious themes helps rationalize his strategy for using the church as a foundation for developing programs with a strong secular orientation."[34] From its basis in Christian institutions and ethics, the program used federal money in an attempt to recast the race-based employment structures of the wider American economy. Its relative success thus raises questions about whether faith-based programs actually sacrifice their core effectiveness—as many advocates claim—when forced to respect boundaries of church-state separation in order to receive public funds.

In any case, the fine points of church-state separation did not greatly concern OIC administrators during the program's early years. By August 1967, the feeder employed a staff of forty-three instructors and twenty-five counselors, and had enrolled more than nine thousand trainees. It achieved this record despite a potentially devastating setback on July 17, 1965, when a fire destroyed the feeder's building, with all its equipment and records. In a demonstration of OIC's growing political influence and popularity, however, Governor William Scranton opened a nearby state armory for the feeder's use, allowing it to resume operations almost immediately. Local print and broadcast media sent out appeals for previous applicants to re-register, and OIC staff and federal VISTA volunteers painstakingly recreated hundreds of individual records. By early September, 94 percent of the pre-fire enrollees had re-registered with OIC. The fire may have even accelerated OIC's growth by providing additional publicity. In 1969, the OIC Feeder Program moved into its own building on North Broad Street, and had a waiting list of more than 10,000 names.[35] OIC's popularity indicated its success as an educational program, but also the magnitude of the problem of jobs that Philadelphia's local industrial and employment policies had to face.

Reaching the Hard-Core Unemployed

The presence of the OIC Feeder Program had important implications for OIC's student population. Most job training programs in the early 1960s lacked the capacity to address issues more complicated than simple lack of skills. As a result, many accepted participants on the basis of previous education and experience. This practice, known as "creaming," usually screened out those who had the greatest need for training. African Americans suffered from particularly high rates of rejection on these grounds.[36] In contrast, the feeder's pre-vocational remedial programs allowed OIC to serve a far higher percentage of Philadelphia's poorest population than other programs. Such individuals, however, still had to find OIC, so program recruiters fanned out into bars, pool halls, barbershops, beauty parlors, pawnshops, and housing projects. In addition, OIC received referrals from welfare and employment agencies, public health centers, churches, and unions. Local radio stations regularly broadcast information, and the Department of Public Assistance mailed OIC brochures with welfare checks. As OIC's reputation spread among Philadelphia businesses, company personnel departments began to refer unqualified applicants to OIC, as did the city's Civil Service Commission. By the end of the program's second year, word-of-mouth referrals accounted for more than a third of all new enrollees. One formerly unemployed trainee reported that he had learned about the program when "he went downstairs to sit on the step, and as he sat, looking dejected and frustrated, a friend came by and struck up a conversation which led to the discussion of OIC and its merits." Both outreach and word of mouth worked, and awareness of the program spread rapidly.[37]

An OIC planning manual observed that recruiting "at a corner bar may attract different persons than if the announcement is made in neighborhood churches."[38] The composition of OIC's enrollment reflected such recruiting techniques. Of the trainees who enrolled in OIC between April 1965 and December 1966, 81 percent lacked a high school diploma, 20.6 percent had less than a ninth grade education, 32.6 percent received welfare or unemployment benefits, 98 percent met the federal definition of poverty, and 75.5 percent were older than twenty-one. The man who learned of OIC from a friend as he sat on his front stoop, for example, was thirty-nine and had never completed high school. "William L.," who heard of OIC on the radio, was forty-four and had left school after the fifth grade. Regardless of previous educational levels, however, the generally poor quality of trainees' past schooling meant that many were functionally illiterate. Further, almost all OIC trainees came from high poverty areas of the city, and one 1968 estimate indicated that 31 percent of OIC students came from among Philadelphia's "hard-core unemployed." OIC thus achieved some success in reaching the most disadvantaged inner city residents, along with people slightly better off but still chronically underemployed.[39]

Although program officials tried to emphasize its multiracial nature, OIC remained primarily an African American program. The program did establish one Spanish-language center during the 1970s. Rather than a full training program, the Spanish-language center offered English as a second language and other basic education classes.[40] OIC officials also considered starting a training center in the all-white, blue-collar Kensington section of Philadelphia, but never implemented the idea. The result was that blacks made up more than 90 percent of OIC trainees throughout the 1960s and 1970s. In failing to broaden its recruitment base into Philadelphia's white neighborhoods, OIC contributed to the racially targeted character of the War on Poverty and, indirectly, to the Great Society's resulting failure to build support among working class whites. In 1969, for example, the representative to the Philadelphia Anti-Poverty Action Committee from largely white Northeast Philadelphia complained that OIC had not even responded to inquiries about establishing a training center in that section of the city, and that white applicants had been rejected "because they are white." While such claims are difficult to validate, they reflected common perceptions about both OIC and the War on Poverty among the white working class. Why OIC did not reach out to poor, working-class whites remains unclear. A commitment to the program's origins in the civil rights movement, along with doubts about the receptiveness of whites to a black-run program, may have limited OIC's inter-racial outreach efforts. Equally probable, however, is that the extensive needs of the black community led OIC officials to concentrate the program's resources on African Americans alone.[41]

Race, however, defined only part of OIC's makeup. Gender also shaped the program in important ways. Between July and September 1965, more than 65 percent of all new OIC trainees were women. This high rate of female participation worried such observers as labor economist Herbert Striner, who argued in 1967 "that Negro teen-age males present a more important employment target than the females." In an attempt to bring this ratio into balance, OIC for a time even gave men priority on the Feeder Program waiting list. Striner, one of OIC's leading advocates in Washington, pointed out with palpable relief that during 1966 and 1967 OIC had "been singularly successful" in increasing its recruitment of black men. This emphasis on male enrollment reflected wider concerns about the social and economic roles of black men, as exemplified in OIC's "male orientation" course. Male enrollment, however, increased only to 43 percent in 1967, and women continued to be a majority. After OIC expanded nationally, women accounted for 64 percent of total enrollments during the program's first decade. In contrast, women made up only 40 percent of the trainees at Philadelphia's primary federal job training facility, a disparity that apparently reflected the Manpower Development and Training Administration's heavy emphasis on traditionally male jobs.[42]

OIC's high female participation rate may have been linked to women's generally greater access to welfare benefits. Particularly in the absence of stipends for participation in OIC, outside public support freed low-skilled

women to enroll in the program. Despite the broadening of welfare programs to include unemployed fathers, men still had access to fewer sources
of financial support outside the labor market. Equally important may
have been the changing structure of the labor market itself, as a more service-oriented economy offered more jobs in traditionally female employment categories, which was reflected in OIC's course offerings. Despite
its early concern, OIC eventually accepted the gender disparity, and by
the early 1970s offered child care services to trainees through an OEO-
funded program.[43]

Race and gender issues aside, two weaknesses undermined OIC's ability to reach Philadelphia's disadvantaged. First, although OIC sought to
move new students into the program quickly to take advantage of their
initial enthusiasm, the backlog of applicants for popular courses created
lengthy waiting lists. At the end of October 1966, for example, the feeder
had a waiting list of 6,671 names. Frequently, students waited anywhere
from two to six weeks before orientation and then experienced an additional two week delay before they could enter the feeder. These delays
arose because OIC grouped students in the feeder by vocational area, but
also allowed them to choose their own area of training. Although important in principle and probably necessary in practice, the interaction
of these two practices created a bottleneck effect in class enrollments.
New students frequently chose popular classes and then languished on
a waiting list when no openings existed. Meanwhile, feeder courses in
less popular areas remained below capacity because of inadequate demand. In March 1967, for example, 85 percent of applicants on the waiting list had registered for one of the ten most popular OIC vocational
areas, such as clerk-typing, power sewing, IBM machine operation, and
sheet metal. The other 15 percent waited for slots in nineteen less popular courses, such as restaurant practices and vending machine maintenance, or difficult classes like computer programming, computer maintenance, chemistry laboratory technician, and drafting. Building trades
such as plumbing and heating, brick masonry, and air conditioning also
had short waiting lists because all-white unions controlled entry into the
trade; students understood that the actual prospects for employment in
these fields would be low.[44] Regardless of their cause, the lengthy waiting
lists performed a kind of self-selection on OIC's recruiting pool, as the delays discouraged applicants who might have succeeded if admitted immediately. By one estimate, only 60 percent of those who initially registered
for OIC actually entered the feeder. While some of these lost applicants

were referred to other training or social services or placed on jobs, most simply dropped out. Many of these were among the most frustrated and least skilled of Philadelphia's poor—exactly the group that OIC hoped to reach.[45]

OIC's policy regarding financial support for trainees created a second challenge. In keeping with its self-help, "no-dole" philosophy, OIC provided no stipends for trainees. Sullivan explained that "we give him no training stipends. Rather a man's motivation is self-respect—for OIC is no WPA program—the realization that if he stays with the program there will be a job at the end."[46] The anti-stipend policy produced unintended and largely negative consequences, as it too functioned as a selection mechanism that discouraged people without autonomous income sources. OEO's consultant concluded that the no-stipends approach "works in favor of employed workers, mainly with daytime occupations, and women who are supported by their families or husbands."[47] This observation overstated the problem, as it ignored the wide participation of unemployed female heads of households, as well as the reality that over half of all OIC trainees were unemployed and almost half received welfare or unemployment payments. Still, while not as severe as the problems that plagued earlier manpower programs, OIC's no-stipends policy and waiting lists prevented the program from reaching an even greater percentage of Philadelphia's hard-core unemployed.[48]

OIC's Job-Training Program

For all of the Feeder Program's innovations, it represented only a preparatory curriculum for OIC's actual skill training.[49] Training courses took place in the old police station at 19th and Oxford, and in three additional branch centers in West Philadelphia, South Philadelphia, and the Germantown section of northwest Philadelphia. This expansion around the city occurred ahead of schedule during late 1964 and 1965, in response both to the high demand for the program and to the sense of crisis that followed the North Philadelphia riots of August 1964. The result was that between February 15 and October 31, 1965, OIC enrolled a total of 644 trainees in the North Philadelphia branch, 467 in the West Philadelphia branch, 161 in the Germantown branch, and 35 in the South Philadelphia branch. As reflected in these numbers, each branch emphasized particular training areas: the original North Philadelphia center focused on machine tooling,

welding, sheet metal, and drafting; the South Philadelphia branch primarily offered courses in printing, graphic arts, and office skills; the West
Philadelphia branch emphasized electronics, computer maintenance, and
secretarial skills; finally, the Germantown branch stressed construction
skills such as plumbing, brick masonry, and electricity installation.[50]

Over 70 percent of OIC's instructors came directly from industry, and
some even worked at OIC on a volunteer, part-time basis while continuing to hold full-time jobs. Although many instructors came to OIC from
the Philadelphia School District, the program required no formal teacher
certification. Instead, OIC adopted the philosophy that "the ability to relate with the trainee and to be able to impart specific skill information
at a level which the trainee can use, is a sounder criterion for selecting
instructors than certification." While this use of nontraditional teachers
broadened the range of talent available to OIC, it contributed to a lack of
standardization in OIC's courses.[51]

The use of instructors from industry helped OIC maintain a close fit
between its course content and the skill requirements of employers. This
became increasingly important between 1965 and 1968, when the Technical Advisory Committees lapsed into inactivity. This meant that OIC
relied almost entirely on instructors for information about current work
conditions and skill demands in industry, with little systematic review of
course content. Beginning in 1968, though, OIC reestablished direct industry contacts through the formation of new advisory committees.[52]

Content aside, all branches operated according to a "job-ready" approach to vocational instruction. Instead of providing complete training in
all aspects of a trade, OIC sought to make its trainees proficient in enough
basic skills to obtain an entry-level job. This approach assumed that even
with a longer, more thorough training experience, changing technological demands would require constant acquisition of new skills. It also prevented employers from completely shifting the cost of training onto OIC.
"Becky H.," a divorced mother who overcame serious financial and personal challenges to complete OIC's commercial art course, exemplified
such relationships. After graduating from OIC, she accepted an on-the-
job trainee position with the Goodway Printing Company. There, she received additional training at the company's expense. Eventually, she received a full-time job with Goodway. Because many trainees came to OIC
having had negative work and school experiences in the past, Thomas
Ritter explained, "job-ready" training was the only practical choice: "We
want to give trainees enough to function in the job they're after, but not

enough to panic them. Most of them had just given up hope when they came here. They've got it now. We don't want to snuff it out."[53]

Depending on the difficulty of the course, training ranged from eight weeks to eighteen months in length, with an average of twenty-two weeks. Students in areas with shortages of qualified workers often found jobs and left OIC without completing formal training. The "job ready" training approach facilitated such choices. Curricular areas prone to such attrition included Power Sewing, IBM Key Punch Operation, and Clerk-Typist training. Overall, a sample of 265 OIC placements indicated that 50 percent finished their program, 25 percent received a job offer before the end of their course, and 13 percent moved directly from the Feeder Program to a job placement with no additional training. OIC accepted this tendency toward early exit both as an inevitable function of the economic stress faced by trainees and as validation of the feeder's motivational, job orientation, and basic education functions.[54]

In principle, the job-ready training concept meant that at the end of a course trainees would be ready to step immediately into a job. In most cases, this worked. Typical OIC courses offered relatively high-quality instruction and fulfilled the goal of providing "job-ready" skills.[55] A few classes even benefited from access to high-quality, modern equipment. These included the teletype course, for which Western Union donated machines and provided curriculum assistance, and the computer technology course, for which UNIVAC donated a new $300,000 system. Successful training, however, did not depend on access to corporate largess, as most courses (drafting, electronics, chemistry-lab technician, clerk-typing, IBM key punch, secretarial skills, laundry and dry cleaning, and commercial art) acquired adequate equipment and provided training that employers considered to be at least satisfactory. A number of other courses, including office machine practices and air conditioning and refrigeration repair, offered high quality training despite problems of poor equipment or inadequate space.[56]

Occasionally, however, deficits in up-to-date machinery, as well as a lack of regular course reviews by the Technical Advisory Committees, compromised OIC's ability to connect the content of the training to actual needs in the workplace. As late as 1967, the machine tool operation class at North Philadelphia, for example, used outmoded machinery at least twenty years old, while the power sewing course at the same branch employed such thoroughly antiquated equipment that trainees found it impossible to handle the powerful new machinery or the fast production

FIGURE 19. Joseph Yermish of Philadelphia's Fenway Machine Company, Inc., demonstrates the company's "Nibbler" electric metal cutting tool to OIC machine tool operations instructor George Bennett, March 19, 1971. Fenway had just donated three Nibblers to OIC's Metal Fabrication course. OIC students are observing the demonstration. Photo courtesy of Temple University Libraries, Urban Archives, Philadelphia, Pennsylvania.

pace in an actual Philadelphia garment factory. In a few cases, equipment problems reached absurd extremes, such as a clerk-typing class that lacked electric typewriters, or an office machine repair class with equipment so ancient that there was "serious doubt that such obsolete machines would have any training value."[57] Students in other courses, such as the brick masonry class in the Germantown branch, endured inadequate lighting and cramped classrooms. A few courses suffered from both space and materials problems, as an evaluation of the North Philadelphia sheet metal class illustrated: "classroom instructional space, which is shared by the welding class, is poorly lighted and provides little or no blackboard space nor adequate space for visual aids. Instructional materials appear to be poor and outdated. Textbooks used are more than 20 years old."[58] These limitations had negative consequences for trainees' performance in actual job situations. A different set of problems affected the commercial cooking, restaurant practices, and printing courses. Students in these classes worked in OIC's cafeterias or filled OIC's internal printing needs, and often these functional responsibilities interfered with the actual training program. This practice veered dangerously close to exploitation.[59]

In a few vocational areas, workplace discrimination overwhelmed OIC's capacity either to develop strong courses or to engage in economic-based civil rights action. A plumbing course at the Germantown branch not only suffered from inadequate funding, equipment, and space, but also from underenrollment; in 1967, the OEO consultant attributed this "to the fact that the plumbing union has been one of the most difficult ones for minority group members to enter. There are few Negroes in the plumbing trade now in Philadelphia, and the likelihood of getting young men interested in this area is slim because of the apprenticeship restrictions and other barriers imposed by the building and construction trades."[60] OIC also received criticism from within Philadelphia's African American community for expending resources on training in the discriminatory construction trades. During the economic boom of the mid- and late-1960s, however, shortages of craftsmen existed in many of the trades, and OIC argued that the availability of skilled African American craftsmen would break down racial barriers by meeting the need for skilled workers in these fields—a variation of the increasingly discredited Myrdalian "breakthough" argument of the 1950s. Nonetheless, the incentive to pursue such breakthroughs remained strong because of the high wages available in the best-paid construction fields: when an OIC-trained mason became the first black to "crack" the all-white Brick Layers Union, he received a salary of $5.40 an hour, "the highest on record for an OIC graduate" as of 1966.[61]

In addition, Sullivan's liberal commitments ran deep, and included dedication to the principle of unionism—extending even to the building trades—that likely derived from his early association with Sleeping Car Porters Union president A. Philip Randolph. When a consortium of non-union black contractors lobbied him in 1968 to form a partnership that would provide the builders with partially trained craftspeople, Sullivan hesitated, agreeing to consider the proposal but insisting that "I am a union man...I want my men in unions." He hinted, however, that he might abandon that principle unless the building trades made progress on integration. Developing an autonomous black sector of the construction industry would soon emerge as a primary strategy for dealing with building trades discrimination, but it would be managed through organizations other than OIC.[62]

Eventually, in cooperation with the Urban League and the Pennsylvania State Employment Service, OIC managed to break down some of the building trades' resistance and succeeded in establishing a union approved pre-apprenticeship program as part of a broader liberal challenge to the racial prerogatives of the trades. In addition, OIC official Robert McGlotten negotiated an agreement under which the Building Trades Council "certified" a number of black contractors, which brought their mostly black employees into the unions.[63] The unions, of course, did not represent the only source of discrimination in the industry. Construction firms, too, resisted hiring African Americans. Placement statistics and personal accounts indicated that OIC continued to have difficulty in attaining jobs for students in the construction courses, and program officials consistently supported the federal government's groundbreaking but controversial "Philadelphia Plan" for affirmative action in the construction industry (chapter 7).[64]

Construction remained a heavily male-dominated field in the 1960s, but the interplay of race, gender norms, and labor-market structure affected all OIC job training programs. When OIC began in the mid-1960s, the feminist movement was still new. The labor market also remained highly gendered, with most jobs clearly demarcated as male or female. OIC responded to the clear structural cues of this labor market, not to mention the expectations of its federal and foundation funding agencies, by directing women and men into gender-determined training tracks. A survey of ninety-three trainees who attended OIC between 1964 and 1966 shows clear, sex-based differences in training, as most women completed courses in office-clerical fields (clerk-typist, secretarial skills, and IBM key punch operation), in female-dominated manufacturing areas (power sewing and electronic assembly), or in service sector fields (merchandising-marketing or restaurant practices). Men, by contrast, typically completed courses in fields such as brick masonry, sheet metal, electrician, air conditioning and refrigeration, machine tool operation, electronics technician, and drafting. Both men and women took teletype and commercial cooking courses, and the merchandising-marketing and key punch courses each had one male participant, but generally very little enrollment overlap existed between male and female students. Significantly, male-dominated job categories paid notably more than women's. Although the survey contained incomplete earnings information, the available data yield a rough estimate of average weekly earnings after placement of $109.84 for men and $73.89 for women.[65]

In one case, the gendered nature of the labor market, combined with family stress, led a female trainee to abandon the male-dominated electronics technician curriculum even though "she was doing very well." She explained her decision on the grounds that "employment as an electronic technician is practically unheard of for women." The woman's children had gone to live with relatives in the South while she and her husband trained at OIC and worked in low-wage jobs. "I miss my children very much," she said. OIC counselors persuaded the woman to transfer to the typically female electronics assembly course instead of dropping out of OIC completely. The assembly course took less than three months to complete, as compared to a year for the technician curriculum, and she soon found employment "as an assembler at a local firm...receiving 'good pay' for her work." Meanwhile, her husband continued to train at OIC while working part-time. Eventually, the couple's children joined them in Philadelphia. The incident illustrated how the constraints of a gendered labor market could combine with family pressures to shape women's training experiences at OIC.[66]

Even a decade later, OIC job placements showed similar patterns. Data on 275 female placements and 190 male placements from 1974–75 indicate that men typically trained for and obtained jobs as welders, machine tool operators, auto mechanics, maintenance workers, construction helpers, laborers, and auto body repairmen. Women, in contrast, still primarily entered office related fields such as clerk-typist, clerk, keypunch operator, secretary, proof machine operator, and bank teller, as well as factory jobs such as sewing machine operator and production worker, and such deeply gendered jobs as "flower arranger."[67] Clearly, OIC worked within existing, gender-based employment patterns that it did not explicitly challenge.

Still, careful review of these data demonstrates that the program did something more than simply reproduce gendered labor market structures. By 1975, a number of women and men used OIC training to cross traditional gender boundaries: albeit in very limited numbers, women received placements as auto mechanics, machine tool operators, and maintenance workers; men were placed as keypunch operators, office clerks, and sales clerks. Even in the survey from the mid-1960s, two women had completed the chemistry lab technician course and found jobs in the field; another had become a commercial artist (Becky H., mentioned earlier). Such exceptions demonstrate that while OIC did not have a transformative effect on gendered employment norms—and did not attempt to do so—it did

FIGURE 20. OIC trainee Esther Davies demonstrates uses an oscilloscope to test a transistor while program founder Leon H. Sullivan observes, January 24, 1965. On a limited basis, a few OIC trainees began transcending traditional gendered employment categories. Photo courtesy of Temple University Libraries, Urban Archives, Philadelphia, Pennsylvania.

provide an avenue of opportunity for both women and men who sought training and employment in nontraditional fields.[68]

Even more significantly, the trainee profiles from the 1960s indicate that many of the female trainees used OIC to establish or maintain autonomous households. At least fifteen of the fifty-one women profiled were single mothers, many of whom relied on welfare. For them, OIC represented a path to independence, even if an imperfect one given the generally low wages in female-dominated fields. While OIC administrators might have preferred the maintenance of traditional family structures and the preservation of the family wage, they soon accepted the reality that single, female parenthood provided the impetus for many trainees to enter

FIGURE 21. Although many OIC trainees pursued training in traditional gender categories, some moved across such lines. In this photo, OIC welding instructor Thomas Smith works with a female welding trainee, Deborah Hall (using blowtorch), January 27, 1978. Photo courtesy of Temple University Libraries, Urban Archives, Philadelphia, Pennsylvania.

OIC. The ability to develop such independence mattered, as it helped to relieve the economic pressures that might otherwise constrain a woman to an abusive or otherwise oppressive marriage or relationship. OIC's 1966 profile of one single mother noted the growing prevalence of such family structures, and, rather than condemn her, celebrated the woman's efforts to better her situation (even as it used the title "Mrs." because the woman had not officially divorced her husband): "In Philadelphia, as in many cities throughout the nation, there is an army of women, young and old, who find themselves the sole breadwinner of the family. In such cases where there is no husband, this family responsibility weighs heavily on the mother. Mrs. Joan W. is a typical example of a mother who rose to meet this responsibility."[69] Just as OIC did not pass judgment on single mothers, it made no effort to impose norms of domesticity, either. Unlike other War on Poverty–era programs such as the Job Corps, the program did not offer courses for women on domestic skills or childrearing practices.[70]

Faced with the reality of changing social and economic structures, OIC once again chose the pragmatic path of taking people as they came to the program and training them for whatever employment might be available in the labor market. In this way, it operated in the mainstream of the twentieth century liberal tradition. Yet OIC also pushed postwar liberalism toward greater engagement with economic issues and adapted traditional cultural values such as self-reliance to the changing family structures and economic challenges of the low-income urban neighborhoods where it worked. As it did so, it began to shift the on-the-ground meaning of such national liberal initiatives as the War on Poverty.

Job Placement and OIC

The test of OIC's strategy for pursuing an economic-based form of civil rights action came when its students attempted to find desirable skilled and semi-skilled jobs. Complete assessment of the program's success in this area is difficult because OIC and other job training programs of the period often kept less than perfect records. OIC's focus was on program development and operation rather than administration, and federal agencies failed to push for improved record keeping during this period. As a result, the statistics cited in this section are approximations that almost certainly overstate the actual number of placements.[71]

Regardless of the exact data, OIC immediately enjoyed significant success in placing trainees. Between February 15 and October 31, 1965, OIC graduated 579 students and claimed to have placed 507 of them in jobs directly related to their training; fifty-two other students took jobs in unrelated fields; twenty remained unplaced as of January 1966 (table 5.1).[72] By the end of 1966, OIC's blend of uplift ideology, remedial education, job preparation, and appeals to both the social responsibility and self-interest of employers seemed to be a successful formula. Job placements accelerated rapidly, increasing from 240 in 1964 to 875 in 1965 and 1,398 in 1966. Out of this total of 2,513 placements, 2,382 were in training related fields. The city's Economic Development Unit found that during 1964–66, OIC received $3,561,500 in federal support and placed 2,290 graduates in jobs and 314 in On-the-Job Training programs funded by the U.S. Department of Labor. In contrast, the federal manpower program conducted at the Board of Education's John F. Kennedy Center received $5,197,285 in federal funds but placed only 1,639 students. OIC, it appeared, was both cheaper and more effective than other programs.[73]

Between February 1964 and April 1967, 888 separate employers ranging from "government agencies and large corporations to the one-man

TABLE 5.1 **OIC Placements Related to Field of Training, February 15 to October 31, 1965**

Course name	Placements related to training	Placements not related to training	Related to training (%)
Welding	16	0	100
Brick Masonry	2	0	100
IBM Key Punch	1	0	100
Wiring	1	0	100
Civil Service Prep.	1	0	100
Home Economics	1	0	100
Power Sewing	120	3	97
Restaurant Practices	77	2	97
Machine Tool	47	2	96
Teletype	24	2	92
Commercial Cooking	10	1	91
Secretarial Science	9	1	90
Electronics Assembly	90	11	89
Drafting	12	2	86
Merchandising	12	2	86
Sheet Metal	75	17	81
Chemistry Lab Tech.	9	9	50
Total	507	52	90

shop" hired OIC trainees. Overall, these firms found OIC trainees satisfactory, and many went out of their way to hire workers from the program—even if they had initially hired OIC graduates only "to avoid charges of discrimination."[74] In 1967, one employer decided to rely exclusively on OIC for future recruitment, and in a number of cases, employers with pressing labor shortages hired all the trainees in a relevant vocational class, regardless of actual progress. Businesses praised the preparation, motivation, and attitude of OIC trainees; as the OEO consultant reported in 1967, "most employers looked upon OIC as a good screening device." Occasional problems occurred in relation to specific skills and work speed, usually attributable to OIC's difficulties in obtaining modern machinery for its courses, but in general employers viewed OIC as the most reliable training program in Philadelphia. As Chamber of Commerce executive director and 1971 Republican mayoral candidate Thacher Longstreth put it, "An OIC stamp on a worker is like a sterling stamp on silver."[75] OIC's continuing placement record indicated that Longstreth's opinion was widely shared among Philadelphia employers. By the end of 1969, OIC reported that 15,084 people had graduated from the Philadelphia program, and that 9,261 had secured some form of job placement.[76]

While employers clearly supported OIC and valued the workers it trained, the benefits derived by the trainees themselves must be the ultimate standard of evaluation. As comprehensive data on the long-term effects of OIC training are unavailable, conclusions must be derived from short-term data and individual case histories. A number of studies provide information on the relationship between OIC training and changes in earnings, although none cover Philadelphia specifically, focusing instead on the centers that the organization soon established elsewhere in the U.S.—in 30 cities by 1967, 59 cities by 1970, and 130 cities by 1976.[77] A 1969 study of internal OIC statistics on pre- and post-training earnings revealed that nationally, average annual income increased from $1,900 to $2,900; an examination of thirteen OIC centers suggested that trainees experienced an increase in earnings of more than $2,000. Two years later, an OIC brochure claimed an increase in average income from $2,094 to $4,277. A detailed 1971 evaluation of the Boston and Oakland OICs revealed that trainees who had been employed prior to enrollment in OIC showed average annual earnings gains of $1,400 in Boston and $1,200 in Oakland, while those who had been unemployed experienced smaller increases of $1,150 in Boston and $900 in Oakland. A separate study of the Boston OIC supported these findings and showed that female trainees experienced greater increases than males, although women still had lower overall incomes. Significantly, the Boston-Oakland study compared OIC to the federal Work Incentive and Concentrated Employment Programs and concluded that "OIC appears to have had the greatest impact."[78] Enrollment, graduation, and job placement figures offer a second measure of OIC's effectiveness. OIC reported that around the United States, it had provided service to 73,424 people between 1964 and 1969; of this number, 49,116 completed training and 28,274 received job placements. Philadelphia remained the largest center of OIC activity, accounting for 31 percent of OIC graduates and 33 percent of job placements.[79]

Post-training job retention rates provide an indication of trainees' ability to function in the workplace. The 1967 OEO study surveyed 116 job placements from the Philadelphia OIC and found that fifty-one left their initial post-OIC job within eight months; among this group, nineteen quit, eleven were laid off, three left because of illness, sixteen were fired for unsatisfactory performance, and no information was available for two.[80] An internal OIC evaluation of job placements made by the Philadelphia OIC between 1964 and 1969 revealed that 75 percent remained on the job after six months. After twelve months, this figure dropped to 50 percent, but the statistics indicated that some improvement in this measure occurred after 1967.[81] These findings demonstrate that OIC training led to relatively permanent work placements for a significant percentage of participants. In combination with the overall placement data, these statistics suggest that OIC succeeded in placing trainees in desirable positions that led to increases in earnings, even if it could not resolve all of the challenges inherent in moving from underemployment to work.[82]

Stories of individual trainees offer a more qualitative measure of OIC's results. The case of a trainee identified as Mildred C. suggests the benefit that OIC provided simply by helping people escape the lowest stratum of the labor market. A single mother, Mildred C. had worked for years as a sorter at a uniform laundry service, a place of hot, dirty work where, in her words, "nobody cared anything about anybody else, and the supervisor treated the help like dirt." Mildred C. heard about OIC on the radio, but was initially intimidated by the idea of a training program and worried about whether she would be accepted by her instructors and fellow trainees. Upon enrolling, however, she found that "they accepted me as I was, and within minutes the strangeness I felt disappeared." Mildred C. moved rapidly through the feeder and the IBM key punch course and accepted a position with a large insurance company as a key punch operator. A summary of her story noted the contrast between "the heat in which she had to work on her former job" and the "air conditioned office she now occupies." It also noted that along with "the highest salary she had ever earned," Mildred C. now received a full range of benefits.[83]

A second trainee entered OIC with a similar work history. Andy Miller dropped out of school in tenth grade and worked at a succession of odd jobs, "pumping gas, parking cars, shifting stock." Immediately before enrolling in OIC at age twenty-seven, he worked in the stock room of a local department store. Married with three children, Miller lived with his family in a public housing project. By the early 1960s, he became frustrated and depressed about his situation: "I got sick and tired of being pushed around and kicked around. People looked at me like I was stupid, talked to me any kind of way. I was mad at everybody, mad at myself, thought I must be pretty dumb not to get the right kind of job." Miller added, "Sometimes I wished I was white, then I wouldn't have these problems." After two unsuccessful attempts at conventional night school classes, Miller enrolled in OIC's evening session shortly after the program opened. During the year that he spent at OIC, Miller worked during the day "ferrying rental cars" to support himself and his family (no information was available about the employment status of Miller's wife). After completing the Feeder Program and the sheet metal course at OIC's North Philadelphia center, Miller was hired by Boeing Aircraft's Vertol Helicopter Division. Reflecting OIC's job-ready training approach, Miller spent most of his first year at Boeing as an apprentice, mastering additional skills necessary to shape metal for the company's military helicopters. After receiving a promotion into a regular production position, Miller's income rose to $140 per week, far above the $65 of his previous stock room job. With this additional income, the Miller family purchased its own home.[84]

Andy Miller's placement at Boeing-Vertol raises a crucial point about OIC's success during the late 1960s: the national economic expansion induced by the Kennedy-Johnson tax cut and Vietnam War spending significantly increased the demand for manufacturing workers, especially among such defense-related companies as Boeing. When the economy slipped into a recession during the 1970s, OIC's job placements declined precipitously. OIC was in part the beneficiary of good timing, as its development took place during a period of economic expansion that made it easier to break down hiring barriers by appealing to employers' self-interest.[85] As the success of PIDC's industrial renewal efforts during the same years further illustrates, urban deindustrialization did not proceed from the 1950s on in an unbroken trajectory of decline. Conversely, however, even the most innovative local industrial and employment policies remained constrained by fluctuations of the wider economy.

Nonetheless, Miller's story provides one indication of OIC's capacity to improve the economic status of disadvantaged inner city residents. Miller had previously held a low-skill, low-wage job with few prospects for advancement, and, given his family status, could certainly be counted among the working poor. His OIC training led to the attainment of a significantly higher income and eventual entry into the middle class. Unfortunately, because of the lack of data on the long-term effects of OIC training, it is difficult to determine whether the improved fortunes of Andy Miller and other OIC trainees persisted once Philadelphia's economy sank into an accelerated decline during the 1970s.[86] Ultimately, OIC's great limitation lay in its vulnerability to such economic changes and in its dependence on the jobs offered by private companies. This dilemma would eventually become the great tragedy of OIC.

In OIC's early years, however, such long-term problems remained secondary to the immediate challenges of building a major new community institution. For many, both in Philadelphia and elsewhere, OIC seemed to offer a pragmatic, if partial, solution to the social and economic problems facing inner cities. When a 1966 OEO evaluation criticized every other

War on Poverty initiative in Philadelphia, it singled out OIC as "an example of an imaginative effort to mobilize community resources in the development of manpower training and employment opportunities" and unequivocally endorsed OIC's new funding requests. By the time of this assessment, OIC's central challenge seemed to be nothing less than how to expand the program as rapidly as possible across the United States.[87]

Government, Business, and OIC's Expansion

OIC quickly attracted the attention of federal officials eager to associate themselves with a program that Pennsylvania senator Joseph Clark celebrated as "the most successful segment, or one might say battalion or regiment or division, of the War on Poverty."[88] Robert Kennedy, John Lindsay, Hubert Humphrey, George McGovern, and Richard Nixon all visited the Philadelphia OIC, and Massachusetts senator Edward W. Brooke cochaired OIC's national fund-raising drive; OIC also received an unwelcome endorsement from the segregationist George Wallace.[89] The program's most significant endorsement, however, came on June 29, 1967, when President Lyndon Johnson and OEO director Sargent Shriver made a surprise visit to OIC's Feeder Program and the North Philadelphia training center. Special assistant to the president Sherwin Markman had met with Sullivan and visited OIC during an undercover "ghetto tour" in the spring of 1967. Along with pointing out the politically salient but increasingly unsustainable fact that Sullivan "is solely concerned with civil rights and does not become involved in Vietnam debates," Markman described OIC "as the pride of Philadelphia's poverty unit" and "the Nation's outstanding ghetto project" and suggested that Johnson associate himself with OIC through a spontaneous but well publicized presidential visit.[90]

Nearly two months later, President Johnson traveled to Philadelphia to meet Sullivan and tour OIC. Speaking to a large audience at the OIC feeder, he linked OIC to his own vision of the Great Society, and implicitly, of twentieth century liberalism—even as he alluded to fears about the forces that had begun to erode both his presidency and the liberal vision itself:

> The Federal Government did not build this center. Neither business, nor labor, nor philanthropy, nor city officials built it. All of us are helping now, and I

FIGURE 22. President Lyndon B. Johnson visiting the North Philadelphia OIC center with Leon H. Sullivan, June 29, 1967. Photo courtesy of Temple University Libraries, Urban Archives, Philadelphia, Pennsylvania.

am proud of the part we are playing. But the spirit built this center—the spirit that wants to say "yes" to life, that wants to affirm the dignity of every man, whatever his origins, whatever his race or religion.

That same spirit has given power and direction to all we have tried to do in our years of national leadership. . . . the problems of poverty, the consequences of discrimination, the ignorance and helplessness that are passed on, generation to generation, are almost too great for us to comprehend or master. Almost too great—for they were all created by the failures of men. There is nothing preordained about them. Being created by men, they can be overcome by men—by the restless spirit that speaks to all of us in the darkest hours, a spirit that says, "Believe in yourself, have pride in yourself. Prepare yourself for the work you must do." . . . I know you have made me feel that we—all 200 million of us—are going to make it.[91]

During this period, as well as during the decline of Great Society liberalism that followed, OIC translated the characteristics that had attracted

Johnson to Philadelphia into a highly successful campaign to secure increased financial support from business and, especially, from government. This successful grantsmanship demonstrated the utility of OIC's reconfiguration of the traditional themes of self-help and self-reliance into a liberal framework for community development. As such, OIC adopted a deeply pragmatic form of liberalism, a form intensely engaged with real economic problems and questions of racial justice, but also sensitive to the wider, mainstream political culture in which both public and private funding sources operated. This cultural deftness increasingly stood in contrast with demands for social change advanced by more radical activists during the mid- and late-1960s, and it helped OIC attain the financial and technical resources necessary to expand its operations. The presence of the activist left on the national political scene actually assisted the program, as the contrast between OIC and black power activists, or with advocates of a generous guaranteed annual income, helped to legitimize OIC as a moderate and reasonable force. OIC's urban liberalism thus provided a realistic framework for building viable large-scale social institutions in the inner city. Whether this pragmatic moderation could advance a truly transformative social and racial agenda, however, remained an open question.

Increased resources allowed OIC to undertake a rapid national expansion. Almost from its inception, the Philadelphia OIC had received inquiries from groups interested in starting centers in other cities. In 1965, the Stern Foundation gave OIC a $50,000 grant to develop such a plan and in 1966 the OIC Board created the OIC National Institute to oversee a national expansion. The Department of Labor (DOL), Department of Health, Education, and Welfare (HEW), and OEO committed $5 million in experimental funds to finance the establishment of new OICs in East Palo Alto-Menlo Park, Erie, Harrisburg, Little Rock, Oklahoma City, Roanoke, Seattle, and Washington, D.C. Additional funding followed the next year, and by October 1967, OIC had opened centers in 30 cities around the United States, with 36 more under development. The program continued to expand, reaching 130 cities in 1976, with development groups in an additional 99 cities. OIC relied on autonomous local groups to create legitimate, community-based organizations; as OIC vice chairman Maurice Dawkins noted in 1972, the new centers were run by "grass roots leaders ranging from Black Panthers to Black Welfare Mothers to Black Moderate Elks and Masons and Black George Wallace supporters." Cities with large OIC programs included Dallas, Baltimore, Seattle, Oakland, Wilmington, and Denver.[92]

Local OIC programs varied significantly in quality. One prominent failure took place in south-central Los Angeles, where an OIC funded by the Ford Foundation and large corporations inspired only opposition from the surrounding community. By 1970, the center closed.[93] Despite such setbacks, OIC's expansion allowed it to play an important national role in OEO's job training efforts: during 1968, for example, OICs around the United States accounted for more than 12 percent of the 91,000 people who received job training through the Community Action Program.[94] At its peak during the early 1980s, OIC had centers in more than 150 cities and 46 foreign countries in the developing world (beginning with Nigeria and Ghana in 1970). Although many centers grew to enroll hundreds or thousands of students, they generally remained smaller than the original Philadelphia OIC.[95]

The new OIC centers received financial support from a variety of public and private sources. In 1970, seventeen centers drew their primary funding from a combination of OEO, HEW, and DOL sources, fifteen from a new DOL initiative known as the Concentrated Employment Program, six from the Economic Development Administration, ten from state governments, and eleven from private business or philanthropic organizations. Overall, the federal government remained by far the largest source of financial support, as from 1964 to 1969, federal funds accounted for $45.9 million of OIC's total $48.5 million funding.[96] Despite the continued rhetorical and technical support of the business community, OIC relied almost entirely on public funding sources.

OIC officials thus consistently merged their emphasis on self-help with claims that the program's continued success depended on activist federal engagement with urban problems. Testifying before a House Subcommittee in 1965, Leon Sullivan left little doubt about the importance of government support: "No program of this description or ambition can be successful without government funds. Philanthropic grants and contributions will be helpful to indigenous community groups in getting programs underway, and volunteers in massive numbers are always quite helpful, but the major financial brunt for the development of qualitative efforts to insure the job being done has to be assumed from public funds."[97]

During the 1970s, as the economy slipped into recession and deindustrialization accelerated, Sullivan and other OIC officials lobbied hard for both national full employment policies and a series of emergency public employment measures. OIC leaders argued that public employment programs should contain a training element to improve the long-term skills of participants, but they also maintained that the federal government should pursue activist policy measures to create full employment through both private and public job creation. Without jobs, training would have little value. Thomas Ritter explained in 1975 that "as a practical matter training with job development for jobs that already exist can and must be supplemented by job creation to provide meaningful work. When private industry is no longer providing a sufficient number of jobs, new jobs can and must be created in the public sector."[98] In OIC's view, African American self-reliance did not conflict with the presence of a strong national state, but instead required it. More specifically, OIC needed three things from the state: first, a reliable source of funding; second, a commitment to employment-focused economic policy; and third, a stable policy environment that consistently supported the autonomy of community-based programs. During the 1960s and 1970s, the federal government generally satisfied the first criteria, but failed to provide the second or third. After 1980, none of these conditions would be met.

Federal funding continued to provide the largest component of OIC's budget. This support allowed OIC to expand, but also drew the program into intricate bureaucratic relationships that constrained its flexibility. Beginning with the 1964 grants from the ARA and the DOL and continuing with the 1965 OEO community action grants, OIC soon established a complex funding structure that drew on categorical grants from multiple federal agencies. Initially, most of OIC's funding came from OEO, DOL, and the Department of Health, Education, and Welfare (HEW) through an unprecedented "tri-agency" funding stream. Because these agencies had little experience with either inter-agency cooperation or community-based organizations, this structure led to significant administrative headaches for OIC. Statutory restrictions on grants, as well as bureaucratic rivalries, made it difficult for the federal agencies to coordinate activities. As a result, "OIC administrators were often subject to triplicate record keeping and reporting, frequent oversight evaluations, and communication with multiple government contract officers."[99]

Attempts to resolve such problems proved largely counterproductive. After 1967, OIC also dealt with a new DOL initiative known as the Concentrated Employment Program (CEP). Designed to improve the coordination of the fragmented training services that drew on DOL funding,

CEP grouped local training programs together and required each to provide specific services on a subcontract basis with the goal of assuring the
best possible mix of services for each trainee. In practice, CEP in Philadelphia merely highlighted conflicts within the local job training system by
creating duplications of effort and clashes of interests between different
training programs. The subcontracting concept proved particularly problematic for OIC, as it allowed the program to provide only one part of
a student's training. This undermined OIC's "on-going process" relationship with trainees. Although not all OIC trainees qualified for CEP support, the policy led to a significant erosion of OIC control. Despite OIC's
earlier success, the DOL viewed the rationalization of job training as a
higher priority than maintaining the integrity of the OIC program. OIC
officials had little choice but to tolerate this change, as the new framework
provided a source of funding separate from the War on Poverty, which by
the late-1960s appeared increasingly vulnerable.[100]

Nonetheless, the relationship with OEO continued to be OIC's most
important governmental tie, as the anti-poverty program contributed the
largest component of OIC's tri-agency funding. In Philadelphia, oversight
of this funding lay with the Philadelphia Anti-poverty Action Committee (PAAC). Although Sullivan and Ritter maintained amiable relations
with the PAAC leadership, damaging tensions did develop at the staff
levels of the agencies. In the spring of 1967, rumors even circulated that
federal officials planned to place Sullivan and OIC in charge of Philadelphia's entire anti-poverty program.[101] This change never took place, but
the underlying tension between OIC and PAAC became public in August 1968 after Congress reduced funding for local community action
agencies. OEO specified that the cut be applied on a proportional basis
among funded programs. PAAC, however, expressly violated this order
and cut OIC's funding by 33.3 percent, an amount disproportional to the
overall 26.7 percent reduction. PAAC chairman John Otto Renemann
argued that because of its national prominence, OIC should be able to
raise the necessary funds elsewhere and complained that "OIC has been
getting the lion's share of the poverty funds during the past three years."
OIC immediately filed an objection with OEO, which threatened PAAC
with the loss of all federal support unless it applied the cuts propor-
tionally.[102]

Despite the centrality of OIC's public funding, the business community continued to play an important role in OIC's operation during the
late-1960s and early-1970s. In part, this reflected business discomfort with

further expansions of the pure public sector, but it also highlighted the
appeal that OIC's emphasis on motivation, attitude, and workplace expectations continued to hold for business leaders who "complained about
the poor work habits, high turnover, and disciplinary problems" of employees hired from job training programs.[103] OIC thus offered an attractive option for corporate executives who felt pressed by the events of
the 1960s to increase their companies' community involvement. The presence of more radical possibilities in the inner cities also drew business to
OIC. Even as it appealed to mainstream political-economic and cultural
discourses amenable to corporate executives, OIC implicitly evoked the
supposed threat of more militant black organizations in order to present
itself as a reasonable, nonviolent alternative. Leon Sullivan's claim that
federal funding would allow OIC to transform the "Burn, Baby, Burn"
slogan into the more acceptable "Build, Brother, Build" provided the
most direct demonstration of this association.[104] OIC liberalism existed
in—even required—a tense balance between accommodation to societal
norms, civil rights activism, and militancy; the maintenance of that balance drew business support.

Sullivan actively sought the involvement of local and national business
executives. In 1968, OIC used these relationships to form a series of new
business advisory committees that included representatives from General
Electric, Chase Manhattan, Boeing, AT&T, IBM, and Coca-Cola, and the
locally based Rohm and Haas, DuPont, Campbell Soup, and Philadelphia
National Bank, as well as officers of two black-owned companies, Johnson Publications (publisher of *Ebony*) and Parks Sausage Company.[105] Inevitably, the extent of OIC's relationships with industry raised concerns.
Some observers concluded that the industry committees constituted a paternalistic co-optation of OIC and an erasure of the program's original
character as a grassroots element of the civil rights movement. According to this view, OIC aided business by supplying trained workers during
peak demand periods, while providing no guarantee that trainees would
have jobs beyond the next downturn. OIC served even broader capitalist imperatives by separating the unemployed and working poor and reinforcing pervasive cultural messages of individualism and the work ethic
while undercutting demands for more radical social and economic change.
This seemed to legitimize a political discourse that had already been deployed, to great national effect, by conservative politicians. Other critics hinted that OIC's ties to powerful corporate figures primarily served

Sullivan's own ego while pulling him away from the communities he claimed to serve.[106]

OIC's job placement rates did fluctuate with the wider economy, and cooperation with OIC never prevented companies from closing plants in inner-city neighborhoods. Nonetheless, a critique that dismisses OIC as nothing more than a complicit partner in the depredations of capitalism, or as simply an enabler of conservative rhetoric, misses the program's significance. OIC's relationships with industry served the needs of OIC at least as much as they did those of business. OIC secured technical advice at no cost, developed job placement connections, and gained access to the equipment necessary to support its activities. In addition, OIC never ceded any element of its autonomy to the business committees. Final authority remained with Sullivan and OIC's board, and both the national and local OIC boards maintained their original, community-based composition.

As such, OIC managed to take advantage of the benefits of industry participation while negotiating the dangers of co-optation. Further, Sullivan and other OIC officials maintained a realistic view of the dangers of capital mobility and tried to develop a strategy that would meet its challenges.[107] OIC's business development project (chapter 6) operated on the premise that African Americans would overcome dependence only if they combined their resources with funds from both government and sympathetic business interests to develop what Sullivan called "community capitalism." Echoing the traditions of black nationalism grounded in economic development that had been promoted a half-century earlier by Marcus Garvey, this strategy did not require separatism, but it did require control.[108] Here again, Sullivan's vision was not one of pure privatism, as the project required the support of the federal government. For all of its backing of OIC, business alone could never be fully trusted.

"A Second Postreconstruction": OIC and the New Federalism

As Lyndon Johnson's Great Society faded into Richard Nixon's New Federalism, job training programs in the United States underwent a sweeping transformation. Since the New Deal, most federal social programs had been funded through categorical grants that could be used only for narrow, federally defined purposes. Categorical grants, for example, supported Urban

Renewal, Community Action, Head Start, the Concentrated Employment Program, Model Cities, and the Special Impact Program. Recipients could be either state or local governments or privately operated programs such as OIC. In the area of job training, categorical grants facilitated the kind of experimentation that generated OIC, but also produced an unwieldy mixture of programs that resisted coordination.[109]

For reasons of both ideology and administrative efficiency, the Nixon administration sought to replace this system with a program of block grants to other levels of government. This "New Federalism" called for giving state and local governments nearly total autonomy over the use of such grants within broadly defined areas such as job training, redevelopment, education, or transportation.[110] Although OIC had long favored the elimination of the awkward tri-agency and CEP funding systems, it lobbied not for block grants but for a more focused system of categorical funding under which OIC itself would receive a single, direct federal grant to support its operations. In 1969, OIC administrators submitted a proposal for such a grant to the Department of Labor.[111]

Nixon had pledged to support OIC during the 1968 campaign, but his New Federalism proposals posed grave dangers for the program, as decentralization would subject OIC to the vagaries of local and state politics.[112] Hoping to discourage such an approach, Sullivan testified against Nixon's proposal in both the House and Senate. He found a sympathetic audience, as House Democrats offered an alternative reform bill with exactly the kind of categorical funding structure that OIC wanted. One account of Sullivan's Senate appearance concluded that "it was a very bad day for the concept of decategorization." Shortly thereafter, an amendment to the Employment and Manpower Act of 1970 named OIC as one of only a few training programs that would receive direct federal funds.[113]

Although Nixon vetoed the 1970 bill because of its public employment measures, the DOL decided that OIC's proposal for categorical funding offered a valuable opportunity for experimentation. In July 1971, it named OIC as a "prime national contractor for the delivery of manpower services" and awarded it $32.6 million for the following year. In both the size of the grant and the autonomy that OIC received in its use, the contract had little precedent in any previous funding arrangement for job training programs—or community-based organizations more generally.[114] As such, it provided a model of an urban policy structure that American liberals might have pursued on a much broader basis. In conjunction with funds that OIC received from the federal Work Incentives Program and a number of local grants, the organization as a whole had a budget of almost $50 million for 1972—"an amount far exceeding that controlled by any other predominantly black community organization."[115]

The only drawback of the prime national contract was its impermanence, as OIC's categorical status lasted for only two years. Between 1971 and 1973, debates continued in Congress over proposals for federal revenue sharing and decategorization. During this period, OIC supporters pushed for legislation to preserve an exception for OIC's categorical funding status. In both 1972 and 1973, Opportunities Industrialization Assistance Acts received some bipartisan support, and in March 1973, a silent, 5,000 person march from the Washington Monument to the Capitol conveyed support for the legislation. Nonetheless, OIC's bill stalled in Congress, and the 1973 session eventually produced new manpower legislation known as the Comprehensive Employment and Training Act (CETA). During debate over the bill, the Senate passed an amendment "to include OIC by name as a recipient of funds to deliver comprehensive manpower services." Attainment of this special categorical status, rather than outright opposition to revenue sharing, was the primary goal of OIC's lobbying strategy. This approach acknowledged that manpower reform was inevitable and sought to protect OIC without alienating the administration.[116]

The House, however, defeated a similar OIC amendment and the conference committee eliminated the measure from the final legislation. Despite OIC's popularity, the categorical funding amendment failed because it undercut CETA's core principles of decategorization and decentralization and invited comparable demands from other community-based organizations. In addition, some legislators expressed concern about OIC's capacity to manage its increasingly far-flung training system. In a compromise, the conference committee included an explanatory statement at the end of the bill that named OIC as an example of the type of community-based program that should receive support.[117]

Passed in December 1973, CETA achieved the Nixon administration's goal of decentralizing federal manpower services. Although it retained federal oversight standards, Title I of the act shifted functional control of job training programs to "local prime sponsors," which could be state or local governments or regional consortiums. Each prime sponsor appointed a manpower planning council that would formulate plans for reorganizing local manpower resources into a single, comprehensive structure that minimized duplication of services. The manpower councils then issued contracts to public or private agencies for delivery of the various service components. More than one such agency might participate in a local program, but no specific service component would be provided by more than one agency.[118]

Despite the failure of the direct OIC amendments, CETA made federal funding contingent on inclusion of local "programs of demonstrated effectiveness" and establishment of "appropriate arrangements with community-based organizations serving the poverty community." In addition, manpower councils had to include "representatives of community-based organizations and of the client community to be served." Crucially, these provisions established a category of preferred service providers that assured OIC of participation and continued funding. Without this clarification, it would also have been impossible for OIC to expand into new cities using CETA funds.[119]

Although these protections assured that CETA would not cause the collapse of OIC, the new legislation posed a serious challenge to OIC's original job-training model. CETA not only tied OIC funding to the politics of local manpower councils, but also eroded its comprehensive, "on-going" process model. Unless a manpower planning council subcontracted all program services to a local OIC center, OIC would lose control of much of the training process. In such a situation, an OIC center might provide some combination of recruitment, counseling, prevocational training, skill training, or job placement, while other agencies handled the remaining services. This made it impossible for OIC to work consistently with trainees over a continuous period of time, within a single philosophical framework, on all of the factors affecting job readiness. In 1977, OIC executive director Elton Jolly explained how CETA undercut OIC's basic principles: "We must be able to offer total services to the whole person if we are to help people. Lack of comprehensiveness hurts our accountability to people. OIC cannot hold other agencies accountable." Another OIC official argued that CETA risked the creation of "a human service assembly line." In major cities like Atlanta and Washington, D.C., this loss of comprehensive control even led to the rejection of OIC's Feeder Program as an unnecessary component of manpower training.[120]

CETA also strained OIC's no-stipends policy, as it provided minimum wage cash allowances for participants. While the no-stipends policy had a mixed and not entirely salutary effect on OIC, its loss exemplified CETA's tendency to erode OIC's defining characteristics (although a few centers including Philadelphia obtained exemptions).[121] Finally, CETA linked job training programs to local patronage politics. Many localities, for example, used their CETA funding to rehire municipal employees laid off during the recession of 1974–75. While such public employment had a place during an economic downturn, it did little to advance job training. Other abuses under CETA had no such economic justification, as in a Philadelphia case in which DOL auditors charged Mayor Frank Rizzo with using CETA funds for patronage hiring. By early 1976, a frustrated Leon Sullivan declared that "if the 1960s were the second reconstruction period…the 1970s have become a second postreconstruction—an era when hope fades under the merciless onslaught of policies of benign neglect and a revival of State's rights adding up to a strategy of a hard-line against black folk."[122]

Still, OIC as a whole actually faired relatively well under CETA: in 1975, 66 of OIC's 110 local centers provided comprehensive services; 17 provided feeder services only, and 27 provided a combination of noncomprehensive services. Although CETA shifted manpower funds from inner cities to suburban and rural areas, OIC still received almost $44 million during the first year of CETA's operation—a substantial increase over the $32 million and $23.4 million that it received in the first and second years of its previous prime national contract. In both 1974 and 1975, OIC received more federal funds under CETA than the Urban League and the Latino Service, Employment, Redevelopment program, two other prominent, community-based programs. A significant percentage of this increased funding, however, supported the CETA stipends for trainees rather than actual OIC program operation.[123]

During this early period of CETA operation, OIC's business connections became increasingly important. Local manpower councils often responded positively to direct lobbying by OIC's business allies because such connections offered the promise of successful job placements.[124] In Washington, however, the limitations of such influence became apparent in 1976 when Pennsylvania senator Richard Schweiker introduced legislation to restore OIC's categorical funding status and link the program directly to federal job creation and economic development initiatives. As proposed, the "Opportunities Industrialization Centers Job Creation and Training Act" would have authorized OIC to actively create jobs for the hard-core unemployed, as well as "to train such individuals to make the transition to permanent employment." The legislation established an official goal of creating one million new jobs in four years and filling them with individuals trained by OIC; federal, state, and local agencies would be required to give OIC efforts "special consideration" as they developed their own programs. Faced with opposition from other community-based organizations (CBOs) that objected to the act's exclusive support for OIC, as well as from inflation hawks, Schweiker accepted an amendment that broadened the bill to cover other established community-based training programs.[125]

The OIC-CBO job creation legislation was part of a renewed public debate during the mid-1970s about full employment policy. This discussion centered on the Humphrey-Hawkins employment bills proposed between 1974 and 1978. When finally passed in 1978, Humphrey-Hawkins had been stripped of substantive elements that would have forced the federal government to implement aggressive full employment policies. Earlier versions of the bill, however, had proposed the use of public service, public works, and private sector jobs programs to reduce unemployment from the nearly 8 percent rate of 1975–76 to 3 percent—and had officially designated the federal government as the employer of last resort. In its most ambitious form, the employment creation measures of Humphrey-Hawkins thus resurrected the "social Keynesianism" abandoned by the Council of Economic Advisors under presidents Kennedy and Johnson and returned to the basic tenets of the "security" liberalism embodied in the 1945 full employment bill.[126]

OIC offered unequivocal support for this national resurgence of a structurally oriented form of American liberalism. In December 1975, Sullivan told a congressional conference on full employment policy, "we believe that the committed goal of this country for both the President and Congress must be a policy of full employment and to commit the resources to meet that goal." Invoking the still fresh memory of the urban unrest of the 1960s—a tactic he never hesitated to deploy—the OIC leader warned that without such a "move towards a policy of full employment, we are going to see insurrections in the cities of this country that are going to make the riots of a few years ago look like little church meetings." The Schweiker OIC-CBO legislation thus formed a supplement to Humphrey-Hawkins, particularly in its suggestion that OIC engage in direct job creation as well as training. Although it gained support with the wider CBO coverage, the bill nonetheless died in committee, leaving yet another road toward coordinated industrial and employment policy untaken.[127]

The failure of the OIC-CBO job creation bill marked the start of a period in which OIC's capacity to navigate CETA politics masked increasingly serious internal weaknesses. The organization's leadership, many of whom were Philadelphia-based ministers who had worked with Sullivan since the Selective Patronage campaigns, generally lacked the managerial expertise to run a program of OIC's scope. The New Federalism only exacerbated this problem, as CETA's emphasis on local control reversed a process of internal centralization that had begun under OIC's prime contract. CETA expanded the autonomy of local affiliates, limited the role of the OIC national administration, and increased the affiliates' dependence on local governments—as the OIC national office did not control the distribution of CETA funds. These changes drastically diminished OIC's ability to enforce uniform national standards for the program. As a result, some OIC branches deteriorated. In San Francisco, Michigan, and Connecticut, local CETA prime sponsors dropped OIC affiliates from their programs because of management incompetence and ineffective or even nonexistent training.[128] By the early 1980s, such problems would threaten the viability of the entire OIC experiment.

Social policy under the Nixon administration represented less a rejection of government engagement in urban problems than a reordering of federalist arrangements between local, state, and federal governments. Nixon opposed the community empowerment strategies of the War on Poverty, and his policies shifted resources in ways that built Republican strength in the South and in suburbs. His administration, however, neither reduced the size of the national state nor engaged in the sweeping anti-government attacks that would be carried out by his more conservative successors. Instead, Nixon pursued a combination of partisan political advantage, governmental efficiency, and expanded local and state policy autonomy.[129] This new autonomy primarily benefited governmental and quasi-public bodies. PIDC, for example, found that the new block grant structure provided important advantages over the old categorical system (chapter 8).

In contrast, community-based organizations such as OIC experienced a significant decrease in flexibility under the New Federalism. In the absence of rigorous local planning in the manner of the National Resources

Planning Board, OIC would have been better served by a structure that provided direct federal grants with little or no intervention by local governmental authorities. OEO's Special Impact Program provided a model for such a system. OIC's work could still have been coordinated with other aspects of local industrial and employment policy, but the program would not have been subject to the loss of administrative and programmatic control that it experienced under CETA. In the actual case of OIC and CETA, however, the key conclusion that can be drawn from this "Nixonian liberalism" is that community-based organizations require direct access to federal financial resources and relative operational autonomy. With its emphasis on local government rather than CBOs, the New Federalism failed to recognize this point.

More broadly, OIC's fundamental insight consisted of the recognition that by emphasizing traditional American discourses of self-reliance and opportunity, liberalism could access significant government and corporate support while still pursuing civil rights activism. When combined with remedial education and counseling, the application of these themes in OIC's innovative Feeder Program helped to prepare disadvantaged and frustrated inner-city residents for the difficulties they would face in skills courses and the workplace. In combination with OIC's "job-ready" training approach, the philosophy provided a basis for appealing to employers to hire OIC graduates on both the moral grounds of civil rights and the pragmatic grounds of self-interest. As such, OIC effectively challenged the wider community, both local and national, to live up to its own ideals and rhetoric.[130] What Leon Sullivan and his associates accomplished was the construction of an effective and viable form of community-based local employment policy—a job-oriented, community-based response to the problems of poverty, discrimination, and deindustrialization in postwar Philadelphia that reshaped older strands of structural, job-oriented liberalism and adapted it for the needs and politics of the 1960s and 1970s. Drawing on the state yet remaining autonomous from it, Sullivan's pragmatic reformulation of American liberalism succeeded, for a time, within the framework to which it was applied. Few other War on Poverty programs, and none in Philadelphia, accomplished so much.

The development of OIC shows that the War on Poverty had the greatest positive effect when it focused on concrete dimensions of the problem of jobs and provided direct, categorical funding for pragmatic, community-based programs. It also suggests a broader conclusion: that the War on Poverty cannot be fully assessed by looking only at formal community action agencies; instead, it is crucial to examine the programs that such agencies funded as autonomous sites of political action, community mobilization, and most important, policy innovation. Much of the War on Poverty's significance rests in the history of such implementation agencies.

CHAPTER SIX

"We had to create jobs": The OIC-Progress Movement and Community Capitalism

In the aftermath of Martin Luther King Jr.'s assassination on April 4, 1968, massive rebellions in urban areas around the United States thrust the racial and economic problems of American cities back into the national consciousness. During the Oregon and Indiana presidential primary campaigns a few weeks later, Republican candidate Richard M. Nixon addressed the crisis in a two-part speech on NBC radio. These "Bridges to Human Dignity" speeches, as the Nixon campaign described them, differed from the "law-and-order" appeals that typified the former vice president's 1968 campaign. Nixon outlined a program of "black capitalism" as a potential solution to the problems of inner-city African American communities. The proposal included federal tax credits for companies that established branches in high poverty areas, a special bank to provide loans for businesses in such areas, the extension of special Small Business Administration (SBA) loan programs to these companies, and training programs for minority entrepreneurs. More broadly, Nixon emphasized that regardless of race, human rights ultimately depended on access to property and economic power: "To have human rights, people need property rights...the economic power that comes from ownership, and the security and independence that comes from economic power.... What most of the militants are asking is to be included as owners, as entrepreneurs, to have a share of the wealth and a piece of the action. And this is precisely what the central target of the new approach ought to be. It ought to be oriented toward more black ownership, for from this can flow the rest—black pride, black jobs, black opportunity and, yes, black power, in the best, the constructive sense of that often misapplied term."[1] Nixon's narrow victory in the 1968 election, however, depended far more on his appeals to the anxieties and resentments of suburban whites than on his Bridges to Human Dignity speeches. The priorities of the new administration reflected this political reality. Significant resources for black capitalism never materialized, and at least at the federal level, the concept never became a central focus of American urban policy.[2]

National contours of public policy, though, do not always define the limits of policy influence across multiple levels of the American state. In Philadelphia, black capitalism followed a different and more important course. During the early and mid-1960s, community activists, city officials, and business leaders became increasingly concerned about the weakness of the city's African American business community. In 1964, a study by the Drexel Institute of Technology revealed that while blacks owned 4,242 businesses in Philadelphia (9 percent of the city's total), only thirteen of these were in manufacturing and only fourteen were in wholesaling. Further, eight of the manufacturers and eight of the wholesalers were either "producers or distributors of beauty products." Hairdressers, barbershops, and restaurants, almost all of them small and "extremely marginal in profit-making, stability and physical conditions," accounted for 46.5 percent of the remaining black-owned businesses in the city. In economic sectors other than manufacturing and wholesaling, only ten black-owned firms had annual revenues of more than $100,000. In predominately African American North Philadelphia, black-owned firms operated only in the retail or personal services fields. Even in black neighborhoods, however, 60 percent of all businesses had white ownership.[3] These grim statistics led both black and white observers to conclude that some form of black economic development was essential to improving the social, economic, and political status of African American Philadelphians.

When the black capitalism concept attained national prominence during the 1968 presidential campaign, "on-the-ground" efforts in this area had thus been underway in Philadelphia's African American community for more than five years. These initiatives ranged from bank lending programs to community-based development projects, all aimed at minority entrepreneurs, and all of which developed despite the federal War on Poverty's general inattention to issues of employment and economic development.[4] The OIC-based Progress Movement, however, proved to be the largest and most significant of Philadelphia's black capitalism initiatives. An effort to develop black-owned manufacturing and commercial businesses, the Progress Movement added an industrial policy component to the community-based employment policy of OIC—and produced far more substantive achievements than the black capitalism programs of the Nixon administration.

The Progress Movement's black-owned businesses varied in their viability, but their existence and partial success demonstrates once again the vibrancy of liberal responses to the problem of jobs in Philadelphia after World War II. As with PIDC and OIC, the best Progress Movement programs contained elements of promise that, if fully developed and adequately supported, might have provided the foundation for a comprehensive institutional response to Philadelphia's postwar economic crisis. Also like PIDC and OIC, the Progress Movement's community capitalism strategy remained constrained by Philadelphia's racially defined, parallel tracks of local economic policy and by the federal government's unwillingness to support job creation as a central component of American urban policy. Although the Progress Movement narrowed the racial divide, it could not create a comprehensive strategy that could draw together local economic policy, or much less, alter federal urban policy or the economic and racial incentive structures that underlay capital mobility. Further, by the 1970s, the quixotic nature of federal policy created new dilemmas for the overall OIC–Progress Movement, as major shifts in the structure of American federalism, followed by significant funding cuts, undermined program quality and reduced available resources even as the national economy weakened. In combination with serious management problems created by the rapid expansion of the 1960s and 1970s, these changes left the OIC–Progress Movement in a dramatically weakened position, with its promise for American cities and for American liberalism largely unfulfilled.

Leon Sullivan and the Progress Movement

The planners of the federal anti-poverty program had assumed that in a high-growth macroeconomic environment, job training could reduce poverty by improving the individual skills and behavioral characteristics of the poor without addressing the racial and spatial imbalances of the wider economy. OIC itself initially embraced this nonstructural orientation. Even its name unintentionally linked the program to the leading sociological idea—opportunity theory—that undergirded the War on Poverty. Although OIC quickly emerged as a model War on Poverty program, Sullivan and other OIC officials became concerned about the limitations of this approach. Increasingly, they recognized that job skills alone would be insufficient to address the employment problems of urban African Americans. Even with improved skills, African Americans remained dependent on the success of macroeconomic policy and the beneficence of white employers. Faced with the harsh realities of ongoing racial discrimination, limited African American control of capital, and Philadelphia's loss of industry, OIC soon rejected the underlying Keynesian assumptions of postwar manpower policy and moved into the field of direct economic development. As Sullivan later explained, "it was not enough merely to *get* jobs. We had to *create* jobs."[5]

Known alternately as the "10–36 Plan" and the "Progress Movement," Sullivan's inner-city economic development program operated from a base of cooperative community investment—what the minister and his allies referred to as "community capitalism"—and grew to include housing projects, commercial developments, and manufacturing firms, as well as nonprofit business training and social service projects. Sullivan had realized that job training constituted only a first step in resolving the economic problems of black Philadelphians, as it neither eliminated African Americans' economic dependence nor reduced their vulnerability. Despite the gains of the civil rights movement, Sullivan maintained, African Americans still had only a "tissue-paper middle class." The cooperative, communal use of what capital the community had, he believed, offered both a possible solution to this problem and a logical extension of the self-help principles of OIC.[6]

Where OIC had operated as a nominally multiracial program, the Progress Movement focused explicitly on the economic needs of African Americans. Unlike civil rights leaders such as CORE's Roy Innis, however, Sullivan rejected racial separatism as the goal of black economic development. In his 1969 autobiography, he argued that "the aim is to keep some of the money at home instead of seeing it all flow out, week after week, into the suburbs, making the wealthy wealthier from the earnings of black folks. This does not mean the creation of a black economy or black nationalization. The realities of economic development in a world going to the moon preclude such intentions, however much we might hope that it could be done." Instead, he continued, blacks had to become simultaneously "self-dependent" and "partners" with whites in controlling the economic system.[7]

The Progress Movement thus sought to achieve racial and social equality, economic integration, and African American self-determination by reducing or even eliminating racially based relationships of economic dependence. Although this approach transcended the narrower goals of OIC, Sullivan's economic development program relied on a strategy similar to that of the job-training program: use the community's resources to establish a base and then call the bluff of white society by accepting its values while demanding the public and private resources necessary to achieve significant social and economic effects. "I believe in the free enterprise system," explained Sullivan in 1971, "but I work *on* that system to get out of it what I can for black people."[8]

The origins of this community capitalism program actually emerged even before the selective patronage campaigns ended. Faced with the dilemma of how to address community economic needs that could not be met solely through a reduction in overt hiring discrimination, Sullivan developed a plan through which limited individual financial resources could be pooled into a significant communal capital base. On June 15, 1962, Sullivan drew on the biblical account of Jesus feeding 5,000 followers with five loaves and two fish as he urged his Zion Baptist congregation to join him in what he called a "10-36-50" plan. Under this plan, fifty Zion Baptist members would contribute $10 a month to a cooperative investment pool for thirty-six months. The money raised during the first sixteen months would go into a trust for scholarships and other community needs, while the funds collected through the remainder would be used to establish new, communally owned, for-profit businesses. At the end of the thirty-six months, members would receive a share of common stock in the enterprise. The response of the congregation far exceeded Sullivan's goal: 227 members joined, and "50" was dropped from the program's name. By 1968, the 10-36 Plan had nearly 4,000 members, with another 10,000 people on a waiting list. By 1977, the plan had raised more than $2.9 million.[9]

During its first three years, the 10-36 Plan operated as a savings program, focusing on the collection of capital rather than on economic development projects. In 1965, the board of directors established Zion Investment Associates (ZIA), which managed all for-profit activities of the Progress Movement. In 1966, ZIA created the Zion Non-Profit Charitable

Trust, which oversaw all nonprofit projects and operated on a tax-exempt basis.[10] As they developed these institutional elements of the plan, Sullivan and his associates launched the new program with vigor. When a landlord refused to rent an apartment to a black couple from Sullivan's congregation, 10-36 Plan members decided to purchase the entire building. Within a week, ZIA acquired the eight-unit building for $75,000. Four years later, in response to an interviewer's query about whether the new landlords evicted the white tenants of the building, Sullivan responded, "No, but we put a whole lot more colored folks in there." The purchase of the apartment building not only presented an opportunity for integration, but also provided a source of revenue that supported the movement's other projects.[11]

With the prospect of access to almost $250,000 upon fulfillment of the 10-36 subscriptions, Sullivan and the other directors of the Progress Movement began to consider a range of possible development projects. A few months after the acquisition of the apartment building, Zion Non-Profit began construction on a new, ninety-six-unit apartment complex in lower North Philadelphia known as Zion Gardens. Built on previously cleared land in the Southwest Temple Urban Renewal Area, the $1-million apartment complex was financed using a combination of 10-36 funds and low-cost private loans guaranteed through a new effort by the Department of Housing and Urban Development to encourage construction of middle-income housing by nonprofit groups. Completed in 1966, Zion Gardens became the first African American–owned apartment complex in Philadelphia. It achieved full occupancy within a year. As with the smaller apartment building, Zion Gardens provided a dependable income stream for the Progress Movement while expanding the supply of affordable housing.[12]

Sullivan and his associates next sought to expand the 10-36 Plan's activities into the commercial sphere. Throughout 1967, they worked to secure financing, land, and tenants for a new shopping center in the North Philadelphia area. Late in the year, ZIA began construction on the $1.9 million Progress Plaza Shopping Center at the corner of Broad and Oxford Streets, also in the Southwest Temple Urban Renewal Area. Upon its opening in October 1968, Progress Plaza became "the first major black-owned, black-developed and black-managed shopping center in the nation."[13]

The Progress Plaza project required that ZIA make a number of significant compromises. As it did with the Zion Gardens project a few blocks away, ZIA built Progress Plaza on land already cleared through urban renewal. Such clearance projects imposed heavy costs on black communities

FIGURE 23. Vista of the OIC Progress Movement's Progress Plaza Shopping Center, with the North Philadelphia skyline of housing towers and loft factories behind it and a lot cleared under urban renewal beside it, December 11, 1969. The Benjamin Franklin Bridge over the Delaware River is visible in the distance. The center had opened in October 1968. Photo courtesy of Temple University Libraries, Urban Archives, Philadelphia, Pennsylvania.

by destroying homes and businesses and by increasing crowding in adjoining neighborhoods. Yet by the time that planning for Progress Plaza and Zion Gardens began, clearance had already been completed in the Southwest Temple Urban Renewal Area. The two projects thus put vacant land back into use while giving African Americans control of the new developments—and much of the profits. In addition, the apartments supplied new housing and the shopping center provided badly needed commercial services for the surrounding community. To Sullivan and his advisors, a refusal to use the land as an act of defiance against urban renewal would have been counterproductive.[14]

ZIA also had to compromise its initial goal of including only black-owned businesses. In order to supplement the 10-36 funds with private financing, ZIA worked with the First Pennsylvania Banking and Trust

Company, a Philadelphia bank that had developed a series of loan programs aimed at African American businesses. Before it would commit to the Progress Plaza development, First Pennsylvania required that ZIA secure leases from large chain stores that would serve as anchors for the center. ZIA attracted an A&P Supermarket, a Bell Telephone office, a Marriott restaurant, a Florsheim shoe store, and branch offices of Pennsylvania Savings Fund Society (PSFS), the black-owned North Carolina Mutual Life Insurance Company, and First Pennsylvania itself.[15]

Inclusion of the chain stores provided a number of benefits. First, ZIA negotiated agreements with each company specifying that the individual stores would have black management and a majority of black employees. In addition, each chain tenant agreed to contribute a percentage of gross profits above a specified amount to the 10-36 program. ZIA used income from the chain leases to provide rental subsidies for the black-owned businesses in Progress Plaza.[16] Second, A&P was the first large supermarket in the North Philadelphia area, and while its presence threatened small neighborhood groceries, many of which were actually owned by nonresidents, the store offered locals lower prices and a wider range of foods. Third, the chain stores attracted customers to Progress Plaza, which provided support for the ten black-owned stores in the center. Finally, the ability to attract such tenants provided ZIA and the Progress Movement with legitimacy in the wider business community. The twenty-year, million-dollar A&P lease, for example, was the largest such contract ever concluded by a black-owned organization.[17]

In operation, Progress Plaza produced a mixed record of successes and setbacks, which typified the challenges that faced the Progress Movement's community-based economic development strategy. The shopping center achieved full occupancy almost immediately and attracted a solid base of customers. With Temple University just two blocks to the north, white customers made up 35 percent of the center's clientele.[18] Still, Progress Plaza as a whole struggled to attain profitability during its early years of operation. While difficulties were concentrated among the smaller stores, the larger chain tenants also failed to attain the levels of sales revenue necessary to trigger the supplementary rent provisions in their leases.[19] Eventually, however, ZIA managed to remedy these issues by replacing the weaker stores and gradually expanding the center's customer base. By 1974, the A&P store ranked as one of the chain's top five grocery stores in the Delaware Valley region. Despite the failure of some of the smaller stores,

FIGURE 24. Pharmacist George B. Lees in his Progress Plaza drug store, October 17, 1969. Photo courtesy of Temple University Libraries, Urban Archives, Philadelphia, Pennsylvania.

ZIA consistently maintained nine or ten black-owned stores at Progress Plaza, and the shopping center as a whole employed 150 people. As this stabilization took place, Progress Plaza gradually began to return positive net profits for ZIA. By the late 1970s, its value rose to almost $3 million. By 1975, ZIA ended its rent subsidization program.[20]

Community Capitalism and Manufacturing

The opening of Zion Gardens and Progress Plaza provided dramatic examples of the Progress Movement's capacity to conceive and implement significant development projects. Sullivan and his associates soon sought to build on this early momentum by extending their activities beyond housing and retail and into economic sectors where blacks in Philadelphia had little presence. One set of programs provided entrepreneurial training and business counseling for inner-city residents. Another channeled federal loans to minority-owned businesses through a nonprofit venture capital corporation. This latter program received financial support from the federal Economic Development Administration, the Small Business

Administration, the Office of Economic Opportunity, and the Office of Minority Business Enterprise, as well as from the Ford Foundation.[21]

The most important of the progress movement initiatives, however, pursued the direct development of manufacturing firms. In considering manufacturing fields to enter, Sullivan and his advisors sought sectors that would create employment to counter inner-city job losses. They also evaluated options in terms of public prominence, prestige, and market opportunities, and sought ventures that would challenge preconceived notions about African American business capabilities. In light of the ongoing American space effort, Sullivan soon focused on creating an aerospace company. "When the first landing on the moon came," he later explained, "I wanted something there that a black man had made."[22]

In April 1968, amidst the uncertainty that followed the King assassination, Sullivan arranged a breakfast meeting with Mark Morton, the vice president of General Electric's Missile and Space Division in Valley Forge, Pennsylvania, who had previously provided equipment for OIC's training programs. At the meeting, Sullivan casually asked Morton "What do you need to start an aerospace company?" and then asked the startled executive for GE's assistance in creating such a company.[23] Although the request "took him slightly aback," Morton presented Sullivan's idea to other GE executives and gained the corporation's support. Sullivan's timing in making the proposal during the same month as the King assassination and Nixon's Bridges to Human Dignity speeches may have played a fortuitous part in GE's decision. Whatever the motivation, Morton quickly arranged for the preparation of reports that explained the requirements for starting an aerospace enterprise.

Among the GE employees who participated in this planning project was Benjamin W. Sallard, a thirty-nine-year-old African American production manager. Shortly after receiving Morton's reports, Sullivan hired Sallard as the general manager of the prospective company. Other GE employees, all but one of them African American, were hired to fill out the new company's management and technical staff. In May 1968, ZIA incorporated the company under the name Progress Aerospace Enterprises (PAE), and on June 26, Sullivan unveiled plans for the venture at a meeting of 10-36 shareholders. As it had with Progress Plaza, First Pennsylvania Banking and Trust provided financing for the new company. Initially, PAE operated out of Sallard's basement, but on July 15, the company moved into an abandoned factory on Windrim Avenue in North Philadelphia.[24]

Along with management personnel and continuing technical support, GE also provided PAE with an initial $2,575,000 contract to produce sub-components for the space program. In its reliance on extensive technical and financial assistance from corporate backers, PAE thus added private corporate resources to the public and philanthropic sources on which the Progress Movement drew for its entrepreneurial training programs. With this foundation in place, PAE attracted additional contracts from NASA for cables and shielding and from the U.S. Air Force for ground support interfaces and helicopter engine harnesses. Seeking to begin production as rapidly as possible, PAE also implemented crash-training programs both at its own plant and at GE's Valley Forge facility. This training provided employees, many of whom were recruited from OIC, with industry-wide proficiency certification. Job Opportunities in the Business Sector (JOBS), a joint project of the U.S. Department of Labor and the National Alliance of Businessmen, funded the program through a $522,000 contract under which PAE agreed "to train 100 hardcore 'unemployables.'" Training and job development had begun to come together.[25]

Production began shortly after PAE moved into the Windrim Avenue plant, and the company delivered its first completed sub-components to GE in August, barely four months after the initial meeting between Sullivan and Morton. Late in 1968, Sullivan described the new venture as both an example of African American economic development and as an extension of civil rights–based demands for opportunity. PAE, he argued, represented "a new direction that will help people get from outside the door of free enterprise to the inside.... all we want is the opportunity to prove that we can do this highly complex work like anyone else." Between August 1968 and the spring of 1970, PAE received additional contracts from Boeing, Philco-Ford, and Westinghouse. Meanwhile, the company's employment rose from fourteen in July 1968 to fifty-four in November 1968 and to one hundred and seven in February 1970. Most of these positions required relatively high skill levels and many employees came from the OIC job training programs.[26] The OIC–Progress Movement's ability to create such jobs and fill them with African Americans trained in the same institutional framework represented an unprecedented achievement in Philadelphia's postwar economic development and manpower policies.

Although the rapid start-up of PAE would have been impressive by itself, the aerospace business was only the first of two companies that ZIA founded during the summer of 1968. At the same time that it incorporated

PAE, ZIA also formed the Progress Garment Manufacturing Company (PGM) as a new entrant in the venerable Philadelphia apparel industry. Sullivan explained that the garment company would balance PAE's work in a high-technology field with a business that required lower skill levels and, theoretically, lower risk.[27] Like PAE, PGM relied on close relationships with large, established firms. In particular, PGM received direct assistance from the Villager Corporation, one of the largest women's clothing labels in the United States. Villager not only "took our black management into their shops to learn the whole garment-manufacturing process" but also provided the new company with subcontracts to produce garments under its label. In addition, the Singer Corporation provided sophisticated sewing, cutting, and pressing equipment, and the International Ladies Garment Workers Union offered technical assistance in setting up PGM's production lines. As with the aerospace company, many of PGM's workers came from OIC.[28]

Operating out of the same Windrim Avenue plant as PAE, PGM began production with sixteen workers on August 5, 1968; the facility offered air-conditioned, well-lit working conditions that exceeded the generally low standards prevalent in the garment industry. Although Villager remained PGM's largest customer, the company also secured contracts with a number of other companies, including Sears Roebuck. Throughout 1969 and into 1970, PGM produced women's skirts for the department store and catalog giant. Late in 1968, PGM even introduced its own line of women's clothing under the label "10-36 Fashions." By early 1970, PGM employed fifty workers and could produce up to 4,000 items of clothing per week.[29]

In February 1970, in the aftermath of the apparently successful start-ups of PAE and PGM, ZIA president Carl L. Hairston launched a chain of inner-city convenience stores known as Our Markets, which offered affordable foods in inner-city areas "deserted by other stores." A $200,000 loan from the Ford Foundation financed the project.[30] At the opening of the first store at 17th and Venango streets, Sullivan cut a ribbon stretched across the front door, made the first purchase, and, in a statement that neatly summarized the quasi-religious, communal capitalism on which the Progress Movement was based, told the crowd that "with God's help we shall open many more ... all wealth to the people." By the spring of 1971, ZIA had opened four Our Markets stores in neighborhoods around the city, each of which operated in a new, specially constructed building and employed African American management and staff. In December 1971,

ZIA's five-year operating plan suggested that the company would open as many as twenty-three new Our Markets by January 1975.[31] Also in 1970, ZIA organized the Progress Construction Company, which it hoped would enter the building industry through a series of joint ventures with existing firms. This strategy proved unrealistic. An initial contract to build a new eight-story office building was abandoned, and the only project that Progress Construction actually completed was a joint venture to rebuild Sullivan's Zion Baptist Church, which was destroyed by a suspicious fire in November 1970.[32]

The OIC–Progress Movement was not alone in its community development efforts in the United States in the late 1960s. Brooklyn's Bedford-Stuyvesant Restoration Corporation, which received support from OEO's Special Impact Program, employed community residents in housing renovation and park construction projects, funded cultural organizations, and invested in more than forty businesses. Cleveland's Hough Area Development Corporation was organized to oversee federal reconstruction funds following six days of violent rebellions in the city's Hough neighborhood. Using an OEO grant and support from the city's African American mayor, Carl Stokes, the Hough group developed housing and a shopping center and opened a factory. After the 1967 rebellions in Newark, Catholic priest William Lindert founded the New Communities Corporation, which undertook similar projects and offered social services. It operated from an explicitly religious basis. Like the Bedford-Stuyvesant Restoration Corporation, it remains in operation today.[33]

A different approach emerged in Oakland. African American activists organized the Justice on BART (JOBART) coalition to fight for jobs for African Americans on the massive project to build the Bay Area Rapid Transit system. They achieved some success, although most of the positions were for unskilled laborers. An even more ambitious initiative emerged when Percy Moore of the Oakland Economic Development Council Incorporated (an offshoot of Oakland's official War on Poverty program), demanded that specific jobs in Oakland companies be reserved exclusively for city residents alone. Moore's claims for community control over job distribution in the private sector met with complete resistance from business and from local, state, and federal officials. These efforts illustrated the limitations of radical, protest-based approaches to the problem of jobs. Soon, however, the OIC–Progress Movement and other CDCs would highlight the equally powerful constraints that faced African American liberals struggling with the same issues.[34]

* * *

In combination with OIC's established reputation, the rapid expansion of the Progress Movement's economic development projects further enhanced Sullivan's image as a pragmatic and effective leader. In January 1971, General Motors asked him to become the first African American member of its board of directors. In a congratulatory phone call to Sullivan, Lyndon Johnson quipped that "now what's good for General Motors really is good for America."[35] In the years that followed, Sullivan emerged as an independent and sometimes controversial voice on the GM board, pushing the automaker to hire minorities, increase African American ownership of its dealerships, and reform its practices in apartheid South Africa. The latter effort led to the minister's formulation of the "Sullivan Principles," which articulated nondiscrimination and human rights standards for companies operating in South Africa.[36] Sullivan's work on the apartheid problem reflected his own increased interest in the African continent, which he pursued in part through the introduction of the OIC program in African countries such as Nigeria, Ghana, Ethiopia, and Kenya. Although the Sullivan Principles represented one of the first anti-apartheid actions within the corporate sector, they drew criticism from activists who called for *total* disinvestment from the country.[37]

During the early 1970s, however, Sullivan's prominence obscured serious problems within the Progress Movement enterprises. Despite rapid growth, the actual viability of the business initiatives remained uncertain. In part, both ZIA and Zion Non-Profit had simply expanded too quickly, often into areas where they had little expertise. In 1980, Sullivan explained that "I thought I could develop business[es] fast. I thought if I could get the resources, I could make those businesses successful . . . I was naïve." Ira Wells, ZIA's legal counsel, recalled that "we started Progress Aerospace with all good intentions . . . Rev. Sullivan is a fantastic man, but when he started that company . . . he didn't have any idea what he was doing—none of us did."[38] The result was that all ZIA enterprises struggled to become profitable. The first major crisis occurred in early 1970 when Villager ended its contract with the Progress Garment Manufacturing Company (PGM) during a slowdown in the apparel industry. Faced with the loss of this "prime customer and consultant" and unable to secure additional contracts, ZIA suspended work at PGM in May 1970. In November, ZIA treasurer William Downes informed the Philadelphia Apparel Producers Association that the company would eventually reopen, but "as of this date we do not know when."[39]

Production finally resumed in March 1971 after PGM received subcontracts from two large apparel firms. Later in the year, it added a contract with the Girl Scouts of America for blouse production. But the garment operation had difficulty attracting skilled workers and struggled with low productivity. Meanwhile, the number and size of PGM's contracts remained too small to produce adequate levels of revenue, and ZIA officials began to consider moving the subsidiary into other lines of business.[40] By the fall of 1971, they decided that the company would enter the commercial electronics field. While there was little skill overlap with garment production, the field had some similarity with PAE's operation. As a result, PGM's new area of work increased the overall coherence of ZIA's business plan. Shortly after the move into electronics, PGM won contracts from Delco and IBM for "single lead production" and, on a significantly larger scale, from General Motors to build electrical harnesses for buses and passenger coaches. The latter contract was probably a consequence of Sullivan's position on the GM board. Subsequently, because of the garment operation's continuing losses and production problems, ZIA permanently closed the garment line and changed the subsidiary's name to Progress Products Company (PPC). By the end of 1972, the General Motors contract accounted for all of PPC's work.[41]

Meanwhile, Progress Aerospace faced a different set of problems. The company accepted new contracts from Litton Industries, Minneapolis Honeywell, Philco-Ford, United Aircraft, and Western Electric, as well as from the Federal Aviation Administration and the U.S. Army, Navy, Air Force, and Coast Guard. By 1972, its products included amplification equipment, electronic modules, printed circuit board assemblies, radio channel control equipment, electrical test equipment, mine test sets, and wire harnesses. In addition, as it developed an increasingly sophisticated range of capabilities, PAE undertook work on complete electrical systems as well as sub-components.[42] To accommodate the increased workload, PAE and the other ZIA subsidiaries moved into a larger industrial complex in Upper North Philadelphia's Nicetown neighborhood in 1972. Despite its growth and variety of customers, however, the company remained dependent on contracts from GE and the federal government. During 1972, 78 percent of PAE's work could be traced to GE and 94 percent originated, "directly or indirectly," from federal sources.[43] The importance of these relationships meant that PAE would be vulnerable to demand fluctuations from either source. In addition, many of the government contracts produced revenues that barely covered production costs.[44] Finally, many of PAE's contracts from both private companies and the government involved defense production. This created a distinctly ironic relation between the intended and actual nature of the company. PAE had been created to improve the economic fortunes and capacities of African Americans as it "integrated," in Leon Sullivan's words, "the race to the moon." In reality, however, the company primarily became a military contractor building weapon systems for a war in which young black men served and died in disproportionate numbers. This tension exemplified the dilemmas at the core of "black capitalism": could African Americans claim a significant place in American capitalism without becoming complicit in the damage that the wider political economic system, at its worst, inflicted on poor and minority communities? In this case, the answer did not seem encouraging.

At a level of lesser ethical consequence, PAE struggled with mundane dilemmas common to many small companies. For all of its growth and technical proficiency, PAE failed to become profitable. Suffering from cost overruns, excessive overhead, production difficulties, and problems in meeting delivery schedules, the company reported losses of $279,885 in 1972 alone.[45] In the face of such losses, as well as those sustained at PGM, ZIA's overall financial situation became increasingly untenable. Nor were these financial problems limited to the manufacturing companies. Our Markets proved to be a disappointment. The stores struggled with high rates of turnover in personnel, failed "to attract good management talent at the store manager level," and suffered from aggressive competition by larger grocery stores that reduced prices to match or undersell Our Markets.[46] Such competition benefited inner-city consumers, but the store chain lost $67,000 during the first nine months of 1971 and $167,395 in 1972. Collectively, ZIA lost more than $2.3 million between 1968 and 1972, culminating in a record loss of $840,298 in 1972.[47] A GE executive who had worked closely with ZIA later recalled that the company had been on the brink of bankruptcy at least four times, and that once, GE made a contract payment early so that PAE could pay its employees on schedule.[48]

These difficulties eventually affected the 10-36 Plan itself. In order to register a nationwide stock offering with the SEC, the plan was forced to make a recision offer to reimburse dissatisfied stockholders. By 1975, 349 10-36 Plan stockholders accepted the offer and withdrew $50,860 from the Progress Movement.[49] The new prospectus included a lengthy list of the risk factors associated with the 10-36 Plan, including low profitability of existing operations, "emphasis on social needs of [the] minority commu-nity," competition from more experienced companies, dependence on "a few large customers," non-refundability of contributions and stock sub-scriptions, and the centrality of Sullivan's personal leadership. For the first time, the new stock subscription failed to sell out, although it did raise over $2 million to fund ZIA's operations.[50]

During this period, ZIA also experienced conflict with its labor force. On April 13, 1973, employees at Progress Aerospace and Progress Prod-ucts voted to join Teamsters Union Local 929. Contract negotiations be-tween ZIA and Local 929 soon broke down, leading to a three-week strike at PAE. Although ZIA's annual report noted that the company "was still able to meet substantially the production requirements of its major cus-tomer, the General Electric Company," ZIA nonetheless reached a set-tlement that granted significant hourly wage increases to workers at both PAE and PPC. The strike, however, did not initiate an extended pattern of conflict, and by 1975, ZIA noted that "relations with Local 929 . . . have never been better."[51]

By the time of the strike, a complete restructuring of the entire ZIA or-ganization had begun. Initially, ZIA's board hesitated to take such a step, suggesting in October 1971 that stockholder concerns could be allayed through publication of "a special brochure" highlighting the company's strengths, the "human benefits" it created, and the "positive trends" in its prospects.[52] A year later, however, it had become clear that while the project had produced social benefits, ZIA could no longer demonstrate the existence of any positive trends. As a result, the company imple-mented a rapid series of changes. Along with the withdrawal of PPC from garment production in 1972, ZIA president Hairston "realigned" the company's management on the basis of a yearlong review by executives from General Motors and General Electric. The company also closed an unprofitable appliance store that it had operated in Progress Plaza and reorganized its entrepreneurial development and training programs.[53]

After these changes, Hairston confidently wrote that "we believe the worst is largely behind us."[54] ZIA's overall sales revenue did increase throughout 1971 and 1972, but the company's losses only mounted pro-portionally. As a result, more sweeping changes ensued during late 1972 and early 1973. ZIA laid off workers, and total employment fell from 360 to 225 between December 1972 and April 1973. The layoffs saved ZIA $415,000, but also demonstrated that a combination of macroeconomic cycles and poor management decisions could constrain any form of urban economic development, regardless of its social purpose. In addition, ZIA closed its unprofitable Our Markets during the winter of 1973.[55]

Finally, in April 1973, ZIA implemented a second, more thorough reorganization of its management team when Frederick Miller replaced Hairston as company president. Miller, a former teacher and long-time Sullivan associate who had developed OIC's Feeder Program and overseen OIC's national expansion, restructured ZIA "to operate as a traditional entrepreneurship with a strong professional chief executive." This meant that Miller implemented a centralized decision-making structure in which final authority rested with top ZIA executives, rather than with the in-plant management of the subsidiaries. He also reduced the size of the company's highly paid management staff and took steps to control costs by introducing "more efficient systems for scheduling, controlling, and monitoring," drastically reducing management at each subsidiary, and replacing ineffective plant managers.[56] Finally, Miller worked with Philadelphia banks to restructure more than $2 million of ZIA's debt, securing an additional $309,990 in working capital. Additional capital came from the Ford Foundation, which directed $500,000 to ZIA by way of Zion Non-Profit.[57]

Gradually, the cumulative impact of these changes had a positive effect on ZIA's performance. In the aftermath of an aggressive marketing effort, Progress Products Company received new contracts from AC Spark Plug, Chrysler, Ford, and IBM, as well as a promise of increased purchases from the company's largest client, the Packard Electric Division of General Motors. The IBM contract reflected PPC's focus on the production of electric cables, which quickly became its primary line of business. PPC also began producing electric cables for automobiles, supplementing the electrical harnesses that it already built for that industry. By the summer of 1973, PPC built "17 different cable assemblies" for GM alone, and became the automaker's only external contractor for cable production.[58]

Although Progress Aerospace continued to struggle with production and management problems, it too received new business, including a contract from the NASA Flight Research Center for a new small aircraft guidance system. Even more important than the company's attraction of new orders was PAE's successful completion of a contract for complex moving target simulators for the Defense Department. During 1974, PAE experienced an increase in business: the company received new contracts

FIGURE 25. Visitors to the OIC–Progress Movement's Progress Products Company, undated, probably 1970s. The woman in the foreground is displaying a rack of the company's electrical cables for the automobile industry. The boxes stacked in the right of the photo are stamped "Packard Electric GM." This General Motors subsidiary was one of Progress Product's largest customers. Photo courtesy of Temple University Libraries, Urban Archives, Philadelphia, Pennsylvania.

from Philco-Ford for automobile air conditioner components, from the U.S. Navy for emergency power centers "used in support of tactical data processing for anti-submarine warfare systems," and from Boeing-Vertol for undercarriage assemblies in light-rail transit systems. In addition, Western Electric renewed a simple but profitable contract for hand trucks used in moving "electric subassemblies between test stations."[59] These contracts demonstrate that unlike PPC, with its focus on electric cables, PAE never concentrated on a specific product area. In the long run, this would hurt the company, but in 1975 PAE's array of contracts proved to be beneficial when GE temporarily suspended a major sub-contract for Minuteman missile cables. Although this sub-contract represented 46 percent of PAE's total revenue in 1974, the other contracts provided a sufficient backlog to sustain the company's operations, even if they could not fully compensate for the immediate loss. PAE recovered relatively quickly, however, as it won an additional $2.6 million in new contracts during 1975, or more than three times the value of the lost GE work.

In part, the company achieved these gains through the federal Small Business Administration's Section 8(a) program, which channeled government contracts to minority-owned firms.[60] ZIA's participation in a federal minority set-aside program illustrates how Sullivan's rhetoric about community and individual uplift actually meant that African Americans should take full advantage of all available political, financial, or social resources. While Sullivan's strategy accepted the basic tenets of the free enterprise system, it also rejected neither government nor the new race-based economic entitlements won through civil rights activism in the late 1960s and early 1970s. From this perspective, acceptance of the benefits of affirmative action did not in any way contradict the underlying principles of the Progress Movement. Such a contradiction would instead have been produced by a rejection of such benefits, or of those available through other sources. By 1979, the Section 8(a) program had channeled $18 million in federal contracts to PAE alone.[61]

After suffering record losses of $1,682,579 in 1973, improvements in performance and efficiency combined with the additional business to produce ZIA's first overall profit, of $547,448 in 1974.[62] This continued, and through 1976, ZIA enjoyed an unprecedented period of prosperity. During these years, PPC emerged as the organization's most profitable subsidiary as a result of its "improvements in production flow, quality control procedures and packaging," as well as its consistent contract base with GM and IBM, and, starting in 1977, its production of dashboard instruments, clocks, and stereo speakers for Chrysler.[63] Meanwhile, PAE became even more engaged in defense-related work, as it accepted contracts from Westinghouse, Raytheon, the Defense Logistics Agency, a number of federal arsenals, and new work from GE. In addition, the company slowly improved its efficiency and implemented cost control measures, placing it in a position to reverse its previous losses. In 1977, PAE successfully bid on a $2.45 million contract to produce padlocks for the army. Awarded through the SBA's minority set-aside program, the contract was "one of the largest . . . ever awarded a minority contractor under Section 8(a)."

The result of these contracts was that each year between 1972 and 1978, *Black Enterprise* magazine ranked ZIA as one of the top 100 African American–owned U.S. companies in terms of total sales revenue.[64] Such accolades, however, proved impermanent. During the late 1970s, PAE and PPC suffered from the weakening national economy, as both experienced a decrease in revenue from existing contracts and greater difficulty in attracting new business. A series of poor management decisions exacerbated these problems. ZIA repeatedly overestimated production capabilities, because of a failure "to bring realism to planning and thinking." As a result, PAE and PPC often failed to fulfill contracts in the allotted time. This raised overhead costs, and because most of the federal contracts were written on a fixed cost basis, such overruns came directly out of profit margins. Even ZIA's core social purpose, "providing employment," had become a drag on the operation, as a consultant noted that it had been pursued without "fully bearing in mind the ramifications on the bottom line." These problems became particularly severe at PAE, which experienced operating losses of $1.24 million in 1978 and $571,053 in 1979.[65]

Even more importantly, ZIA as a whole still carried a burden of $2.375 million in debt as a result of its start-up costs and large losses. ZIA primarily owed this debt to a group of Philadelphia banks, which, as a result of their recognition of the Progress Movement's social importance, proved accommodating to the company's needs. In 1975, the banks forgave $600,000 of ZIA's debt and reduced the interest rate on the remainder to 1 percent until 1977. Despite their interest in ZIA's success, the banks would not maintain this flexibility indefinitely. After the expiration of the reduced rate arrangement, the banks required ZIA to make regular quarterly payments of 5 percent of the principal plus full interest, totaling $1,547,000 by 1980.[66]

ZIA failed to make most of these payments, as it once again experienced overall losses. In September 1980, an analyst noted that "the firm is technically in default on significant amounts of debt and could be classified as bankrupt." Although PPC and Progress Plaza managed to remain marginally profitable, ZIA as a whole lost $284,957 in 1977, $395,000 in 1978, and $369,000 in 1979. These losses came almost entirely from PAE. By 1980, the combination of debt pressure, decreased revenues, and operating losses placed the company in an inescapable dilemma. In order to meet its contract commitments and generate adequate revenue, PAE needed greater working capital to cover overhead expenses and basic input costs such as payroll and materials. ZIA's existing debt burden, however, made it impossible to obtain such capital. In turn, this limited the company's production capacity, preventing it from generating the revenue necessary to meet its debt obligations.[67]

Trapped in a cycle of debt, PAE was unable to replace faulty machinery and experienced serious production problems and cost overruns on its padlock contract with the U.S. Army. In the fall of 1980, the company found itself unable to fulfill either the padlock contract or a contract to produce electronics for army field communications vans. With no prospect for profitable operation, ZIA's board of directors decided on September 22, 1980, to close PAE. Sullivan personally delivered the news to the company's eighty-four remaining employees, and the company ceased operations on October 15.[68] This action did not resolve the overall problem, however, as ZIA remained liable for much of the $2.45 million padlock contract, as well as other guaranteed work that PAE left uncompleted. Although both PPC and Progress Plaza managed to earn small profits during this period, they could not cover even ZIA's existing debt, let alone these additional obligations.[69]

By 1982, the uncertainty of this situation made it increasingly difficult for PPC to attract new contracts. In addition, the lack of new capital investment meant that the company's production lines had not been modernized in years. PPC president Emmanuel Malone reported that the company was "20 years behind" and pointed out that its higher costs prevented it from matching the lower contract bids of more efficient competitors. Although PPC managed to extract minor wage concessions from the union during the summer of 1982, the company's lack of work rapidly destroyed its profitability and it closed shortly later.[70] In the end, Sullivan's experiment to extend African American enterprise into the high-tech fields of aerospace and electronics had been brought down, at least in part, by the consequences of a relatively a low-tech contract for padlock production.

ZIA continued to exist even after the failure of the manufacturing subsidiaries and, under the new name of Progress Investment Associates (which it adopted in 1977), still manages the Progress Plaza shopping center and has approximately 4,000 shareholders. The company made its first small dividend payment to 10-36 Plan members in 1991, but in 1998 the anchor grocery store closed, leaving the future of Progress Plaza in jeopardy. In the spring of 2007, following an internal reorganization, Progress Investment Associates broke ground on a $16.1 million renovation of the shopping center. Along with new office and retail space and the rehabilitation of parts of the existing center, the project will replace the original 18,000-square-foot grocery store with a new 42,000-square-foot facility. The state of Pennsylvania provided $5 million for the project, part of which came from the new Fresh Food Financing Initiative, a state program that subsidizes grocery store construction in urban and rural areas lacking access to healthy food. Along with a small city contribution, most of the remaining financing came from the Reinvestment Fund, a nonprofit community investment group.[71] The new venture thus marked at least a partial revival of Leon Sullivan's vision of spurring community-based economic development through the establishment of communally owned businesses.

Big Too Fast? The Decline of OIC

By 1980, the OIC job training program also faced increasing difficulties. Despite the overall increase in funding that OIC received under CETA, the combination of rapid growth, operational decentralization, and a weak national economy meant that the program increasingly could not meet its financial needs. OIC had always operated on a narrow financial margin: as early as 1969, it had slipped more than $1 million into debt, including $435,000 in unpaid withholding taxes to the IRS.[72] A combination of generous federal support and effective fund-raising resolved such early problems, but in the mid-1970s the financial pressure on OIC became more serious. During this period, the Philadelphia OIC accrued city, state, and federal tax debts of over $587,000 in unpaid withholding taxes that had been deducted from paychecks but never submitted. The program also accrued a debt of $520,000 to an employee-pension fund, as well as a $420,000 backlog in unpaid local property and school taxes. In 1978, only a last minute deal with the city revenue department saved OIC's headquarters from a sheriff's sale. In all three cases, the Philadelphia OIC redirected the money to maintain programs and pay salaries. Even so, the Philadelphia staff had to be cut from 400 to 233 between 1978 and 1980. Such financial difficulties became common at OIC centers around the country, and OIC executive director Elton Jolly estimated in 1980 that the survival of 53 of OIC's 143 affiliates remained in doubt. Sullivan admitted that OIC "got big too fast, and now I've got to catch up with it. ... I think that we are going to have to professionalize the operations of the OIC or else we will not be able to make it." Other program officials took a more aggressive stance: Thomas Ritter suggested that as a nonprofit, public service agency, OIC did not "have any business paying taxes anyway" and argued that the tax debts should be forgiven.[73]

During the 1970s, Sullivan himself became increasingly focused on national and international issues, including apartheid, and less involved in OIC–Progress Movement operations. In 1971, an article in the business-oriented *Philadelphia Magazine* observed that "Sullivan is probably the most respected black in Philadelphia, but he cannot be said to exercise real power at this time. He is considered something of a lone wolf and has, in fact, gone national in scope."[74] Sullivan's vision had always extended beyond the city, as could be seen in the national expansion of the OIC–Progress Movement, and in many respects this visionary quality lay at the core of his effectiveness. Still, without Sullivan's day-to-day presence, local business support declined and course content in the local program gradually slipped out of date. With business contacts weakened amid a sluggish economy, the Philadelphia OIC placed only 321 of 900 graduates in jobs; ten years earlier, the Philadelphia OIC claimed to have placed 2,085 trainees in jobs. Sullivan's presence alone, of course, might not have stemmed this decline.[75]

Along with such indications of diminishing effectiveness, questions emerged about the integrity of OIC's reporting procedures. Critics charged that at both the local and national levels, OIC had made exaggerated claims about the number of students trained and placed in jobs. In other cases, OIC's lack of centralized control under CETA contributed to fiscal irregularities. A 1980 DOL audit revealed that under the 1971–73 prime contract, which had been the high point of OIC centralization, local OIC affiliates had nonetheless charged $1.5 million in non-allowable expenses to the federal government. DOL denied an OIC appeal of the audit and identified an additional $220,728 in unjustified expenses that had to be repaid. While the DOL audit could be partially explained as the consequence of actions taken by OIC affiliates, the Department of Education soon disallowed $771,437 in "unreasonable" rental charges that the Philadelphia OIC's Germantown center had paid to an OIC subsidiary and then billed to the federal government. This charge brought the issue of accounting irregularities to the Philadelphia core of the OIC program.[76]

In November 1980, the *Philadelphia Bulletin* ran a four-part investigative series that described OIC as a "troubled giant" and detailed many of the agency's problems both locally and nationally. The series produced angry countercharges that Sullivan and OIC were the targets of a racially motivated smear campaign, and African American ministers and political leaders prepared for a potential boycott of the *Bulletin*. Although Sullivan initially lashed out at the *Bulletin*, warning that the newspaper was "playing with the wrong Negro now," he soon rejected the idea of a boycott (much to the relief of the newspaper, which was itself in serious

financial jeopardy and would cease publication in 1982).[77] Published only
two weeks after Ronald Reagan's victory in the 1980 presidential election, the tenor of the *Bulletin* series was in part a product of the conservative, anti-government moment in which it was written. Independent
assessments conducted by the DOL and a committee of OIC business
supporters, however, confirmed some of the newspaper's findings.[78]

During the 1980s, OIC's difficulties became more severe, as the organization's weakened ties to business failed to protect it from the Reagan
administration's elimination of CETA and federal revenue sharing. Sullivan had recognized from the very beginning that OIC required an activist
federal government, and during the national retrenchment of the 1980s
and 1990s, more than half of OIC's local centers closed. As the twentieth
century came to an end, OIC still existed, but with a far smaller organization, a less influential position, and an uncertain vision of its future role
in American society.[79] Few contrasts better demonstrate the changes in
American public policy structures, political economy, and social philosophy than that between OIC in 1973 and OIC in 2000.

Despite its decline, OIC's legacy for American job training efforts
remains important. Founded in 1967, the OIC branch in Santa Clara County,
California, has since evolved into an independent program known as the
Center for Employment Training (CET), which now operates throughout the western United States. Although no formal ties remain between
the two programs, CET's origin in the OIC system is reflected in its programming: its emphasis on remedial education as well as vocational training, its self-paced "open-entry open-exit" model, its focus on attitude and
motivation, its "embeddedness" in the community and in broader social
movements, and in its close ties to networks of employers. In a direct continuation of the OIC model, the program maintains Industrial Advisory
Boards and Technical Advisory Committees at each of its branches. CET
is now widely regarded as one of the most effective job training programs
in the United States.[80]

Although the Nixon administration never followed through in a meaningful way on the black capitalism proposals of the 1968 "Bridges to Human Dignity" speeches, the concept of black capitalism (or in Sullivan's
preferred formulation, community capitalism) focused on an aspect of
American social policy that had been underemphasized by the ostensi-
bly pro-urban Great Society. In its most basic form, the black capitalism strategy tried to address the intertwined relationship between racial

discrimination in employment, deindustrialization, and the availability of decent work opportunities for inner-city residents. As the major Philadelphia manifestation of the concept, the OIC–Progress Movement's development of commercial and manufacturing businesses constituted a far more serious exploration of the policy possibilities that flowed from these relationships than anything undertaken by the Nixon administration. The outcome of the OIC–Progress Movement's experiment in community economic activism demonstrates both the real potential and the distinct limitations of black capitalism, and of community-based local industrial policies more generally, as a response to the racial and structural employment problems of U.S. cities.

Through Progress Plaza and the ZIA subsidiaries, Leon Sullivan's 10-36 Plan showed that the pooling of community resources could produce significant, highly sophisticated business ventures in poverty-stricken minority areas. The success of the shopping center in attracting outside tenants, of the manufacturing companies in securing public and private contracts, and of the nonprofit programs in gaining government and business support provide further evidence that such communities could attract outside resources and economic development through the same political and discursive strategies that OIC employed in its job training program. By emphasizing traditional American ideological discourses of self-reliance, uplift, and the creation of opportunity, while also directly challenging the wider community to meet its long-ignored moral, ethical, and economic obligations to African Americans, the OIC–Progress Movement offered an important liberal response to the pressing question of how African Americans might achieve full economic empowerment following the political and in some measures social triumph of what Bayard Rustin described as the "classical" phase of the civil rights movement. It offered an innovative urban liberalism, updated and made relevant for the postwar United States.

Sullivan's community-based industrial and employment policies were also an important precursor to the community development corporations that emerged in many American cities during the 1970s and 1980s. These organizations proved to be one of the few effective strategies for improving conditions in inner-city neighborhoods. The OIC–Progress Movement programs, though, also foreshadowed difficulties that CDCs would have with urban economic development.[81] More significantly, the communal basis and sense of social responsibility that lay at the root of Leon Sullivan's version of capitalist development provided an alternative to the increasingly rootless economic model that came to dominate the American economy in the last decades of the twentieth century.

This alternative form of capitalist development, however, in turn demonstrated the constraints on liberal urban economic activism. The failure of PAE and PPC reflected not only mistakes by ZIA management—although such mistakes played a large part—but also the extraordinary difficulty of operating a profitable manufacturing enterprise in an inner-city environment such as Philadelphia. ZIA and other Philadelphia companies faced competitors who could take advantage of the availability of low cost, non-union labor elsewhere in the United States and abroad, as well as direct or indirect government subsidies for such moves. City tax levels, which rose to meet the growing costs of city services, personnel, and infrastructure, added further to the financial pressure on inner city firms. As a result, even community-oriented companies had few protections against either poor management decisions or macroeconomic fluctuations. Any business, whether minority- or white-owned, would have faced a challenging path in attempting what the OIC–Progress Movement undertook: rapidly starting and operating complex businesses in varied fields, all within a wider context of rapid economic restructuring and industrial exodus. The process of urban deindustrialization, in short, paid little heed to a company's form of organization or social purpose.

ZIA and the wider Progress Movement also continued the racialized patterns of economic development already identified in regard to PIDC and OIC. While OIC maintained some direct connections with both the local business community and the local War on Poverty, the Progress Movement worked primarily with the federal government and national corporations and had little or no interaction with PIDC, Philadelphia's formal War on Poverty, or the city's economic planning initiatives. Even more than OIC, the Progress Movement operated on one side of a racial divide that separated parallel but potentially complementary tracks of local industrial and employment policy. Both of the policy tracks included useful, innovative, and even effective responses to the problem of jobs, but ultimately, each remained only a partial solution. Yet without a formal economic planning or coordinating function, such as that proposed by local economists Kirk Petshek in the 1950s or Elizabeth Deutermann and John Culp in the 1960s, no mechanism existed to draw agencies such as PIDC into active engagement with social movements such as the OIC–Progress Movement. Instead, each initiative, one largely white and the other primarily African American, pursued its own particular agenda on each side of the divide, with no thought for how the abilities of one might assist the other. Without a comprehensive, citywide approach to economic development, neither "black" programs such as the OIC–Progress Movement nor "white" programs such as PIDC could address the full range of factors amenable to local action. Also absent, of course, was a wider federal framework of support for either industrial policy or fully articulated employment policy. These burdens, from management mistakes to the racial bifurcation of policy to the endlessly shifting nature of federal urban policy, proved in the end too great for the OIC–Progress Movement.

While the OIC–Progress Movement's economic development projects suggest the limits of what community-oriented, urban development efforts can accomplish, they also extend and complicate currently prevailing histories of post–World War II American liberalism. With its structural analysis of the interaction of discrimination, poverty, and economic change, its commitment to the deployment of public and private resources to generate inner-city jobs, and its attempt to create a restructured model of capitalism based on community control and social responsibility, the OIC–Progress Movement embodied a strain of postwar liberalism that directly addressed problems of economics, and in particular, the often devastating interaction of racial and employment issues that shaped much of the problem of jobs in U.S. inner cities. Its most ambitious components, the ZIA manufacturing companies, went a step beyond even this, as they sought to maintain an urban manufacturing base in the face of a wider shift to an economy based on services, information, and technology.

In undertaking such challenges, the OIC–Progress Movement built on a legacy of liberal African American economic activism that extended at least to the Garveyite movement of the 1920s, and that continued forcefully in the 1960s freedom struggle through initiatives as varied as Martin Luther King's Poor People's Campaign, Rustin and A. Phillip Randolph's Freedom Budget for All Americans, Oakland activists' attempt to gain control of private hiring decisions, and early Community Development Corporations in Brooklyn, Cleveland, and elsewhere. These and many other ambitious initiatives kept economic issues at the center of local liberalism and the civil rights movement into the 1970s.

Finally, the OIC–Progress Movement's job training and job creation programs indicate that local institutions could transform federal policy. The movement used the base of community control provided by the distinctly nonstructural War on Poverty to develop a structural, employment-focused, and community-based apparatus of local employment and industrial policy that pursued both economic security goals and a civil rights-based challenge to discrimination. Local activists, in other words, deployed the tools provided by federal programs—community action and job training grants, small business programs, and set-asides—to shift the basic orientation of federal policy itself. What the movement lacked was the support of either a similarly committed national liberal state or a closely coordinated set of comprehensive local economic policies. As a result, the OIC–Progress Movement found that it had little to fall back on as its financial troubles mounted and its political and corporate backers lost interest.

CHAPTER SEVEN

The Philadelphia Plan: Affirmative Action and the Problem of Jobs

During the years of the early republic, Philadelphia's First Bank of the United States had been the focus of bitter debate over Alexander Hamilton's centralizing plans for national economic development. In late June 1969, the marble-clad, neoclassical bank building very briefly became the site, once again, of controversy about the authority of the federal government. This time the question was how to balance the demands of racial justice with the customs of labor unions and the stringencies of economic change. The occasion was an announcement by assistant secretary of labor Arthur Fletcher that his department would institute a program of affirmative action in the local construction industry that would pressure contractors to employ black workers and pressure all-white building trades unions to admit blacks as members. Known as the Philadelphia Plan, this policy replaced an earlier version that had been declared illegal by the U.S. comptroller general. Together, these two plans constituted the first fully developed affirmative action program in the United States. Fletcher, the highest-ranking African American in the Nixon administration, spoke in the large banking room on the building's first floor, beneath a columned rotunda with a lighted glass dome, and explained the provisions of the new plan: contractors would be required to make a "good faith effort" to hire minority workers for specified percentages of their workforces on federally financed construction projects worth more than $500,000; these percentages would be carefully crafted as ranges rather than absolutes to avoid violation of the Civil Rights Act's ban on hiring quotas. Fletcher acknowledged that "it might be better, admittedly, if specific goals weren't required...but it is imperative that we face facts and dedicate ourselves to ending discrimination in employment in this country."

As Fletcher concluded his remarks, the stately quality of the ceremony quickly dissipated into a debate among members of the audience. Joseph Burke, president of Sheet Metal Workers Local 19, requested "special privilege" to speak about the plan and stated that "I protest strongly what's being done. We're going to have to work with it, but the employers and the unions weren't even contacted to get their thoughts on the plan. I protest and I protest strongly. I beg you not to put the plan into effect until both the contractors and the unions sit with the people involved and see if we can be helpful." Burke's remarks spurred an angry response from Charles Bowser, formerly head of the Philadelphia Anti-poverty Action Committee and at the time director of the Philadelphia Urban Coalition: "it's been postponed for 300 years." Burke then walked out, claiming that his objections were not to integration but to the policy process behind the Philadelphia Plan and to the burdens that it placed on his industry and union.[1]

The Philadelphia Plan provided a crucial starting point in the national development of affirmative action. Yet it also reshaped liberal politics and policy in Philadelphia itself, both in relation to the specific policy questions posed by the problem of jobs, and in the context of the liberal reform coalition that in the late 1940s and 1950s had mirrored the national New Deal coalition (minus, of course, Southerners) and that had pursued policy initiatives reflective of a liberalism very different from what had come to predominate nationally. By the late 1960s, Philadelphia's liberal reform coalition had begun to fall apart as Mayor Tate and other factions of the feuding city Democratic Party reasserted an older style of urban organizational politics, and as broader questions of race and power within the urban polity increasingly strained the liberal order. The racial bifurcation of industrial and employment policy in the city marked a more subtle but even more critical manifestation of this pattern. On the issue of the Philadelphia Plan, however, the liberal political, business, and civil rights communities remained deeply engaged with the problem of integrating the local construction industry. Despite its often polarizing character nationally, affirmative action in Philadelphia generated new forms of liberal activism that narrowed the divide between Philadelphia's racially bifurcated responses to the problem of jobs and drew parts of the liberal coalition back together. At times, the Philadelphia Plan even drew radicals into the coalition. This tightening of liberal bonds resulted partially from the Philadelphia Plan's engagement with issues of racial justice, but also from its engagement with the consequences of economic change, if not with their underlying structural basis. Yet because the latter focus on economic justice did not extend sufficiently far, the Philadelphia Plan exacerbated divisions between liberals (of all races), and key elements of the city's white working class, which had been an important part of the reform coalition locally and the New Deal coalition nationally. Just as Joseph Burke walked out on the Philadelphia Plan announcement at the First Bank of the United States, "hard hat" unionists and their sympathizers would soon depart the house of liberalism, locally and nationally.

The Building Trades, the Civil Rights Movement, and the First Philadelphia Plan

As Philadelphia lost manufacturing jobs during the 1950s and early 1960s, and as the federal urban renewal program financed both public and private construction projects, the local construction industry became an increasingly important employer. African Americans, however, had little access to skilled jobs in the industry. Building-trade unions had long relied on closed recruiting and apprenticeship systems based on family and neighborhood networks. Labor agreements with contractors allowed the unions to control the training and hiring process for the industry, and both job openings and spots in apprenticeship programs went almost entirely to the relatives and close acquaintances of union members. Often, specific ethnic groups dominated a particular trade. As one union member explained in 1970, "it's a neighborhood thing. We all know each other. When you work as long as we have to make a good thing, you want to hand it on to somebody you know. Not everybody who gets in is the son of somebody but he's some kind of relative, brother-in-law or something."[2] Although the construction unions claimed they did not discriminate, this closed system relegated African American construction workers to low-paying positions as unskilled laborers—if they were hired at all.[3]

Beginning in the mid-1950s, the Philadelphia NAACP, the Urban League, the Council on Equal Job Opportunity (CEJO), and the Quaker American Friends Service Committee lobbied construction contractors and unions to accept blacks as apprentices, union members, and workers. The contractors and unions resisted these appeals, and the city's Commission on Human Relations (CHR) took no action. In the early 1960s, the Philadelphia AFL-CIO's Human Rights Committee, chaired by black labor activist and liberal reform ally James H. Jones, fought unsuccessfully to convince the building trades that they should adopt a voluntary integration program. In the winter and spring of 1963, however, with new civil rights protests in Birmingham, Alabama, and the selective patronage movement well underway in Philadelphia, the city's building trades unions attracted new public attention when the business and political monthly *Greater Philadelphia Magazine* published an investigation of the failure of the CHR, the liberal reformers, and the organization Democrats to confront the problem of discrimination in the construction industry.[4]

Later that spring, the Congress of Racial Equality (CORE), along with the newly radicalized NAACP chapter led by the militant attorney Cecil B. Moore, staged a series of sit-ins, marches, and pickets to protest the absence of skilled blacks working on the new Municipal Services Building adjacent to City Hall and on a new school in the largely black Strawberry Mansion neighborhood. The protests culminated on May 31 when, with negotiations still underway, two hundred police in full riot gear charged a line of forty picketers at the school site. The resulting clash sent twelve picketers and nine police to the hospital, but also pushed the two sides toward an agreement. Within hours of the skirmish, the school board and the building trades accepted Moore's demands that they hire five black workers for skilled jobs at the school and that they establish a joint committee to monitor hiring practices, union membership rules, and apprenticeships. For his part, Moore agreed not only to end the NAACP pickets but also to discourage any other groups from engaging in protest actions against the industry. The latter move infuriated CORE, but was designed to assert Moore's predominance as the leading force in the Philadelphia civil rights movement.[5]

Resistance to integration, though, remained strong among both union leaders and rank-and-file members. The CHR worked with the unions to develop a minority-hiring plan, but the latter pursued a policy of carefully circumscribed tokenism. Meanwhile, Moore and the NAACP moved on, first to other fields of employment discrimination, such as the post office and interstate bus companies, and then to a bitter fight over the integration of Girard College, a boys' orphanage and school in North Philadelphia that accepted only whites because of restrictions in the will of founder Stephen Girard. This rapidly evolving, politically driven strategy meant

FIGURE 26. African American workers enter a school construction site in North Philadelphia's Strawberry Mansion neighborhood after unions and contractors agreed to NAACP and CORE demands that a limited number of blacks be added to the project's skilled workforce. The agreement followed a violent confrontation between African American picketers and police hours before. Note the cheering protestors in the background. May 1963. Photo courtesy of Temple University Libraries, Urban Archives, Philadelphia, Pennsylvania.

that Moore and the NAACP exerted little additional pressure on the building trades. Ultimately, despite their drama, the 1963 construction protests yielded no real remedy, as recalcitrant unions and complicit contractors devised effective ways to avoid integration.[6]

This stalemate, though, did not bring the issue to a close. President Kennedy responded to the upheaval in Philadelphia, as well as to similar protests that followed in New York, Trenton, Newark, and Cleveland, by banning discrimination on all construction projects built with federal

funds (Executive Order 11114). The following year, Title VII of the Civil
Rights Act outlawed private employment discrimination on the basis of
race, national origin, religion, and sex and created the Equal Employment Opportunities Commission to adjudicate complaints. It also effectively prohibited explicit racial hiring quotas. Title VI of the act banned
discrimination in all federally assisted programs, but relied on a vague
process of referral to the Justice Department for enforcement.[7] Nearly a
year later, in a June 1965 commencement address at Howard University,
President Johnson called on the nation to move beyond such straight-
forward verities of color-blind equal opportunity to address the social
and economic consequences of slavery, segregation, and discrimination:
"You do not take a person who, for years, has been hobbled by chains
and liberate him, bring him up to the starting line of a race and then say,
'You are free to compete with all the others,' and still justly believe that
you have been completely fair. . . . equal opportunity is essential, but not
enough, not enough."[8] In September, Johnson acted on his Howard address with Executive Order 11246. This order created a new Office of
Federal Contract Compliance (OFCC) in the Department of Labor and
authorized its director to "adopt such rules and regulations and issue such
orders as he deems necessary and appropriate" to achieve equal opportunity in the workforces of federal contractors. In effect, the order authorized the OFCC to implement "affirmative" hiring programs on federal
work sites, and to cancel contracts if contractors failed to integrate their
crews.

Understaffed and underfunded, OFCC spent much of 1966 and 1967
experimenting with prototype affirmative action programs. In 1966, it required contractors on St. Louis's Gateway Arch and the San Francisco
Bay Area Regional Transit system (BART) to develop minority recruitment and training plans prior to the award of contracts. The St. Louis
Plan led to an immediate union walkout before being preempted by a federal Title VII discrimination lawsuit, while the San Francisco Plan, which
lacked specific compliance standards, produced few measurable minority
employment gains. Shifting its focus to Cleveland in early 1967, OFCC
abandoned such "paper compliance" plans for a results-oriented approach that required the low-bidding contractor to use "manning tables"
to specify in advance how many minorities would be hired in each skill
area during each stage of a project. Although the manning table requirement skirted Title VII's quota ban, it led to revised bids from Cleveland
area contractors who promised to hire more than 100 African American

workers, or more than 25 percent of projected workforces, on upcoming federal projects worth more than $125 million.[9]

By fall 1967, OFCC turned its attention to Philadelphia. In contrast to the earlier plans, the impetus for this extension came not from Washington but from the Philadelphia Federal Executive Board (FEB), a coordinating body of regional federal agency administrators. Philadelphia FEB chair Warren Phelan, from HUD, pushed for an interagency effort to force integration in the building trades unions by way of economic pressure on contractors. Phelan correctly perceived the contractors as the point in the construction industry most susceptible to federal influence. Prior to implementing the new approach, Phelan oversaw a survey of area union membership that indicated many of the fifty-five building-trade unions already had some minority members or were so small as to be insignificant. Seven of the eight largest, best-paid, and highest-skilled building trade locals, however, showed a different pattern: out of a combined membership of approximately 9,000, the electricians, sheet metal workers, plumbers, roofers, structural ironworkers, steamfitters, and elevator constructors together had "no more than 25 to 30 minority journeymen, and 15 minority apprentices / helpers-tenders." One union, the elevator constructors, had no minorities at all. This meant that African Americans had almost no representation in the most important segments of the Philadelphia-area construction industry. Both the symbolic and economic significance of such exclusionary practices made the seven unions an inviting target for the FEB.[10]

With the explicit support of the OFCC and other federal agencies, Phelan's FEB drafted a new Philadelphia Plan for affirmative action in the building trades. Released on October 27, 1967, after a summer that saw violent inner city upheavals in Newark, Detroit, Tampa, Cincinnati, Buffalo, and elsewhere, the Philadelphia Plan applied to all federal contracts of more than $500,000 and followed the Cleveland Plan in its requirement that low bidding contractors submit manning tables showing how they would employ a "representative number" of minorities "in all trades on the job and in all phases of the work." The contract would be offered to the next lowest bidder in the event that a contractor proved unable or unwilling to supply such a table. Defined as targets rather than rigid quotas, these goals were established in post-bid discussions between contractors, the regional federal agency offering the contract, and an FEB Contract Compliance Committee. As in the Cleveland Plan, the Philadelphia Plan thus withdrew the government from direct negotiations with the building-trade unions and shifted responsibility to the contractor, who was "expected to use the same resourcefulness in making opportunities available to minorities as he applies to other aspects of his business." Contractors could integrate their workforces however they preferred, but they had to achieve results.[11]

The main innovation of the plan, however, was its reliance on local implementation through the Philadelphia FEB, where the Cleveland Plan relied on direct oversight from Washington. OFCC would provide support, but as Phelan noted on the day of its release, "this plan offers a firm, new approach for the local community to apply local solutions" and "will aptly demonstrate the essence of 'creative federalism'"—a phrase that President Johnson had emphasized when he laid out the principles of the Great Society in 1964. In keeping with this idea, the plan would also be implemented in close cooperation with the city's Commission on Human Relations. In another significant difference from Cleveland, the operational guidelines explicitly targeted the seven trades identified in the FEB survey, noting that "*most* of the necessary *compliance effort* activity will involve the higher paid trades. . . . No program can be acceptable which does not deal satisfactorily and specifically with these trades."[12] The Philadelphia FEB thus sought to tackle employment discrimination in a highly visible and economically significant field that presumably could have a substantive effect on the economic fortunes of inner city African Americans.

By the spring of 1968, the Philadelphia Plan began to affect construction operations. At the beginning of May, Phelan's FEB had suspended more than $19 million in federal construction funds in the area, including a new classroom building at the Drexel Institute of Technology, a housing development in suburban Bucks County, and the renovation of an industrial building that would provide a new home for the Spring Garden Institute, a local technical training school.[13] The largest single contract suspension blocked for six months the construction of the Girard Point Bridge that would carry Interstate 95 over the Schuylkill River. The Girard Point case involved Operating Engineers Local 542, whose members operated heavy equipment such as cranes and bulldozers. Local 542 had been identified by the FEB the previous year as a possible candidate for the plan, but had ultimately been excluded from the list of critical trades because its 5,000 members included between 800 and 900 blacks. While this percentage was far higher than the other leading trades, it masked the internal operations of a union job assignment process in which fixed seniority rules combined with racism to limit black members' access to desirable jobs, as well as their total work hours. Joyce Rush, whose husband was a member of Local 542 and whose involvement in the issue had been spurred by her husband's periodic unemployment, noted at a 1969 federal hearing that "those blacks who are able to gain entry...are the last hired, the first laid off. Many of them average six-month lay-offs, from three- to six-month lay-offs, each year....Endless hours are spent in the hiring hall waiting for jobs."[14] Union membership mattered, but it did not assure actual employment, and the Girard Point Bridge case showed the first of many layers of complexity that the federal government sought to unravel through the Philadelphia Plan. With more than $96 million in highways funds jeopardized statewide, the state highway department eventually brokered a compromise under which the unions and contractors agreed to hire a "representative number of blacks" and implement minority apprentice recruitment efforts and journeyman upgrade programs.[15]

Late in April, an even more consequential dispute—in terms of both symbolism and the size of the contract involved—emerged over a new U.S. Mint facility on Independence Mall in Center City. In this case, which took place only weeks after the King assassination, the Philadelphia Plan applied to a large, highly visible federal facility being built just a few hundred yards from the site of the nation's founding. During the last week of April, federal officials threatened to sanction the $30 million contract of McCloskey and Company, the prime contractor on the project, who also happened to be one of Philadelphia's largest builders and a major contributor to the local and national Democratic Party. McCloskey, the government announced, had to hire ten black electricians. McCloskey responded immediately and on May 2, 1968, administered a journeyman qualifying examination to eleven African Americans to identify candidates who would satisfy the Philadelphia Plan requirements.[16]

This process, however, had been so rushed that not all of the candidates even understood the purpose of the exam: one twenty-one-year-old man who had electrical experience from the military had taken the exam on the assumption that it would allow him to qualify for a union apprenticeship, rather than journeyman status. Afterward, the man knew he had not passed. Another candidate, however, spoke to the tremendous difficulties faced by skilled African Americans in Philadelphia and much of the urban United States. Thirty-nine years old, he had spent thirteen years as an electrician's mate in the U.S. Navy, but had worked only intermittently in the field since returning to civilian life, mostly in large manufacturing companies or at the Philadelphia Navy Yard. At the time of the Mint exam, he earned $1.60 an hour as a janitor. Following the examination, he expressed his frustration with union dominance of building-trades employment: "the electricians local is too hard to crack. Several times I inquired about joining it."[17]

The electricians union, meanwhile, lashed out at the process. Electricians Local 98 charged that the OFCC had undertaken a "direct perversion of the country's dedication to equal opportunity regardless of race, color, or creed" and indicated that "we will not allow the combination of racial discrimination and outright union-busting which the Philadelphia Plan represents to go unchecked." The union also threatened a court challenge against "this comic opera, political power play of the government."[18] The situation deteriorated further when McCloskey announced that although none of the test takers had achieved a qualifying journeyman's grade, three candidates had been offered employment on the basis of their "background and experience." On May 3, two of the black, non-union electricians arrived on site and began work. Immediately, twenty-five union electricians walked off the job. Although the union did not authorize the walkout, its legal counsel Bernard Katz described the process as "an unbelievable wrong...that is making a sham of our apprentice training program."[19] Another dimension of the dispute involved the few African Americans who were already members of Local 98. According to the OFCC and McCloskey, two to four black electrician apprentices already worked at the Mint site (which employed approximately seventy to ninety electricians).[20] Katz later commented on their response to the Philadelphia Plan hires: "The unionized black apprentice electricians, working at less than the journeyman rate because they were in the apprenticeship training program...were furious. They knew more than these instant journeymen and they were being penalized by virtue of the fact that they were in a unionized program undergoing the necessary training. Financially, they would have been temporarily better off had they been non-union and had they capitalized on the 'instant journeyman' concept of the Office of Federal Contract Compliance."[21] Whether Katz accurately depicted the feelings of the black apprentices is impossible to assess, but he clearly expressed the unions' fear that the Philadelphia Plan would harm the economic interests of their members, black and white, and their belief that they should be allowed to manage the integration of their membership. For civil rights activists, though, and indeed for most others in the liberal coalition, four black apprentices in a seventy-person workforce would no longer suffice. Over the following days, four additional African Americans accepted employment at the Mint site. In early June, two of the newly hired black electricians were fired "because of a question of competency." The two immediately filed a complaint with the CHR that charged a subcontractor and the electricians union with discrimination.[22]

Meanwhile, Local 98 made its next move not in the courts, as threatened, but at the level of local equal employment enforcement. On May 7, the union filed a complaint with the CHR, charging that three white electricians had been denied employment at the Mint in favor of less qualified African Americans. In one move, Local 98 had linked local and national equal employment institutions, and had posed claims of merit against those of equality and charges of reverse discrimination against claims of institutionalized segregation. For nearly two weeks, the dispute simmered as the CHR reviewed the case. At the same time, Reverend Ralph Abernathy brought the late Martin Luther King Jr.'s Poor People's Campaign to Philadelphia, where participants held an enthusiastic rally, attended by both Mayor Tate and Police Commissioner Rizzo. The marchers spent the night camped on an empty lot in North Philadelphia before proceeding to Washington D.C., where they built Resurrection City on the national mall and lobbied Congress for additional funds and services to combat poverty.[23]

On May 20, the CHR dismissed Local 98's complaint on the legally sound but politically evasive grounds that it lacked jurisdiction over the claim because of the federal role in the Philadelphia Plan. Although Local 98 indicated it would refer the claim to the courts, events preempted what might otherwise have been a landmark affirmative action case. First, the new Mint facility was nearly complete and would be dedicated on September 18, rendering the issue of construction employment moot.[24] Second, the continuation of the Philadelphia Plan itself would soon be cast into doubt.

The first sign of trouble for the plan came when U.S. comptroller general Elmer Staats ruled the similar but less expansive Cleveland Plan illegal because it violated federal competitive bidding regulations by relying on post-bid negotiations, rather than specifying minority hiring standards in initial bidding notices. The ruling posed a grave threat to the Philadelphia Plan, which relied on a similar process of post-bid, pre-award negotiations. On November 18, Staats ruled the Philadelphia Plan illegal on the grounds that it too violated competitive bidding rules. Entering their final months in office, President Johnson and secretary of labor Willard Wirtz had little incentive, or political capacity, to challenge the ruling.[25]

At the time of its apparent demise, the initial Philadelphia Plan had produced only minor gains in African American employment. The regional OFCC coordinator reported that as of late September, the plan had been applied to twenty-five separate construction projects, worth $25 million; agreements on manning tables had been reached in nineteen of those cases, producing commitments to hire 132 minorities in the seven critical trades, out of 529 workers on the covered job sites.[26] These numbers highlighted the limitations of focusing on construction employment: while jobs in the critical trades offered high wages, 132 positions would not resolve the wider problem of jobs for African American Philadelphia, even in the midst of a federally funded construction boom. Far more jobs would be needed, far beyond construction. Even more problematically, the jobs obtained under the plan did not actually represent 132 new positions for African Americans previously outside the building trades; unions and contractors frequently engaged in a practice known as "motorcycling," in which the few blacks in a union would be shifted from one job site to another as needed to demonstrate compliance with federal standards. In a 1969 hearing on the Philadelphia Plan, an assistant secretary of labor described this practice: "when they felt the compliance officer was going to come around they would take the one [minority] craftsman they had and put him on a motorcycle and scoot him to the next job just ahead of the compliance officer. Consequently there was a chance that all these jobs would have a craftsman on them, but as a result of that fleeting motorcycle." At the same hearing, Joyce Rush described her husband's experience: "my husband is an operating engineer—and I hope he'll be one tomorrow—but last year [1968] they motorcycled him from the end of Philadelphia to the top of Philadelphia, from the east to the west." OFCC and the FEB simply lacked the staff to monitor such abuses.[27]

Nonetheless, the first Philadelphia Plan had two important consequences, one direct and one indirect. First, because of the plan, the building trades unions in Philadelphia initiated new minority recruitment and apprenticeship programs. Not coincidentally, this process began the day before McCloskey and Company administered special exams to qualify black electricians for employment at the U.S. Mint. Following a heated, three hour debate that day, the Philadelphia Building and Construction Trades Council voted to launch an official recruitment program, funded

by a DOL grant, to bring African Americans into their apprenticeship programs. Although the measure passed, thirty of the hundred delegates voted
against even undertaking such a program. An African American delegate from Laborer's Local 332 reported that the opposition was based
on "unfounded fears that under it locals will become all black." Simultaneously, the Building and Construction Trades Council passed a resolution that opposed the Philadelphia Plan as "an illegal quota system."[28] Six
days later, the council finalized an agreement with the General Building
Contractors Association and the Negro Trade Union Leadership Council
(NTULC) to begin a joint minority apprentice recruitment effort. Mayor
Tate, long a strong labor ally, attended the meeting and endorsed the
new initiative, which became part of a wider national partnership between the AFL-CIO and the NTULC known as the Apprentice Outreach
Program.[29]

The Apprentice Outreach Program received a $60,000 grant from the
Department of Labor and began operation in late August. It continued
even after Elmer Staats ruled against the Philadelphia Plan. The schools,
the state employment service, and community organizations such as OIC
all referred candidates for the newly opened apprenticeships. During
the outreach program's first eight months, the building trades unions recruited a total of sixty-five apprentices, a small number relative to the
need for jobs in Philadelphia. Further, fifty of these new apprentices entered programs in unions not covered by the Philadelphia Plan, while
the plan's seven critical trades, with their higher pay and steadier employment, recruited only eight apprentices.[30] Despite official AFL-CIO
sanction for outreach, locals retained nearly complete discretion over the
initiation and operation of their individual programs—and locals in the
critical trades moved with notable slowness. The Steamfitters, for example, did not even begin accepting applications for apprenticeships until
January 6, 1969, provided only a week's notice before the enrollment period began, and then accepted applications only until January 10. The
African American *Philadelphia Tribune* provided a free advertisement of
the openings, and published a front-page editorial that noted the steamfitters' $6 per hour wage, proclaimed that "the walls which have kept blacks
from these high-paying jobs must be torn down," and warned interested
readers not to "let this opportunity pass you by. It may not come again
soon." By April, the Steamfitters had recruited only two black apprentices; the plumbers four; the structural and ornamental ironworkers two;
the four remaining critical trades none.[31]

The City Plan for Affirmative Action

Gradually, however, and particularly after the comptroller general's ruling, the outreach programs began to affect union practices. In part, this
took place because of pressure that remained on the key building trades
from a second consequence of the federal plan. This pressure came from
the city government's implementation, through the CHR, of a *local* Philadelphia Plan. This local plan actually had more significance for Philadelphia's local liberalism than the initial federal plan did, especially for the
liberal response to the problem of jobs and for the formation of policy
and activist coalitions.

The CHR, under executive director Clarence Farmer, drafted the city's
affirmative action plan in late 1967 and early 1968 after the announcement
of the federal plan. At a basic level, the city plan reflected the same constraint that shaped the federal plan, as it had to avoid direct minority employment quotas that would violate Title VII. The CHR's solution, however, took a form that was simpler, less specific, and broader: it avoided
the complex pre-award manning table negotiations of the federal plan,
required only that "representative numbers" of minorities be hired, covered fields other than construction, and was applicable beyond government agencies. Functionally, the plan operated through an employment
survey sent in May 1968 to all firms holding city contracts, including service providers and suppliers as well as construction contractors. Any firm
that did not return the survey automatically went on a list of companies
prohibited from receiving further city business; any company that replied
but that did not report a "representative number" of minority employees
could enter into negotiations with the CHR over what that number should
be and how an affirmative action program to attain such a goal would be
implemented. Failure to negotiate or to comply with an agreement would
lead to placement on the banned contractors list. The CHR maintained
that this nonprescriptive, consensus-based approach "allows for flexibility
and adaptation to the diversified companies which are affected." A
$14,000 grant from the federal Equal Employment Opportunity Commis-
sion supported staffing for the new program.

The city plan went beyond the federal plan in one other area, as it required that any company doing business with the city had to "hire and
train hard-core unemployed persons so that they may become an integral
part of his workforce." In implementing this rule, the CHR developed

the standard that for every hundred employees in a company's workforce, one unemployed worker had to be hired and trained.[32] This policy meant that the city plan not only challenged discrimination, but also sought to expand the pool of jobs available to the poor. Inclusion of such an active employment policy component was far from incidental, as it highlighted an understanding of the problem of jobs distinctly different from that of the federal plan. While the FEB's Philadelphia Plan focused narrowly on the enforcement of equal employment opportunity, the city plan sought to address the economic status of inner city communities as well as to eliminate employment discrimination. Yet it also defined such discrimination in terms more sophisticated than those of the FEB, viewing it as institutionalized rather than overt and as manifest in barriers such as culturally biased entrance exams, stringent but irrelevant prerequisites, and automatic disqualification for petty crimes. Addressing the structural and spatial rationales for affirmative action in city-funded employment, the city plan noted that despite widespread prosperity in the United States and low overall unemployment, "there exists in Philadelphia, as in most urban centers . . . a virtual economic depression for a disproportionate number of black and Puerto Rican citizens." As a result, city contracts "will be expended only with those contractors who are willing to participate in this program to fight hard-core unemployment and institutionalized discrimination."[33] By developing a city plan that gave so much attention to structural economic concerns, and specifically, to how spatially concentrated economic stagnation interacted with institutionalized employment discrimination, the CHR based its model of affirmative action on a realistic understanding of the dilemmas that faced inner city African Americans. Local liberalism in Philadelphia—in this case embodied by the CHR—thus outdid its national counterparts by embedding affirmative action policy in a rigorous structural analysis of the city's problem of jobs, and in the process broke through a key limitation of Great Society liberalism.

Two other elements of the city plan also pushed beyond the federal Philadelphia Plan. At the immediate, pragmatic level of increasing the number of jobs affected by affirmative action, the city plan covered not just construction but all suppliers and service providers doing business with the city. Such companies actually formed the initial priorities in enforcement of the plan.[34] Also, the CHR successfully convinced not just city agencies, but also semi-autonomous municipal authorities and large private institutions to adopt the city plan. By mid-1969, the Board of Education, the Philadelphia Gas Works, the major universities, the YWCA, the United Fund, the Federation of Jewish Agencies, the Archdiocese of Philadelphia, and numerous churches and synagogues all accepted the city plan as an official standard for contracting policy. Whether PIDC adopted the plan remains unclear.[35] This broad participation in the city plan meant that it applied to a far greater number of contracts, employers, and jobs than the city alone could have generated, and—despite the significance of federally financed construction—far more than that encompassed by the limited reach of the federal plan.

The CHR's citywide affirmative action plan had another important effect for the wider trajectory of liberalism in Philadelphia. It sparked a strengthening of the old liberal civil rights coalition—or, more accurately, parts of that coalition, as the unions remained notably absent. This renewed alliance first emerged as the CHR worked to achieve the widest possible adoption of its plan. In doing so, the commission relied on lobbying both by city agencies such as the Commission on Higher Education and by liberal citizens groups such as the Council on Equal Job Opportunity, an umbrella organization that had long been involved in challenges to discrimination. In the fall of 1968, for example, Commission on Higher Education chairman Brother Daniel Bernian wrote to every institution of higher learning in the city, noted CEJO's campaign "to encourage business, industry, and public agencies to take affirmative action leading toward employment of minority persons," and urged universities and colleges to do likewise. He received uniformly positive responses, typified by that of University of Pennsylvania president Gaylord Harnwell, who assured Bernian that his institution "is in complete accord with the view expressed by the Commission." Meanwhile, CEJO also worked to convince "religious, charitable, and non-profit groups" to adopt the plan, and coordinated its efforts with the CHR's work in surveying the employment practices of contractors and suppliers in the city.[36]

By early 1969, Farmer praised the "widespread adoption" of the city Philadelphia Plan. Later in the year, CHR deputy director Richard Levin explained to a DOL hearing that the plan had focused on "the service and supply contractors, and has been quite successful in that area." He conceded, however, that most progress in construction, if any, had been the result of the more rigorous federal Philadelphia Plan, and called for its reinstatement.[37] Although construction, as Levin implied, exposed the limits of local policy capabilities, the city plan nonetheless provided a means to maintain pressure on the unions to expand their outreach programs after the Staats ruling. The School District of Philadelphia quickly became the main battleground in this struggle, in part because it had begun a building program to replace many of the city's crumbling schools. The Board of Education had full, state-sanctioned authority over the schools, and initially hesitated to adopt the plan out of reluctance to cede any element of its closely guarded autonomy to the city government, and because it was already engaged in a contentious dispute over school desegregation. Also, the superintendent of schools, Mark Shedd, expressed uncertainty over "just what the Philadelphia Plan entails" in terms of actual contracting practice.[38] Faced with demands from a coalition of community groups for an even more aggressive affirmative action policy, however, the board finally adopted the city plan in the fall of 1968.

Superintendent Shedd—who had undertaken a controversial school reform program in partnership with board president (and former mayor) Richardson Dilworth—then launched a campaign to force the seven critical building trades to integrate their apprentice programs. Shedd and Dilworth had powerful leverage because the union apprentice programs relied on the free use of school facilities, as well as on teachers supplied by the board. After a series of unsuccessful meetings with union officials during the fall, Shedd ordered the Sheet Metal Union out of Bok Vocational School in December. Shedd also informed Steamfitters union officials that unless they increased minority enrollments, their apprentice program would be evicted from the schools on March 7. The local, however, made little progress, and with only one African American in an apprentice class of nineteen, the union program was ordered to vacate school facilities in February. Shedd followed with similar sanctions against the other critical trades as well as the Operating Engineers. With this added pressure, previously recalcitrant building trades locals began to implement stronger recruitment programs and to advertise the openings in black newspapers. By June, even the Sheet Metal Workers opened their apprentice program to minority applicants and applied for reentry to Board of Education facilities.[39]

Despite the efforts of the liberal–civil rights coalition and the added pressure from the Board of Education, the city's overall progress in opening jobs funded through public contracts remained torturously slow. Each case involved struggles both on the street and in conference rooms around the city. A notably successful case during the summer and fall of 1969 involved the A. B. Dick Company, one of the city's largest distributors of supplies for duplicating and photocopying machines. In mid-July, A. B. Dick fired two black workers who, ironically, had attempted to organize a unionization vote in the company's trucking and warehousing division. Three of the men's co-workers joined them in what soon became a small-scale protest strike. The case became intertwined with the anti-discrimination effort when the strikers, with the assistance of the Consumers' Education and Protective Association (a local advocacy group), publicized the racial makeup of the company's workforce: 90 percent of the trucking and warehouse workers at A. B. Dick were black, while nearly 98 percent of the clerical and sales workers were white. Meanwhile, the federal National Labor Relations Board (NLRB) began an investigation not of the company's firing of the union organizers, but of possible intimidation of other employees by the strikers.[40]

City government and institutions proved more responsive than the NLRB. After the strikers picketed both the CHR offices and the Board of Education, the CHR found A. B. Dick's hiring practices unacceptable and removed the company from its approved bidders list.[41] The elimination of A. B. Dick's business with all signatories of the city plan had a powerful effect. On October 10, the CHR announced that A. B. Dick had accepted an eleven-point plan: the company would "hire a number of hardcore unemployed and adopt an employment policy of nondiscrimination on race," advertise itself as an equal opportunity employer, retain all applications for a 120-day period, inform the CHR of the rationale behind all rejected applications, accept employment applications even when it had no vacancies, and "interview all minority persons" during recruiting visits to schools or colleges. Of even greater significance for institutionalized discrimination, A. B. Dick agreed both to cease accepting any referrals of white employment candidates from its white employees, and to review all of its qualification requirements for relevance to actual job performance. These latter points addressed two of the most frequently cited minority complaints about hiring practices in the city, and their inclusion indicated that the CHR could adapt the city plan to actual conditions. In the aftermath of the agreement, three of the five strikers returned to the company, one resigned, and one remained, for an unexplained reason, unemployed. The three who resumed work intended to continue their organizing campaign.[42]

Beyond Integration: Minority Contractors
and Philadelphia's Liberal Coalition

Even as the initial federal Philadelphia Plan foundered, participants in a new local partnership began to develop an alternative strategy to challenge construction industry discrimination. As the local branch of a newly organized national organization, the Philadelphia Urban Coalition drew on city government, the private sector, liberal labor groups, and African American community organizations to develop one of the first truly cross-racial liberal responses to any employment issue in Philadelphia. More broadly, the Urban Coalition reflected the unifying effect that the Philadelphia Plan had for many liberals. Although it lacked the authority to implement a fully coordinated set of policy responses to Philadelphia's problem of jobs, the Coalition's construction-industry programs successfully operated not only across boundaries between the public and private sectors but also across the city's racialized, parallel tracks of local industrial and employment policy. Its activities in the construction field thus provided a partial demonstration of the potential efficacy of coordinated, comprehensive responses to employment related urban problems.

The national Urban Coalition had been organized by prominent political, labor, business, and religious leaders in the aftermath of the 1967 uprisings in Newark and Detroit. Mayor Tate served on the steering committee for the national organization. At the founding meeting in August 1967, A. Phillip Randolph read the coalition's "Statement of Principles, Goals, and Commitments," which called for cooperative government-industry efforts to address urban problems, a renewed pursuit of the 1949 U.S. Housing Act's goal of "a decent home for every American," and the creation of one million "meaningful" and "socially useful" public works jobs on urban reconstruction projects. The last item was a direct endorsement of a $2.8 billion emergency jobs program that had been proposed in the Senate by Pennsylvania Senator and former Philadelphia Mayor Joseph Clark, but that was opposed by the Johnson administration.[43]

The Philadelphia version of the Urban Coalition started work in early 1968 when Tate organized a local chapter and appointed African American deputy mayor Charles Bowser (the former PAAC leader) as its executive director.[44] The local Coalition rapidly became one of Philadelphia's most active public-private organizations, with projects in economic development, education, health, welfare, housing, and job training. While this broad approach offered the promise of a comprehensive attack on urban problems, it also risked superficiality and attenuation of the organization's limited resources.[45] But in its economic development and job training activities, the Coalition made substantive progress by engaging key racial dimensions of the problem of jobs that other quasi-public initiatives such as PIDC had ignored.[46]

In particular, the Coalition focused on the issue of black participation in the building trades. In late 1968, as Elmer Staats prepared to block the federal Philadelphia Plan, the Coalition organized a minority contractors association known as the General and Specialties Contractors Association of Philadelphia (GASCAP), which offered a revolving loan and collateral fund and provided management assistance and training. Most importantly, GASCAP also pursued construction contracts for its members. In early 1970, the Coalition used a $700,000-grant from Philadelphia's struggling Model Cities Administration to create the Minority Contractors Assistance Program (MCAP), which provided financial support and technical advice to minority-owned construction firms. MCAP expanded GASCAP's loan and collateral programs and between January and June of 1970 provided $25,659 in direct loans and $480,000 in loan guarantees for minority contractors.[47]

Along with this financial support, staff members and expert volunteers from the Coalition's "Action Construction Team" offered management and financial counseling for participating minority contractors. They also ran a weekly series of "Job Control Clinics" that addressed contractors' specific, on-the-job problems. In addition, MCAP worked with institutions such as the University of Pennsylvania to encourage minority contractors to bid on large, institutional construction jobs. A number of the MCAP contractors secured major contracts through this program. This initiative also inadvertently highlighted the costs of the wider bifurcation of economic policy in the city. MCAP contractors could have benefited greatly from construction contracts linked to PIDC, which during this period remained extremely active in industrial development. Given the Coalition's quasi-public character, and the overlap of at least some of its leadership with PIDC, such a link could likely have been forged.

GASCAP remained active as well. Its members organized a cooperative that allowed minority contractors to obtain building materials at reduced costs and offered lines of credit that assisted members in making such purchases. After discovering that tax issues constituted one of the most difficult problems facing many minority contractors, MCAP and GASCAP developed a system to help in maintaining payroll records and

establishing structured tax depository accounts for both back taxes and
quarterly payments. Almost immediately, these initiatives produced dramatic results: during the first twenty-four weeks of MCAP's operation, the
144 participating contractors earned $7 million, compared to only $4 million during the entire previous year.[48] By the spring of 1972, the program
provided assistance to 200 minority contractors who received more than
$12 million in contracts despite a slowdown in the industry. During that
year, the federal Office of Minority Business Enterprise provided grants
worth $314,915 to expand MCAP on a regional basis.[49]

The success of MCAP and GASCAP indicates that continued opposition to integration created significant costs for the unions. These programs
bypassed the traditional union-contractor arrangements by creating an
autonomous, non-union African American sector within the industry. With
little commitment to the existing union-based system, African American
contractors would presumably hire non-union black (as well as white)
workers. During the urban-renewal building boom of the mid- and late-
1960s, the building trades could afford the costs of such an oppositional
stance toward integration. In later periods of lower activity, however,
the presence of a large, non-union African American sector, justified by
the moral and social imperative of ending discrimination, would severely
weaken the trades.

As it worked to develop a base of independent African American contractors, however, the Urban Coalition did not abandon the union integration effort. Instead, it actively sought to break down patterns of discrimination in union apprenticeships, membership, and hiring structures.
In an effort to work cooperatively with the unions, the Coalition in 1970
added the business manager of the Building Trades Council of Philadelphia to its board and, in an attempt "to generate catalytic action to deepen
the involvement of the Philadelphia labor movement in its activities,"
created a Labor Advisory Council with representatives of most major
Philadelphia unions. Bowser also reached out to the Building Trades
Council to develop a Coalition program that upgraded the skills of minority craftsmen so they could qualify for union journeyman status. The effort met with some acceptance and lessened some tensions. Cooperation,
though, had limits. At Urban Coalition board meetings, Bowser defended
the constitutionality of the Philadelphia Plan against labor and contractor objections and argued that lawsuits brought by groups such as the
Contractors Association of Eastern Pennsylvania were nothing more than
unjustifiable delaying tactics. Under Bowser's direction, the Coalition

also provided legal and lobbying support for the campaign to sustain the Philadelphia Plan through the legal challenges that followed the Nixon administration's 1969 resurrection of affirmative action.[50]

In an area of minority job development unrelated to the construction industry dispute, the Coalition supported the regional transit agency SEPTA in an unsuccessful effort to get a $250,000 grant from the U.S. Department of Transportation (DOT) to provide low-fare transit service from North Philadelphia to outlying industrial parks in Northeast Philadelphia and the suburbs. The DOT, however, denied the request, leading the Urban Coalition to charge "that the underlying reason for rejecting the proposal was to prevent Black and Spanish-speaking persons from obtaining jobs in white suburbs." Calls for a congressional probe of the decision went unanswered, however, and inadequate bus service remained the only nonautomobile option for reaching the northeast industrial parks. In the following months, the Coalition lobbied against an increase in SEPTA fares and urged the agency to reject a $7-million DOT grant for the purchase of new metroliner commuter trains, which the Coalition argued would primarily benefit suburban commuters; Coalition Manpower Task Force chair Joseph Harvey maintained that after DOT's rejection of the "relatively miniscule" low-fare grant, acceptance of the equipment grant would endorse the federal agency's "'cynical disregard' for the needs of the ghetto jobless."[51] Unlike PIDC, the Coalition was willing to challenge spatially embedded relationships between race, residence, and employment in both the city and the region. In large part, these positions reflected the influence of the increasingly militant Bowser, who transcended his earlier PAAC and City Hall incarnations and moved to the forefront of African American politics in the city (he would run for mayor in 1975 and 1979).

More generally, however, the Urban Coalition's loose coalition of community, business, political, and labor representatives began to bridge the racial gaps that had previously bifurcated Philadelphia's response to the problem of jobs into parallel, racially defined tracks. Although it sometimes dispersed its financial and human resources over a broad and almost unmanageable range of social, cultural, and economic activities, and of course never linked its programs to PIDC, the Coalition at its best served as coordinator for cooperative, public-private strategies to address the many facets—structural, political, racial, and physical—of Philadelphia's problem of jobs. As a result, its primary legacy consisted of demonstrating the potential benefits of socially conscious economic strategies, and of creating new channels of communication across the racial divide that had separated industrial and employment policy in Philadelphia during the previous decade. Support for affirmative action, and for the development of an autonomous black construction sector, was a core component of this coalescence of liberal and civil rights interests.

The Second (Federal) Philadelphia Plan

By the time that the Urban Coalition implemented its construction industry programs, the struggle over affirmative action in Philadelphia had been transformed by the unexpected revival of the federal Philadelphia Plan. When Elmer Staats rejected the original FEB Philadelphia Plan in November 1968, it seemed improbable that the plan would be resurrected by an incoming Nixon administration that had targeted its campaign strategy to voters disaffected by racial integration and anti-war protests. By June 1969, however, the unlikely had occurred, as new secretary of labor George Schultz and assistant secretary Arthur Fletcher strengthened the OFCC and unveiled the revised Philadelphia Plan in the contentious press conference at the First Bank of the United States building.

The Nixon administration's motivation in reviving the Philadelphia Plan has been the subject of extensive debate, but the decision ultimately arose from a mixed set of impulses ranging from legitimate concerns for racial justice on the part of Fletcher and, to a lesser extent, Schultz, to a cynical effort on the part of the president and domestic policy advisor John Ehrlichman to splinter the New Deal coalition by dividing unions from civil rights groups. In practice, the revised plan obviated Staats's objection to the violation of competitive bidding rules, as Fletcher and his staff eliminated post-bid negotiations over manning tables and instead specified that detailed hiring requirements would be spelled out in pre-bid project specifications. They also deflected the question of Title VII's quota ban by establishing percentage *ranges* for minority participation in each skill rather than fixed targets. Over a three-year period, gradual increases in those ranges would draw minority participation in the building trades into line with the overall area population makeup. To further differentiate these "goal" ranges from illegal quotas, the plan required that contractors simply had to make a demonstrable "good-faith" effort to fulfill the hiring obligation. Contractors could show such "good-faith" by working with community groups, job training programs, or government agencies to find qualified workers or apprentices, and by requiring sub-contractors to meet hiring goals.[52] Supporters saw OFCC's differentiation of goal-based employment ranges from quotas as a nuanced balancing of the law with legitimate social justice concerns. As a *Washington Post* editorial put it, a quota "means a ceiling... the goals embodied in the Philadelphia Plan constitute a floor, not a ceiling; they constitute an agreement to enlarge job opportunities for minority workers, not restrict them; and so they are in complete conformity with the essential spirit and purpose of the Civil Rights Act." Opponents, including Staats, viewed the distinction as a dubious semantic device designed to evade Title VII's quota ban.[53]

By late summer, Staats and the administration were engaged in open conflict over the Philadelphia Plan's legality.[54] At the same time, debate over the plan raged in Philadelphia. Among civil rights activists and non-union liberals, the effort to implement the revised plan provided a source of renewed unity, to an even greater extent than the earlier FEB and city plans. This cooperative work began even before the OFCC publicly announced its intent to issue the revised plan. In late March, at a meeting in the offices of the Urban League, a coalition that included the CHR, the ACLU, the Council on Equal Job Opportunity (CEJO), the Council of Black Clergy, People for Human Rights, the Episcopal Diocese, and Wives for Equal Opportunity (a group organized by Joyce Rush) agreed to pursue "a campaign for testing the suspension of the Philadelphia Plan." On April 29, CHR director Clarence Farmer and Urban Coalition Director Bowser joined members of Philadelphia's congressional delegation for a discussion of the plan with Staats and OFCC officials. Farmer and Bowser argued that affirmative action in construction constituted a crucial priority for the city, both in addressing unemployment among minorities and in maintaining racial peace. In a June follow-up letter, Farmer made the latter point explicit when he cautioned Staats that blocking the soon to-be-released revised plan would "cause tensions which may erupt into demonstrations or civil disorders." In the aftermath of the revised plan's release, the *Philadelphia Tribune* credited this local lobbying effort as a significant factor in the decision to revive the plan.[55] Liberal white organizations such as the New Democratic Coalition joined the cause as well; *Philadelphia Magazine* described this group as "the aspiring liberal conscience of the city's Democratic party" because of its cross-racial alliances with the Black Political Forum (which had begun preparations to run a black mayoral candidate in 1971) and its grassroots efforts to unseat entrenched ward leaders.[56]

This mobilization of the liberal-civil rights coalition spanned political ideologies from moderate to militant. In mid-July, fifteen "civil rights and community groups" ranging from the staid Urban League to the pragmatists of OIC to the increasingly radical Model Cities Area–Wide Council (chapter 8) attended a meeting with regional OFCC officials at which they discussed details of the revised Philadelphia Plan and offered suggestions about the specific employment ranges that federal officials should apply. Ben Stahl, the local director of the AFL-CIO's Human Resources Development Institute (HRDI), also attended the meeting as a representative of labor; a few weeks before, Stahl had dismissed the Philadelphia Plan as "a slogan, not a plan," but he now acknowledged that it had "rallied civil rights groups and others who want to see the logjam broken."[57]

The pro-plan coalition, however, soon left even progressive unionists such as Stahl behind. CEJO executive director H. Louis Evert publicly urged the federal government to broaden the plan to cover all construction unions and all forms of federal contracting. He also called on the unions not just to open their apprenticeships but to transform them. He urged them to eliminate nonessential entry requirements such as high school graduation, to completely restructure written and oral qualifying examinations or replace them with "post-employment testing," to drastically shorten the multi-year apprentice programs, and to implement journeyman upgrade programs for non-union minority craftspeople.[58] A member of CEJO himself, Stahl countered privately that such proposals offered "a negative and basically insignificant approach to the problem" that would merely lower standards. In a comment that highlighted the cost to the liberal coalition of marginalizing the unions, Stahl also argued that "any expansion of employment requires expansion of work opportunities, and CEJO and other groups must be concerned with a full employment economy and cannot ignore current trends." In particular, he urged, CEJO should fight against President Nixon's recently proposed cutbacks in federal construction spending. Whatever recalcitrance they displayed on racial integration, the unions at the end of the 1960s still supported the revival of a job-centered, structurally focused liberalism, a liberalism without which the problem of jobs could not be solved. While the Philadelphia Plan tightened and strengthened the liberal-civil rights coalition, the increasing separation of the "hard hats" from that coalition came at significant cost.[59]

By the time assistant secretary Fletcher arrived in Philadelphia on August 26 to hold hearings on the revised plan, the two sides had developed opposite positions. Representatives of the building trades remained deeply hostile to the Philadelphia Plan, as were many of the contractors. They argued that the number of qualified African American craftsmen, or even experienced union helpers who could be easily upgraded to journeymen, remained so small that the contractors could not possibly meet the plan's standards. Benjamin Dyess of the General Building Contractors Association informed Fletcher's panel that if "the problem is caused by a lack of minority individuals not already employed in the industry who possess the skills necessary to be qualified for employment in these crafts, only training is the answer. We believe [that] situation is the cause of the problem."[60] From this view, minority employment could only increase through the expansion of the union outreach programs, which the unions claimed were operating successfully. Building Trades Council attorney Bernard Katz pointed out that the initial Apprentice Outreach Program contract with the Department of Labor had required the placement of only fifty minority applicants in apprentice programs during the entire first year of the program, but that the trades had already accepted eighty-three such apprentices. Union representatives also challenged the premise that their locals excluded anyone on the basis of race, pointing out overall membership and apprentice percentages, but eliding questions about which trades minorities had actually been able to enter, what status they had reached, what type of work they did, and how frequently they could obtain it. This led, inevitably, to the old canard that discrimination could not exist unless specific, overt cases of exclusion could be documented.[61] Finally, the unions warned that the plan would lower both quality and safety standards by forcing them to accept unqualified members.[62]

Supporters of the plan countered that qualified minority tradesmen could be found, or at least that numerous non-union craftsmen and union helpers could be easily upgraded. OIC job development manager Rennie Morgan estimated that OIC alone could supply between 5,000 and 8,000 qualified candidates in a year. He added that an OIC program that upgraded craftsmen to journeyman skill levels had run into a wall of union resistance—as trainees in the program had warned beforehand: "[trainees] came to us because they had confidence in us, but they told us then that they didn't believe that anything would come of it; and a little while later we found out that nothing would come of it."[63] Many observers also noted that repeated frustration in attempting to gain entry had thoroughly alienated much of the black community from the building trade unions. Joyce Rush pointed out that "there is a severe lack of trust as far as the black community is concerned because of the fact that those of us who have dedicated ourselves to trying to open up the unions and the jobs that are supposed to be available through these unions have had a wall and many walls put before us." Rush explained that even for those few blacks who did gain admission to the unions, actual work opportunities remained scarce: "black union members don't work in some cases even half a year. So being a union member is not automatically seen as desirable." Despite lower wages, non-union contractors offered more consistent work, and with it, the opportunity for higher earnings over an annual cycle. Liberal city councilman David Cohen offered similar observations from conversations with blacks in his district.[64]

The Building Trades' outreach program garnered no more enthusiasm. Describing the outreach program implemented by the Operating Engineers, Rush concluded that "this program was theatrics.... the training program was set up in order to avoid being put under the Philadelphia Plan."[65] Even with outreach in effect, it remained a pre-apprentice program with no guarantee of admission to apprenticeships, much less to union membership, journeyman status, or eventual employment.

More subtle issues affected assessments of the Philadelphia Plan as well. The relationship between gender, work, and family life was a prominent undercurrent that ran through much of the debate, though it was rarely discussed directly. Here, the Philadelphia Plan interacted in unexpected and sometimes problematic ways with the transformation of gender roles underway by the end of the 1960s. Union speakers defended their traditional training and membership practices as necessary to protect what they saw as a clear social good: the ability of men to earn a "family wage" sufficient to support dependent women and children. As Katz explained, "when a union accepts members—regardless of their racial background, regardless of their ethnic background—it also becomes their job to do everything possible to keep those members in a position of being able to support their wives and their families and to keep them employed."[66] Female African American activists in the Wives for Equal Employment Opportunity group, however, also claimed the moral authority of the family wage as they fought to secure affirmative action in the male-dominated construction industry. As Rush explained, "from personal experience...when a man cannot go out of his front door and go to work (peace of mind, you know) and know that he doesn't have to break his neck to compete with other white individuals to stay on the job,

he can come home with the same peace of mind and function as a male
and as the head of his family. But in many instances wives must go out
to work and leave the children with other people so that they can supplement the family income." As the founder of a policy advocacy group that
lobbied for the transformation of hiring practices in a major industry—an
industry in which her own husband worked—Rush clearly saw a role for
women outside the home and had personally forged such a life for her-
self. Yet her involvement in the Philadelphia Plan, she noted, stemmed
from the fact that male unemployment and limited earning power "created problems with the family structure and with children. And this is
our interest, how this problem can be solved through the Philadelphia
Plan."[67]

Rush's analysis highlighted how for much of the African American
community, the concept of the male-earned "family wage" still held appeal, even at a time when welfare rights activists offered a radically different and in some ways more realistic vision that sought to create alternative
relationships between work, state support, and family structures.[68] For
the social structure outlined by Rush to function, however, the need to secure, or even reassert, the masculinity of African American males became
paramount, and played a significant part in the emphasis of the northern
civil rights movement on gaining access to employment in the unquestionably "manly" field of construction. Postwar local liberalism could not
readily separate the issues of race and economic structure raised by discrimination and deindustrialization from the questions of gender raised
by changing family norms and work roles. Rush's testimony touched on
the exact issues that had exploded into public consciousness following the
publication of the Moynihan report four years earlier. The controversy
surrounding that report's discussion of "pathological" matriarchal family
structures in the black community had obscured a crucial point that Rush
now made with far more grace: the availability of decent jobs for black
men mattered greatly for the lives of many black women and children.
Although Rush clearly normalized the role of wife and mother as home-
maker, her argument made clear that large numbers of unemployed and
underemployed males did not serve the interests of any community—and
building trades jobs offered a seemingly promising way to combat that
problem.

As OFCC moved to implement the revised Philadelphia Plan, the building
trades issue became increasingly contentious nationally. Even as Fletcher

proceeded with hearings in Philadelphia, protests against construction discrimination began in Pittsburgh and soon led to violent clashes between activists and union members. A few weeks later in Chicago, fist-fights broke out before one of Fletcher's hearings. The confrontations led to five injuries and nine arrests and delayed the hearing for a day.[69] Meanwhile, the national Building Trades Convention passed a resolution that rejected the revised Philadelphia Plan and blasted it as a quota system, "high-handed, ambiguous, and in definite conflict with the Civil Rights Act of 1964." Speaking at the convention, AFL-CIO president and plumber's union member George Meany accused the Nixon administration of making a racial "whipping boy" out of the building trades.[70]

Nonetheless, in October OFCC approved the first contract under the revised Philadelphia Plan, to Bristol Steel and Iron Works of Richmond, Virginia for an addition to Children's Hospital of Philadelphia. By mid-January 1970, a total of seven contracts, worth $34 million, had been written under the plan.[71] Further implementation, however, moved slowly, impeded by a widely anticipated court challenge. This came on January 8, when the Contractors Association of Eastern Pennsylvania charged in a U.S. District Court suit that the revised plan established a racial quota, and as such violated both the Civil Rights Act and the Constitution's equal protection clause. Although it rejected the claims, the DOL indicated that it welcomed the suit as a means to clarify the plan's cloudy legal standing.[72] Joining the DOL, the city of Philadelphia filed a brief that called for dismissal on the grounds that the plan's "good faith" provision meant that the contractor "is not obligated to guarantee any specific number of jobs to minority group members," only to "broaden his recruitment base beyond trade unions if the unions don't furnish sufficient minority employees." While expected, the city's stance nonetheless showed again how the Philadelphia Plan, and affirmative action more generally, reinforced key parts of the liberal-civil rights coalition. In this case, the Tate administration sided with the integrationists, rather than with the building trades unions who had long been among the mayor's key supporters. This apparent discrepancy may be explained by two factors: first, Tate had also drawn equally crucial votes from the African American community, and, although he had more recently pursued a "law-and-order" strategy targeted at ethnic whites, he still hoped to maintain black support; second, more speculatively, the 1968 ouster of Tate ally James O'Neill as president of the Philadelphia Building Trades Council by a rival faction within the council may have cost the unions an important link to the mayor's office.[73] Although widely disparaged by liberal reformers (with justification in such areas as fiscal management), Tate remained at base a liberal politician, committed not just to ward-based organizational politics but also to the use of the state to address social inequities. In the case of the General Contractors Association suit, the mayor's political calculations coincided with his policy goals, and Tate's organization Democrats lined up once again, as they had during the 1950s, with both the reform liberals and the civil rights community.

The position proved to be a winning one. On March 14, District Court judge Charles Weiner ruled that because it did not require the hiring of a fixed number or percentage of minority workers, the Philadelphia Plan violated neither law nor constitution. Denying the contractor's request for an injunction, Weiner described construction employment as an "unpalatable situation" that had "fostered and perpetuated a system that has effectively maintained a segregated class. That concept, if I may use the strong language it deserves, is repugnant, unworthy and contrary to present national policy." The contractors filed an appeal, but in April 1971 the U.S. Court of Appeals upheld Weiner's ruling; in October, the Supreme Court refused to hear an appeal. These decisions effectively dismissed the objections of both the comptroller general and the unions and cleared the way for the revised Philadelphia Plan to proceed, checked only by the limited enforcement capacity of the OFCC, the continuing resistance of unions and contractors, and the shifting political interests of the Nixon administration.[74]

Such constraints proved significant. Despite the court challenge, the DOL in 1970 began to deploy the Philadelphia Plan nationally as a stick to encourage the adoption of voluntary "hometown plans" that Secretary Schultz indicated he preferred and that had already been drafted in Chicago and Pittsburgh. By February 1970, DOL identified eighteen cities as primary candidates for an imposed Philadelphia-style plan if they did not implement acceptable voluntary plans. Immediate priorities for the summer construction season included Boston, Newark, Atlanta, Detroit, Seattle, and Los Angeles. On June 1, DOL imposed a mandatory plan in Washington, D.C., after negotiations to develop a voluntary plan failed— and applied the requirements not just to federal contracts, but to all of a contractor's work in the Washington area. By July, however, only Boston, Denver, and Indianapolis had forged hometown plans, with tentative arrangements pending in New Orleans and St. Louis. The DOL then added seventy-three additional cities to its list.[75]

In Philadelphia, meanwhile, enforcement of the plan had gone poorly. Underfunded, understaffed, and hampered by the continuing court case, the OFCC regional office struggled to assure that contractors complied with contracts issued under the plan. By May, the plan had been applied to nine projects covering $42 million, but many contractors had not met their hiring goals and most unions had simply refused to cooperate. Regional OFCC director Bernard Stalvey acknowledged that "there is no doubt that the contractors are behind in compliance," and indicated that the federal departments that actually issued the contracts would begin to press for progress. Two months later, Philadelphia Urban League director Andrew Freeman charged that "the plan is a failure because the compliance office has not had the staff to monitor it and the contracting agencies, like H.E.W. and H.U.D. are not committed to compliance."[76] In September, when DOL issued a blithely optimistic report claiming that the plan had achieved a minority participation rate of nearly 23 percent in five of the critical trades, CEJO President Thomas Rowe blasted the figures as "unwittingly deceiving the public." Rowe noted that the survey covered only 180 jobs spread over twenty-five projects; further, the procedures of the survey had been such that contractors had engaged in extensive "motorcycling" to achieve a fraudulent compliance.[77]

The unions adopted an equally dismissive view of the DOL survey. Ben Stahl wrote to a colleague that "I would still have to say that no new minority worker has been put to work as a result of the Philadelphia Plan." Stahl also recognized the reality of motorcycle compliance, but drew a different conclusion about it: "this is the major fallacy of the Philadelphia Plan. . . . this is why it is impossible to have an area-wide program covering all construction, and why stress should be laid on machinery and training programs that will bring minority workers into the industry." As evidence for this point, Stahl claimed that those minorities who *had* been identified by the DOL survey were there as a result of the Apprentice Outreach Program, the recent unionization of two black contractors, and a special iron workers permit program—but not from the Philadelphia Plan.[78]

While such criticism from both sides reflected the frustrations generated by the plan, CEJO's position demonstrated once again that the court case and the difficulties associated with implementation maintained the revived alliance among liberals and civil rights activists. Beginning in the spring of 1970, organizations including CEJO, the Urban League, the League of Women Voters, the NAACP, North City Congress, and the Philadelphia Tutorial Project formally allied in support of the plan through a new umbrella group known as the Action for Jobs Committee. Action for Jobs emerged as the primary pro-plan lobbying force, and, with the understaffed OFCC unable to put large numbers of inspectors in the field, served a vital function in bringing contractor and union failures to the government's attention.[79]

OFCC increasingly responded to such complaints with alacrity. In late June, OFCC revised the plan's compliance system, requiring monthly reporting of "the minority percentage of man-hours per craft, by contract." If those percentages fell below the contractor's minimum goal, the federal contracting agencies would issue a "show cause" notice requiring the contractor to demonstrate legitimate, specific factors that had prevented them from meeting the commitments. Failure to show such cause could lead to the suspension or revocation of a federal contract, and a ban on future work. Within two weeks, HEW issued six "show cause" orders in the Philadelphia area and HUD issued one. OFCC director John L. Wilks implicitly acknowledged the role of community groups such as Action for Jobs: "This is the first overt enforcement action we've taken. Because of the debate over the plan's workability, some segments of the public apparently felt we'd let the plan drift. But we have no intention of letting it drift." The action also brought a new actor into the struggle, as it affected not only the contractors and unions targeted by the plan, but also had direct consequences for the institutions that would benefit from federally financed work. The six HEW show-cause orders, for example, involved building projects at Children's Hospital, the University of Pennsylvania, and Temple University in Philadelphia, and Villanova University, Pennsylvania Military College, and Lincoln University in the suburbs. None of these institutions wanted their projects delayed, none had a particular interest in preserving the prerogatives of the building trades unions, and some faced intense pressure from students, faculty, and neighbors to demonstrate greater racial sensitivity. All would willingly place additional pressure on their contractors.

In August, the first actual cancellation of a contract occurred when Edgely Air Products of suburban Levittown lost the remainder of a $43,000 subcontract for sheet metal work on Penn's new medical laboratory building (only about $5,000 worth of work remained); more significantly, the company would be "debarred," meaning that it could receive no future federal contracts until it corrected its hiring procedures. Edgely, whose workforce on the project included no minorities, appealed the ruling, claiming that as a small company with only ten employees it had no vacancies. Administrative hurdles within HEW delayed a final decision until September 1971, at which point HEW secretary Elliot Richardson cancelled the contract and debarred Edgely on the grounds that it had not made good faith efforts such as hiring minority replacements for workers on vacation. The ruling showed the potential power of Philadelphia Plan sanctions: company owner Leonard Nucero glumly told reporters that the action would "cripple" his company because of its dependence on government work.[80]

By March 1971, HEW had issued more than twenty such orders, but by mid-1972, only two additional firms had actually been debarred. This reflected, in part, the Nixon administration's decision in the fall of 1970 to deemphasize the Philadelphia Plan in order to build support among blue collar workers who appeared increasingly supportive of the administration's Vietnam policy following the spring "hard hat riot" in which New York City construction workers attacked and routed an anti-war protest. Extension of mandatory "Philadelphia-style" plans to other cities slowed, and after his 1972 reelection, Nixon appointed New York Building Trades president Peter Brennan as Secretary of Labor. CEJO president William Gutman and CEJO director Louis Evert later charged that the administration effected this policy shift to "woo the labor vote in the elections of November 1970," and further claimed that "from that point on no one ever felt threatened by the Philadelphia Plan. In fact, it seemed to be embarrassing to the administration."[81]

Despite the low rate of debarments and contract cancellations, Gutman and Evert somewhat overstated the case for such abandonment. In February of 1971, the DOL awarded two contracts to the Philadelphia Urban Coalition "to recruit, train and place 180 trainees in five construction trades." The first contract, for $188,400, would involve cooperation with the Negro Trade Union Leadership Council and would cover recruitment of minority construction workers who could be upgraded to journeymen. Skill evaluations would be conducted to determine the credit that each participant should receive for past work experience, and employment counseling and follow-up services would be offered. DOL indicated that it would "encourage" area construction contractors to implement training programs that would complete the journeyman upgrades for the program's participants, but if they failed to do so, the Urban Coalition would receive a second, $460,000 contract to conduct the training itself. In addition, assistant secretary Fletcher issued DOL Revised Order 4, which stated that federal contractors would be required to meet the plan's minority hiring requirements in their nonfederal work. CEJO had lobbied for adoption of this standard since 1969.[82]

Finally, the OFCC began to perform unannounced compliance checks at Philadelphia Plan construction sites. These checks explicitly sought to counter "motorcycle compliance." As CEJO's Gutman and Evert wrote, OFCC "has never had the supportive manpower needed to oversee such a vast undertaking" as the Philadelphia Plan, and the spot compliance checks approach maximized the resources that the agency did have available. When the spot checks exposed failures to fulfill contract requirements, OFCC issued show-cause orders against the offending contractors. Even though the orders produced few actual contract cancellations, they frequently led to direct negotiations with contractors in which "almost all of the firms agreed to correct discriminatory practices" and add blacks to their workforces.[83]

Gradually, these efforts began to produce positive results. A carefully controlled compliance check of seventy-four federal projects in September 1973 showed that minorities had made inroads into the building trades, including the six critical trades targeted by the Philadelphia Plan. Overall, the checks revealed that minorities accounted for 929 of the 2,752 total workers on the projects (33.8 percent); in the critical trades, minorities held a significantly lower share, 115 out of 713 (16.1 percent), but it still far exceeded their negligible representation when the first Philadelphia Plan had been announced in 1967. Further, OFCC determined that 1,137 minorities had become full members of the critical trades, up from 283 in 1969. Overall, contractors reported that from January through October 1973, minority workers accounted for 21 percent of hours worked in the critical trades (13,692 out of 65,338), easily within the 1973 goal range of 19.8–23.8 percent. Four of the six crafts met or exceeded their goals, ranging from highs of 33 percent for the Steamfitters (20–24 percent goal) and 31 percent for the Ironworkers (22–26 percent goal) to 22 percent each for the Plumbers (20–24 percent goal) and Elevator Constructors (19–23 percent goal); those that fell below their goals included the Electrical Workers, with 17 percent (19–23 percent goal), and the long-recalcitrant Sheet Metal Workers, with 12 percent (19–23 percent goal). These percentages all remained below the black share of population in Philadelphia (although not the region), and some may have reflected persistent motorcycle compliance or other forms of statistical padding. Nonetheless, they showed that the Philadelphia Plan had produced real gains for minority employment in the building and construction trades.[84]

Earlier in 1973, a study by the CHR revealed a wider picture of employment integration beyond the construction industry. In particular, the CHR sought to illustrate the effects of the city affirmative action plan. Although the survey revealed some progress, the overall results were sobering. A broad survey of 232 companies, "in finance, sales, manufacturing, transportation, construction, hostelry, and utility services," showed that blacks held just 6 percent of the jobs considered most desirable. Yet they dominated the low-end categories of operatives, laborers, and service workers, with 33, 52, and 23 percent of these positions respectively. A subset of the study examined 60 companies for whom the CHR had also collected data in 1968, and this analysis showed that blacks had made gains in desirable job categories, but still held a share far below their proportion in the total population: black employment as "officials and managers" increased from 1.8 percent to 4.3 percent of jobs in the field; for technicians, from 3.9 to 7.6 percent; for sales positions, from 4.5 to 8.0 percent; for clerical jobs, from 8 to 12 percent. Hispanics registered almost no increase, and held only 191 positions at the sixty firms.[85] The CHR study thus indicated that while racial barriers in employment had decreased during the years of the federal and local Philadelphia Plans, the pace of change remained slow and the lingering effects of long-term discrimination and unequal education remained powerful. The deterioration of the overall city economy loomed over these concerns, and here the racial bifurcation of industrial and employment policy in Philadelphia continued to matter: PIDC, the city's primary strategy for addressing structural economic problems, never offered any form of direct support or participation in either the city or federal Philadelphia Plans.

The real but limited gains identified by the CHR analysis highlighted a significant drawback of the Department of Labor's heavy emphasis on integration of the construction industry. The six critical trades offered well-paid if physically difficult and somewhat irregular jobs. Construction was a highly desirable career for working class men, and a visible target for federal officials and civil rights activists seeking viable strategies to secure employment integration. Unfortunately, the field did not employ enough people to resolve, even partially, the African American problem of jobs in Philadelphia, even if full integration could be achieved. At the 1969 DOL hearings, for example, CHR deputy director Richard Levin pointed out that even a proportional share of existing jobs in the critical trades would produce barely 2,000 positions for minorities. While far from irrelevant, construction was just one part of the solution to a far larger problem. As such, Levin added that "in several ways the amount of time and effort being spent on the construction industry is unfortunate."[86] Observers less sympathetic to the Philadelphia Plan also noted this problem. James Loughlin, business manager for the Philadelphia Building Trades Council, replied to a question about whether the unions would double their membership if presented with sufficient numbers of qualified minority applicants: "when you talk about doubling their present membership does that mean we would have unemployed within the ranks of organized labor, to take in more than the quota of people that will be able to do the work?"[87] Such positions had a self-serving component, reflecting the unions' desire to control entry into their trades, but the underlying point remained a pressing one. Ben Stahl noted the basic numerical constraint when he pointed out that "even if all the new apprentices indentured this coming year were black, only a small dent would be made in meeting the job problems of minority workers."[88] Donald Slayman, director of the national AFL-CIO Human Rights Department, brought the issue into even sharper focus during a testy exchange at the 1969 hearings: "what good will it do if [blacks are] 48% in construction and remain 1% in television, radio, banking, newspapers?" Slayman's comment identified very real limitations to relying on construction employment as a solution to the problem of jobs for inner city African Americans. His comments also spoke to the resentment and alienation that the Philadelphia Plan had produced by targeting the building trades. The union official also noted, however, that minority expectations about construction unemployment actually might not be unrealistic, subject to the key contingency of maintaining the full-employment liberalism that the unions favored: "If the federal government will bring about its promises—Congressional action and other promises of investing the kinds of money in building this country that communities need: building the houses, rebuilding the cities, putting into effect the Model Cities program"—then integration could occur "without hurting a single worker in the existing industry."[89] The limitations of focusing on the building trades as a source of minority employment became even more apparent by the mid-1970s, as the economy slipped into recession and construction employment in Philadelphia collapsed.

Slayman's comment about full employment, however, illustrates that at the close of the 1960s, the building trades unions, and the labor movement generally, remained very much a part of the national liberal coalition in terms of economic policy. While hostile to affirmative action, as well as in many cases to the cultural style and political positions of Black Power activists, the New Left, and the anti-War movement, the unions remained supportive of direct federal intervention in the economy, both in terms of structural reform and job creation. The AFL-CIO's Ben Stahl, for example, repeatedly wrote about economic policy in reports to his advisory council. During the summer of 1970, Stahl noted the "high correlation between full employment and fair employment"; a month later, after pointing out recent increases in black unemployment in Philadelphia, he suggested that "it is perhaps time to re-read *A Freedom Budget For All Americans* proposed by the A. Philip Randolph Institute back in 66."[90]

Nor was this a passing emphasis. In November 1971, following Frank Rizzo's election as mayor in a racially bruising campaign, Stahl observed that Philadelphia had lost 42,000 jobs over the previous eighteen months, "mostly in manufacturing," and argued that "full employment and sound manpower policies point the way toward uniting a divided community. Reunification of the labor-minority coalition, temporarily shaken, is another immediate order of the day."[91] Here was the core dilemma that liberalism faced in addressing the problem of jobs in Philadelphia, and increasingly, nationally: both the labor and African American components of the old New Deal coalition suffered severely from the effects of deindustrialization and cyclical economic problems, but blacks bore the extra weight of racial discrimination in employment (exacerbated by housing segregation, which limited black access to jobs); legitimate, rights-based efforts to alleviate the latter problem, especially as it applied to black men, could easily alienate labor constituencies with a vested interest in the benefits derived from existing patterns of hiring and promotion. Yet these same unions, even the "hard hat" construction locals central to the subset of working-class whites who drifted away from the New Deal coalition during the Nixon years, were still progressive on many key structural, job-related issues, and still supported many of the older liberal economic and employment policy goals. Although the issue of affirmative action in construction unified much of the liberal-civil rights coalition in Philadelphia and elsewhere for future battles in the 1970s and 1980s, it came at the cost of pushing away key elements of working class white America that in other respects remained sympathetic to liberal goals.

Scholars have recently identified racial fractures in the New Deal coalition dating back to at least the late 1940s over issues such as neighborhood integration and public housing in the north, not to mention Jim Crow segregation in the south. As a result, many have deemphasized the significance of the late 1960s and early 1970s in the eventual collapse of the New Deal coalition. After all, if that coalition had been so divided before 1950, its strength seems diminished, and its demise nearly preordained. Such arguments are valid, as these fractures were real and divisive; further, they have provided valuable nuance to simplistic accounts that emphasized a "backlash" against the excesses of the 1960s. Nonetheless, they require qualification, because well into the late 1960s and beyond, the same working class whites and union members who had opposed open housing for two decades remained dedicated supporters of much of the New Deal economic agenda. The old coalition, at least in its northern segments, could still find unity around traditional liberal economic issues such as full employment, infrastructure development, and active social policies, and continued to vote accordingly.

By the end of the 1970s, this was no longer true. As the account of the Philadelphia Plan in its home city makes clear, something *had* happened in the late-1960s, something that introduced powerful new social and political currents of rights-conscious liberalism into northern cities. The Philadelphia Plan (or even affirmative action more generally) did not by itself bring the triumph of conservatism, but it did exacerbate preexisting fractures, disaffect key liberal constituencies, and take its place as one of a number of events that widened preexisting cracks in the New Deal coalition to the point that they would soon shatter—even as it sought, with great justification, to rectify injustice and to strive for solutions to the racial dimensions of the problem of jobs.

"You'll never pull it off in this city": Model Cities, Racial Conflict, and Local Industrial Policy

D espite the partial success of PIDC and the more dramatic, if ultimately temporary, results of the OIC–Progress Movement, a mood
of increasing pessimism gripped both elite and working class Philadelphia during the late 1960s and early 1970s. With the "renaissance" of the
Clark and Dilworth years receding into memory, Philadelphia struggled
with the same problems of racial conflict and economic dislocation that
plagued other American cities during the period. The disputes regarding
the Philadelphia Plan more accurately characterized the city's social and
political atmosphere than did the wider optimism of PIDC and the OIC–
Progress Movement. In addition, although Philadelphia after 1964 avoided
the massive uprisings that Newark, Los Angeles, Detroit, and other cities
experienced, it did so at a high cost. Prior to his 1967 re-election, Mayor
Tate used an array of city services, municipal employment, and War on Poverty programs to secure massive support in the city's black neighborhoods.
During and after the 1967 campaign, however, Tate sought to shore up his
uncertain base in Philadelphia's white ethnic wards by gradually adopting
a law-and-order agenda that granted increasing autonomy to police commissioner Frank Rizzo, who enjoyed tremendous popularity among working class ethnic whites. Philadelphia thus escaped most of the physical destruction of the "long hot summers" of 1967 and 1968 not because of an
absence of underlying social tensions, but instead because of an emergency declaration issued by Tate that barred groups of more than twelve

people on city streets and because of Rizzo's willingness to repress the slightest hint of disorder, especially in African American neighborhoods.[1]

Mayor Tate had never enjoyed more than the tacit support of either the elite businessmen of the Greater Philadelphia Movement (GPM) or the liberal, reform wing of the Democratic Party. His embrace of Rizzo, especially when combined with a cycle of wage and benefit concessions to municipal employee unions followed by increases in the city wage tax, only reinforced the division between the mayor and these groups.[2] At the time, however, the influence of the formerly powerful GPM had begun to fade. Not only did the group lack the direct access to the mayor that it had enjoyed under Clark and Dilworth, but it also suffered from the death or retirement of many of the business leaders who had formed its core during the 1950s and early 1960s. The decline of Philadelphia as a corporate headquarters location reduced the pool of talent available to replace these leaders, and as a result, it remained uncertain whether such uncompleted, large-scale public-private projects as the Market East mall in Center City or the University City Science Center in West Philadelphia would receive the cohesive elite political support that had once been provided for the Food Distribution Center, Society Hill, and even PIDC. In a 1971 assessment of the state of the city's "establishment," *Greater Philadelphia* magazine concluded that "Philadelphia is currently virtually without leadership, other than that minimum that is needed to repair its potholes and to bake its daily bread. Establishment power has frozen to death, a victim of the chill in City Hall and its own rigidity." Other possible sources of leadership offered little promise of filling this void. The major labor unions remained factionalized and largely depoliticized, while the African American community, despite exceptions such as Leon Sullivan's programs and a new black political action committee, had not yet developed an autonomous center of power capable of translating the social movements of the 1960s into citywide political or economic leadership.[3]

Meanwhile, the national economy began to suffer from an inflationary spiral that would eventually collapse into recession in 1970 and 1971. These macroeconomic changes brought the war-induced prosperity of the 1960s to an end, and the flight of factories and jobs out of Philadelphia accelerated as the new decade began. The end of the Vietnam military buildup exacerbated this trend, and between 1967 and 1972 Philadelphia lost another 724 industrial firms and 61,300 manufacturing jobs. The number of census tracts in Philadelphia characterized by intense, concentrated poverty increased at a rate that equaled or exceeded any other major American city.[4]

Despite both the growing sense of despair among the city's elite and the overall bleakness of the city's social and economic position, the early 1970s actually brought a number of developments that suggested cooperative public, private, and community efforts might still be able to address the city's problem of jobs. Ironically, the most vibrant example of such possibility emerged from a program that had been widely derided as a hopeless public failure. This was the city's Model Cities program, from the ruins of which came a cooperative operation with PIDC that finally drew together the previously separate, racially defined tracks of local industrial and employment policy. By themselves, such initiatives could by no means solve the problems of jobs, housing, or race in 1970s Philadelphia. Yet they did demonstrate that community mobilization, local industrial and employment policies, and targeted federal funding could still create opportunities for meaningful local action—even during a period when most observers on both the political right and left dismissed such strategies as irrelevant hangovers from a discredited era of liberal planning and social action.

PIDC and the Service Sector

In the aftermath of PIDC's temporary loss of its federal tax exemption in 1967–68, city officials and PIDC board members raised new questions about the quasi-public corporation's relationship to the changing Philadelphia economy and, more broadly, about its future goals and direction. They observed both that PIDC had slowed but not reversed the decline of Philadelphia's manufacturing sector during the 1960s and that the base of the national economy had begun to shift from manufacturing to services. This led both city and Chamber of Commerce participants in PIDC to question whether the nonprofit corporation should continue to focus exclusively on industrial development or expand its operations into services.[5]

In February 1970, Mayor Tate's cabinet discussed PIDC's situation and reached a "general agreement that it must be expanded to meet the changing times and conditions. . . . PIDC should progress, serving not only in industrial but in commercial, wholesale, retail and service areas."[6] Deputy commerce director David G. Davis later explained that "the concept is that PIDC should be able to assist in the relocation and expansion of most businesses in addition to strictly industrial firms, as well as the attraction of new businesses of any type to Philadelphia, including corporate headquarters and other strictly office-type functions."[7]

PIDC's Chamber of Commerce participants had been thinking in similar terms. On February 20, Chamber president John P. Bracken informed Mayor Tate that "I do not think that there is any need to appoint a special committee to study this; action is more important at the moment than study."[8] Richard McConnell, now PIDC's senior vice president, and city commerce director Harry Galfand both insisted on a slower and more carefully considered decision-making process. Shortly after Bracken met with Galfand and McConnell to discuss the issue, PIDC commissioned a study of the idea from the consulting firm Economic Research Associates (ERA). Completed in July 1970, ERA's report noted that the Philadelphia region's economy had not moved as far toward the service sector as the nation's other large metropolitan areas. As a result, Philadelphia had not fully shared in the twenty million service jobs created nationally during the period. On this basis, the consultants reasoned that "if Philadelphia could attain a services employment share similar to that of other major cities and metropolitan areas, approximately 112,000 jobs would be added to the city's economy. At average annual per capita earnings of $5,143, these jobs would represent an estimated $576 million in payrolls."[9] Such growth, ERA promised, would produce a $23.5 million increase in local income tax revenue and a $20.7 million rise in property tax revenue. While Philadelphia possessed numerous human, cultural, and institutional resources that would be helpful in attracting service industries, the effort would also require something far more concrete: the creation of sixteen million square feet of new office space. To meet this need, as well as to engage in the marketing needed to attract services, Philadelphia would have to pursue a "concerted and comprehensive" development program focused on commercial and office space. No other local organization was better suited to this task than PIDC, ERA concluded, "largely because of the skills and capabilities it has developed in the related field of industrial expansion." As such, the consultants offered an unqualified endorsement of the plan to expand PIDC's activities.[10]

PIDC's board endorsed these recommendations, and at a luncheon for "business and civic leaders" at the Bellevue-Stratford Hotel (the same hotel where, almost eleven years earlier, PIDC had hosted the "groundbreaking" ceremony for West Wholesale Drug) on February 17, 1971,

PIDC executive vice president Edward Martin announced "that for the first time in any major city the corporation was offering 100 percent financing at low interest rates to nonmanufacturing industries." At the luncheon, Mayor Tate commented on the national shift to service activities and explained that "we should not try to hide from change, but we should look this change right in the eye and find out how we can benefit...we should support the construction of office buildings for finance, insurance, and real estate businesses."[11] PIDC based its goals for the new program, quite literally, on the ERA report's estimates of the gains from a service-oriented program: sixteen million square feet of office space, 112,000 new jobs, and a $44 million increase in city tax revenues. A few days later, Martin explained the rationale for PIDC's new service program to the *Philadelphia Bulletin*. PIDC would focus on firms that provided business services and "basic protection," on the theory that this would eventually yield "the prize catch: corporate headquarters. These are the biggest consumers of business services. If we can supply enough services here to attract them in the first place, then they'll generate a huge demand for more services in turn."[12] Martin's comment delineated a transformation in PIDC's strategy: rather than preserving the city's job and tax base solely through the provision of new or renovated industrial facilities, Philadelphia would rely on a supposedly self-reinforcing cycle of business service provision and corporate office expansion.

The economic events of the following decade would make the flaws in Martin's analysis brutally evident, but the expansion of PIDC's program into the service sector did possess a pragmatic rationality. By the early 1970s, the American economy was in the midst of a profound and difficult transformation, and attention to service as well as manufacturing industries provided an opportunity to take advantage of an area of possible job growth and tax-base expansion. Still, the decision entailed a significant downside. Desirable service jobs required higher levels of education and skills than manufacturing jobs, while low-skilled service positions paid far less than their generally unionized industrial counterparts. Low-income African Americans in particular, and the poor more generally, would inevitably be hurt by such changes. Further, many of the best office positions would go to suburban residents, as a result of underlying differences in educational levels as well as the persistence of racial discrimination in hiring decisions. While the city would still benefit from the wage taxes derived from commuters, such jobs would do relatively little to reduce city unemployment or poverty. For both these reasons, PIDC's new emphasis on the service sector represented a problematic response to the opportunities for public action available in the urban economy of the 1970s.

The underlying pragmatism of the move, however, contributed to a notable increase in PIDC's rate of transactions. By June 1971, PIDC already had twenty commercial transactions under consideration, and between 1971 and 1976 PIDC completed 494 total transactions, although 402 of these were industrial.[13] At the same time, however, the new strategy was a more indirect approach to Philadelphia's underlying problems of unemployment, poverty, and economic decline than the quasi-public corporation's previous strategy of focusing exclusively on manufacturing and related industries.

In view of PIDC's decision to expand into the service and commercial sectors, it would be easy to dismiss the quasi-public corporation's role during the following years as little more than a familiar example of a pro-growth urban development organization. Beginning with the 1972 construction of a new headquarters building on Independence Mall for the Royal Globe Insurance Company, PIDC helped to finance many of Philadelphia's most prominent downtown development projects during the next three decades. Among others, these included renovation of the Medical Tower Building, multiple new downtown office buildings, the Market East shopping center, the Center City commuter tunnel, the Penn's Landing waterfront complex, parts of the University City Science Center, numerous downtown parking garages, movie theaters, restaurant facilities, and, in the 1980s and 1990s, a massive health sciences center on the abandoned site of Philadelphia General Hospital. The organization also supported the renovation and modernization of many smaller downtown office buildings that had begun to deteriorate with age, and under a new feature of the federal tax code, it provided low-cost financing for pollution control equipment at the oil refineries along the Schuylkill River.[14] These activities did create, or at least preserve, some jobs in the city, which in itself was a notable achievement in the depressed economy that gripped Philadelphia for much of the 1970s. As examples of downtown-oriented redevelopment, however, many also generated the liabilities and problematic social and policy characteristics identified by scholars who have analyzed the activities of urban pro-growth coalitions.[15]

Despite its engagement in such projects, however, a simple equation of PIDC in the 1970s with an exclusively downtown-oriented, pro-growth agenda neglects key characteristics of the program. These suggest a more nuanced interpretation of its role in an increasingly stagnant local economy. Even with its new commitments in the commercial and service sectors, PIDC continued its involvement with the city's declining industrial sector: between 1971 and 1974, PIDC completed 136 transactions with manufacturing firms, which exceeded its highest total for any previous four-year period; it also completed 102 transactions with warehouse or wholesale firms, 40 with firms in the service category, and 29 with firms in the finance, insurance, and real estate category; from 1972 to 1976, the quasi-public agency financed investments of $176.4 million in industrial projects, or 69.3 percent of its $254.7 million total during the period; meanwhile, it financed investments of $78.3 million in commercial projects, or 30.7 percent of the total. As late as 1983, the industrial sector accounted for 60 percent of PIDC's work.[16] Even more significantly, PIDC for the first time began to address the relationship between economic change and the city's social problems. As such, it began to close the gap between the racially defined, parallel tracks of local industrial and employment policy that had emerged during the 1950s and 1960s. Ironically, PIDC's work with the largely discredited economic program of the city's Model Cities administration provided the primary vehicle for this change, even though Model Cities itself had been the venue for one of the city's most bitter struggles over racial power during the late 1960s.

Model Cities, Racial Politics, and the Collapse of Economic Planning

During the early years of the federal War on Poverty, the liberal economists who advocated a comprehensive economic planning program for Philadelphia failed in their efforts to include such a system in the city's anti-poverty campaign. By the time that another opening for such planning arose, Philadelphia would be well advanced in the process of creating parallel tracks of local economic policy, one white and one black, and both inadequate to address the city's problem of jobs. This second chance at coordination came in the context of the Model Cities program. Its immediate outcome would be largely determined by the racial divisions that increasingly dominated local politics in Philadelphia. Over the longer term, however, the closing stages of Model Cities would provide a chance to draw the parallel policy tracks together, although largely too late and on an inadequate scale.

The Demonstration Cities program, better known as Model Cities, had originally been formulated in 1964 by President Johnson's Task Force on Metropolitan and Urban Problems. The Task Force's plan, which was extensively promoted by United Auto Workers President Walter Reuther, envisioned an "urban TVA" that would revitalize cities through the concentrated application of public, private, and community resources to specific urban neighborhoods. As a second stage of the federal War on Poverty, Model Cities (as the Johnson administration renamed the program to avoid associations with urban riots) represented an opportunity to apply lessons learned in the Community Action Program, as well as in more than fifteen years of urban renewal. Signed into law on November 4, 1966, Model Cities differed from these predecessors in that it sought to adopt a comprehensive but concentrated approach to urban problems. The program required cities to develop a detailed plan for attacking the interrelated physical, social, and economic problems of a severely disadvantaged neighborhood through the coordinated application of physical rebuilding, social services, health care, job training, and economic development.[17]

The final Model Cities legislation, though, included features that ultimately undermined its effectiveness. In order to insure passage of the legislation, the program had been extended to 63 cities, in contrast to the 6 that Reuther had recommended; eventually, 108 cities received Model Cities funds. Meanwhile, Congress reduced appropriations from the original bill's $2.3 billion over five years to slightly more than $900 million over two years. As a result, none of the cities received the level of funding necessary to implement the sweeping, long-range strategies initially envisioned. Further, although cities would be expected to draw on existing federal programs and services, the legislation provided no mechanism for coordinating Model Cities participation by relevant federal departments and agencies, or even for ensuring their cooperation.[18] Most seriously of all, the legislation failed to resolve the conflicts over participation that had plagued community action. The Economic Opportunity Act's emphasis on community control over federal anti-poverty programs had inspired bitter power struggles between community groups and mayors, but rather than define a clear federal position regarding the participation dispute, the Model Cities Act finessed the issue once again: the legislation emphasized the continuing importance of "meaningful" community participation but also stated that the program should allow for "the exercise of leadership by responsible elected officials." Model Cities did not clearly situate authority with either the community or city hall, and in Philadelphia the resulting uncertainty, along with attenuated and inadequate funding, generated conflicts that undermined both the program's overall effectiveness and its potential as a comprehensive planning device.[19]

In late 1966 and early 1967, however, the inadequacy of the legislation had not yet become apparent and Philadelphia officials felt confident that they had an excellent chance of receiving a substantial share of Model Cities funds. As the president of the National League of Cities, Mayor Tate played a key role in lobbying for the legislation; William L. Rafsky, the executive vice president of the Old Philadelphia Development Corporation and former city development coordinator, served on the Presidential Task Force that drafted the Model Cities Act; finally, Philadelphia congressman William Barrett, a long-time Tate ally, chaired a key housing subcommittee in the House.[20]

As the legislation moved toward passage during the fall of 1966, Tate appointed a task force to develop Philadelphia's application for Model Cities planning funds, on the belief that the city's chances for a large grant would be maximized by meeting all HUD deadlines and being first in line for funding. To chair the task force, Tate appointed city economist Joseph Oberman, who also served as director of the city's new Economic Development Unit, a body established earlier in the year with a grant from the U.S. Economic Development Administration and tasked with coordinating the city's economic development policy as called for in the earlier CRP and OEDP proposals. The mayor himself chaired a policy advisory group that would review the recommendations of Oberman's task force. Patrick McLaughlin, who had formerly served as Philadelphia's chief lobbyist in Washington, moved into a dual position as city development coordinator and Model Cities administrator. In the latter post, McLaughlin oversaw the actual writing of the planning grant application.[21]

In its haste to complete the application, however, the Tate administration made a crucial mistake: it did not include any community representatives on the planning task force or the policy advisory group. The administration feared that organizing an inclusive planning body might delay submission of Philadelphia's proposal, and, in the aftermath of community action, Tate had little interest in such participation anyway. From the perspective of the community, the resulting 350-page draft application, which focused on a 2,000-block area of North Philadelphia, thus appeared out of nowhere in January 1967. Already unhappy about their exclusion from the planning process, community leaders took offense at the paternalistic tone that the draft document adopted in regard to North Philadelphia residents and their organizations, churches, and other institutions. Faced with community demands for "equal partnership" in the Model Cities program, McLaughlin apologized for the previous lack of participatory planning and Tate agreed to include twelve community representatives on the task force subcommittees that would revise the city proposal to meet a March 1 federal deadline. A coalition of community groups accepted the offer, on the condition that the city maintain an "equal partnership" with them through the remaining phases of Model Cities. Coming in the aftermath of Tate's domination of the local Community Action Program, this initial planning period nonetheless established an atmosphere of distrust from which Philadelphia's Model Cities effort never recovered.[22]

Despite these difficulties, Oberman's task force managed to complete a substantially revised, shortened, and focused planning grant application and Philadelphia became the only city in the United States to meet the federal deadline. Even with community participation, the revised draft retained some of the problematic language of the original, as it described North Philadelphia as a "miasmic environment" and emphasized the "social disorganization" and "widespread and self-perpetuating social indifference and personal apathy" of the community.[23]

In other respects, the grant application was a remarkable document. It recognized, in a manner that echoed Elizabeth Deutermann and John Culp's earlier proposals for coordinated economic planning, the existence of a relationship between poverty, the availability of employment, and the social and physical problems that affected urban neighborhoods. Rejecting the culture of poverty thesis, it argued that urban poverty resulted less from the characteristics of the individual than from the interaction of "poor education, poor health, slum housing, racial discrimination and a multitude of other social ills" that "inhibit the individual from escaping poverty." While only a comprehensive policy that addressed each of these areas could have any hope of success, the application argued that such initiatives alone would not be enough to overcome the skepticism engendered in North Philadelphia by previous top-down public actions. Such distrust could be countered only by the city's acceptance of participation by area residents, through "a real offer of the real power to exercise a determining voice in planning for definitively scheduled improvement of their community and their own lot."[24] In order to extend such a real offer of real power, the application proposed the creation of a new community organization known as the North Philadelphia Area-Wide Council (AWC). Organized around sixteen smaller neighborhood "hubs," the AWC would bring community members together to set goals, create plans, facilitate resident participation, and evaluate proposals developed by the city. The membership of AWC's hubs included more than 150 settlement houses, churches, and neighborhood groups; each hub would appoint representatives to the sixty-four-member AWC executive board.[25]

This offer of power, however, had distinct limits, as the city retained significant control over Model Cities. The position of Model Cities administrator would continue to be held by city development coordinator Patrick McLaughlin. Crucially, the administrator would be tasked with bringing AWC's efforts into line with those of city, state, and federal agencies. A fifteen member policy committee, composed of six AWC representatives, six city representatives, and one each from the state, the Board of Education, and the North City Congress (a publicly funded community organization) would finalize the program's policies and goals, distribute funds, and provide overall direction. Finally, regardless of the rhetorical attention to meaningful community participation, the application stated that final "responsibility for the conduct of the program" would rest with the mayor.[26] When briefed on these aspects of the proposal, even the Greater Philadelphia Movement's representative to the Economic Development Unit's Advisory Council questioned whether the centralization of authority might "dilute efforts toward the goal of grass-roots participation" and repeat "the mistakes that have troubled the poverty program."[27]

Despite such concerns, the strategy of developing a broad, coordinated policy for addressing multiple community problems nonetheless placed the revised Model Cities planning grant application within the trajectory that had begun with Kirk Petshek in the 1950s and continued in the 1960s with the plans that Deutermann and Culp had developed for the Community Renewal and Overall Economic Development programs. This trajectory reflected a number of core principles that linked Philadelphia's local liberalism to the broader national tradition of reform liberalism, as well as to concerns about social equity in American society as a whole. Quoting almost directly from the recently completed final report of the CRP program, the Model Cities planning application emphasized that a decent urban society should insure that all of its members enjoyed at least four minimum standards:

- *A home and environment* which are safe, comfortable, and accessible to places of work and to community facilities;
- An *income* which is sufficient to live decently and respectably;
- An *education* which prepares each individual to engage in useful work, to take part in community affairs, and to enjoy his leisure.
- Underlying these three requirements, there is a fourth which applies to them all—*equal opportunity, social mobility.*[28]

Reminiscent of Franklin Delano Roosevelt's 1943 Economic Bill of Rights, this statement aptly summarized key tenets of mid-twentieth-century American liberalism. Implementation of such goals, however, would prove a challenge.

In a manner similar to what Deutermann and Culp had proposed in the CRP and OEDP economic reports, but unlike the War on Poverty, Philadelphia's Model Cities planning grant application built on these four principles by emphasizing the role of jobs in a comprehensive approach to inner-city problems. Along with preliminary proposals for health services, education, recreation, crime reduction, welfare, social services, and housing construction, rehabilitation, and desegregation, the application established a goal of reducing unemployment in the target area by 50 percent within five years. This target would be reached through job creation and job training, the development of businesses owned by community residents, and efforts to match residents with jobs throughout the region. It also called for linking together the city's disparate range of existing job-related initiatives, so that coordinated job training, job creation, and job retention programs could be geared specifically toward providing employment for residents of the Model Cities area. In effect, the proposal called for elimination of the racial bifurcation of local industrial and employment policy in Philadelphia. During the process of preparing the revised application, Deutermann and other members of the Economic Development Unit's Advisory Council even argued that job development should be made the primary focus of the *entire* Model Cities program in Philadelphia. Although this did not happen, the employment orientation of the actual document reflected the intellectual position and the policy influence that Joseph Oberman and the Economic Development Unit exerted on the process of drafting the application.[29]

Proposals for specific programs remained relatively vague, but the application sketched out both ideas and general goals for each stage of Model Cities. Within the economic area, immediate efforts might include contacting "every unemployed resident" within the Model Cities neighborhood, providing direct public employment on neighborhood reconstruction projects, creating a computerized clearing house for job-opening information, and establishing job training programs in "at least two new manufacturing installations in rehabilitated industrial structures." Over an intermediate term, additional programs would be established to place residents in jobs elsewhere in the region (and find them housing), provide venture capital for area small businesses, plan for the physical expansion of firms within area industrial districts, create "management academies" to train residents in entrepreneurial skills, and challenge discrimination by employers, unions, and banks. Over a longer term, goals included the creation of a $2-million venture and working capital fund "for existing and would-be target area entrepreneurs," a manufacturing plant that would provide on-the-job training for both management and production workers, and the establishment of business service centers for "the resident entrepreneur."[30]

While the potential viability of these ideas varied, collectively they provided a vision of how Philadelphia's public, private, and community sectors might cooperate to address the problem of jobs in North Philadelphia. By focusing intensely on employment as a core issue, the Model Cities application diverged markedly from the War on Poverty's emphasis on restructuring local political and social service relationships and improving individual skill sets. The grant application instead reflected postwar local liberalism's core concern with the structure of the economy and with the social consequences of political economic relationships.

Within months, however, persistent conflict between demands for community self-determination and the Tate administration's determination to maintain control effectively undercut the promise of Philadelphia's Model Cities application. Inadequate funding exacerbated such problems. Although HUD delayed a final decision on the planning grants until November 1967, it informally notified the city in April that it would receive only half of the requested $750,000 planning grant. Such funding decreases limited the program's capacity to address the target area's problems, while the lack of concrete progress eroded the community's confidence that the rhetoric of Model Cities planners would ever be matched by on-the-ground results.[31]

On November 16, HUD finally awarded Philadelphia a Model Cities planning grant of only $178,000, an amount even smaller than expected.[32] The next day, the racial and political tensions that had formed an implicit background to the planning process finally exploded and destroyed the tenuous partnership between AWC and the city. The most proximate cause of this development lay not with the Model Cities planning process itself but in the Philadelphia Police Department's response to a campaign to push the Board of Education to hire African American teachers and principals and to increase attention to African American culture and history within its curriculum. On November 17, approximately 3,500 black high school students marched to a protest rally on these issues at the Board of Education Building along the Benjamin Franklin Parkway. With Mayor Tate vacationing in Florida, police commissioner Frank Rizzo exerted his own brand of racialized, authoritarian control. When protestors gathered around plainclothes officers arresting a student who had run across the roofs of parked cars, Rizzo reportedly ordered a squad of heavily armed riot police to "get their black asses!" The police then charged into the crowd, violently beating protestors and African American bystanders alike. As many as thirty needed medical attention, with fifteen requiring hospitalization. Some of the protestors fled into Center City a few blocks away, breaking windows and injuring twenty-seven pedestrians as they ran. A total of twelve police officers suffered injuries during the morning's violence as well.[33]

Mayor Tate, who had been re-elected less than two weeks before on a margin provided largely by black voters, initially saw the incident as an opportunity to fire Rizzo, whom he had never particularly liked. In the following days, however, the city's white ethnic neighborhoods produced a visceral outpouring of support for the police commissioner. This response convinced the mayor that removing Rizzo would be politically disastrous. On November 22, Tate thus endorsed Rizzo's actions during the protest and his overall handling of race relations. In December, the mayor solidified his hold on the "law and order" issue by fulfilling a campaign promise to re-appoint Rizzo as police commissioner. In 1971, Tate would designate Rizzo as his preferred successor.[34]

The Board of Education demonstration also had immediate repercussions for the Model Cities program. Shortly after the incident, press reports revealed that AWC assistant director Walter Palmer had been authorized to use AWC mimeograph machines for the production of leaflets

advertising the rally. Palmer, a black power activist, had been hired specifically to build connections between AWC and young, militant segments
of the African American community. In assisting with the rally, he had
thus simply been doing his job. Tate nonetheless criticized the AWC's
"haphazard" hiring processes and Model Cities administrator McLaughlin announced a city audit of AWC's use of public money. HUD officials
also criticized the community group. The AWC, however, defended its
right to engage in political and protest activities, arguing that such participation represented a necessary part of an inseparable continuum between "community planning and community participation." This position
clearly indicated that AWC had no intention of following Samuel Evans's
Philadelphia Anti-Poverty Action Committee (PAAC) in becoming an
adjunct of Tate's political organization.[35]

These events made the existing gap between the city and AWC ir-
reparable. AWC refused to turn over meeting minutes for the city audit, and on December 10, citing the reduced federal planning grant, the
city announced that AWC's funding would remain at $13,000 per month
rather than being increased to a promised $21,000 per month. AWC re-
fused to accept this funding level, and the city in turn threatened to appoint PAAC as the community participation arm of the Model Cities program. In January 1968, the two sides agreed to a compromise funding
level of $18,000 per month, but the city-AWC relationship had already
been fatally compromised.[36] In January 1968, Philip Kalodner replaced
McLaughlin as development coordinator and Model Cities administrator,
but the change in personnel did little to improve relations between the
two sides. In March 1968, Kalodner provided a public demonstration of
this distrust when he submitted two sets of program proposals to HUD,
one prepared by city officials and one by AWC. HUD officials found the
extent of the rift disturbing. They requested the resubmission of a single,
supplemental application by December 31.

When Kalodner proved no more capable of working with the AWC
than McLaughlin, Mayor Tate not only fired him but also decoupled the
posts of development coordinator and Model Cities administrator. He
placed the former office under the control of city planning director Edmund Bacon and named Robert Williams, an African American lawyer,
newspaper publisher, and politician to the latter position. For a brief period, Williams improved relations with AWC. Through the fall of 1968,
with HUD's December 31 deadline for the submission of detailed project

plans looming, the Model Cities Administration, the city Economic Development Unit, and AWC cooperated in a sometimes tense process of finalizing the detailed project plans. AWC insisted that its existing program proposals be included and that an earlier request for a $49 million Model Cities program budget not be reduced.[37] The city accepted these terms, even though it had already been informed that HUD would provide no more than $25 million. AWC itself, however, had begun to splinter into factions. A member of the moderate group later recalled the final months of 1968 as a period in which "we worked night and day, weekends, and holidays to put together our ideas and the city's ideas. We had many differences in approach, but with our partnership arrangement, we were able to trade off so that they got some of their priorities, but so did we." In contrast, a more radical group of AWC members remained unhappy with the process. The night before the application would be submitted to HUD, individuals from this group forced their way into the city's printing plant and "upset tables, threw papers on the floor, and tried to hinder the duplicating process" in an attempt to prevent the document's completion.[38]

Nonetheless, the city met the deadline and submitted a program application that retained the basic projects suggested by the AWC. At the core of the new application lay proposals for seven new nonprofit community corporations that would oversee programs in housing development and rehabilitation, health services, education, redevelopment, and economic development. AWC members would exercise majority control over the board of directors of some of the corporations and share control over the remainder.[39] The project plans also specified that half of the city's Model Cities funding would be devoted to economic development projects. A detailed economic development proposal drafted originally by city economist Oberman and revised by African American attorney Ragan Henry specified that the primary goal of the Model Cities economic development project would be the creation of a viable, community-controlled capitalism in the area. Specifically, the economic development plan called for the creation of an "internal economy" for North Philadelphia, in which at least 50 percent of all businesses would be owned by area residents.[40] This "internal economy" reflected a more inward looking strategy than that of the OIC–Progress Movement's community capitalism effort.

Three of the proposed community corporations would focus on economic development; of these, two would exist primarily as financing vehicles. A third, known as the Model Cities Economic Development Corporation (MCEDC), would pursue the internal economy goal by renovating abandoned industrial buildings in which it would establish "incubators" for new manufacturing ventures operated and owned by residents of the Model Cities neighborhood. These facilities would be staffed by "experts in the various aspects of plant management, and ... divided into areas devoted to various kinds of industrial and manufacturing activity." Within sub-sections of the building, separate model plants would be established and operated by "owner-trainees" who would receive training in business operation and management. Over the course of each business's occupancy of the incubator facility, its operation would be conducted on an increasingly independent basis, culminating with the owner-trainee's move to a separate facility. Similar incubators would be established to support the creation of new commercial and retail businesses. Financing for these new businesses would be provided by existing organizations ranging from the Small Business Administration to PIDC. The plans for MCEDC also envisioned the establishment of a land exchange program that would seek to create separate residential and industrial districts through a program of clearance and reconstruction of both housing and factories—the modernist ideal of single-use planning, appearing even in Model Cities.[41]

Although the AWC would not exercise majority control over the corporation, it would have significant influence, as the board would consist of eight AWC members and nine appointees from a range of other interested local groups. PIDC would be among these organizations. Along with the Model Cities Administration and the city economist, other groups represented on the board would include the North City Congress, the Urban Coalition, public utilities, the Chamber of Commerce, and representatives of the banking and savings and loan industries. This wide participation indicated that the Model Cities program sought to close the racial gap between Philadelphia's parallel tracks of industrial and employment policy. Yet that gulf nonetheless remained, as the new Model Cities corporation failed to include OIC, the single largest black effort to address the problem of jobs in Philadelphia, and an institution then operating at the height of its influence and popularity.[42]

The project plans for MCEDC and the two financing corporations echoed both the general goals outlined in the 1967 planning grant application and the increasingly popular idea of a black capitalism tied to the wider economy but controlled within the North Philadelphia community. With its attention to job and business development, the compromise

Philadelphia program thus sought to reverse the War on Poverty's earlier inattention to job creation. Like the federal Special Impact Program, the economic elements of Philadelphia's supplemental Model Cities application reflected a local liberalism that was far more attuned to structural economic issues and problems than its national counterpart. If implemented as planned, the proposed program would have transferred a broad array of productive resources to a disadvantaged community, and as such, would have represented a significant experiment for twentieth century American liberalism. By the time that HUD actually considered the revised Philadelphia application, however, a new presidential administration had come to power that shared little of its predecessor's tendency toward equivocation regarding community participation in anti-poverty programs. Instead, the newly inaugurated Nixon administration made it clear that direct community involvement would play no part in its urban policy.[43]

Changes within Philadelphia's Model Cities structure reinforced this shift. In March 1969, Model Cities administrator Robert Williams resigned to run for a Common Pleas Court judgeship, and Mayor Tate named Goldie Watson to the position. Watson had followed a unique path in Philadelphia African American politics. In the late 1940s, she had been part of a left-wing African American group that temporarily won control of the local NAACP. In 1954, she was fired from her job as a public school teacher after refusing to testify before the House Un-American Activities Committee about her involvement with the communist party, stating instead that "I can only hope and pray that the stand I have taken will awaken Negro Americans to the threat to Democracy. If our rights as guaranteed by the First Amendment continue to be violated, my people will find it impossible to continue the struggle for first class citizenship and complete equality." Six years later, the Pennsylvania Supreme Court overturned the firing and reinstated her. The U.S. Supreme Court then declined to hear the Board of Education's appeal. By that point, however, Watson had opened a successful dress shop and become a partner in a ballroom and catering business in North Philadelphia. She also formed an alliance with African American politicians such as state senator Herbert Arlene and party officials such as Johnny Sills, who oversaw patronage operations in the African American community. Increasingly active in Democratic ward operations in her own right, she eventually emerged as a key North Philadelphia operative for Tate and in

1967 served as the mayor's North Philadelphia campaign coordinator, delivering African American votes that helped Tate narrowly defeat Arlen Specter.[44]

Widely influential in North Philadelphia, Watson had little interest in ceding any control to AWC. She thus found HUD's new policy perfectly acceptable. When Nixon's HUD objected to the supplemental program application's "unusually heavy reliance on new corporations...heavy [AWC] involvement in these operating corporations...[and] insufficient involvement of the City...and established institutions," Watson immediately restructured the program by limiting the AWC's representation on the nonprofits' boards to one-third of total members and reducing AWC's role in the overall program to "community organization, planning, evaluation, and community advocate activities." AWC rejected a contract that codified the new structure and sued the city and HUD for violation of the original Demonstration Cities Act's community participation provisions. Meanwhile, Watson's effort to appease HUD failed, as the agency rejected all Model Cities projects associated with the community corporations and funded only $3.3 million of the $25 million that Philadelphia expected—and the $49 million that the AWC wanted.[45]

In November 1969, a District Court dismissed the AWC suit, and almost immediately, Watson moved to replace AWC with a new interim citizens' committee. By this point, AWC's intransigence and its domination by the most militant faction of its membership had alienated significant segments of the city's African American community. In a reflection of this frustration, nineteen of the thirty-five members of the interim committee were former AWC board members, and their participation in the new group demonstrated their willingness to ally with Watson and Mayor Tate against their former AWC colleagues.[46] In part, this shift in alliances resulted from Goldie Watson's own popularity in North Philadelphia. As one observer noted, Watson's influence in city hall made her a badly needed community "success symbol." More broadly, the dispute reflected the question of whether African Americans should pragmatically work with the white power structure or seek confrontation in the name of securing complete control over the resources provided by the federal government. With Watson's replacement of AWC, pragmatism won out.

With AWC effectively defeated, HUD compromised and accepted the original community corporation structure as modified by Watson, and over the following four years, Philadelphia's Model Cities program

FIGURE 27. Philadelphia Model Cities administrator Goldie Watson speaking at a North Philadelphia street protest at the corner of Broad Street and Girard Avenue, July 11, 1973. The crowd had gathered to protest delays in the payment of welfare checks. Watson informed them that she had arranged for a "flying squad" of city workers to process the late checks. Such actions, and her capacity to deliver on such promises because of her influence with mayors Tate and Rizzo, made Watson one of the most powerful figures in the city's African American community during the late 1960s and 1970s. Her management of the Model Cities program, however, drew criticism. Photo courtesy of Temple University Libraries, Urban Archives, Philadelphia, Pennsylvania.

received more than $75 million in federal program funds. In February 1972, AWC won a pyrrhic victory when the Third Circuit Court of Appeals ruled that the city had acted inappropriately in restructuring the Model Cities program. The court, however, provided only the limited remedy of a new election to choose representatives for the Citizens Advisory Committee. With AWC largely discredited and reduced to a small organization, allies of Watson easily won the election.[47]

By the early 1970s, Philadelphia's Model Cities program devolved into a political tool controlled primarily by Watson and secondarily by Tate and his successor, Frank Rizzo. Although the program had real accomplishments in such areas as lead paint abatement, rat control, subway station renovations, and provision of summer programs for children, most of its projects operated on a small scale and often at high costs.[48] In many cases, Watson simply channeled federal funds directly into city operating agencies without community involvement of any kind. Even Rizzo's violence-prone police department received funds through this technique. Although part of her purview, the Model Cities Economic Development Corporation was never a priority for Watson and suffered particularly from inattention and exploitation for patronage purposes. The corporation did not even begin operations until 1971, and after that its activities remained limited to granting loans to a few existing small businesses. By early 1973, the corporation's staff included Cecil B. Moore's daughter, Robert Williams's wife, the cousin of one of Watson's assistants, the nephew of a congressman, friends of city council members, the widow of a policeman, and at least four close associates of a politically influential lawyer. Shortly before a scheduled audit, a suspicious fire destroyed the corporation's headquarters.[49]

Despite these limitations, the final stages of the Model Cities economic program would play an important part in finally bringing the social, the physical, and the economic together in a manner that ideally might have been pursued from the beginning of the Great Society in 1964, if not from the initial victory of Philadelphia's reform liberals in 1951. Ironically, this development was the direct result of a crisis for Mayor Rizzo and Watson that placed the Model Cities economic project in particular jeopardy. As 1972 closed, newly elected Republican city controller and local basketball legend Tom Gola issued a scathing audit of the Model Cities Economic Development Corporation: "The project...failed to accomplish many portions of its program objectives," Gola contended. "The major reason for this failure is that policies, guidelines, procedures and delegations of authority were not established prior to the rapid development of the project. Other causes included . . . ineffective leadership in the overall direction and supervision of the project, lack of proper internal controls, poor communications within and between the operating agency and subcontractors, lack of project publicity, and the hiring of unqualified personnel." Gola also accused Watson of channeling a $115,000-contract to a partner in her personal catering business. Responding to these charges, HUD informed the city that the corporation would lose all federal funding unless it was completely reorganized. Hoping to salvage the program and its federal grants, the Rizzo administration turned to PIDC for help in restructuring the Model Cities Economic Development Corporation.[50]

This decision led to significant changes for the Model Cities program, for PIDC, and for the overall character of local urban policy in Philadelphia. The most notable accomplishment of the new policy direction would be its closure of the racially defined, parallel tracks of local industrial and employment policy in Philadelphia, a change that would partially resolve the major dilemma that had previously plagued the city's response to the problem of jobs. Unfortunately, the length of the learning process that had preceded this development meant that such changes came at the start of a long period of retrenchment in federal urban policy. More generally, however, the 1973 Model Cities–PIDC partnership provided a demonstration of the policy strategy that all levels of government should have pursued throughout the Great Society. This approach consisted of providing federal funds for economically oriented local programs, restricted only by civil rights safeguards that created jobs in low-income, inner-city communities. Only the very limited Special Impact Program implemented such a policy on a program-wide basis. A wider application of such policies would not have resolved all the problems that resulted from the political economy of race and deindustrialization in Philadelphia, or elsewhere, but it would have placed the problem of jobs at the forefront of public concern and deployed available resources in a way that directly affected the economic life of the inner city. The lesson of the War on Poverty, Model Cities, and the problem of jobs in Philadelphia is that public policy, especially when deployed from the federal level, does best when it reinforces innovative local programs and viable local resources, subject to basic community participation requirements and strict civil rights enforcement.

A Few Who Remained: Somerset Knitting Mills, the Garment Center, and PIDC During the 1970s

Initially, the Model Cities program had perpetuated the racial divide in Philadelphia's economic development efforts. Although the original 1968–1969 plans for the project specified that a representative of PIDC would be appointed to the board of directors of the Model Cities Economic Development Corporation, PIDC did not even receive a request for such participation until April 1971. While the PIDC board dutifully appointed a representative at that time, the agency's initial participation was minimal.[51] In the aftermath of Controller Gola's 1972 critique of the Model Cities economic program, however, Mayor Rizzo requested that PIDC evaluate how the project could be reorganized. Walter D'Alessio, who served as PIDC executive vice president throughout this period, described PIDC's initial interaction with the Model Cities administration, as well as the racial tensions that pervaded both the Lower North Philadelphia area and the Model Cities program itself:

> We went out to talk to the Model Cities people and . . . asked the question have you surveyed the industry in the Model Cities area? Do you know who you are working with? Who is hiring the Model Cities residents now? What are you doing with them? [Model Cities officials answered:] No, we don't want to talk to them. They are not very well received in the community. They are largely Jewish owned business[es]. We never liked them anyway and we'll form our own Black-owned industries. We [PIDC] said that's not practical. If you don't like them, fine. We said take . . . the $3 million you have left [from HUD's initial $6,594,277 grant], put a million dollars of it into an account for grants. No salaries to be paid out of it, no expenses, what we want is access to that money to put on a grant basis, no loans, into projects that will expand businesses that are now in the impacted neighborhoods. And they said ok.[52]

PIDC thus proposed a fundamental alteration in the Model Cities economic program, away from the original goal of generating employment through the development of black capitalism and toward the assistance and preservation of existing businesses that already employed community residents, regardless of their ownership. Although this change compromised the ideal of community self-determination, the Philadelphia Model Cities administration had demonstrated little capacity to achieve such goals. PIDC's proposed alternative at least involved the immediate expansion of employment opportunities for residents of North Philadelphia.

Despite their limited prior engagement with Model Cities itself, D'Alessio and his staff had long been active in the Lower North Philadelphia area and had a number of possible projects ready for such a partnership.[53] Among these, the Somerset Knitting Mills Company provided the key opportunity to bring PIDC's ideas into actual operation. A producer of men's sweaters, Somerset had been founded in Philadelphia in 1935. In a 1963 PIDC transaction, the company had moved into a shared nine-story building on North Broad Street, the main north-south artery through central Philadelphia. In 1968, in a typical example of the acquisition of formerly Philadelphia-owned firms by nonlocal corporations, Somerset was purchased by the New York–based Philips-Van Heusen Corporation. Despite the economic problems that began to plague the apparel industry in the early 1970s, Somerset continued to prosper and by 1972 needed additional space for modernization and expansion. The company already operated a subsidiary in southern New Jersey, and Philips-Van Heusen planned either a consolidation there or a move to a low-cost, anti-union state such as North Carolina, South Carolina, or Alabama. In a rare example of local managerial independence, Somerset president Donald E. Cutler challenged this approach and argued that the company should resist the industry's trend of moving urban plants to rural areas. Cutler, who had financed his education at Yale by working as a sweater salesman, noted that most of the company's employees lived in the immediate neighborhood and used public transportation to get to the plant. Even a move to New Jersey would thus require replacing most of the workforce, and Cutler contended that in an industry that had long been characterized by a limited supply of trained labor, such a decision would be inefficient and possibly disastrous. Presented with this analysis, Philips-Van Heusen agreed to build a new plant in Philadelphia—on the condition that Cutler find an appropriate, affordable site.[54]

Cutler turned to PIDC's D'Alessio, who by early 1973 identified a vacant eight-acre site on the south side of Spring Garden Street in the Franklin-Callowhill East Urban Renewal area. Following a helicopter tour of industrial locations in the city, Cutler agreed to pursue the site. Although a $2,540,000 low-interest PIDC loan reduced Somerset's costs, the $70,000 per acre cost still remained approximately $30,000 per acre higher than what company leaders judged affordable. By this point, PIDC had begun its work with the Model Cities Administration, and D'Alessio suggested that Somerset might be an appropriate candidate for grant funds from the program's beleaguered economic project. Although the site actually lay across the street from the Model Cities area, eighty to eighty-five percent of the company's 400 employees were African American or Puerto Rican residents of the Model Cities area (many of them women). The location of the workers' residences made the project eligible for Model Cities funding, and Goldie Watson soon agreed to provide a $300,000 grant toward the company's purchase of the land. PIDC and Cutler also involved the plant's Knit Goods Workers Union local in planning for the project.[55]

On August 7, 1973, PIDC's board approved the transaction, and on January 10, 1974, Cutler and Mayor Rizzo unveiled plans for the $7.5 million, 250,000-square-foot plant. The new facility was the largest garment factory built in Philadelphia since the 1920s. At the public announcement of the project, Cutler praised the assistance he had received, noting that "I've never dealt with a government agency before. . . . friends of mine said 'Don't do it. You'll never pull it off in this city.' But the cooperation was incredible. There was a sense of urgency and things got done." Cutler also challenged assumptions about the spatial dimensions of industrial movement in the garment industry: "contrary to what people think, the future of the [apparel] industry lies in New York and Philadelphia. This is a people-oriented industry and it's in the cities that the people are."[56] During the months that followed, Somerset's local state-sponsored challenge to the industry's migration away from northern cities and unionized workforces extended to the aesthetic character of the workplace itself. The city required that 1 percent of the cost of all construction projects should be spent on art work; as a reporter for the *Philadelphia Inquirer* noted, in most cases this meant that the developer "put something stainless steel and expensive outside the building." In contrast, Somerset met the one percent art requirement by painting walls in the plant's production areas with brightly colored murals and geometric designs, some of them evoking "a vague abstract impression of skeins of yarn being whirled through complex machines," with the express purpose of creating a pleasant work environment, raising morale, reducing employee turnover—and, not least, enhancing productivity.[57]

Somerset moved into its new building in 1975 and immediately prospered, as annual sales rose from $17 million to $20 million. In 1977, the company expanded its operations by purchasing machinery and patent rights for the Coleseta shirt label from a defunct Florida company, and

FIGURE 28. Donald E. Cutler, president of Somerset Knitting Mills Company, with an artist's sketch of the company's new plant in the Franklin–Callowhill East urban renewal area, December 10, 1974. The plant would be built with assistance from an innovative partnership between PIDC and the Philadelphia Model Cities Administration. In exchange for a PIDC-administered grant of Model Cities economic development funds to defray construction costs, Somerset agreed to employ residents of the neighborhoods surrounding the new plant. Photo courtesy of Temple University Libraries, Urban Archives, Philadelphia, Pennsylvania.

added another one hundred workers. At the time of this expansion, Somerset vice president Thomas E. Cahill rejected any form of spatial determinism in industrial location decisions: "it's not the location that kills a firm, it's poor management." Continuing, he also placed the company's growth in the context of overturning stereotypes about the inner-city poor: "rather than welfare problems, the unemployed minority populations of the city, as well as the white poor, can be a tangible asset." Proving Cahill's point—at least about inner city workers—Somerset Knitting Mills remained in its Spring Garden Street Building until 1992, and at its peak level of operation employed as many as 500 workers.[58]

Somerset's example indicates that traditional manufacturing firms could survive in inner-city locations, even in a supposedly postindustrial age. It also shows that local public policymakers could help them do so by lowering effective costs while also requiring social responsibility from the firm that received aid. Prior to the mid-1970s, PIDC typically accomplished the former by using federal tax incentives to cut finance costs. In the case of Somerset Knitting Mills, however, the quasi-public organization devised a way to deploy federal grants to reduce land acquisition costs. Either way, the effect was that a manufacturing firm remained in the city without any local subsidy. The key to such a strategy lay in the availability of unrestricted finance tools and the direct accessibility of federal development funds for innovative local agencies and programs, along with imposition of the critical new condition that the recipient firm employ neighborhood residents. The wider result was that the local state had restructured the industrial real estate market to counter the problem of jobs.

The Somerset project marked only the beginning of a period of even more extensive cooperation between PIDC, the garment industry, and the Philadelphia Model Cities Administration. After a period of relative stability in the mid-1960s, the Philadelphia apparel industry struggled with serious problems during the early 1970s. Faced with increasing competition from both overseas producers and domestic competitors in non-union states, local industry officials also struggled with obsolete and increasingly decrepit loft factories. Not only were these plants inefficient, they also featured terrible working conditions that often drove employees to leave the industry for other work at their first opportunity. As a result, during the mid- and late-1960s many apparel firms actually experienced the seemingly contradictory dilemma of facing a labor shortage amidst high inner-city unemployment. In addition, a high percentage of Philadelphia apparel firms had traditionally been located in the central core of the city, where they were vulnerable to displacement by urban renewal projects during the 1950s and 1960s. Many small, family-owned firms simply never reopened after being removed from their original locations. Increasing competition from large corporate conglomerates often cemented such decisions. By the early 1970s, clearance of older buildings in the eastern half of Center City for the construction of the Market East and Gallery shopping centers threatened another 4,500 jobs.[59] Together these factors meant that garment industry employment in Philadelphia fell from 47,000 in 1964 to 41,100 in 1967 to 33,500 in 1972. It was during this period that the OIC–Progress Movement shifted its apparel company out of the garment industry and into electronics. With the textile industry already decimated, however, apparel nonetheless remained Philadelphia's largest industrial employment sector. Further, the industry employed a high ratio of city residents, most of whom by the 1970s were black or Puerto Rican, and many of whom were women. Industry analysts recognized that if past patterns persisted, Philadelphia would soon lose most of its remaining apparel firms and jobs.[60]

Many of these trends had been pointed out in a widely circulated 1966 study of the apparel industry by Edward B. Shils, chairman of the Department of Industry at the University of Pennsylvania's Wharton School of Business and later president of the Knitted Outerwear Manufacturers Association. Shils had urged that the city government, the business community, and the garment workers unions should undertake a joint project to train workers and provide financing and space for the creation of as many as six "garment centers" that would offer modern facilities, improved working conditions, and economies of scale. PIDC prepared a feasibility study in 1967 that endorsed the concept, but with the industry not yet in crisis and with numerous other development and anti-poverty endeavors competing for attention, the project made little progress.[61] In the early 1970s, however, with firms closing, jobs disappearing, and union membership declining, pressure increased on all parties to take action. PIDC, the Old Philadelphia Development Corporation, and the ILGWU collaborated on the organization of the Philadelphia Garment Industry Board in 1973. Composed of city and state officials and representatives from the city's major economic development and business organizations, unions, and the local industry's leading firms, the Garment Board soon formulated a three-phase program designed to revitalize the industry and establish Philadelphia as the "style center of the world."[62]

Along with a number of immediate cosmetic steps, such as improved lighting and subway stops in a newly designated "Garment Square" district along North Broad Street, the key intermediate component of the Garment Board's program consisted of the construction of a new Garment Center on the edge of Center City that would serve as the focal point of the local industry. Publicity for the project claimed that it would stimulate the city's apparel industry as the Food Distribution Center had invigorated the food processing industry a decade earlier. PIDC and Model Cities played a central part in the project, as PIDC coordinated its own low-interest financing with a $450,000 Model Cities grant for acquisition of the land from the RA. As with the new plant for Somerset Knitting Mills, the project qualified for Model Cities funds because as many as 80 percent of workers would come from the Model Cities area in Lower North Philadelphia. Opened in early 1976, the $4.9 million, six-story garment

FIGURE 29. Philadelphia mayor Frank Rizzo with Greater Philadelphia Movement chairman Stephen S. Gardner, and Philadelphia Dress Joint Board (International Ladies Garment Workers' Union) manager William Ross at a meeting regarding the Philadelphia Garment Industry Board's new Garment Center project. The eight-story Garment Center would be built with PIDC–Model Cities funds. The William Penn statue atop the City Hall tower is visible in the background. Photo courtesy of Temple University Libraries, Urban Archives, Philadelphia, Pennsylvania.

center included manufacturing, retail, and office space, a health care center, and, in what Mayor Rizzo described as the center's "most unusual aspect," a training center and a child care center. As the mayor noted, "students will be on the job right there ... and some workers will be able to have lunch with their own children." At the time of its opening, firms in the center employed 475 workers, but the building had a capacity of "650 industrial workers, 650 commercial office workers, 200 retail personnel, and 10 training supervisors," as well as facilities for 500 trainees a year.[63]

Evaluated together, the Somerset Knitting Mills and Garment Center projects demonstrated the value in bridging the gap between the racially defined, parallel tracks of Philadelphia's response to the problem of jobs. Throughout the 1970s and 1980s, PIDC continued to pursue such initiatives in conjunction with its more prominent efforts at service sector development and its traditional industrial financing activity. In 1975, when the federal government merged urban renewal, Model Cities, and other urban programs into the Community Development Block Grant (CDBG) program, Mayor Rizzo appointed PIDC as an administrator of several key economic aspects of Philadelphia's grant. Under CDBG, PIDC managed what it called the Model Cities Land Development Program "to assist in the retention and expansion of industry in the Model Cities area." As with its earlier incarnation, this version of the program concentrated on land acquisition for firms that would provide employment for Model Cities residents. By April 1976, PIDC had completed eight grants worth $979,000 to firms employing 1,439 workers. PIDC also initiated a second program, the City-Wide Land Development Program, which pursued similar goals throughout Philadelphia, beginning with a $384,000 project in southwest Philadelphia's Eastwick urban renewal area.[64] During the 1980s, PIDC continued its efforts by participating in the federal Urban Development Action Grant (UDAG), Mortgage Loan, and SBA 504 loan programs, and the Pennsylvania Enterprise Zone and Capital Loan Fund programs. With the resulting funds, PIDC developed inner-city industrial projects in such areas as the Parkside section of West Philadelphia, Hunting Park, and along the American Street corridor. Between 1983 and 1988, the American Street project alone created approximately 1,700 new jobs.[65]

These projects gradually merged the physically based projects that PIDC had pursued since the early 1960s with the social concerns that it had largely ignored during the initial period of its operation. Ironically, their significance and relative success gives a rough measure of the cost exacted by the collapse of local economic planning during the early years of PIDC and the War on Poverty. If such planning proposals had been implemented, Philadelphia's racially bifurcated tracks of local industrial policy might have been drawn together as early as the mid-1960s and could have provided a crucial structural base for the local War on Poverty.

PIDC's continuing policy innovations aside, other aspects of local public policy under Rizzo dramatically worsened the city's economic situation. Although the mayor supported initiatives such as the Garment Center, the Somerset Knitting Mills project, and the establishment of a tariff-free trade zone in the Eastwick and Penrose Industrial Parks, he failed to expand such episodic interventions into a truly comprehensive local economic policy. Instead, the Rizzo administration shaped public policy on an opportunistic basis closely tied to political considerations. During Rizzo's first term, this approach included cooperating with downtown business interests to facilitate the construction of the Market East urban shopping mall and the Center City commuter tunnel. These projects helped Center City retain a high level of vitality during an era in which many central business districts suffered devastating economic downturns, but they also placed great fiscal stress on the city's capital budget and strained the Rizzo administration's already tenuous relationship with activists who lobbied for greater attention to neighborhood problems. Despite the promotion of Goldie Watson to deputy mayor in 1974, racial tensions only exacerbated these divisions.[66] Rizzo, meanwhile, sought to secure his own political base by granting generous wage and benefit increases to the city's municipal employee unions. This continued a pattern that had begun under Mayor Tate a decade earlier. In combination with economic stagnation and increasing city service needs, such concessions produced a record city budget deficit of $86 million (not revealed until after Rizzo's 1975 reelection) and forced the mayor to push through a $250 million increase in wage and property taxes.

Along with Rizzo's continuing exacerbation of racial tensions, such actions produced bitter divisions between the mayor, the business community, African Americans, and white liberals. In the aftermath of the 1976 tax increase, a recall petition to remove Rizzo from office gathered more than 200,000 signatures. The petition never reached the ballot, though, because the city solicitor rejected more than 115,000 of the signatures on technicalities. Despite the defeat of the recall petition, a similar alliance between business, African Americans, and white liberals blocked Rizzo's 1978 campaign to change the charter to allow him to run for a third term. The recall and "Charter Defense" alliances laid the groundwork for the successful mayoral campaigns of William Green in 1979 and W. Wilson Goode, the city's first African American mayor, in 1983.[67]

The weak economy, increasing domestic and overseas competition, and local tax increases all contributed to an even greater erosion of Philadelphia's economic base. The wage tax, which rose from 2 percent in 1969 to 4.3 percent after the 1976 Rizzo increase (and reached 4.96 percent in 1984), proved to be particularly controversial. Despite PIDC's efforts, the city lost 138,814 jobs during the two terms of the Rizzo administration, including more than 77,600 in manufacturing. Unemployment rose from 4.6 percent in 1970 to 11.2 percent in 1980, and the percentage of the city's population on welfare rose from 14 percent at the start of the decade to 20 percent at its close. Meanwhile, Philadelphia's population fell by 13 percent. Beginning in 1976, the number of service industry jobs in Philadelphia exceeded the total in the manufacturing sector. Much of the growth in service jobs occurred in health care, as Philadelphia evolved into one of the nation's leading medical centers. This development could be traced in part to the work of the city Hospital Authority, which oversaw the renovation, expansion, or construction of twenty-seven hospitals during the Rizzo years. One of the authority's most important projects, the Philadelphia Center for Health Care Sciences, occupied the former site of Philadelphia General Hospital in West Philadelphia, a major public hospital that Rizzo had closed during the budget crisis of the mid-1970s. By the end of the 1980s, the health care and education sectors emerged as leading sources of employment in Philadelphia.[68]

Despite the positive dimensions of PIDC's work in the decades following the 1971 expansion of its mission, the best opportunities for local policies to redirect the course of Philadelphia's economy had in many respects passed with the end of the late-1960s economic boom. Few examples better illustrate this dilemma than the fate of the Garment Center project. This building offered manufacturers an efficient modern facility and workers a range of services unprecedented in any Philadelphia manufacturing establishment. Further, it was created through a partnership of business, labor, and government with funding from a federal social program and a local quasi-public development entity. As such, it constituted a model of the kind of cooperative public-private partnership that, with wider vision, might have been implemented ten to fifteen years earlier. Unfortunately, the center was too little and too late to save the Philadelphia garment industry. In 1966, Edward Shills had suggested that as many as six such buildings would be needed immediately to resolve the industry's problems. In 1973, an analyst for the Greater Philadelphia Movement suggested that the Garment Industry Board should be even more aggressive in aiding the industry. The unnamed analyst pointed out that the new Garment Center would serve only a fraction of the firms and workers displaced by the Market East project alone, noting, "I fear that GPM may be endorsing something whose goals are admittedly cosmetic in the short run and perhaps not ambitious enough in the long run." The third proposed phase of the Garment Board's program involved detailed research studies of the industry, and the analyst warned that with such a process "we won't have definite impact upon the industry until 1977–78 at the earliest. That may simply be too late."[69]

Events soon proved the GPM observer right. The Garment Center quickly found tenants, but the overall industry collapsed in Philadelphia, eviscerated by the shift of production to low-wage, low-cost locations first in Mexico and Central American and then in Asia. By 1979, membership in the apparel unions fell to below 8,000, and by 1982, total employment in the industry declined to 18,200; by 1997, it had reached 5,269.[70] Whether earlier and more aggressive action by the kind of development partnership that emerged in the 1970s could have saved even some part of the Philadelphia garment industry cannot be definitively assessed. Given the nature of the global competition the local industry faced, apparel might well have been beyond saving, at least in the long-term. Such a strategy, however, would have maximized the chances of attaining such a result, would have saved more firms on a temporary basis, and, much more importantly, could have been applied on a citywide basis across a range of other industries more viable than apparel. In any case, both the Somerset and Garment Center projects, along with PIDC's industrial development efforts elsewhere in the city, clearly illustrated that such possibilities continued to exist far into the era of what is usually assumed to be the postindustrial American economy.

Whether inevitable or preventable, the decline of industries such as apparel exacted very real human costs. Shortly before Somerset closed, seventy-seven year old Regina Marucci, who had worked at the plant since 1975 and in the apparel industry since 1929, described what would be lost: "It's like home. Those girls are a part of you. They tell you their problems, and you tell them theirs. Several of the girls came to the viewing for my husband. We don't know if we'll see each other again." Ten years later, a reporter at a Philadelphia Labor Day Parade met one former Somerset employee and recorded an exchange that captured another consequence of the loss: "'They don't have a union where I work now,' Joe said, 'It's too small, but they take care of us pretty good.' 'Hey, you got no pension,' his Dad piped in." Regina Marucci's experience of a loss of community as the plant prepared to close, and Joe's sense of diminished economic security ten years later, captured much of what deindustrialization and the problem of jobs meant for so many Philadelphians.[71]

And All the World Was Philadelphia

In 1968, historian Sam Bass Warner chose the phrase "if all the world was Philadelphia" as the title for what would become a classic essay about the promise and limitations of urban history as a field of historical inquiry.[1] By the end of the twentieth century, accelerated global capital mobility meant that "all the world" had in many respects become Philadelphia. Like Philadelphia during the 1950s and 1960s, communities in the southern and western United States that had once drawn manufacturing plants from the older industrial regions of the Northeast and Midwest increasingly struggled to address the loss of such industry, and the relatively well-paying jobs that it provided, to low-wage regions in the developing world. For such communities, the experience of postwar Philadelphia offers key insights into the possibilities for social, political, and policy action in this still new world.

In the decades after World War II, Philadelphia liberals responded to the city's problem of jobs with surprising insight, forgotten activism, and unrecognized accomplishment, but also with crucial shortfalls of vision. As early as the mid-1950s, local liberals realized that creeping deindustrialization and persistent employment discrimination threatened both the economic security of working class Philadelphians and the fiscal stability of the city government. To address these problems, they created a series of state-based and state-funded policy strategies. These local initiatives included the industrial and employment policies of PIDC and the OIC–

Progress Movement, the Urban Coalition's efforts to work both with and outside of the local and federal "Philadelphia Plans" for construction industry integration, and the proposals for coordinated local economic planning that circulated in parallel with the very different War on Poverty and Model Cities initiatives of the Great Society.

This local liberalism produced a striking series of accomplishments that neither resolved the problem of jobs nor stopped the process of deindustrialization, but did succeed in preserving viable elements of the city's old manufacturing base, in shaping the specific character of its economy, and in establishing precedents and models for community-based urban development strategies. In broader terms, they demonstrated that during the post–World War II period, urban liberals in Philadelphia implemented the kind of public intervention in the private economy that their federal counterparts during the postwar period remained mostly unwilling to contemplate. Unfortunately, tragic missed opportunities accompanied these local industrial and employment policies, particularly the racial bifurcation of local industrial and employment policy. The resulting parallel policy tracks significantly constrained the city's ability to address the problem of jobs in a coherent, comprehensive fashion.

By the mid-1970s, liberal policymakers had completed a lengthy and rather painful learning process in Philadelphia. The Somerset and Garment Center projects represented the material outcome of this process, but also, and more importantly, they reflected the underlying policy lessons that could be derived from Philadelphia's experience. The first lesson was that successful urban social policy had to take the problem of jobs seriously. Issues of community empowerment, service provision, and urban poverty could never be adequately addressed by programs that ignored employment issues. Efforts to improve housing, reorganize social services, or empower poor communities rapidly unravel without some form of viable local economic base. In addition to its pragmatic necessity, a work-based approach to social policy offers a potentially valuable political benefit. As Leon Sullivan recognized, liberal assertions of the centrality of work and, importantly, access to jobs, resonate with fundamental American ideological tenets. Emphasis on the significance of work to American social, civic, and economic life may allow liberals to open new societal discussions about both the meaning of economic security and the social and political structures through which it might be achieved for all citizens. In his 1944 "Economic Bill of Rights," Franklin D. Roosevelt outlined such a course for postwar liberalism. Since the era of the Great

Society, however, liberals have too often ignored the political and policy possibilities that might be derived from a clear emphasis on work as a fundamental American value—and potentially, on decent, rewarding employment as a core American right.

The second lesson constituted a partial converse of the first: job creation programs such as PIDC might have a positive effect even without attention to social issues, but their value could be multiplied if they concentrated their effort on key social problems in areas of the city that had both distinct needs and clear opportunities. Despite the postwar decline of Philadelphia's old industrial belt, many areas of the city retained such potential even as the century came to a close. Economic development should be closely linked to neighborhoods, but must also be connected to broader economic networks, both in the city and beyond; even more centrally, economic development must remain, as Philadelphia's OEDP planners wrote in 1964, "a means to achieving social and welfare objectives."

The third lesson is based on the recognition that local industrial policy, and local liberalism generally, required the provision of direct financial resources and positive incentives by the federal government. Neither local nor philanthropic funding sources could ever supply the quantity of resources that quasi-public agencies like PIDC and community organizations like OIC required. Further, the exact structure of such support not only mattered but varied among different types of recipients. Quite simply, the experiences of PIDC and OIC, as well as of the wider War on Poverty in Philadelphia, demonstrate that some forms of intergovernmental relationships work better than others. In each of these cases, federal urban policy was most effective when it provided direct grants to innovative local programs that addressed local needs, and in particular, employment issues. These arrangements characterized OIC's early categorical grant support and its "prime national contractor" status of the early-1970s, as well as the PIDC–Model Cities partnership of the mid-1970s that completed the Somerset Knitting Mills, Garment Center, and other industrial projects. In contrast, federal policies consistently failed when they sought to address urban problems by restructuring urban political systems. This pattern persisted both in the direct case of the Community Action and Model Cities programs of the 1960s, and more subtly in CETA's redirection of power away from community-based job training programs such as OIC and toward "prime sponsors" based in local governments. As a concept, community action worked tremendously well when used to empower innovative activists and organizations, but proved far more problematic when applied to political reorganization.

As such, dispersal of resources and policy authority to local institutions, both governmental and nongovernmental, may offer the outlines for a powerful form of liberal federalism that works with rather than against basic constitutional structures and ideological presuppositions of American society. Postwar Philadelphia's experiments in local state building offer an important precedent for such an approach. Regardless of the structural arrangements of federal policy, however, a strong federal commitment both to funding such policies and to enforcing civil rights laws will remain a vital prerequisite for the successful implementation of even the most innovative local programs. The resources that can be derived from local, philanthropic, and charitable sources will never be enough to sustain effective policy, and unchecked localism will likely remain vulnerable to the toleration of discrimination.

The issue of local political power and control over development policy weighs heavily on these questions of urban funding and development strategy. The War on Poverty's federally sponsored effort to reorganize local politics through community action and empowerment proved to be in many respects unrealistic, even if desirable in principle. As the careers of such African American leaders as Wilson Goode and John Street have demonstrated in Philadelphia during the past three decades, political power can only be created "the old fashioned way": by building it over time through a combination of activism, community organizing, and at times, painful compromise. The same pragmatist principles apply to development policy. Unlike the sweeping (if always underfunded) political and social objectives of the War on Poverty, direct grant relationships offered few promises of transformative policy change. As the experiences of PIDC and OIC demonstrate, however, such relationships provided one of the few viable strategies for making significant interventions in the problem of jobs with which Philadelphia and similar cities continued to struggle as the twenty-first century came to a close. Ultimately, such tests of actual effectiveness provide the standard for evaluating both local and federal policies and community-based initiatives. Philadelphia's local industrial and employment policies did not, and could not, resolve the problem of jobs, but they mitigated its severity and improved the overall economic situation of the city and its residents.

Finally, this study's focus on the local state yields important insights about postwar liberalism and the broader sweep of postwar American history. Among the most important is the recognition that after World War II, local liberals continued to focus on the structural economic considerations that national liberals gradually abandoned. This structural orientation formed the basis for PIDC's program of rehabilitating inner-city factories and building urban industrial parks. Industrial renewal in Philadelphia had limitations of scope, capacity, and perspective, but the inescapable fact remains that as early as the late-1950s, liberal policymakers in the city were attempting to address urban deindustrialization through the public provision of new or modernized industrial facilities. During the entire post–World War II period, no policy undertaken at the federal level matched the ambitiousness of this local engagement with structural economic problems.

In a similar fashion, Leon Sullivan's job training and business development initiatives exhibited a willingness to attack the problems created by both deindustrialization and the wider political economy of race in northern cities. Sullivan's efforts addressed overt and covert employment discrimination, the inadequate educational opportunities available to African Americans, and the limited control of capital by Philadelphia's black community. Perhaps most interestingly, Sullivan and his associates confronted the deeply held ideologies of individualism and self-reliance that persistently bedeviled American advocates of state-centered social policy throughout the twentieth century. Rather than attempting to overturn such cultural characteristics, the OIC–Progress Movement inverted the problem by assertively embracing these ideals and challenging American society to live up to its own rhetoric, while also embedding them in an alternative form of community capitalism. Throughout the late-1960s and 1970s, Sullivan and the OIC–Progress Movement used this discursive strategy to build a series of community-owned economic institutions controlled by African Americans. In a period that would soon generate not a radical transformation of American society but a resurgent conservatism that achieved political success by celebrating traditional ideological orientations, Sullivan's pragmatic approach offered American liberalism a viable set of alternative social, economic, and rhetorical strategies. The race-based approach of the Philadelphia Plan marked a point where local liberalism came together with the wider trajectory of postwar liberalism, unifying many Philadelphia liberals but also delineating the structural as well as cultural limitations of both race-based and economic-based approaches to the problem of jobs.

These developments, of course, took place within wider frames of post-war U.S. urban history. Philadelphia's local liberalism, and the policy initiatives it generated, cannot easily be placed on a simple continuum of urban political ideology. Through the 1950s and 1960s, Philadelphia stood clearly to the left of cities such as Los Angeles or Oakland, where right-wing, business-dominated coalitions controlled much of local politics and policy. Cities like Detroit experienced a period of conservative political control, driven by a homeowners' politics that resisted racial integration. By the 1960s and 1970s, however, Detroit's politics would move leftward as the city's economic plight deepened, whites departed, and African Americans demanded political power. The politics of homeowner reaction extended to Chicago (and elsewhere), although it never led to conservative capture of that city's government. Philadelphia too shared aspects of race-driven homeowners' politics. While this fatally undermined the city's public housing policies, it did not prevent the local engagement of a structural economic liberalism left largely unattended by postwar national liberals.[2] Leon Sullivan and the OIC–Progress Movement even recast powerful cultural ideas about self-reliance and self-help as state-supported strategies of liberal uplift. Community development organizers in cities such as New York and Cleveland pursued similar rhetorical and strategic tacks to a greater degree than has been previously recognized, as did employment-oriented civil rights campaigners and advocates of workplace gender equity. Activists in cities like New York, though, also moved in directions far more radical than that of Sullivan and Philadelphia liberalism, remaining engaged for at least a time after the war with the American communist movement and far later, with an aggressive local trade unionism or, separately, black power.[3] Yet such radical urbanism did not necessarily accomplish more than Philadelphia's local liberalism.

Superficially, at least, Philadelphia liberalism's non-transformative, non-revolutionary character, its racial bifurcation of policy, and (in the case of the OIC–Progress Movement) its embrace of self-help suggest that its closest parallel might be the moderate, supposedly color-blind centrism that emerged during the 1960s and 1970s in "New South" cities such as Atlanta and Charlotte. This comparison falters, however, when it is extended to Philadelphia liberals' eventual embrace of the racially compensatory Philadelphia Plan, to their development of neighborhood employment requirements in projects such as Somerset Knitting Mills, to the racial and ultimately redistributive orientation of OIC, and to the structural, economic orientation of their key economic policies. In contrast, New South moderates, and in fact suburbanites nationwide, embraced integration in theory while preserving a myth of suburban racial innocence and rejecting nearly all forms of compensatory state-based intervention in housing, employment, or education.[4] Philadelphia's postwar liberals never overcame housing segregation, but in response to the problem of jobs, they shaped a nuanced form of urban moderation that was both more interventionist and, ultimately, more racially focused than its possible counterparts in the New South.

Unlike political ideology, it may be possible to establish at least at rough continuum of social and economic outcomes among cities similar to Philadelphia. While most older industrial cities had areas of high poverty and extreme segregation as the twentieth century closed, Philadelphia stood at something of a middle position in economic outcomes. While ultimately less successful than high-tech areas such as Boston or San Francisco, Philadelphia's local liberalism helped retain a degree of economic vibrancy that placed it, despite its severe problems, in a better position than Detroit, St. Louis, Cleveland, or Baltimore. Local politics, local policies, and local liberalism all mattered greatly in shaping such outcomes.

Such observations, about cities specifically and postwar liberalism generally, lead to a broader final judgment about liberal political strategy. The ultimate measure of both urban policy and urban activism is on-the-ground accomplishment. Neither PIDC nor the OIC–Progress Movement solved the problem of jobs in Philadelphia. Neither effort even presented a particularly thorough analysis of the political economic, racial, and spatial issues that caused urban deindustrialization. Nonetheless, both created highly functional programs that had positive effects on the economic lives of working class Philadelphians. Both found pragmatic ways to work effectively within the limits of available resources and political institutions. Both demonstrated that it is as valid to take an immediate, if limited, action to address a specific problem as to work indefinitely for an ideal solution that may or may not emerge at some unknown future moment. Sullivan's record, in particular, indicates that liberals must learn to take advantage of the culture in which they live rather than struggling against it: instead of rejecting the mainstream emphasis on work, jobs, and self-reliance, the OIC–Progress Movement demanded the resources necessary to fulfill these ideals for all Americans.

Ultimately, American liberals must find ways to gain support for efforts to address urban issues, and the problem of poverty more generally, in a political culture that is fundamentally conservative. Organization, activism, and critical analysis are crucial to the process. American liberalism will always require a vital left that creates new opportunities by challenging the boundaries of political possibility. The history of the twentieth century United States, however, offers little hope for quick transformative change. In such an environment, liberal strategies that work around the constraints of culture and political economy offer the real prospect of implementing projects that can actually secure meaningful, immediate progress. The legacy of local liberalism in postwar Philadelphia rests on exactly this insight. PIDC and the OIC programs had distinct limitations, but they succeeded in building factories, providing job training, and creating African American–owned businesses. Few others in postwar Philadelphia, or the United States, were doing more.

List of Abbreviations

Temple University Urban Archives, Philadelphia, Pennsylvania (TUUA)

ACWAR	Amalgamated Clothing Workers of America Records
BCR	Black Coalition Records
CCCPR	Citizens' Council on City Planning Records
EPACR	Eastwick Project Area Committee Records
FCR	Fellowship Commission Records
GPC	General Pamphlet Collection
GPMR	Greater Philadelphia Movement Records
GPPR	Greater Philadelphia Partnership Records
HADV-NURA	Housing Association of the Delaware Valley Records, Neighborhood and Urban Renewal Area Files
HADV-OF	Housing Association of the Delaware Valley Records, Office Files
HRDI	AFL-CIO Human Resources Development Institute
JLCR	Jewish Labor Committee Records
OICAR	Opportunities Industrialization Centers of America Records
KRPP	Kirk R. Petshek Papers
PBCC	*Philadelphia Evening Bulletin* News Clippings Collection
PCCAR	Philadelphia Council for Community Advancement Records
FCR	Fellowship Commission Records
WMPP	Walter M. Phillips Sr. Papers
POHP	Walter M. Phillips Oral History Project
TWUAR	Textile Workers Union of America Records
ULR	Urban League Records

City of Philadelphia, Department of Records, City Archives, Philadelphia, Pennsylvania (CA)

CPCR	City Planning Commission Records
DC-BSF	Department of Commerce, Business Services Division Files
DC-IDF	Department of Commerce, Industrial Development Division, Project Files 1953–70
DC-IDC	Department of Commerce, Industrial Development Division, Correspondence, 1952–60, 1968
DMD-HF	Deputy Managing Director for Housing Files
MD-FC	Managing Director, Files and Correspondence
MCF	Mayor's Correspondence and Files

Historical Society of Pennsylvania; Philadelphia, Pennsylvania (HSP)

AMGP	Albert M. Greenfield Papers
CCLF	Chamber of Commerce Loose Files

Federal Agencies

DOL	U.S. Department of Labor
USCCR	United States Commission on Civil Rights

Newspapers and Magazines (abbreviated titles only)

NYT	*New York Times*
PB	*Philadelphia Evening and Sunday Bulletin*
PI	*Philadelphia Inquirer*
PDN	*Philadelphia Daily News*
PT	*Philadelphia Tribune*
PM	*Philadelphia Magazine; Greater Philadelphia: The Magazine for Executives; Greater Philadelphia Magazine*
WSJ	*Wall Street Journal*
WP	*Washington Post*

Notes

Introduction

1. "Whitman Starts Plant; Ground Broken on Roosevelt Blvd.," *PB*, April 7, 1960; Joseph M. Guess, "Whitman's to Build Plant on Boulevard; Chocolate Firm Reverses Its Plan to Move to N.J.," *PB*, January 28, 1960.

2. "Drug Company Abandons Plan to Leave City; West Wholesale to Build New Plant at Front & Luzerne," *PB*, September 8, 1960; Joseph M. Guess, "Firm Decides to Stay in City; PIDC Helps Finance New Drug Plant," *PB,* February 23, 1960.

3. For the continued relevance of the local state in American political history, Thomas J. Sugrue, "All Politics Is Local: The Persistence of Localism in Twentieth Century America," in *The Democratic Experiment: New Directions in American Political History,* ed. Meg Jacobs, William J. Novak, and Julian Zelizer (Princeton: Princeton University Press, 2003), 301–26; Philip J. Ethington, "Mapping the Local State," *Journal of Urban History* 27:5 (July 2001): 686–702; Eric H. Monkkonen, *The Local State: Public Money and American Cities* (Stanford: Stanford University Press, 1995).

4. Clifford Geertz, *The Interpretation of Cultures* (New York: Basic Books, 1973), 23.

5. Paul Starr, *Freedom's Power: The True Force of Liberalism* (New York: Basic Books, 2007); William A. Galston, *Liberal Purposes: Goods, Virtues, and Diversity in the Liberal State* (New York: Cambridge University Press, 1991).

6. David A. Hollinger, *In the American Province: Studies in the History and Historiography of Ideas* (Baltimore: Johns Hopkins University Press, 1989); Gary Gerstle, "The Protean Character of American Liberalism," *American Historical Review* 99:4 (October 1994): 1043–73; Louis Menand, *The Metaphysical Club* (New York: Farrar, Straus and Giroux, 2001); James T. Kloppenburg, *The Virtues of Liberalism* (New York: Oxford University Press, 1998).

7. Robert H. Zieger, *The CIO, 1935–1955* (Chapel Hill: University of North Carolina Press, 1995); Ellen Schrecker, *Many Are the Crimes: McCarthyism in America* (Princeton: Princeton University Press, 1998); Paul Lyons, *Philadelphia Communists, 1936–1956* (Philadelphia: Temple University Press, 1982); Lyons, *The People of This Generation: The Rise and Fall of the New Left in Philadelphia* (Philadelphia: University of Pennsylvania Press, 2003), 10–11; Sherman Labovitz, *Being Red in Philadelphia: A Memoir of the McCarthy Era* (Philadelphia: Camino Books, 1998).

8. Michael Tomasky, "Party in Search of a Notion," *American Prospect* 17:5 (May 2006): 20–28; Gary Gerstle, "The Protean Character of American Liberalism," *American Historical Review* 99:4 (October 1994): 1043–73; Ira Katznelson, *When Affirmative Action Was White: An Untold History of Racial Inequality in Twentieth Century America* (New York: W.W. Norton, 2005).

9. Gunnar Myrdal, *An American Dilemma: the Negro Problem and Modern Democracy* (New York: Harper & Brothers, 1944); Thomas J. Sugrue, "Affirmative Action from Below: Civil Rights, the Building Trades, and the Politics of Racial Equality in the Urban North, 1945–1969," *Journal of American History* 91 (June 2004): 145–73; Risa L. Goluboff, *The Lost Origins of Civil Rights* (Cambridge, MA: Harvard University Press, 2007).

10. Martha Biondi, *To Stand and Fight: The Struggle for Civil Rights in Postwar New York City* (Cambridge: Harvard University Press, 2003); John D'Emilio, *Lost Prophet: The Life and Times of Bayard Rustin* (New York: Free Press, 2003); Nancy MacLean, *Freedom Is Not Enough: The Opening of the American Workplace* (Cambridge: Harvard University Press, 2006); Thomas F. Jackson, *From Civil Rights to Human Rights: Martin Luther King, Jr., and the Struggle for Economic Justice* (Philadelphia: University of Pennsylvania Press, 2007); Kent Germany, *New Orleans after the Promises: Poverty, Citizenship, and the Search for the Great Society* (Athens: University of Georgia Press, 2007); Robert O. Self, *American Babylon: Race and the Struggle for Postwar Oakland* (Princeton, NJ: Princeton University Press, 2003); Christina Greene, *Our Separate Ways: Women and the Black Freedom Movement in Durham, North Carolina* (Chapel Hill: University of North Carolina Press, 2005); Annelise Orleck, *Storming Caesar's Palace: How Black Mothers Fought Their Own War on Poverty* (Boston: Beacon Press, 2005); Matthew Countryman, *Up South: Civil Rights and Black Power in Philadelphia* (Philadelphia: University of Pennsylvania Press, 2005).

11. Kloppenburg, *The Virtues of Liberalism*, 100–23; Alice O'Connor, "Swimming against the Tide: A Brief History of Federal Policy in Poor Communities," in William T. Dickens and Ronald F. Ferguson, eds., *Urban Problems and Community Development* (Washington, D.C.: Brookings Institution Press, 1999); Margaret Weir, *Politics and Jobs: The Boundaries of Employment Policy in the United States* (Princeton: Princeton University Press, 1992); Weir, "The Federal Government and Unemployment: The Frustration of Policy Innovation from the New

Deal to the Great Society," in *The Politics of Social Policy in the United States*, ed. Weir, Ann Shola Orloff, and Theda Skocpol (Princeton: Princeton University Press, 1988), 149–90.

12. Robert M. Collins, *More: The Politics of Economic Growth in Postwar America* (New York: Oxford University Press, 2000); Gareth Davies, *From Opportunity to Entitlement: The Transformation and Decline of Great Society Liberalism* (Lawrence: University Press of Kansas, 1996); Thomas F. Jackson, "The State, the Movement, and the Urban Poor: The War on Poverty and Political Mobilization in the 1960s," in Michael B. Katz., ed., *The "Underclass" Debate: Views From History* (Princeton: Princeton University Press, 1993), 403–39; Judith Russell, *Economics, Bureaucracy, and Race: How Keynesians Misguided the War on Poverty* (New York: Columbia University Press, 2004).

13. Alan Brinkley, *The End of Reform: New Deal Liberalism in Recession and War* (New York: Alfred A. Knopf, 1995); Steve Fraser and Gary Gerstle, eds., *The Rise and Fall of the New Deal Order, 1930–1980* (Princeton: Princeton University Press, 1989); Colin Gordon, *New Deals: Business, Labor, and Politics in America, 1920–1935* (New York: Cambridge University Press, 1994); Christopher L. Tomlins, *The State and the Unions: Labor Relations, Law, and the Organized Labor Movement in America, 1880–1960* (Cambridge: Cambridge University Press, 1985); Katznelson, *When Affirmative Action Was White*.

14. Jason Scott Smith, *Building New Deal Liberalism: The Political Economy of Public Works, 1933–1956* (New York: Cambridge University Press, 2006); Margaret Pugh O'Mara, *Cities of Knowledge: Cold War Science and the Search for the Next Silicon Valley* (Princeton: Princeton University Press, 2004); Jordan A. Schwartz, *The New Dealers: Power Politics in the Age of Roosevelt* (New York: Alfred A. Knopf, 1993).

15. Meg Jacobs, *Pocketbook Politics: Economic Citizenship in Twentieth-Century America* (Princeton: Princeton University Press, 2005); Lizabeth Cohen, *A Consumers' Republic: The Politics of Mass Consumption in Postwar America* (New York: Alfred A. Knopf, 2003).

16. Thomas J. Sugrue, *The Origins of the Urban Crisis: Race and Inequality in Postwar Detroit* (Princeton: Princeton University Press, 1996); Gary Gerstle, "Race and the Myth of the Liberal Consensus," *Journal of American History* 82:2 (September 1995): 579–86; Arnold R. Hirsch, *Making the Second Ghetto: Race and Housing in Chicago 1940–1960* (New York: Cambridge University Press, 1983).

17. Matthew D. Lassiter, *The Silent Majority: Suburban Politics in the Sunbelt South* (Princeton: Princeton University Press, 2005); Kevin M. Kruse, *White Flight: Atlanta and the Making of Modern Conservatism* (Princeton: Princeton University Press, 2005); Self, *American Babylon*; Becky M. Nicolaides, *My Blue Heaven: Life and Politics in the Working-Class Suburbs of Los Angeles, 1920–1965* (Chicago: University of Chicago Press, 2002); Lisa McGirr, *Suburban Warriors: The Origins of the New American Right* (Princeton: Princeton University Press, 2001).

18. Hirsch, *Making the Second Ghetto*; John F. Bauman, *Public Housing, Race, and Renewal: Urban Planning in Philadelphia, 1920–1974* (Philadelphia: Temple University Press, 1987); Sugrue, *Origins of the Urban Crisis*. For an important reconsideration of such perspectives, Sylvie Murray, *The Progressive Housewife: Community Activism in Suburban Queens, 1945–1965* (Philadelphia: University of Pennsylvania Press, 2003).

19. Industrial policy can be defined as a "menu of subsidies and sanctions" applied to business by government; it focuses on "*industrial* or *producing* sectors of the economy" rather than consumers. Aaron Wildavsky, "Industrial Policies in American Political Cultures," in *The Politics of Industrial Policy*, ed. Claude E. Barfield and William A. Schambra (Washington, D.C.: American Enterprise Institute for Public Policy Research, 1986), 27; Harvey A. Goldstein, "Why State and Local Industrial Policy? An Introduction to the Debate," in *The State and Local Industrial Policy Question*, ed. Harvey A. Goldstein (Washington, D.C.: Planners Press, 1987). Employment policy may be defined as any policy designed to promote employment, ranging from skill training to direct public creation of jobs. Weir, *Politics and Jobs*; Gary Mucciaroni, *The Political Failure of Employment Policy 1945–1982* (Pittsburgh: University of Pittsburgh Press, 1990).

20. Geertz, *Interpretation of Cultures*, 23.

21. Alice Kessler-Harris, *In Pursuit of Equity: Women, Men, and the Quest for Economic Citizenship in 20th-Century America* (New York: Oxford University Press, 2001).

22. James R. Grossman, *Land of Hope: Chicago, Black Southerners, and the Great Migration* (Chicago: University of Chicago Press, 1989); Nicholas Lemann, *The Promised Land: The Great Black Migration and How It Changed America* (New York: Knopf, 1991); James N. Gregory, *The Southern Diaspora: How the Great Migrations of Black and White Southerners Transformed America* (Chapel Hill: University of North Carolina Press, 2005);

23. For an important account of African American suburbs, Andrew Wiese, *Places of Their Own: African American Suburbanization in the Twentieth Century* (Chicago: University of Chicago Press, 2004). James Wolfinger, *Philadelphia Divided: Race and Politics in the City of Brotherly Love* (Chapel Hill: University of North Carolina Press, 2007).

24. Kirk R. Petshek, *The Challenge of Urban Reform: Policies and Programs in Philadelphia* (Philadelphia: Temple University Press, 1973), 8–40, 286–99; William W. Cutler, III, "The Persistent Dualism: Centralization and Decentralization in Philadelphia, 1854–1975," in *The Divided Metropolis: Social and Spatial Dimensions of Philadelphia, 1800–1975*, ed. Cutler and Howard Gillette, Jr. (Westport, CT: Greenwood Press, 1980), 249–84; Bauman, *Public Housing, Race, and Renewal*, 102–3,118–23; Sam Bass Warner Jr., *The Private City: Philadelphia in Three Periods of Its Growth*, rev. ed. (Philadelphia: University of Pennsylvania Press,

1987), ix–xxvi, 214–23; Carolyn Adams, David Bartelt, David Elesh, Ira Goldstein, Nancy Kleniewski, and William Yancey, *Philadelphia: Neighborhoods, Division, and Conflict in a Postindustrial City* (Philadelphia: Temple University Press, 1991); Walter Licht, *Getting Work: Philadelphia, 1840–1950* (Philadelphia: University of Pennsylvania Press, 1992), 208–19.

25. Petshek, *Challenge of Urban Reform*, 15–16; for Dewey and American liberalism, see Kloppenburg, *The Virtues of Liberalism*.

26. The clearest articulation of these ideas can be found in National Resources Committee, *Our Cities: Their Role in the National Economy* (Washington, D.C.: GPO, 1937), 73–81.

Chapter One

1. "Noisy Democrats Cheer Victor and Boo Dark Union League," *PB*, November 7, 1951.

2. Peter McCaffery, *When Bosses Ruled Philadelphia: The Emergence of the Republican Machine, 1867–1933* (University Park: Pennsylvania State University Press, 1993), 135; James Reichley, *The Art of Government: Reform and Organization Politics in Philadelphia* (New York: Fund for the Republic, 1959), 3–13, 107–12; Russell F. Weigley, ed., *Philadelphia: A 300-Year History* (New York: W. W. Norton, 1982), 608–9, 619–23, 650–53; John F. Bauman, *Public Housing, Race, and Renewal: Urban Planning in Philadelphia, 1920–1974* (Philadelphia: Temple University Press, 1987), 29–32, 97–103; Kirk R. Petshek, *The Challenge of Urban Reform: Policies and Programs in Philadelphia* (Philadelphia: Temple University Press, 1973), 14–28; S. A. Paolontonio, *Rizzo: The Last Big Man in Big City America* (Philadelphia: Camino Books, 1993), 41–45.

3. Petshek, *The Challenge of Urban Reform*, 28–40, 50–51; Reichley, *The Art of Government*, 9–16; Nancy Kleniewski, "Neighborhood Decline and Downtown Renewal: The Politics of Redevelopment in Philadelphia, 1952–1962" (Ph.D. diss., Temple University, 1981), 99–119.

4. Jon C. Teaford, *The Rough Road to Renaissance: Urban Revitalization in America, 1940–1985* (Baltimore: Johns Hopkins Press, 1990), 54–66.

5. Thomas J. Sugrue, *The Origins of the Urban Crisis: Race and Inequality in Postwar Detroit* (Princeton: Princeton University Press, 1996); Martha Biondi, *To Stand and Fight: The Struggle for Civil Rights in Postwar New York City* (Cambridge, MA: Harvard University Press, 2003); Eric Avila, *Popular Culture in the Age of White Flight: Fear and Fantasy in Suburban Los Angeles* (Berkeley: University of California Press, 2004).

6. Paul Lyons, *Philadelphia Communists, 1936–1956* (Philadelphia: Temple University Press, 1982); Lyons, *The People of This Generation: The Rise and Fall*

of the New Left in Philadelphia (Philadelphia: University of Pennsylvania Press, 2003), 10–11; Sherman Labovitz, *Being Red in Philadelphia: A Memoir of the McCarthy Era* (Philadelphia: Camino Books, 1998).

7. Carolyn Teich Adams, *The Politics of Capital Investment: The Case of Philadelphia* (Albany: State University of New York Press, 1988), 31.

8. Petshek, *The Challenge of Urban Reform,* 14–17.

9. CPC, *Planning Study No. 2: Economic Base Study of the Philadelphia Area* (Philadelphia: City Planning Commission, August 1949).

10. Federal Reserve Bank of Philadelphia, *Business Review* (January 1953–September 1954), and "Industrial Employment Is Declining in Pennsylvania," *Business Review* (March 1954), 3–7.

11. Chamber of Commerce of Greater Philadelphia, *Greater Philadelphia Facts: Business and Civic Statistics, Edition of 1966* (Philadelphia: Chamber, 1966), 19; Arleigh P. Hess Jr., "Unemployment in the Philadelphia Labor Market Area: A Study of Changes in Employment During the First Eight Months of 1954, and a Discussion of Possible City Government Program to Reduce Unemployment," n.d., WMPP, Acc. 527, Box 17, Report: Unemployment in Philadelphia, 1954, TUUA, 11–28, 31.

12. Robert C. Goodwin, "Telegraph to the Honorable Joseph S. Clark Jr.," June 4, 1954, MCF, RG 60-2.3, Box A-470, Folder 104, City Archives (hereafter CA); Patrick H. McLaughlin, "Memo to Walter M. Phillips; Subject: Unemployment," April 30, 1954, MCF, ibid.; Kirk R. Petshek, "Memo to Walter M. Phillips; Subject: Unemployment," July 25, 1955, MD-FC, RG 61.2, Box A-710, Confidential Cabinet Meetings,1954, CA, 2.

13. Chamber of Commerce, *Greater Philadelphia Facts,* 9.

14. Teaford, Rough Road to Renaissance.

15. Philadelphia Department of Commerce, "Toward Greater Prosperity in Philadelphia: The Story of the Department of Commerce of the City of Philadelphia 1952–55," n.d. [1956?], WMPP, Acc. 527, Box 17, Phila. Comm. Dept. Printed Material 1957–61, TUUA, 3, 26; Walter M. Phillips, "Weekly Report to the Mayor," January 14, 1955, MD-FC, RG 61.2, Box A-713, Confidential Weekly Reports, City Representative, 1955, CA, 1; Kirk R. Petshek, "Memo to Walter M. Phillips; Subject: The City's Economic Problems," November 22, 1955, MD-FC, RG 61.2, Box A-710, Confidential Cabinet Meetings 1954, CA, 1, 4–5; Petshek, "Annual Report Economic Development" [1955], n.d., WMPP, Acc. 527, Box 17, Industrial Development Memos, 1953–54, 3; Petshek, *The Challenge of Urban Reform,* xi.

16. Kirk R. Petshek, "Memo to Walter M. Phillips; Subject: Unemployment," July 25, 1955, MD-FC, RG 61.2, Box A-710, Confidential Cabinet Meetings 1954, CA, 1–3.

17. Kirk R. Petshek, "Memo to Walter M. Phillips; Subject: The City's Economic Problems," November 22, 1955, MD-FC, RG 61.2, Box A-710, Confidential

Cabinet Meetings 1954, CA, 1,3–5; Petshek, "Annual Report Economic Development" [1955], 2.

18. Emily Lewis Jones, ed., *Walter M. Phillips: Philadelphia Gentleman Activist* (Swarthmore, Pennsylvania: Portraits on Tape, 1981), xi, 47, 61–62, 81; Weigley, ed., *Philadelphia: A 300-Year History*, 608–9, 619–23.

19. Walter M. Phillips, "Report of the City's Department of Commerce on the Promotion and Development of Commerce and Industry in Philadelphia; January 1952 to June 1955," n.d., WMPP, Acc. 527, Box 17, Reports under Clark Admin., 1952–55, TUUA, 1.

20. Walter M. Phillips, "A Proposal for Using City-Owned Land in Strengthening Philadelphia's Industrial Base," December 19, 1953, and "Recommended Method for Assuring Availability of Land for Industrial Development in Philadelphia," June 3, 1954, WMPP, Acc. 527, Box 17, Industrial Development Memos, 1953–54, TUUA; Phillips, "A Program for Industrial Land Development within the Corporate Limits of Philadelphia," September 20, 1954, MCF, RG 60-2.5, Box A-490, Industrial Land Development, CA.

21. CPC, *Planning Study No. 2: Economic Base Study of the Philadelphia Area* (Philadelphia: CPC, August 1949), 34. Also, Urban Land Institute (ULI), *Technical Bulletin No. 19: Planned Industrial Districts, Their Organization and Development* (Washington, D.C.: ULI, 1952); Richard Harris, *Unplanned Suburbs: Toronto's American Tragedy, 1900–1950* (Baltimore: Johns Hopkins University Press, 1996), 51–85.

22. Phillips, "A Proposal for Using City-Owned Land in Strengthening Philadelphia's Industrial Base," 2.

23. Robert O. Self, *American Babylon: Race and the Struggle for Postwar Oakland* (Princeton, NJ: Princeton University Press, 2003), 23–34; Sugrue, *Origins of the Urban Crisis*, 125–78; Joseph Heathcott and Maire Agnes Murphy, "Corridors of Flight, Zones of Renewal: Industry, Planning, and Policy in the Making of Metropolitan St. Louis, 1940–1980," *Journal of Urban History* 31:2 (January 2005): 151–89.

24. Phillips, "A Program for Industrial Land Development within the Corporate Limits of Philadelphia," 1–5, 8–9; Phillips, "A Proposal for Using City-Owned Land in Strengthening Philadelphia's Industrial Base," 2–4; Phillips, "Recommended Method for Assuring Availability of Land for Industrial Development in Philadelphia," 2, 6.

25. Edmund N. Bacon to Walter M. Phillips, June 8, 1954, and July 2, 1954, CPCR, RG 145.2, Box A-6390, Land Use - Industrial, 1952–56, CA, 1–2; CPC, *Preliminary Far Northeast Physical Development Plan* (Philadelphia: City of Philadelphia, January 1955); Walter M. Phillips to Edmund N. Bacon, January 21, 1955, MD-FC, RG 61.2, Box A-709, City Planning Commission 1955, CA, 1–8; William L. Rafsky, "Memo to Peter Schauffler," February 8, 1955, MCF, RG 60-2.3, Box A-473, CA, Folder 18: City Planning Commission 1955, CA; Paul A. Wilhelm, "Statement of the Department of Commerce Regarding Preliminary Far Northeast

Physical Development Plan," February 28, 1955, MCF, RG 60-2.5, Box A-490, Industrial Land Development, CA; "Chronology of Industrial Development Program Activities," December 1955, WMPP, Acc. 527, Box 17, Industrial Land Documents, 1952–56; 1961, TUUA, 2–3.

26. Walter M. Phillips, interviewed by Kirk R. Petshek, March 24, 1965, transcript, KRPP, Acc. 202, Box 5, TUUA, 1; "Chronology of Industrial Development Program Activities," 3–8.

27. Walter M. Phillips, interviewed by Petshek, March 24, 1965, 10; Mike Byrne, interviewed by Petshek, December 16, 1964, transcript, KRPP, ibid., 1–2; Joseph Turchi, interviewed by Petshek, December 16, 1964, transcript, KRPP, ibid., 1; Paul Croley, interviewed by Petshek, December 10 [1964], transcript, KRPP, ibid., 3; Warren Eisenberg, "Enter the Age of Tate," *PM*, January 1964, 88; Robert L. Freedman, *A Report on Politics in Philadelphia* (Cambridge, MA: Joint Center for Urban Studies of the Massachusetts Institute of Technology and Harvard University, 1963), II:24–27.

28. Walter A. Phillips, "Memo to Joseph S. Clark Jr.; Subject: Budget Message," September 7, 1955, MCF, RG 60-2.4, Box A-473, Folder 10: Budget For 1956, CA, 1.

29. Phillips, interviewed by Kirk R. Petshek, March 24, 1965, 4; Peter Schauffler, interviewed by Petshek, November 13, 1964, transcript, KRPP, Acc. 202, Box 5, TUUA, 1.

30. Phillips, interviewed by Kirk R. Petshek, March 24, 1965, 1; "Chronology of Industrial Development Program Activities," 3–8; Joseph M. (Mac) Guess, interviewed by Petshek, n.d. [1964–65], transcript, KRPP, Acc. 202, Box 5, TUUA, 1–2; Paul Wilhelm, interviewed by Walter M. Phillips, August 12, 1976, transcript, POHP, Box 9, TUUA, 4; Department of Commerce, Industrial Development Division, "1955 Annual Report," WMPP, Acc. 527; Box 17; Industrial Land Documents 1952–56, 1.

31. Schauffler, interviewed by Petshek, November 13, 1964, 1; David Berger, interviewed by Petshek, January 29, 1965, transcript, KRPP, Acc. 202, Box 5, [Interviews], TUUA, 1; Petshek, *The Challenge of Urban Reform*, 55–61; Freedman, *Report on Politics in Philadelphia*, II:23–24.

32. Frederic R. Mann, "Weekly Report for the Two Weeks Ending January 13, 1956," January 13, 1956, MD-FC, RG 61.2, Box A-708, Confidential-Weekly Reports, City Representative's Office, 1956, CA, 2–3; Frederic R. Mann, "Weekly Report to the Mayor," February 3, 1956, ibid., 2.

33. Berger, interviewed by Kirk R. Petshek, January 29, 1965, 1; Richardson H. Dilworth, interviewed by Petshek, March 21, 1965, transcript, KRPP, Acc. 202, Box 5, TUUA, 2,5.

34. Guian McKee, "Blue Sky Boys, Professional Citizens, and Knights-in-Shining-Money: Philadelphia's Penn Center Project and the Constraints of Private Development," *Journal of Planning History* 6:7 (February 2007).

35. Guian McKee, "Liberal Ends through Illiberal Means: Race, Urban Renewal, and Community in the Eastwick Section of Philadelphia, 1949–1990," *Journal of Urban History* 27: 5 (July 2001): 547–83.

36. Harold Wise, "Community Renewal Program, City of Philadelphia: Industrial Renewal: Requirements and Outlook for Philadelphia," December 1964, CPCR, RG 161.5, Box A-3605, CRP: Industrial Renewal, CA, 24–26, 39–40.

37. Philadelphia officials repeatedly testified in favor of relaxing the restriction on nonresidential projects. "The Rationale for Liberalization of the Provisions for Industrial Redevelopment of Urban Renewal Legislation," n.d. [1959?], KRPP, Acc. 202, Box 4, PIDC, TUUA.

38. Heathcott and Murphy, "Corridors of Flight, Zones of Renewal"; Teaford, *Rough Road to Renaissance*, 149–50, 311.

39. RA, *Summary Report on the Central Urban Renewal Area (C.U.R.A.)* (Philadelphia: City of Philadelphia, March 1956); Development Committee of the Philadelphia Redevelopment Authority, "INTERIM REPORT," December 17, 1952, KRPP, Acc. 202, Box 2, RA Development Areas, TUUA, i,1; William L. Rafsky, "Memo to Mayor Joseph S. Clark on progress of evaluation of the City's redevelopment program," July 22, 1955, MCF, RG 60-2.3, Box A-478, Folder 41D, CA; RA, "Summary Statement on Urban Renewal Policy and Program (Draft)," n.d., ibid.; CPC Comprehensive Planning Division, "Summary Report on the Central Urban Renewal Area (Preliminary Draft)," February 1956, HADV-NURA, Box 1, Folder 12, TUUA; CPC Staff, "A Suggested Approach to the Problem of Urban Renewal," January 1957, ibid.

40. Development Committee of the Philadelphia Redevelopment Authority, "INTERIM REPORT," 3–6; RA, *Philadelphia Renewal Patterns 1957; Annual Report* (Philadelphia: City of Philadelphia, 1958), 28; David Wallace, "Renaissancemanship," *Architectural Forum* 26:3 (August 1960), 160–61; Bauman, *Public Housing, Race, and Renewal*, 107–15, 125–35, 140–43.

41. An estimated $60 million in urban renewal funds would be available to Philadelphia in the immediate five- to six-year period. RA, *Summary Report on the Central Urban Renewal Area (C.U.R.A.)*, 46–70; RA, "Summary Statement on Urban Renewal Policy and Program (Draft)," 1–4; Office of the Development Coordinator, "A New Approach to Urban Renewal for Philadelphia," March 1957, GPC 529–3, TUUA, 1–3.

42. Ibid., 3–6; William L. Rafsky to Henry C. Beerits, May 9, 1957, KRPP, Acc. 202, Box 2, Urban Renewal, 1–5; Wallace, "Renaissancemanship," 160–61.

43. "Segregation: Inside Story of Philadelphia's Racial Housing Problem, as Told by the Mayor," *House and Home*, March 1958, 67–68; "Philadelphia's New Problem," *Time*, February 24, 1958, 18–19. For later uses of "white noose," see Self, *American Babylon*, 256, 370.

44. Office of the Development Coordinator, "A New Approach to Urban Renewal for Philadelphia," 3, 6; CRP, *Technical Report #6: The Redevelopment*

Authority Program, 1945–1962: Dollars Acres and Dwelling Units, prepared under the direction of Marcia J. Rogers, September 1963, 2.

45. Petshek, *The Challenge of Urban Reform*, 185–91; Greater Philadelphia Movement (GPM), "Philadelphia's Food Distribution Center; Prepared for Members of City Council of the City of Philadelphia," June 1955, GPMR, Acc. 291, 296, 307, 311, Box 12, FDC: Gen. Reports, etc., 1957–58, TUUA, 2; FDC Corporation, "How Philadelphia Created the World's First Complete Food Distribution Center," 1967, GPC 475–3, TUUA, 5, 10–15; "Food Distribution Center in S. Philadelphia Nearing OK; City Council Ready to Give Consent to Distribution Unit," *PI*, November 4, 1955; Food Distribution Center, "An Appeal to [Directors of the Fels Foundation]," May 10, 1957, GPMR, Acc. 291, 296, 307, 311, Box 12, FDC: Gen. Reports, etc., 1957–58, TUUA, 11.

46. For a critique of quasi-public agencies, Gail Radford, "From Municipal Socialism to Public Authorities: Institutional Factors in the Shaping of American Public Enterprise," *Journal of American History* 90:3 (December, 2003): 863–90.

47. CCCP, "1961–1966 Capital Program, Philadelphia Department of Commerce, Industrial Land Development," July 1960, CCCPR, Box 39, URB 10/XI/482, 1961–66 Capital Program Analysis - Industrial Land Develop., TUUA, 2; Institute for Urban Studies, University of Pennsylvania, *Industrial Land and Facilities for Philadelphia: A Report to the Philadelphia City Planning Commission* (Philadelphia: City of Philadelphia, 1956), 42.

48. Peter Schauffler, interviewed by Petshek, November 13, 1964, transcript, KRPP, November 13, 1964, Acc. 202, Box 5, TUUA, 1; Frederic R. Mann, "Activity Report[s] to the Mayor," August 18–31, September 1–14, September 15–28, September 29 – October 26, November 24 – December 26, 1957, MD-FC, RG 61.2, Box A-708, Confidential Weekly Reports, City Representative's Office, 1957, CA; Chamber of Commerce, "Minutes of Executive Committee Meeting," November 4, 1957, KRPP, Acc. 202, Box 4, PIDC, TUUA, 1–2; PIDC, "Minutes of Philadelphia Industrial Development Corporation Organizational Meeting of Board of Directors," February 26, 1958, ibid.; KRPP, Acc. 202, Box 4, PIDC, TUUA, 4; Chamber of Commerce of Greater Philadelphia, "Executive Committee Meeting," October 7, 1957, KRPP, ibid.; Chamber, "Board of Director's Meeting," December 3 and 16, 1957, KRPP, ibid.

49. PIDC, "Minutes of Philadelphia Industrial Development Corporation Organizational Meeting," 4–5; "Wm. F. Kelly Named Head of City Development Corp.," *PB*, February 26, 1958.

50. [Keeton Arnett], "Executive Vice President's Report to Board Of Directors," May 20, 1963, CCLF, Box: 1962–63 A-G, Board of Directors, May 1963, HSP, 3–4; Chamber of Commerce Advisory Committee to Commission on Human Relations, "Project No. CI-5," 1962–63, ibid., 1–2.

51. Keeton Arnett, retirement speech, [June] 1964, CCLF, Box: 1963–64 A-F, Arnett, Keeton; Farewell Speech 1964, HSP, 1.

52. Ted Beatty, interviewed by Petshek, December 14, 1964, transcript, KRPP, Acc. 202, Box 5, TUUA, 7.

Chapter Two

1. Gaeton Fonzi, "So Long Sam," *PM*, December 1967, 78–84.

2. Richard Graves to Peter Schauffler, April 15, 1958, KRPP, Acc. 202, Box 4, PIDC, TUUA; Paul Wilhelm, interview by Walter M. Phillips, August 12, 1976, transcript, POHP, Box 9, TUUA, 5–6; Ted Beatty, interviewed by Petshek, December 14, 1964, transcript, KRPP, Acc. 202, Box 5 [Interviews], TUUA, 7; Jan Staebler [*sic*], interviewed by Petshek, January 18, 1965, transcript, KRPP, ibid., 1,3; Citizens' Council on City Planning, "1961–1966 Capital Program, Philadelphia Department of Commerce, Industrial Land Development: Addendum," July 21, 1960, CCCPR, Box 39, URB 10/XI/482, 1961–66 Capital Program Analysis: Industrial Land Develop., TUUA, 2.

3. Chamber of Commerce of Greater Philadelphia, *Greater Philadelphia Facts: Business and Civic Statistics, Edition of 1966* (Philadelphia: The Chamber, 1966), 6; Walter Licht, *Getting Work: Philadelphia, 1840–1950* (Philadelphia: University of Pennsylvania Press, 1992), 3–16.

4. Richard Graves, "Memo to PIDC board of directors; Financing the Proposed Industrial Parks for Small Companies," March 18, 1960, DC-IDPF, RG 64.18, Box A-5193, Phila. Industrial Park 1959–62, CA; Frank Rosen, "'Industrial Park For Small Firms Planned by City," *PI*, February 7, 1960, 1,8; Richard Graves to Robert Tishman, March 23, 1961, DC-ID Files, RG 64.18, Box A-5193, Phila. Industrial Park 1959–62, CA.

5. Mayor's Economic Advisory Committee (MEAC), "Statement of Criteria for Industrial Park Development at the North Philadelphia Airport," December 9, 1960, KRPP, Acc. 202, Box 4, E.A.C., TUUA.

6. MEAC, "Summary of Discussion: Private Financing for Redevelopment," November 20, 1958, KRPP, Acc. 202, Box 4, EAC, TUUA, 2; Graves to Tishman, March 23, 1961, 1–2; Graves, "Memo to PIDC board of directors; Financing the Proposed Industrial Parks for Small Companies." For the history of IRBs, Gail Radford, "From Municipal Socialism to Public Authorities: Institutional Factors in the Shaping of American Public Enterprise," *Journal of American History* 90:3 (December, 2003): 863–90; Alberta M. Sbragia, *Debt Wish: Entrepreneurial Cities, U.S. Federalism, and Economic Development* (Pittsburgh: University of Pittsburgh Press, 1996), 163–79.

7. Lester W. Utter, "Memo to Walter Stein, re: Ruling T:R:I-FCD-5, Philadelphia Industrial Development Corporation," July 15, 1959, DC-IDPF, RG 64.18, Box A-5192, Internal Revenue Service '67, CA; Graves, "Memo to PIDC Board of Directors; Financing the Proposed Industrial Parks for Small Companies," 3–4;

Andrew Young, interview by Walter M. Phillips, October 12, 1978, transcript, POHP, Box 9, TUUA, 2–3; Wilhelm, interview by Phillips, 6.

8. PIDC bore no liability at any stage of the transaction, as both the firm's assets and the building itself were offered as collateral. PIDC transactions on city-owned land relied on the Industrial Redevelopment Fund (the "revolving fund"), which reimbursed the city for infrastructure costs up to the amount assessable for the improvements if the land had been privately held; the fund would then be re-imbursed from the proceeds of the land sale. Under this system, the city's expenses were limited to non-assessable infrastructure costs, its contributions to PIDC's operating budget, and debt service on the bonds used to finance the revolving fund. Michael L. Strong, "1961–1966 Capital Program; Philadelphia Department of Commerce; Industrial Land Development," July 1960, CCCPR, Urb 10/XI, Box 482, 1961–66 Capital Program Analysis—Industrial Land Development, TUUA, 4; PIDC, "Outline of Typical Industrial Build-Lease Project with the Philadel-phia Industrial Development Corporation as Owner, Lessor, And Mortgagor," n.d. [1959–61], KRPP, Acc. 202, Box 4, PIDC, TUUA; Robert Morrow Mitchell, "Industrial Development Activities in the City of Philadelphia: An Analysis of the Intergovernmental Relationships," (MA thesis, University of Pennsylvania, 1968), 12–15.

9. Richard McConnell, interviewed by Kirk R. Petshek, November 11, 1964[?], transcript, KRPP, Acc. 202, Box 5, 9–10.

10. Discussing industrial development (or revenue) bonds, which operated on the same principal as PIDC's industrial mortgages, one analyst noted that "a sig-nificant feature of IDB cost savings is that most of the subsidy comes from the fed-eral government while the IDB is issued by a local government that has virtually no associated costs." Matthew R. Marlin, "Industrial Development Bonds at 50: A Golden Anniversary Review," *Economic Development Quarterly* 1:4 (November 1987): 393.

11. MEAC, "Minutes, Economic Advisory Committee Meeting," October 9, 1959, KRPP, Acc. 202, Box 4, EAC, TUUA, 4; Office of the City Representative, Division of Public Information, *News Release: Office of the Mayor*, May 22, 1958, ibid.

12. David Melnicoff to Mr. Kirk Petshek, October 5, 1959, KRPP, Acc. 202, Box 4, EAC, TUUA 2; John W. Seybold, "Possible Public Statement by Eco-nomic Advisory Committee (draft of outline for same by John W. Seybold)," n.d. [1959?], KRPP, ibid.; MEAC, "Minutes of a Sub-Committee of the Mayor's Eco-nomic Advisory Committee with guests interested in study design," December 10, 1959, KRPP, ibid., 1–4; D. P. Eastburn, "Memo to Kirk R. Petshek; Ultimate Goals for Philadelphia: What Kind of City Do We Want?," March 4, 1959, KRPP, ibid.; [Kirk R. Petshek?], "Comments on Questions on Page 2 of Eastburn's Statement," March 1959, KRPP, ibid.; MEAC, "Minutes of the Mayor's Economic Advisory Committee," June 3, 1959, KRPP, ibid., 6; F. N. Sass, "Confidential: Suggested

Economic Goals for the City of Philadelphia; Mayor's Economic Advisory Committee ," November 3, 1960, KRPP, ibid., 3.

13. Wilhelm, interviewed by Phillips, 9.

14. MEAC, "Minutes, Economic Advisory Committee Meeting," October 11, 1960, KRPP, Acc. 202, Box 4, E.A.C., TUUA, 2.

15. PIDC officials argued that the transactions generated revenue for the revolving fund and met a legitimate need for warehouse space near the airport. They also argued the Gulf Oil land was low-lying and unsuitable for manufacturing, and that PIDC needed to demonstrate its viability to local bankers. Wise, interviewed by Petshek, November 1, 1964, transcript, KRPP, Acc. 202, Box 5, Interviews, TUUA, 7; Beatty, interviewed by Petshek, 5; Wilhelm, interviewed by Phillips, 7. Later events largely bore out the critics' claims: Sun Ray went bankrupt and left the city with significant mortgage obligations, while Gulf chose to refocus its operations on the Houston area and returned the tract to the city. [H. & W. Sylk], "Description of Sun Ray Drugstores transaction in Penrose Industrial Area," n.d. [1968], MCF, RG 60-2.5, Box A-4607, Phila. Industrial Development Corporation, CA, 1–3; Isadore Gottlieb, Esq., "History of Penrose Industries Lease and Option Submitted by Isadore Gottlieb, Esquire," October 7, 1971, DC-IDPF, RG 64.18, Box A-5193, Sun Ray Lease, CA; David G. Davis, "Memo to S. Harry Galfand; Gulf Oil Property: Penrose Tract," September 25, 1968, DC-IDPF, RG 64.18, Box A-5202, Gulf Oil 1968, CA.

16. MEAC, "Meeting of September 15, 1960 [minutes]," September 15, 1960, KRPP, Acc. 202, Box 4, EAC, TUUA; Allan G. Mitchell to Mr. Kirk R. Petshek, December 22, 1959, ibid.

17. PIDC, "1960 Summary of PIDC Activities," March 15, 1961, KRPP, Acc. 202, Box 4, PIDC, TUUA, 1; Beatty, interviewed by Petshek, 1–2,5; Wilhelm, interviewed by Phillips, 9; MEAC, "Minutes, Economic Advisory Committee Meeting," October 9, 1959, 2–5, 9.

18. Robert O. Crockett, "Memo to Files; Criteria for Choice of Industry in Franklin Redevelopment Area," June 2, 1959, KRPP, Acc. 202, Box 2, Industry, TUUA; MEAC "Minutes, Economic Advisory Committee Meeting," October 9, 1959, 3–9; Mitchell to Petshek, December 22, 1959, 1–2; David Melnicoff, "EAC Discussion," October 11, 1960, KRPP, Acc. 202, Box 4, EAC, TUUA; MEAC, "Minutes, Economic Advisory Committee Meeting," October 11, 1960, 3–5.

19. Beatty, interviewed by Petshek, 2–3; PIDC & Tishman Realty & Construction Company, "Agreement," March 29, 1961, DC-IDPF, RG 64.18, Box A-5193, Phila. Industrial Park 1959–62, CA; Robert V. Tishman, "Memo to Mr. Richard Graves; Re: North Philadelphia Airport Property," August 8, 1960, DC-IDPF, ibid.; Frank Binswanger to Richard Graves, August 10, 1960, DC-IDPF, ibid.; Binswanger Corporation, "Release after 12 noon," June 20, 1961, DC-IDPF, ibid., 1–2; "Big Deal on the Boulevard," *PM*, July 1961, 52–54; Kirk R. Petshek, *The*

Challenge of Urban Reform: Policies and Programs in Philadelphia (Philadelphia: Temple University Press, 1973), 210–11.

20. Keeton Arnett and Richard J. McConnell, "Memo to Members and Directors of the Philadelphia Industrial Development Corporation; Background Information on the Tishman Agreement," n.d. [1964], DC-IDPF, RG 64.18, Box A-5201, Phila. Industrial Park 1963–65, 1966, CA, 1–3; Beatty, interviewed by Petshek, 2–4; Wise, interviewed by Petshek, 4–6; Binswanger to Graves, August 10, 1960.

21. Kirk R. Petshek, "Memo to William L. Rafsky; Questions for Developer of North Philadelphia Airport," October 27, 1960, KRPP, Acc. 202, Box 4, PIDC, TUUA, 1–4; MEAC, "Statement by Mayor's Economic Advisory Committee Re: Use of Private Developer for North Philadelphia Airport," December 9, 1960, KRPP, Acc. 202, Box 4, EAC, 2–3.

22. MEAC, "Statement of Criteria for Industrial Park Development at the North Philadelphia Airport," December 9, 1960, KRPP, Acc. 202, Box 4, EAC, TUUA, 1–6; Petshek, *The Challenge of Urban Reform*, 211–14.

23. National Resources Committee, *Our Cities: Their Role in the National Economy* (Washington, D.C.: GPO, 1937), 73–81; Mark I. Gelfand, *A National Of Cities: The Federal Government and Urban America, 1933–1965* (New York: Oxford University Press, 1975), 90–98; Alice O'Connor, "Swimming Against the Tide: A Brief History of Federal Policy in Poor Communities," in William T. Dickens and Ronald F. Ferguson, eds., *Urban Problems and Community Development* (Washington, D.C.: Brookings Institution Press, 1999), 92–99.

24. David C. Melnicoff, "Memo to Mayor's Economic Advisory Committee," March 6, 1961, KRPP, Acc. 202, Box 4, EAC, TUUA; Kirk R. Petshek, "Memo to John P. Robin; Redevelopment Authority: Tishman Contract (RA Meeting May 5)," May 1, 1961, KRPP, Acc. 202, Box 4, PIDC, TUUA; PIDC, "Outline of Provisions for Inclusion in Any Contract between PIDC as the Redeveloper of the North Philadelphia Airport Lands and Any Selected Developer-Investor," December 8, 1960, DC-IDPF, RG 64.18, Box A-5193, Phila. Industrial Park 1959–62, CA; Richard Graves to Robert Tishman, March 23, 1961, DC-IDPF, ibid.; PIDC & Tishman Realty & Construction Company, "Agreement," March 29, 1961, 4–6.

25. "Taken from 'Minutes of the Meeting of the Board of Directors of the Philadelphia Industrial Development Corporation," February 10, 1961, DC-IDPF, RG 64.18, Box A-5193, Phila. Industrial Park 1959–62, CA; "Agreement ('Contract approved at PIDC Annual Mtg., 3/29/61')," March 29, 1961, DC-IDPF, ibid.; Binswanger Corporation, "Release after 12 noon," 1–2; Daniel F. O'Leary, "$70 Million Center for Industry to Ring North Phila. Airport; Will Cover 538-Acre Tract," *PB*, June 20, 1961; "Big Deal on the Boulevard," *PM*, July 1961; Frederic R. Mann to Walter Stein, Esquire, January 16, 1962, DC-IDPF, RG 64.18, Box A-5193, Phila. Industrial Park 1959–62, CA.

26. Although PIDC itself did not offer real estate commissions, brokers received their normal commissions from any PIDC industrial clients with whom they worked; PIDC usually included such commissions in the financing of the transaction. PIDC, "Report of Activities, November 1958 through February 1960," March 4, 1960, KRPP, Acc. 202, Box 4, PIDC, TUUA, 6; PIDC, "Outline of Typical Industrial Build-Lease Project," 2–3; PIDC, "1960 Summary of PIDC Activities," 1–2.

27. PIDC assisted distribution, wholesaling, and warehousing firms that either directly supported manufacturing or involved large scale operations with many jobs. Richard McConnell, who succeeded Graves in 1961, explained that "each case must be looked at individually. . . . it's the right mix of functions which has to be achieved. You can't decide a priori; you've got to find out whether or not it fits into the picture." Richard McConnell, interviewed by Petshek, November 11, 1964[?], transcript, KRPP, Acc. 202, Box 5, [Interviews], TUUA, 11–12.

28. PIDC, "Confidential: Special Meeting of the Board of Directors: PIDC Financing of Transactions Involving Companies which are Strong Financially," March 29, 1965, MFC, RG 60-2.5, Box A-4488, Philadelphia Industrial Development Corporation, CA, 2; PIDC, "Outline Of Typical Industrial Build-Lease Project," 1; McConnell, interviewed by Petshek, 11.

29. PIDC, "Minutes of the Meeting of the Executive Committee of the Philadelphia Industrial Development Corporation," May 7, 1963, CCLF, Box 1963–64, F: PIDC. Exec Committee; May 7, 1963, HSP, 3; PIDC, "Minutes of the Meeting of the Executive Committee of the Philadelphia Industrial Development Corporation," November 19, 1963, CCLF, Box: 1963–64, PIDC. Exec. Committee November 19, 1963, HSP, 5–6.

30. PIDC, "Taken from Minutes of the Executive Committee Meeting of PIDC," April 6, 1965, DC-IDF, RG 64.18, Box A-5201, Bethlehem Steel Company '65, CA; PIDC, "Agenda, Board of Directors Meeting," April 20, 1965, ibid.; PIDC, "News Release," n.d., ibid.

31. For these classifications, PIDC, "Analysis of Real Property Transactions Financed Through PIDC" [1975], GPPR, Acc. 612, Box 12, PIDC Annual Report, TUUA, 74–75.

32. Frank G. Binswanger Jr. to Richard J. McConnell, March 21, 1966, DC-IDPF, RG 64.18, Box A-5201, Phila. Industrial Park 1963–65, 1966, CA, 4; PIDC, "PIDC/1968: Ten Years of Progress in Philadelphia [annual report]," GPC, Box 509-8, TUUA [2, 5]; "Little Ground Left at Phila. Industrial Park," PB, May 3, 1970, 9; PIDC, "Red Lion Industrial District" promotional pamphlet, [1976], GPC, Box 555-11, TUUA, 1–2; PIDC, "Philadelphia Industrial Complex" promotional pamphlet, n.d. [1976], GPC, Box 555-13, TUUA, 1–2; PIDC, "fifteen years of productive growth: annual report 1972," GPMR, Acc. 294, Box 6A, Garment Industry Development, TUUA; CPC, Issue Paper: Industrial Philadelphia: A Study of Industrial Land Use (Philadelphia: City of Philadelphia, 1990), 6, 16–17, 24.

33. PIDC, "Now There Are 6 PIDC Industrial Districts for Your New Plants in Philadelphia" [1962], MFC, RG 60-2.5, Box A-6337, Industrial Development Corp., CA; Eastwick Project Area Committee (EPAC), "Minutes of the PAC Planning Committee," January 25, 1973, EPACR, Acc. 870, Box 1, PAC Info, TUUA, 1; CPC, *Review of the Eastwick Urban Renewal Plan* (Philadelphia: City of Philadelphia, April 1982), 14.

34. PIDC, "Taken From the Agenda for the Executive Committee Meeting of the PIDC," November 17, 1964, DCIDF, RG 64.18, Box A-5201, Crescent Box Corporation 1965, CA; Philadelphia Industrial Park, "News Release," April 21, 1965, ibid. For other early park occupants, Department of Commerce, "Summary Status and Performance Report on the Philadelphia Industrial Park as of July 8, 1964," DC-ID Files, RG 64.18, Box A-5201, 1965–66, F: Phila. Industrial Park 1963–65, 1966, City Archives, 4.

35. Douglas Karsner, "Aviation and Airports: The Impact on the Economic and Geographic Structure of American Cities, 1940s–1980s," *Journal of Urban History* 23:4 (May 1997): 406–36.

36. Program and Budget Committee, "Promoting Philadelphia Industrially: A Program of the Philadelphia Industrial Development Corporation," received June 11, 1958, Vertical Files, Van Pelt Library, University of Pennsylvania, 1–2; PIDC, "Now There Are 6 PIDC Industrial Districts," 2; PIDC, "1965/PIDC's $100 Million Milestone Year [annual report]," KRPP, Acc. 202, Box 4, PIDC, TUUA, 3.

37. Wilhelm, interviewed by Phillips, 10.

38. PIDC, "Now There are 6 PIDC Industrial Districts," 2; Joseph M. Guess, "Firm Decides To Stay in City; PIDC Helps Finance New Drug Plant," *PB*, February 23, 1960; PIDC, "Taken from the Minutes of the Meeting of Members of the PIDC," May 25, 1960, DC-IDPF, RG 64.18, Box A-5201, Frank's Beverages 1966, CA; PIDC, "Agenda and Minutes, Meeting of the Executive Committee," October 22, 1963 and July 14, 1964, DC-IDPF, RG 64.18, Box A-5201, Macke Variety Vending 1965, CA; PIDC, "1965/PIDC's $100 Million Milestone Year," 3.

39. Nearly half of the acreage in the Riverside project remained undeveloped because of a poorly designed contract with a private development consortium. PIDC Special Riverside Committee, "To: Philadelphia Industrial Development Corporation Executive Committee; Subject: Meeting with Riverside Industrial Center Developers," February 2, 1965, DC-IDPF, RG 64.18, Box A-5195, Riverside Industrial Park 1962–65, CA.

40. Arthur D. Little, Inc., *The Usefulness of Philadelphia's Industrial Plant: An Approach to Industrial Renewal; Report to the Philadelphia City Planning Commission* (January 1960), 159–66. PIDC, "Fifteen Years of Productive Growth: Annual Report 1972," 8.

41. PIDC, "Confidential: Special Meeting of the Board of Directors," 2.

42. "Container Corp. to Expand on Erie Avenue," *PB*, December 17, 1965; PIDC, "Minutes of Executive Committee Meeting," April 5, 1966, DCIDF, RG 64.18, Box A-5202, Standard Paper Company 66, CA.

43. PIDC, "Minutes of the Meeting of the Board Of Directors of the PIDC," December 15, 1964, DCIDF, RG 64.18, Box A-5202, Pincus Bros. '66, CA; PIDC, "Minutes of the Meeting of the Executive Committee of the PIDC," July 13, 1965, ibid; PIDC, "Minutes of the Meeting of the Executive Committee of the PIDC," August 3, 1965, ibid.; "Clothing Firm To Move To Independence Mall Area," *PB*, April 6, 1966; Harold Brubaker, "367 Jobs Go The Way of the Suit At Work," *PI*, March 13, 2001.

44. Anthony Zecca to Richard McConnell, October 22, 1964, MCF, RG 60-2.5, Box A-4419, Philadelphia Industrial Development Corporation, CA; Richard McConnell to James Tate, October 22, 1964, ibid.; PIDC, "Minutes Of A Special Meeting of the Board Of Directors of the Philadelphia Industrial Development Corporation," November 9, 1964, ibid.; "Allied Kid's Earnings Fell in 3rd Quarter; Unit Blamed May Go," *WSJ*, November 10, 1965; "Allied Kid Estimates Fiscal '66 Net Rose Slightly," *WSJ*, July 27, 1966.

45. PIDC, "Taken from Report of Meeting of Executive Committee," November 16, 1964, MCF, RG 60-2.5, Box A-4419, Philadelphia Industrial Development Corporation, CA.

46. David W. Bartelt, "Housing the 'Underclass,' "in *The Underclass Debate: Views From History*, ed. Michael B. Katz (Princeton: Princeton University Press, 1993), 118–57,125–37. Lenora E. Berson, *Case Study of a Riot: The Philadelphia Story* (New York: Institute of Human Relations Press, 1966); S. A. Paolantonio, *Frank Rizzo: The Last Big Man in Big City America* (Philadelphia: Camino Books, Inc, 1993); Matthew J. Countryman, *Up South: Civil Rights and Black Power in Philadelphia* (Philadelphia: University of Pennsylvania Press, 2006), 154–78.

47. Walter D'Alessio, "Memo To: Honorable Frank L. Rizzo, Mayor; Subject: 1972 Activity," January 10, 1973, MFC, RG 60-2.6, Box A-3426, PIDC, CA, 2; PIDC, *1971: New Directions for PIDC in Philadelphia*, Free Library of Philadelphia, GDC, Cities P53-1320 1971, 5.

48. The remaining transactions could not be identified from the records consulted; because of the range of sources used in compilation of the database, there does not appear to be any systematic bias in the type of transactions that are missing. Philadelphia Evening Bulletin Newsclipping Collection, TUUA, "Philadelphia Industrial Development Corporation" (clippings filed in annual envelopes); DC-IDPF, RG 64.18, Boxes A-5201 & A-5202, CA; MFC, RG 60-2.4 & RG 60-2.5, PIDC and industrial development annual files, 1959–70, CA; PIDC, "PIDC Looks Back, Looks Ahead"; PIDC, "1963: Another Headline Year for PIDC" (annual report), KRPP, Acc. 202, Box 4, PIDC; PIDC, "1965/PIDC's $100 Million Milestone Year" (annual report); PIDC, "1967: PIDC's Big Year In New Plant

Construction" (annual report), GPC, Box 509-6, TUUA; PIDC, "PIDC/1968—
Ten Years of Progress in Philadelphia"; PIDC, "Over 100 new industrial plants for
Philadelphia . . . created by an all-community effort," n.d. [1967], GPC, Box 871-5,
TUUA; Dalton Corporation, *1970 Dalton's Greater Philadelphia Industrial Directory* (Philadelphia: Dalton Corp., 1970); *Dalton's Directory, Business and Industry
1980* (Haverford, PA: Dalton's Directory, 1980); Dalton's Directory, *1990 Dalton's Philadelphia Metropolitan Directory Business/Industry Philadelphia/Suburbs
South Jersey/Delaware* (Philadelphia: Dalton's Directory, 1990); Commonwealth
of Pennsylvania (various departments), *Industrial Directory of the Commonwealth
of Pennsylvania 1956, 1962, 1968, 1972, 1975, 1980* (Commonwealth of Pennsylvania, semiannual).

49. Chamber of Commerce, *Greater Philadelphia Facts: Business and Civic
Statistics*, 16.

50. Edward Schwartz, "Economic Development as if Neighborhood Mat-
tered," in *Community and Capital in Conflict: Plant Closings and Job Loss*, ed.
John C. Raines, Lenora E. Berson, and David McI. Gracie (Philadelphia: Temple
University Press, 1982), 272–73 (emphasis original).

51. PIDC, "Analysis of Real Property Transactions Financed Through PIDC,"
[1975], 14; PIDC, "material from review of PIDC operations," n.d [1975], GPPR,
Acc. 612, Box 12, PIDC Annual Report, TUUA, 35.

52. During the 1970s PIDC undertook a project to preserve the apparel indus-
try (chapter 8). U.S. Bureau of the Census, *Census of Manufacturers 1963 Volume
III, Area Statistics* [Pennsylvania] (Washington, D.C.: U.S. Government Printing
Office [GPO], 1966), 35; U.S. Bureau of the Census, *Census of Business, 1963 Volume 5, Wholesale Trade: Area Statistics* [Pennsylvania] (Washington, D.C.: GPO,
1966), 27; U.S. Bureau of the Census, *1982 Census of Manufacturers, Geographic
Area Series: Pennsylvania* (Washington, D.C.: GPO, May 1985), PA 90-91; U.S.
Bureau of the Census, *1982 Census of Wholesale Trade: Pennsylvania* (Washing-
ton, D.C.: GPO, November 1984), PA 42–43.

53. Census reports probably understated the Puerto Rican population; in 1970
the census reported 45,788 Spanish speakers in Philadelphia, and the true num-
ber of Puerto Ricans in the city probably lies somewhere between the two figures.
CPC, *Socio-Economic Characteristics; 1960 and 1970 Philadelphia Census Tracts*
(Philadelphia: City of Philadelphia, 1973), 120–21; CPC, *Population Characteris-
tics; 1960 and 1970 Philadelphia Census Tracts* (Philadelphia: City of Philadelphia,
July 1972), 12–13; Carmen Teresa Whalen, *From Puerto Rico to Philadelphia:
Puerto Rican Workers and Postwar Economies* (Philadelphia: Temple University
Press, 2001), 183–86.

54. Of the 354 transactions included in the database, 242 involved moves within
Philadelphia; seventy firms used PIDC aid to expand on site or acquire a secondary
facility, with no relocation; eight newly organized firms started operations in a

facility acquired with PIDC assistance; five existing, non-Philadelphia firms relocated to the city with help from PIDC; no information could be found about the original addresses of twenty-nine firms.

55. PIDC and CPC, *Survey of Industry 1975* (Philadelphia: City of Philadelphia, 1975), 39,108–9; CPC, *Population Characteristics*, 12–13.

56. It should also be noted that the movement of a firm to one of PIDC's peripheral industrial parks did not automatically mean that it would have no African American neighbors. The area surrounding the State Road–Torresdale Industrial Park had a predominantly African American population, while the Penrose and Eastwick industrial parks lay next to the racially mixed neighborhoods of Eastwick.

57. David W. Bartelt, "Housing the 'Underclass,'" 118–57; Kenneth T. Jackson, *Crabgrass Frontier* (New York: Oxford University Press, 1985), 195–218, 231–45.

58. The geographic descriptions in this section are based on the Planning Analysis Sections established by the Philadelphia City Planning Commission. They do not refer to the more colloquial neighborhood names used earlier in this chapter.

59. West Philadelphia, another section with a majority black population and continuing racial turnover, provided a partial exception, as it had sixteen move-ins or expansions and twenty losses. This was the highest net negative impact anywhere in the city.

60. IUS, *Industrial Land and Facilities for Philadelphia*, 147, 286.

61. A 1966 assessment found that the Independence Mall project had displaced 245 businesses; 194 had been relocated in Philadelphia, thirty had left the city, and twenty-one had closed. Community Renewal Program, City of Philadelphia, "Technical Report 19: Relocation of Business and Industrial Firms (preliminary draft)," December, 1966, DC-IDPF, RG 64.18, Box A-5193, Relocation of Business and Industrial Firms, CA, 11.

62. Joel Rast, *Remaking Chicago: The Political Origins of Urban Industrial Change* (DeKalb: Northern Illinois University Press, 1999).

63. CPC, Comprehensive Planning Division, "Callowhill: A Proposal for a Centrally Located Industrial Urban Renewal Area," September 1957, KRPP, Acc. 202, Box 4, Industry Documents, TUUA; RA, "Urban Renewal Plan for the Franklin Urban Renewal Area," July 1964 (rev. January 28, 1965), GPC, Box 457-3, TUUA.

64. PIDC, "News Release," September 8, 1964, DCIDF, RG 64.18, Box A-5201, American Bag and Corporation, '65, CA; PIDC, "Taken From The Minutes of the Executive Committee Meeting Of PIDC," May 4, 1965, ibid.

65. Bureau of the Census, *Census of Manufacturers 1963 Volume III*, 35; Bureau of the Census, *Census of Business, 1963 Volume 5*, 27; U.S. Bureau of the Census, *1992 Census of Manufacturers: Pennsylvania* (Washington, D.C.: GPO, 1994), PA-63; U.S. Bureau of the Census, *1992 Census of Wholesale Trade - Pennsylvania* (Washington, D.C.: GPO, October 1994), pp. PA-49–50.

66. Because the industrial directories provide no indication of changes in company names, such as might occur after acquisition or takeover, this analysis probably overstates the rate of closure for PIDC-assisted firms.

67. U.S. Bureau of the Census, *1992 Census of Manufacturers: Pennsylvania*, PA-63. PIDC's post-1970 activities are discussed in chapter 8.

68. Harvey Schultz, Gail Garfield Schwartz, and Anne Fribourg, "Planning for Jobs: New York City Attempts to Retain and Create Blue Collar Jobs," *Planners Notebook* 2:1 (1972): 6.

69. June Manning Thomas, *Redevelopment and Race: Planning a Finer City in Postwar Detroit* (Baltimore: Johns Hopkins University Press, 1997), 72–81.

70. Jon C. Teaford, *The Rough Road to Renaissance: Urban Revitalization in America, 1940–1985* (Baltimore: Johns Hopkins Press, 1990), 149–50; John T. Cumbler, *A Social History of Economic Decline: Business, Politics, and Work in Trenton* (New Brunswick: Rutgers University Press, 1989), 167–70; Joseph Heathcott and Maire Agnes Murphy, "Corridors of Flight, Zones of Renewal: Industry, Planning, and Policy in the Making of Metropolitan St. Louis, 1940–1980," *Journal of Urban History* 31:2 (January 2005): 151–89.

71. Robert O. Self, *American Babylon: Race and the Struggle for Postwar Oakland* (Princeton, NJ: Princeton University Press, 2003), 153–55, 205–9.

72. Schultz et al., "Planning for Jobs," 1–6; Joshua B. Freeman, *Working Class New York: Life and Labor Since World War II* (New York: New Press, 2000), 149–50. For the earlier period, Joel Schwartz, *The New York Approach: Robert Moses, Urban Liberals, and the Redevelopment of the Inner City* (Columbus: Ohio State University Press, 1993).

73. Barry Bluestone and Mary Huff Stevenson, *The Boston Renaissance: Race, Space, and Economic Change in an American Metropolis* (New York: Russell Sage Foundation, 2000), 68–73; Lawrence W. Kennedy, *Planning the City Upon a Hill: Boston Since 1630* (Amherst: University of Massachusetts Press, 1992), 236. For an important study of state efforts to stem industrial decline in Massachusetts, see David Koistinen, "Public Policies for Countering Deindustrialization in Postwar Massachusetts," *Journal of Policy History* 18:3 (2006): 326–61.

74. Milwaukee experienced a similar denial. James H. J. Tate to Richard J. McConnell, November 5, 1965, MFC, RG 60-2.5, Box A-4488, Philadelphia Industrial Development Corporation, CA; PIDC, "Minutes of the Special Meeting of the Board Of Directors of the PIDC," February 3, 1967, DC-IDPF, RG 64.18, Box A-5193, PIDC - Internal Revenue Service Rulings '67, CA; Walter D'Alessio, interview by Walter M. Phillips, June 7, 1977, transcript, POHP, Box 3, 8.

75. William A. Forsythe, "Graves Expects To Quit PIDC, Enter Business," *PB*, September 20, 1961; Office of Development Coordinator, "Summary of Activities," July 5, 1962, MFC, RG 60-2.5, Box A-6350, Weekly Reports - Development Coordinator, CA, 1; William L. Rafsky, int. by Petshek, March 22, 1965, transcript, KRPP, Acc. 202, Box 5, [Interviews], TUUA, 2.

76. Many observers felt that Graves had been an appropriate administrator for the start-up phase of PIDC's operations, but that McConnell was better suited to running an established organization. McConnell, interview by Petshek, 8–12; Staebler [*sic*], int. by Petshek, 1,3,6–8; Beatty, int. by Petshek, 1–2,7; Wise, int. by Petshek, November 1, 1964, 9; Young, int. by Phillips, 2,4,7–11; Wilhelm, int. by Phillips, 6,10.

77. Charles MacNamara, "A Tale of Two City Bosses," *PM*, June 1971; Warren Eisenberg, "Enter the Age of Tate," *PM*, January 1964, 34; James Reichley, *The Art of Government: Reform and Organization Politics in Philadelphia* (New York: The Fund for the Republic, 1959), 17–18.

78. Warren Eisenberg, "Enter the Age of Tate," *PM*, January 1964; MacNamara, "A Tale of Two City Bosses," 46; Al Hart, interviewed by Petshek, January 25, 1965, transcript, KRPP, Acc. 202, Box 5, [Interviews], TUUA, 6; David Rogers, *The Management of Big Cities: Interest groups And Social Change Strategies* (Beverly Hills, CA: Sage Publications, 1971), 84–88.

79. McConnell, int. by Petshek, 13–14.

80. Thacher Longstreth, interview by Petshek, January 22, 1965, transcript, KRPP, ibid., 3–4; Carolyn Teich Adams, *The Politics of Capital Investment: The Case of Philadelphia* (Albany: State University of New York Press, 1988), 49.

81. Young, interviewed by Phillips, 10–11; PIDC, "News Release (draft)," January 5 (9), 1968, MCF, RG 60-2.5, Box A-4607, Phila. Industrial Development Corporation, CA.

82. "Croley Takes Job of Running City's PIDC," *PB*, April 4, 1968; John P. Bracken to James H.J. Tate, January 29, 1970, MCF, RG 60-2.5, Box PRSC 42,702, Phila. Industrial Development Corp., CA; D'Alessio, interview by Phillips, 10; Young, interviewed by Phillips, 4–5,10–11, 23; PIDC, "News Release," May 5, 1970, DC-IDPF, RG 64.18, Box A-5193, PIDC, CA; Walter Stein, "Memorandum to the Members and Directors of the Philadelphia Industrial Development Corporation," February 13, 1968, MCF, RG 60-2.5, Box A-4607, Phila. Industrial Development Corp., CA; PIDC, "Minutes of the Meeting of the board of directors of the Philadelphia Industrial Development Corporation," February 20, 1968, ibid.

83. Young, interviewed by Phillips, 4.

84. Sbragia, *Debt Wish*, 163–179; Anthony Zecca to Richard J. McConnell, March 5, 1965, MFC, RG 60-2.5, Box A-4488, Philadelphia Industrial Development Corporation, CA.

85. John W. Littleton to Philadelphia Industrial Development Corporation, July 5, 1966, DC-IDPF, RG 64.18, Box A-5193, PIDC - IRS Rulings '67, CA; PIDC, "Taken from Minutes of Executive Committee Meeting Of PIDC," August 3, 1966, DC-IDPF, ibid.

86. At a meeting with Under Secretary of the Treasury Joseph W. Barr, Philadelphia officials learned that because "St. Louis and Milwaukee have been unable to get a favorable tax ruling, great pressure was put on I.R.S. to remove PIDC's tax exemption." PIDC, "Minutes of the Special Meeting of the Board Of Directors,"

February 3, 1967, CA, 1–4. Also, PIDC, "Taken From Minutes Of Executive Committee Meeting Of PIDC," March 21, 1967, DC-IDPF, ibid.; Joseph R. Daughen, "PIDC Is Given Permission to Process Loans," *PB*, February 3, 1967.

87. Edward G. Bauer to Frank Sullivan, April 17, 1968, MFC, RG 60-2.5, Box A-4607, Phila. Industrial Development Corp., CA, 1–2.

88. Margaret Weir, *Politics and Jobs: The Boundaries of Employment Policy In The United States* (Princeton: Princeton University Press, 1992), 8–12, 61–83; Alice O'Connor, "Swimming Against the Tide: A Brief History of Federal Policy in Poor Communities," in William T. Dickens and Ronald F. Ferguson, eds., *Urban Problems and Community Development* (Washington, D.C.: Brookings Institution Press, 1999), 103–104.

89. PIDC, "Minutes of the Meeting of the Executive Committee," May 21, 1968, MFC, RG 60-2.5, Box A-4607, Phila. Industrial Development Corporation, CA, 2,10–11; PIDC, "Agenda for the Board of Directors Meeting of the PIDC;... Report of special Loan Committee," June 18, 1968, MFC, ibid., 2–6; "State Law Lays Ground For PIDC To Reactivate Development Programs," *Greater Philadelphia Chamber of Commerce News*, September 7, 1967, WMPP, Acc. 527, Box 23, Pennjerdel—Economic Development, 1965–67, TUUA, 1,8; Dorothy Byrd, "PIDC Forms New Agency to Fund Projects; Device Will Allow Continued Use of Low-Interest Loans," *PB*, August 4, 1968; William R. Spofford to James H. J. Tate, April 29, 1970, MFC, RG 60-2.5, Box PRSC 42,702, PIDC, CA.

90. Transactions involving private land and existing buildings declined from forty-three in 1966 to fourteen in 1967 and one in 1968. "Taken From 'Minutes Of Meeting Of Newly Elected Board Of Directors Of PIDC," February 21, 1967, 1–2; "State Law Lays Ground," 8; D'Alessio, "Memo To: Honorable Frank L. Rizzo, Mayor; Subject: 1972 Activity," January 10, 1973, 2.

91. Office of the Mayor, "News Release: Remarks by Mayor James H.J. Tate, PIDC Luncheon, Bellevue-Stratford Hotel," February 17, 1971, DC-BSF, RG 64.18, Box A-5197, PIDC '70–'74, CA, 2; D'Alessio, interview by Phillips, 12.

92. Mike Wallace, *A New Deal For New York* (New York: Bell & Weiland, 2002), 31–46; Daniel J. Luria and Joel Rogers, *Metro Futures: Economic Solutions For Cities and Their Suburbs* (Boston: Beacon Press, 1999); Rast, *Remaking Chicago*.

93. Strikes in the Philadelphia region peaked in 1952–1953. Chamber of Commerce of Greater Philadelphia, *Greater Philadelphia Facts: Business and Civic Statistics, Edition of 1966* (Philadelphia: The Chamber, 1966), 20. For the immediate, post-World War II strike wave in Philadelphia, see: Philip Scranton and Walter Licht, *Work Sights: Industrial Philadelphia, 1890–1950* (Philadelphia: Temple University Press, 1986), 257–265. On the Philadelphia labor movement generally, Robert L. Freedman, *A Report on Politics in Philadelphia* (Cambridge, Mass.:

Joint Center for Urban Studies of the Massachusetts Institute of Technology and Harvard University, 1963), V:12–16.

94. George Sternlieb, "Is Business Abandoning The Big City," *Harvard Business Review* 39:1 (January–February 1961), 6–25.

95. In 1971, *Philadelphia Magazine* described Toohey as a "show unionist" and a "nonentity," but characterized Cortigene as "the union leader with real pull right now" and claimed that he "controls about half of labor's political clout." Charles MacNamara, "The Power Crisis: In a city with a lame duck mayor and a tired Establishment, who's running the store?," *PM*, November 1971, 145; James H. J. Tate to Edward F. Toohey, March 29, 1965, MCF, RG 60-2.5, Box A-4488, Philadelphia Industrial Development Corporation, CA; PIDC, *Annual Reports* (contain lists of board members).

96. Robert H. Speck, Jr., "Memo to Edward J. Martin; Progress Report on the Company Visitation Program," October 19, 1971, DC-BSF, RG 64.18, Box A-5197, PIDC 1970–74, CA.

97. Philadelphia AFL-CIO Council, "Minutes," January 14, 1970, JLCR, Acc. 480, Box 18, Philadelphia AFL-CIO Council Misc 1969–70, TUUA, 2; Philadelphia AFL-CIO Council, "Minutes," March 10, 1971, JLCR, Acc. 480, Box 18, Philadelphia AFL-CIO Council Misc. 1970–71, 4.

98. "Agreement to Merge the Philadelphia Industrial Union Council C.I.O. and the Central Labor Union Of Philadelphia and Vicinity into the Philadelphia Council of the AFL-CIO," 1960, JLCR, Acc. 480, Box 18, Philadelphia AFL-CIO Council Misc. 1962, TUUA; Harry Block to All Delegates Philadelphia Council AFL-CIO, n.d. [February 1965], JLCR, Acc. 480, Box 28, Philadelphia Council of Industrial Organizations 1964–67; Douglas Bedell, "AFL-CIO Expands Role in Community Affairs," *PB*, May 20, 1969; Warren Eisenberg, "Labor's Tried Blood," *PM*, March 1964, 28–31,70–79.

99. "Agreement between Textile Workers Union of America, C.I.O., and Anchor Dyeing & Finishing Company, Inc.," August 23, 1950, TWUA Records, Urb 54, Box 12, 3–Anchor Dyeing & Finishing-Agreements, 1950–75, TUUA, 11; "Agreement between Textile Union Workers of America, C.I.O. and Atlas Fabric Corporation," January 22, 1951, TWUA Records, Urb 54, Box 13, 9–Atlas Fabrics Co.-Agreements, 1951–71, TUUA, 11; ACWA, "Meeting of Philadelphia Joint Board A.C.W.A.; Manager's Report ," January 7, February 3, May 5, and December 1, 1955, ACWAR, Acc. 519, Box 2, Minutes, 1955, TUUA.

100. This conclusion is based on review of PIDC Board and Executive Committee minutes, many of which are available in Mayor Tate's Correspondence and Files at the Philadelphia City Archives (RG 60-2.5), as well as an examination of the CEJO Records and the Jewish Labor Committee's HRC and HRDI files at the Temple University Urban Archives: AFL-CIO Human Rights Committee Minutes, 1961–65, in JLCR, Acc. 480, Box 18, Philadelphia AFL-CIO Council

Misc. 1961, 1962, 1963, 1964, 1965, TUUA; AFL-CIO Human Resources Development Institute documents, in JLCR, Acc. 480, Box 19, AFL-CIO HRDI 1969–77,
TUUA; CEJO membership lists, in FC Records, Acc. 626, Box 31, 3–Meeting Attendance and Membership Lists, TUUA.

101. The OEDP sought, unsuccessfully, to establish a system of coordination
for Philadelphia's increasingly chaotic mix of job creation and training programs.
Richard J. McConnell to James H. J. Tate, June 9, 1964, MCF, RG 60-2.5, Box A-
4419, Philadelphia Industrial Development Corporation, CA; see also PIDC 1964
board meeting minutes in this and other annual files.

102. Mitchell, "Industrial Development Activities in the City Of Philadel-
phia," 74–75; Philadelphia Urban Coalition, "Action 70 (annual report)," [1971],
ACWAR, Acc. 519, Box 22, Sec-Treas. Phila. Urban Coalition (1968–Feb. 1970),
TUUA.

103. Ragan A. Henry to Clarence Farmer and Paul Crowley [sic], August 30,
1968, MFC, RG 60-2.5, Box A-4607, Philadelphia Industrial Development Corporation, CA; GPEDC, *Final Report of Greater Philadelphia Enterprises Development
Corporation for Funding Period June 27, 1968 through October 31, 1970* (Philadelphia: GPEDC, 1973), 1; Patricia L. Mallory, Economic Development Unit, "Review of Economic Development Unit Staff Participation with Greater Philadelphia Enterprises Development Corporation," November 1968, GPC, Box 791–4,
TUUA.

104. D'Alessio, interviewed by Phillips, 6–7.

Chapter Three

1. Kirk R. Petshek, *The Challenge of Urban Reform: Policies and Programs in
Philadelphia* (Philadelphia: Temple University Press, 1973), 169.

2. City of Philadelphia, *Community Renewal Program: Major Policies and Proposals* (Philadelphia: City of Philadelphia, February 1967), ii–iv.

3. Economic Development Committee (EDC), "Overall Economic Development Program: City of Philadelphia," June 1964, GPC, Box 293-4, TUUA, 9; Community Renewal Program (City of Philadelphia), "Technical Report 13: Economic
Development," December 1964, Fine Arts Library, University of Pennsylvania, 1.

4. Unemployment in Philadelphia remained at almost 9 percent in 1962 and
1963, far above the 4-5 percent of the region and the United States as a whole.
EDC, "Overall Economic Development Program," 26, 47, 50–51; CRP, "Technical
Report 13," December 1964, 16, 18–18, Table 5-II.

5. EDC, "Overall Economic Development Program," 47–51; CRP, "Technical
Report 13," 16–19.

6. EDC, "Overall Economic Development Program," 22–23, 67–77, 106–117;
CRP, "Technical Report 13," 3–4, 26–28, 32–46, 54–55. For Philadelphia's effort

to promote scientific research, Margaret Pugh O'Mara, *Cities of Knowledge: Cold War Science and the Search for the Next Silicon Valley* (Princeton: Princeton University Press, 2004).

7. EDC, "Overall Economic Development Program," 14–17, 23–24, 95–105; CRP, "Technical Report 13," 25–28.

8. CRP, "Technical Report 13," 27–28.

9. EDC, "Overall Economic Development Program," 17–19, 24, 101–2.

10. CRP, "Technical Report 13," 54; EDC, "Overall Economic Development Program," 122.

11. EDC, "Overall Economic Development Program," 11; also, 1–2, 8–9, 17, 20–25; CRP, "Technical Report 13," 25–29, 51–55.

12. This agency actually operated through two legal entities, the Southeastern Pennsylvania Economic Development Corporation and the Southeastern Pennsylvania Development Fund. William Zucker, interviewed by Petshek, December 31, 1964, transcript, KRPP, Acc. 202, Box 5, (Interviews), TUUA; Sean Ryan, "Developer Sees Ring of Industries," *PI*, August 30, 1964; Charles MacNamara, "The Man From SPEDCO," *PM*, April 1967, 61–68. On the early stages of regional transportation planning, Kirk R. Petshek, *The Challenge of Urban Reform: Policies and Programs in Philadelphia* (Philadelphia: Temple University Press, 1973), 121–30.

13. EDC, "Overall Economic Development Program," 21–22.

14. EDC, "Overall Economic Development Program," 22, 125–26.

15. CRP, "Technical Report 13," 51–55; City of Philadelphia, *Community Renewal Program*, 7; Petshek, *The Challenge of Urban Reform*, 175–81.

16. EDC, "Overall Economic Development Program," 20.

17. This development-programming concept would eventually become the central recommendation in the final 1967 Community Renewal Program report. CRP, "Technical Report 13," 51–52, 55; City of Philadelphia, *Community Renewal Program*, 7; Petshek, *The Challenge of Urban Reform*, 175–81.

18. CRP, "Technical Report 13," 51–55.

19. Otis Graham, Jr., *Toward a Planned Society: From Roosevelt to Nixon* (New York: Oxford University Press, 1976); Alice O'Connor, "Swimming Against the Tide: A Brief History of Federal Policy in Poor Communities," in William T. Dickens and Ronald F. Ferguson, eds., *Urban Problems and Community Development* (Washington, D.C.: Brookings Institution Press, 1999), 92–95.

20. "Annual Message to the Congress on the State of the Union, January 8, 1964," *Public Papers of the Presidents of the United States: Lyndon B. Johnson, 1963–64* (Washington, D.C: GPO, 1965).

21. Ewan Clague and Leo Kramer, *Manpower Policies and Programs: A Review, 1935–75* (Washington, D.C.: W. E. Upjohn Institute for Employment Research, 1976), 6–7. For varying assessments of automation, Allen J. Matusow, *The Unraveling of America* (New York: Harper and Row, 1984), 103–5; Gareth Davies,

From Opportunity to Entitlement: The Transformation and Decline of Great Society Liberalism (Lawrence: University Press of Kansas, 1996), 37–38; Thomas J. Sugrue, *The Origins of the Urban Crisis: Race and Inequality in Postwar Detroit* (Princeton: Princeton University Press, 1996), 7, 130–38, 156.

22. Margaret Weir, *Politics and Jobs: The Boundaries of Employment Policy in the United States* (Princeton: Princeton University Press, 1992), 62–67; Alice O'Connor, *Poverty Knowledge: Social Science, Social Policy, and the Poor in Twentieth-Century U.S. History* (Princeton: Princeton University Press, 2001), 144–49.

23. Sar A. Levitan, *Federal Aid to Depressed Areas: An Evaluation of the Area Redevelopment Administration* (Baltimore: Johns Hopkins Press, 1964); O'Connor, "Swimming Against the Tide," 97–99; Margaret Weir, "The Federal Government and Unemployment: The Frustration of Policy Innovation from the New Deal to the Great Society," in Weir, Ann Shola Orloff, and Theda Skocpol, eds., *The Politics of Social Policy in the United States* (Princeton: Princeton University Press, 1988), 170–76.

24. James T. Patterson, *America's Struggle Against Poverty 1900–1994* (Cambridge: Harvard University Press, 1994), 126–29.

25. Weir, "The Federal Government and Unemployment," 162–71; O'Connor, *Poverty Knowledge*, 140–41.

26. Weir, "The Federal Government and Unemployment," 171–80, and *Politics and Jobs*, 58–61; Judith Stein, *Running Steel, Running America: Race, Economic Policy and the Decline of Liberalism* (Chapel Hill: University of North Carolina Press, 1998), 70–76, 313–14; Clague and Kramer, *Manpower Policies and Programs*, 11–15.

27. Weir, "The Federal Government and Unemployment," 171.

28. Weir, *Politics and Jobs*, 69–75.

29. Henry J. Aaron, *Politics and the Professors: The Great Society in Perspective* (Washington, D.C.: Brookings Institution, 1978), 16–25; O'Connor, *Poverty Knowledge,* 113–29; Patterson, *America's Struggle Against Poverty 1900–1994,* 99–125.

30. Michael L. Gillette, *Launching the War on Poverty: An Oral History* (New York: Twayne Publishers, 1996), 1–26; Stein, *Running Steel, Running America,* 73–76; Weir, *Politics and Jobs,* 67–78; Matusow, *The Unraveling of America,* 119–25, 257–60; Alice O'Connor, "Community Action, Urban Reform, and the Fight Against Poverty: The Ford Foundation's Gray Areas Program," *Journal of Urban History* 22:5 (July 1996): 586–625; Davies, *From Opportunity to Entitlement.*

31. Stein, *Running Steel, Running America,* 314. On the effect of Johnson's "overblown" rhetoric on the War on Poverty, Michael B. Katz, *The Undeserving Poor: From the War on Poverty to the War on Welfare* (New York: Pantheon Books, 1989), 88–90.

32. Lenora E. Berson, *Case Study of a Riot: The Philadelphia Story* (New York: Institute of Human Relations Press, 1966); Matthew J. Countryman, *Up South: Civil Rights and Black Power in Philadelphia*, (Philadelphia: University of Pennsylvania Press, 2006), 154–65.

33. In the 1967 mayoral primary, Smith supported Tate's opponent. After Tate easily won the nomination, Smith refused to support him in the general election. When Tate narrowly won re-election over district attorney Arlen Specter, Smith resigned as chairman. Joseph S. Clark, Jr. and Dennis J. Clark, "Rally and Relapse 1946–1968," in Russell F. Weigley, ed., *Philadelphia: A 300-Year History* (New York, W. W. Norton and Co., 1982), 662–63.

34. Mayor's Anti-Poverty Program, "Functional Statements," n.d. [November 23, 1964], MCF, RG 60-2.5, Box A-4489, Poverty Program, CA, 1–5 and organizational chart.

35. Ibid., 2–3; H. Kristal, "The Great Poverty Snafu: Political Hanky-panky Has Snarled up the City's Limping Program," *PM*, September 1965, 80–82; Warren Eisenberg, "Bungle in the Jungle," *PM*, December 1964, 103–4; Peter Marris and Martin Rein, *Dilemmas of Social Reform: Poverty and Community Action in the United States*, 2nd ed. (Chicago: Aldine Publishing Co., 1973), 113–15.

36. William J. Daniels, "Negro Named to Million $ Study after Protest by Tribune, NAACP," *PT*, January 19, 1963; Daniels, "North Phila. Citizens Solidly Behind NAACP Tribune Poll Reveals; Aroused Community Members Praise Moore, Blast Dash, Negro Leaders," *PT*, January 26, 1963; PCCA, "Annual Report to the Ford Foundation 1963; Part I," 1963, PCCAR, Acc. 675, Box 1, PCCA–Acty Ford Foundation Grant: Annual Report 1963, Part I, TUUA, 8–9; Countryman, *Up South*, 126–29.

37. Paul Ylvisaker to Abraham L. Freedman, April 1, 1964, PCCAR, Acc. 675, Box 2, PCCA–ACTY Grant Letters, TUUA; James H. J. Tate to Freedman, April 27, 1964, PCCAR, Acc. 675, Box 1, PCCA–AD Board of Director's Biographical Data, TUUA, 2; Kristal, "The Great Poverty Snafu," 80–82; Eisenberg, "Bungle in the Jungle," 103–4; Marris and Rein, *Dilemmas of Social Reform*, 113–15.

38. Mayor's Anti-Poverty Program, "Functional Statements," 1–5 and org. chart.; "City Has 10 Plans Ready For U.S. Poverty Grants," *PB*, September 17, 1964, 1, 14; Eisenberg, "bungle in the jungle," 104; David Greenstone and Paul E. Peterson, *Race and Authority in Urban Politics: Community Participation and the War on Poverty* 2nd edition (Chicago: University of Chicago Press, 1976), 26, 139, 265.

39. Marris and Rein, *Dilemmas of Social Reform*, 115; William F. Haddad, "Mr. Shriver and the Savage Politics of Poverty," *Harper's Magazine*, December 1965, 44.

40. Ibid.

41. "City Has 10 Plans Ready for U.S. Poverty Grants," *PB*, September 17, 1964; Orrin Evans, "PCCA Dropping Out of City Antipoverty Program," *PB*,

November 20, 1964; "City to Resubmit Poverty Program," *PB*, November 30, 1964; "City Meets U.S. Legal Requirements, Seeks to Meet Antipoverty Deadline," *PB*, December 23, 1964; PCCA, "Minutes of the Meeting of the Board of Directors," February 26, 1965, PCCAR, Acc. 675, Box 1, PCCA-AD Board of Directors Meeting Minutes, 1965, Feb. 26, 73; Haddad, "Mr. Shriver and the Savage Politics of Poverty," 44.

42. In early 1965, opponents of the Mayor's anti-poverty program formed an emergency committee; members included the local AFL-CIO, CORE, SNCC, the Urban League, North City Congress, the Jewish Labor Committee, the ADA, the Federation of Needy Neighborhoods, the Labor–Civil Rights Coordinated Movement, Leon Sullivan's OIC, and numerous CIO locals. Lawrence O'Rourke, "U.S. Approves 2 Parts of City Poverty Plan; Catholic Program Is Rejected on Church-State Rule," *PB*, December 31, 1964; "New Direction for Poverty War," *PB*, January 30, 1965; O'Rourke, "City Faces Another Rebuff In Visit by U.S. Poverty Aides," *PB*, January 31, 1965; Citizens Emergency Committees on Anti-Poverty (CECAP), Donald Hill, Chairman, "For Immediate Release," February 6, 1965, MCF, RG 60-2.5, Box A-4489, Poverty Program, CA; Douglas Bedell, "Antipoverty Citizens Group Formed Here: 15 Organizations Hope to Gather Facts from Poor," *PB*, February 6, 1965.

43. "City to Get $105,000 for Poverty Fight," *PB*, December 16, 1964; James H. J. Tate to Joseph T. Kelley, February 3, 1965, MCF, RG 60-2.5, Box A-4489, Poverty Program, CA; Samuel L. Evans to James H. J. Tate, January 7, 1965, ibid.; Nochem S. Winnet to James H. J. Tate, January 22, 1965, ibid.; Greenstone and Peterson, *Race and Authority in Urban Politics*, 156–57, 206, 263, 285.

44. Evans to Tate, January 7, 1965, MCF, RG 60-2.5, Box A-4489, Poverty Program, CA.

45. Fred T. Corletto, "Memo to James H. J. Tate; Subject: Anti-Poverty Reorganization," January 28, 1965, MCF, RG 60-2.5, Box A-4489, Poverty Program, CA; Lawrence O'Rourke, "U.S. Gives City Conditional OK on Poverty Aid," *PB*, February 5, 1965; Jerome Cahill, "Indigent Win Role in City's Antipoverty Bid," *PI*, February 6, 1965; Office of the Mayor, "News Release," February 10, 1965, MCF, RG 60-2.5, Box A-4489, Poverty Program, CA, 1–3.

46. Lawrence O'Rourke, "U.S. Urges Freedom for Poverty Unit Here," *PB*, February 7, 1965; CECAP, "The Following Telegram Was Sent to Sargent Shriver, Director of the Office of Economic Opportunity," February 8, 1965, MCF, RG 60-2.5, Box A-4489, Poverty Program, CA; "Citizens Group Raps Tate's Poverty War, Maps Own Program," *PI*, February 20, 1965; Martin J. Herman, "War on Poverty Group Says It Will Be Watchdog," *PB*, March 25, 1965; "Citizen Panel Commends PAAC," *PB*, April 12, 1965; "Job Director Explains City Poverty Plan," *PB*, April 15, 1965; Philadelphia Anti-Poverty Action Committee Subcommittee On Community Action Councils, "Proposals on Responsibilities of Area Community Action Councils," June 28, 1965, MCF, RG 60-2.5, Box A-4489, Phila.

Anti-Poverty Action Committee, CA, 1; Arthur B. Shostak, "Promoting Participation of the Poor: Philadelphia's Antipoverty Program," *Social Work* 11:1 (January 1966): 64–66.

47. Lawrence O'Rourke, "300,000 Urged to Attend Meetings Wednesday on Poverty Program," *PB*, April 25, 1965; "City's Poor Are Cynical of Poverty War, ADA Says," *PB*, April 28, 1965; O'Rourke, "PAAC Willing to Set Up 48 Public Rallies," *PB*, May 4, 1965; O'Rourke, "War-on-Poverty Vote Hailed Here as Success," *PB*, May 27, 1965; Malcolm Poindexter, "Election Winners Plan Priorities in Poverty Fight," *PB*, May 27, 1965; Martin G. Berck, "Call Me by My Rightful Name; And It Isn't POOR," *New York Herald Tribune*, May 30, 1965; Harry A. Bailey, Jr., "Poverty, Politics, and Administration: The Philadelphia Experience," in Ershkowitz and Zikmund, eds., *Black Politics in Philadelphia* (New York: Basic Books, Inc., 1973), 174–76.

48. Nicholas Stroh, "26,000 Poor Vote in PAAC Election Here; Turnout Doubles '65 Balloting but OEO Wants 'Close Look,'" *PB*, July 23, 1966; "U.S., Local Leaders Divide on Meaning of Poverty Vote Figures, *PB*, July 24, 1966; Stroh, "Election Turnout of 17,546 Disappoints Poverty Staff," *PB*, September 8, 1967; Bailey, "Poverty, Politics, and Administration," 176–77.

49. Elliott White, "Articulateness, Political Mobility, and Conservatism: An Analysis of the Philadelphia Antipoverty Election," in Ershkowitz and Zikmund, eds., *Black Politics in Philadelphia*, 200; Lawrence O'Rourke, "Local Leaders Plan to Keep Control of Poverty War," *PB*, April 27, 1965; "Introduction to Part III," in Ershkowitz and Zikmund, eds., *Black Politics in Philadelphia*, 165.

50. Shostak, "Promoting Participation of the Poor," 66–68; "Poverty Program Misses Whites, PAAC Panel Told," *PB*, July 5, 1967; Nicholas Stroh, "Poor in Northeast Get Little Help From City's Biggest Poverty Area," *PB*, May 12, 1968; Bailey, "Poverty, Politics, and Administration," 171–73.

51. Clark and Clark, "Rally and Relapse 1946–1968," 663; Charles A. Ekstrom, "The Electoral Politics of Reform and Machine: The Political Behavior of Philadelphia's 'Black' Wards, 1943–1969," in Ershkowitz and Zikmund, eds., *Black Politics in Philadelphia*, 89, 100–102.

52. Tina V. Weintraub, "Memo to the Honorable James H. J. Tate; Subject: Anti-Poverty Program," February 11, 1965, MCF, RG 60-2.5, Box A-4489, Poverty Program, CA; Thomas W. Rogers, "Memo to Mayor James H. J. Tate; Subject: Isaiah W. Crippins and Charles W. Bowser," March 9, 1965, MCF, RG 60-2.5, Box A-4489, Isaiah Crippens (Poverty), CA; Greenstone and Peterson, *Race and Authority in Urban Politics*, 206–7; Kristal, "The Great Poverty Snafu," 83; Maria S. Bowser, ed., *Urban Commentaries: Selected Speeches, Articles and Poetry of Charles W. Bowser* (Philadelphia: Camino Books, 1999), xv.

53. Matusow, *The Unraveling of America*, 257; John McCullogh, "Politicians Watch Anxiously as Poverty Program Begins; They're Wary of Rising of New Leaders," *PB*, April 25, 1965; Nicholas Stroh, "U.S. Baffled by Report on Poverty

Jobs," *PB*, August 14, 1966; CAP Evaluation Team, "Memorandum to Middle Atlantic Regional Director; Subject: Findings of the Philadelphia Evaluation Team," August 30, 1966, MCF, RG 60-2.5, Box A-4527, Office of Economic Opportunity, CA, 3; Nicholas Stroh, "U.S. Poverty Aid Tied to Control of Evans," *PB*, November 24, 1966; Jerome Cahill, "Apathy Found in Poverty War Here," *PB*, December 26, 1966; Greenstone and Peterson, *Race and Authority in Urban Politics*, 28–29, 207–8.

54. White, "Articulateness, Political Mobility, and Conservatism," 201; Nicholas Stroh, "Mrs. Page Quits PAAC Committee, Says Evans Usurped Her Authority," *PB*, December 19, 1966.

55. Tate received 72.3 percent of the vote in black wards ranked in the lowest third by socioeconomic status. Ekstrom, "The Electoral Politics of Reform And Machine," 98–102; White, "Articulateness, Political Mobility, and Conservatism," 200–201; S. A. Paolantonio, *Frank Rizzo: The Last Big Man in Big City America* (Philadelphia: Camino Books, Inc, 1993), 84–122.

56. CAP Evaluation Team, "Memorandum to Middle Atlantic Regional Director," 1–4; Harry Toland, "PAAC Goes Secret," *PB*, July 18, 1966; Nicholas Stroh, "Antipoverty Committee Warns Staff Not to Talk with News Reporters," *PB*, July 14, 1966.

57. CAP Evaluation Team, "Memorandum to Middle Atlantic Regional Director," 1.

58. Ibid., 3.

59. Office of Economic Opportunity–Community Action Program, "Special Condition: Philadelphia Anti-Poverty Action Committee; Grantee No. CG-2059; Progr Yr. A / Action No. 23; Component No. 7-42," n.d. [August 1966], MFC, RG 60-2.5, Box A-4527, Office of Economic Opportunity, CA; Edward G. Bauer, Jr., "Memorandum to James H. J. Tate; Subject: Memoranda to Middle Atlantic Regional Director of OEO," November 14, 1966, MFC, ibid.; Nicholas Stroh, "Obey New U.S. Rules or Lose Aid, PAAC Told," *PB*, December 16, 1966.

60. Nicholas Stroh, "Crippins, Miss Weems Face Loss of Antipoverty Jobs," *PB*, December 7, 1966; Stroh, "Bowser Assails U.S. Guidelines, Threatens to Quit Antipoverty Post," *PB*, December 8, 1966; Stroh, "Bowser Rejects OEO Demand for Apology," *PB*, December 11, 1966; Orrin Evans, "Miss Weems, Unruffled under Fire, Defends Right to Antipoverty Job," *PB*, December 11, 1966; Stroh, "PAAC Agrees to Shakeup, Moore Quits," *PB*, December 28, 1966.

61. Nicholas Stroh, "Poverty Plan Here Delayed by Red Tape," *PB*, March 9, 1968; Harry Toland, "City Hall Power Play," *PB*, March 11, 1968; Stroh, "PAAC Board Refuses to Give Seat to CORE," *PB*, April 17, 1968; White, "Articulateness, Political Mobility, and Conservatism," 201. OEO, "The Office of Economic Opportunity during the Administration of President Lyndon B. Johnson; November 1963–January 1969," 1969, Special Files: Administrative Histories, Box 1, "Volume I, Part II; Narrative History (3 of 3)," LBJ Library, 598–604.

62. Nicholas Stroh, "PAAC Is Said to Fail to Reach Poor in Slums," *PB*, July 15, 1966; Stroh, "Rival Faction and PAAC Chart Collision Course," *PB*, August 5, 1966; Paul Grimes, "Poverty Official Says Too Few Will Share Civic Responsibility," *PB*, August 20, 1968.

63. The reality of such relationships between immigrant political organizations and social ascent had actually been far less direct, and, in any case, where African Americans such as Chicago congressman William Dawson and Harlem Congressman Adam Clayton Powell had built black political machines, they had not been able to translate such gains into the widespread transformation of their communities. Stephen Erie, *Rainbow's End: Irish-Americans and the Dilemmas of Urban Machine Politics, 1840–1985* (Berkeley: University of California Press, 1988).

64. Charles W. Bowser, untitled report, September 9, 1965, MCF, RG 60-2.5, Box A-4489, Phila. Anti-Poverty Action Committee, CA; PAAC, "Progress Report," n.d. [1966], GPC, Box 333-17, TUUA, 34–39, 52–54; PAAC, "Summaries of Programs Funded by OEO," n.d. [1966], GPC, Box 564-3; PAAC, "Progress Report Supplement; June 1, 1966–August 15, 1967," n.d., GPC, Box 529-9, TUUA; PAAC, "The War on Poverty: Questions and Answers Compiled by the Philadelphia Anti-Poverty Action Committee," n.d. [1966], GPC, Box 529-1, TUUA, 22–25; "Poverty War Expectations," *PB*, November 28, 1965.

65. Arthur L. Silvers, "The Philadelphia Economic Development Program: Evaluation and Perspectives for Planning," February 1967, KRPP, Acc. 202 Box 2, Misc. Papers, TUUA, 24–26.

66. Ibid., 25–26; Kathryn L. Kindl, "Boosters of Black Business in Philadelphia," in Federal Reserve Bank of Philadelphia, *Business Review* (April 1970): 18.

67. James H. J. Tate to Richard J. McConnell, February 9, 1965, MCF, RG 60-2.5, Box A-4489, Poverty Program, CA; McConnell to Tate, February 11, 1965, ibid.

68. Margaret Weir, *Politics and Jobs: The Boundaries of Employment Policy in the United States* (Princeton: Princeton University Press, 1992), 61–63; Michael B. Katz, *The Undeserving Poor: From the War on Poverty to the War on Welfare* (New York: Pantheon Books, 1989), 91–94.

69. Abt Associates, Inc., *An Evaluation of the Special Impact Program: Phase 1 Report; Volume 1: Summary* and esp. *Volume II: Analysis of Program Performance* (Washington, D.C.: Office of Economic Opportunity, March 1972), 1-1 to 1-4, 2-1 to 2-11. Supported by SIP funding, Brooklyn's Bedford-Stuyvesant Restoration Corporation emerged as a key model for the CDC movement around the United States. Nels J. Ackerson, Lawrence H. Sharf, and Robert M. Hager, "Community Development Corporations: Operations and Financing," *Harvard Law Review* 83 (1970): 1595–1600; Geoffrey Faux, "Politics and Bureaucracy in Community-Controlled Economic Development," *Law and Contemporary Problems* 36 (Spring 1971): 277–96; Faux, *CDCs: New Hope for the Inner City: Report*

of the Twentieth Century Fund Task Force on Community Development Corporations (New York: Twentieth Century Fund, 1971), 67–74, 85; Stewart E. Perry, *Federal Support for CDCs: Some of the History and Issues of Community Control* (Cambridge, MA: Center for Community Economic Development, 1973), 1–6, 16; Lawrence F. Parachini, Jr., *A Political History of the Special Impact Program* (Cambridge, MA: Center for Community Economic Development, 1980).

70. Perry, *Federal Support for CDCs*, 4, 29; Faux, "Politics and Bureaucracy," 283, 292.

71. Perry, *Federal Support for CDCs*, 12–15; Robert F. Clark, *Maximum Feasible Success: A History of the Community Action Program* (Washington, D.C.: National Association of Community Action Agencies, 2000), 260; Robert Zdenek, "Community Development Corporations," in Severyn T. Bruyn and James Meehan, eds., *Beyond The Market and the State: New Directions in Community Development* (Philadelphia: Temple University Press, 1987), 112–15; Sara E. Stoutland, "Community Development Corporations: Mission, Strategy, and Accomplishments," in Dickens and Ferguson, eds., *Urban Problems and Community Development*, 193–201.

Chapter Four

1. "Welcome to the Everybody Can 'Be Somebody' Spectacular" (event program), October 11, 1972, OICAR, Acc. 688, Box 34, Government Office; OIC Day ... Program Activities, TUUA; "OIC Fact Sheet," 1972, ibid., 1–2; James Bacon, "All-Star Salute to OIC," *PI*[?], October 12 [?], 1972, clipping, ibid.; Henry Mitchell, "A Closed Circuit Evening," *WP*, October 12, 1972, ibid., D1-D2.

2. "Welcome to the Everybody Can 'Be Somebody' Spectacular," October 11, 1972, 2; "OIC Fact Sheet," 1; Bernard E. Anderson, *The Opportunities Industrialization Centers: A Decade of Community-Based Manpower Services*, Industrial Research Unit Wharton School, University of Pennsylvania, Manpower and Human Resources Studies, no. 6 (Philadelphia: Trustees of the University of Pennsylvania, 1976), 64; David Rogers, "Organizing Manpower Delivery Systems in Big Cities," in Robert L. Aronson, ed., *The Localization of Federal Manpower Planning* (Ithaca: New York State School of Industrial and Labor Relations, Publications Division, 1973), 32.

3. In the sole instance of slight advantage in a desirable job category, nonwhite men accounted for 26.5 percent of Philadelphia's skilled male operatives and nonwhite women for 34.5 percent of skilled female operatives. U.S. Bureau of the Census, *U.S. Census of Population: 1960. Vol. I, Characteristics of the Population. Part 40, Pennsylvania* (Washington, D.C.: U.S. Government Printing Office, 1963), 40–372, 431.

4. Leonard Rico, "The Negro Worker in Philadelphia," in Herbert R. Northrup and Richard L. Rowan, eds. *The Negro and Employment Opportunity: Problems and Practices* (Ann Arbor: Bureau of Industrial Relations, Graduate School of Business Administration, University of Michigan, 1967), 364–68.

5. The CHR had been created by the 1951 City Charter, which gave it the authority to pursue not only individual discrimination complaints but also discriminatory policies and general practices. In theory, this allowed the CHR to consider broad patterns of employment discrimination and freed the agency from the difficult task of proving discrimination on the basis of individual cases. This "general practices" provision was more expansive than any previous FEP law. The CHR had been preceded by a local Fair Employment Practices Commission, established by City Council ordinance in 1948. Paul H. Norgren and Samuel E. Hill, *Toward Fair Employment* (New York: Columbia University Press, 1964), 97–113, 123–24; Norgren, "Fair Employment Practice Laws: Experience, Effects, Prospects," in Arthur M. Ross and Herbert Hill, eds., *Employment, Race, and Poverty* (New York: Harcourt, Brace and World, 1967), 547–50; Pennsylvania Economy League: Bureau of Municipal Research, *Philadelphia Government 1956* (Philadelphia: PEL-BMR, 1956), 14–15, 138–46; August Meier, "Civil Rights Strategies for Negro Employment," in Ross and Hill, eds., *Employment, Race, and Poverty* (New York: Harcourt, Brace and World, 1967), 188; Matthew J. Countryman, *Up South: Civil Rights and Black Power in Philadelphia* (Philadelphia: University of Pennsylvania Press, 2006), 40–41, 58–68; Thomas J. Sugrue, "Affirmative Action from Below: Civil Rights, the Building Trades, and the Politics of Racial Equality in the Urban North, 1945–1969," *Journal of American History* 91:1 (June 2004).

6. Thomas J. Sugrue, "The Tangled Roots of Affirmative Action," *American Behavioral Scientist* 41: 7 (April 1998): 886–97.

7. John Hadley Strange, "Blacks and Philadelphia Politics: 1963–1966," in Miriam Ershkowitz and Joseph Zikmund II, eds., *Black Politics in Philadelphia* (New York: Basic Books, 1973), 124–25; Walter Licht, *Getting Work: Philadelphia, 1840–1950* (Philadelphia: University of Pennsylvania Press, 1992), 208–19.

8. Norgren, "Fair Employment Practice Laws," 553, 556; Countryman, *Up South*, 102–3.

9. Leon H. Sullivan, *Build Brother Build* (Philadelphia: Macrae Smith Company, 1969), 66–84; Hannah Lees, "The Not-Buying Power of Philadelphia's Negroes," *Reporter* 24:10 (May 11, 1961): 33–34; Countryman, *Up South*, 171–88.

10. Sullivan, *Build Brother Build*, 31–43.

11. Ibid., 44–52; Anderson, *The Opportunities Industrialization Centers*, 21–22.

12. Sullivan, *Build Brother Build*, 64–65; Anderson, *The Opportunities Industrialization Centers*, 22; Countryman, *Up South*, 84–86.

13. Sullivan, *Build Brother Build*, 66; Michael Baran, Flournoy A. Coles, Jr., John K. Harris, Alfred P. Parsell, and Carol E. Smith (System Development

Corporation), "OIC-Philadelphia: Final Report of the SDC Task Force," February 25, 1966, GPC, Box 499-2, TUUA, 3.

14. Countryman, *Up South*, 96–103; Sullivan, *Build Brother Build*, 6–68; Anderson, *The Opportunities Industrialization Centers,* 23.

15. Sullivan, *Build Brother Build*, 66–67.

16. "The War on Poverty: Andy Miller Moves Up," *Look*, June 13, 1967, 27.

17. Countryman, *Up South*, 98–101, 106–7.

18. "Spreading Negro Boycott," *PM*, May 1962, 55; Sullivan, *Build Brother Build*, 70, 86; Lees, "The Not-Buying Power of Philadelphia's Negroes," 34; John D. Pomfret, "Negroes Building Boycott Network; 'Selective Patronage' Plan Is Led by Clergy: Aim Is to Cut Job Discrimination," *NYT*, November 25, 1962, 1, 67; Anderson, *The Opportunities Industrialization Centers*, 27.

19. Sullivan, *Build Brother Build*, 70–75, 86; Lees, "The Not-Buying Power of Philadelphia's Negroes," 33; Pomfret, "Negroes Building Boycott Network," 1, 67.

20. Countryman, *Up South*, 106–7. Early national coverage of the selective patronage movement included Lees, "The Not-Buying Power Of Philadelphia's Negroes," and "Negro Consumer: He Is Getting More Attention from Big National Advertisers," *Wall Street Journal*, June 30, 1961, 1. No local coverage occurred until April 15, 1962, when a local television-radio station "broke" the story of the *Bulletin* boycott. The *Bulletin* found itself forced to respond, and the selective patronage movement received local coverage thereafter. It also received sympathetic coverage in the *New Republic, New York Times*, and *Fortune*: "Selective Patronage," *New Republic* (July 9, 1962), 6–7; Pomfret, "Negroes Building Boycott Network"; Charles E. Silberman, "The Businessman and the Negro," *Fortune* (September 1963), 186, 191.

21. "Spreading Negro Boycott," *PM*, 55; Pomfret, "Negroes Building Boycott Network," 1.

22. Pomfret, "Negroes Building Boycott Network," 67; Sullivan, *Build Brother Build*, 74, 83–84; Lees, "The Not-Buying Power of Philadelphia's Negroes," 33; "Spreading Negro Boycott," *PM*, 55–56.

23. Sullivan, *Build Brother Build*, 69, 83–84; Lees, "The Not-Buying Power of Philadelphia's Negroes," 33; "Spreading Negro Boycott," *PM*, 55–56; Countryman, *Up South*, 104–5.

24. Lees, "The Not-Buying Power Of Philadelphia's Negroes," 33–34; "Spreading Negro Boycott," *PM*, 55–56; Sullivan, *Build Brother Build*, 83; Peter H. Binzen, "Tasty Adds Civic Action to Its Production List," *PB*, September 23, 1973; Countryman, *Up South* 104–6.

25. "Pastors Set to Lower Boom on Oil Companies; Esso, Atlantic, Gulf, All Under Clerics' Scrutiny," *PT*, January 10, 1961, 1, 8; "Spreading Negro Boycott," *PM*, 53, 55–57; Chris J. Perry, "400 Local Pastors Cease Boycott on Sun Oil Company; Battle Ends with Giant Corporation Surrendering on Every Issue," *PT*, June

13, 1961, 1–2; "1961 Summary of Activity in Our Fight for Equality," *PT*, January 2, 1962, 3,9; Chris J. Perry, "Inquirer Yields to Pastors for 15th Selective Patronage Victory," *PT*, July 17, 1962. For employment categories emphasized by the ministers, see Pomfret, "Negroes Building Boycott Network," 67.

26. Perry, "400 Local Pastors Cease Boycott on Sun Oil Company," *PT*, 1; Sullivan, *Build Brother Build*, 74, 76, 85–86.

27. Randy Dixon, "Gulf Ends Job Bias; Ministers Close Campaign; 400 Pastors Tell Congregations to Begin Patronage," *PT*, January 24, 1961, 1. The ministers steadily increased their demands as selective patronage proceeded; as a result, the *Philadelphia Inquirer* hired thirty-three black workers, and Sun Oil hired twenty-five. Perry, "Inquirer Yields to Pastors," *PT*, 1; Perry, "400 Local Pastors Cease Boycott on Sun Oil Company," *PT*, 1.

28. Sullivan, *Build Brother Build*, 78–79.

29. Ibid., 79

30. Ibid., 74, 78–79; Lees, "The Not-Buying Power of Philadelphia's Negroes," 33–34; Pomfret, "Negroes Building Boycott Network," 67.

31. "Statement of Rev. Leon H. Sullivan," in Congress, Senate, Subcommittee on Executive Reorganization of the Committee on Government Operations, *Federal Role in Urban Affairs*, 89th Cong., 2nd sess., December 12, 1966, 2576; Sullivan, *Build Brother Build*, 76–77.

32. Dr. Maurice A. Dawkins, "Remarks (Representing Rev. Leon H. Sullivan) at the Pre-Convention Hearing on Rights, Opportunity, and Political Power, Democratic Platform Committee, St. Louis, Missouri," June 17, 1972, OICAR, Acc. 688, Box 24, OPD Resource Center; Speeches; 1967–69, TUUA, 4; Sullivan, *Build Brother Build*, 76–77; Allen J. Matusow, *The Unraveling Of America: A History of Liberalism in the 1960s* (New York: Harper and Row, 1984), 209–10; "Selective Patronage," *New Republic*, 7.

33. Countryman, *Up South*, 103–4.

34. Hannah Lees, "Self-Help in Philadelphia," *Reporter* 31:11 (December 17, 1964): 15; "Statement of Rev. Leon H. Sullivan," December 12, 1966, 2576.

35. Sullivan, *Build Brother Build*, 86.

36. Baran et al., "OIC-Philadelphia: Final Report," 4; Lees, "Self-Help in Philadelphia," 15.

37. Anderson, *The Opportunities Industrialization Centers*, 30–31.

38. Sullivan, *Build Brother Build*, 86.

39. "Negro Group Forms Training Program to Turn Out Technicians and Craftsmen," *PB*, July 30, 1963; "Tower of Strength in the Ghetto," *Business Week*, November 2, 1968, 103.

40. Baran et al., "OIC-Philadelphia: Final Report," 3–4; Lees, "Self-Help in Philadelphia," 15–16.

41. Sullivan, *Build Brother Build*, 87.

42. Opportunities Industrialization Centers, Inc. (OIC), "Philadelphia Opportunities Industrialization Center: Its People, Performance and Promise," n.d. [1967], GPC Box 865-17, TUUA, 1.

43. L. D. Reddick, *The Essence of OIC: Manpower Training for Disadvantaged Adults* (Washington, D.C.: Department of Health, Education, and Welfare, 1971), 12.

44. "Statement of Rev. Leon H. Sullivan," December 12, 1966, 2574. In 1972, a federal evaluation of OIC noted that "observers have commented that the Philadelphia OIC owes much of its success to the fact that the people served by OIC feel that, since they volunteer to serve it and help pay for it, it is theirs and that, as a result, OIC has become a symbol of achievement for the poor in Philadelphia's ghetto community." Comptroller General of the United States, *Report to the Congress: Assessment of Operations and Management of Opportunities Industrialization Centers; B-146879* (Washington, D.C.: General Accounting Office, April 20, 1972), 7. Also, Anderson, *The Opportunities Industrialization Centers,* 31–33.

45. OIC, "How to Start a Feeder," March 1972, OICAR, Acc. 688, Box 76, Feeder Program 3/1972, TUUA, 1–2; OIC, "OIC: The Way Out," [1971?], OICAR, Acc. 688, Box 24, OIC Program Descriptions, TUUA; "OIC Fact Sheet," 1972, OICAR, Acc. 688, Box 34, Government Office; OIC Day . . . Program Activities, TUUA, 2.

46. Jerome S. Cahill, "$458,000 in U.S. Aid Helps N. Phila. Group Pioneer Job Training," *PI,* December 18, 1964.

47. "Negro Group Forms Training Program to Turn Out Technicians and Craftsmen," *PB,* July 30, 1963; "Philadelphians Get Thousands for Job Training," *St. Louis American,* December 5, 1963, OICAR, Acc. 688, Box 20, Folder 32, TUUA; "New Hope through Self-Help," *Ebony,* May 1964, 34; Lees, "Self-Help in Philadelphia," 15; OIC, "Philadelphia Opportunities Industrialization Center" [1967–68], 1; PCCA, "Employment Training Proposal Developed by 'Opportunities Industrialization, Inc.,'" January 23, 1964, PCCAR, Acc. 675, Box 2, PCCA–Acty Ford Foundation Grant, 3.

48. Sullivan, *Build Brother Build,* 87–90; OIC, "Philadelphia Opportunities Industrialization Center," 1; PCCA, "Employment Training Proposal Developed by 'Opportunities Industrialization, Inc.,'" 2–3.

49. Clifford J. Campbell, "Memo to Mr. Paul Ylvisaker; Subject: Comments and recommendations in connection with the Quarterly Review of the Program of 'Opportunities Industrialization Center, Inc.,' 19th and Oxford Streets, Philadelphia, Pennsylvania," June 23, 1964, PCCAR, Acc. 675, Box 2, PCCA-ACTY Grant Letters, TUUA, 2; Baran et al., "OIC-Philadelphia: Final Report," 18; OIC, "Philadelphia Opportunities Industrialization Center," 1; "Philadelphians Get Thousands for Job Training," *St. Louis American,* December 5, 1963; "New Hope Through Self-Help," 34; Anderson, *The Opportunities Industrialization Centers,* 33.

50. Lees, "Self-Help in Philadelphia," 15; "Statement of Rev. Leon Sullivan," in Congress, House, Subcommittee on Labor of the Committee on Education and Labor, *Manpower Act of 1969; Hearings; Part I*, 91st Cong., 1st & 2nd sess., February 26, 1970, 379; Countryman, *Up South*, 130–48; Thomas J. Sugrue, "Affirmative Action from Below: Civil Rights, the Building Trades, and the Politics of Racial Equality in the Urban North, 1945–1969," *Journal of American History* 91:1 (June 2004).

51. Anderson, *The Opportunities Industrialization Centers*, 93–95.

52. Lees, "Self-Help in Philadelphia," 16; Sullivan, *Build Brother Build*, 92.

53. Sullivan, *Build Brother Build*, 92; Lees, "Self-Help in Philadelphia," 16; Baran, et al., "OIC-Philadelphia: Final Report," 69.

54. Greenleigh Associates, Inc., *A Pilot Study of the Opportunities Industrialization Center, Inc. Philadelphia, Pennsylvania* (New York: Greenleigh Associates, August 1967), 115–16; "Philadelphians Get Thousands for Job Training," *St. Louis American*, December 5, 1963; Cahill, "$458,000 in U.S. Aid Helps N. Phila. Group Pioneer Job Training," December 18, 1964, 26; Lees, "Self-Help in Philadelphia," 16; Sullivan, *Build Brother Build*, 93.

55. Clifford J. Campbell, "Memo to Mr. Paul Ylvisaker; Subject: Comments and recommendations in connection with the Quarterly Review of the Program of 'Opportunities Industrialization Center, Inc.,' 19th and Oxford Streets, Philadelphia, Pennsylvania," June 23, 1964, PCCAR, Acc. 675, Box 2, PCCA-ACTY Grant Letters, TUUA, 3; Baran et al., "OIC-Philadelphia: Final Report," 62.

56. Sullivan, *Build Brother Build*, 94; Baran et al., "OIC-Philadelphia: Final Report," 62; Greenleigh Associates, *A Pilot Study*, 73–85.

57. Lees, "Self-Help in Philadelphia," 16; Clifford J. Campbell, "Memo to Mr. Paul Ylvisaker; Subject: Comments and recommendations in connection with the Quarterly Review of the Program of 'Opportunities Industrialization Center, Inc.,' 19th and Oxford Streets, Philadelphia, Pennsylvania," June 23, 1964, PCCAR, Acc. 675, Box 2, PCCA-ACTY Grant Letters, TUUA, 2,5; Baran et al., "OIC-Philadelphia: Final Report," 60; "Employment: Solving the Q.N. Problem," *Time*, March 3, 1967, 25.

58. Richard D. Jordan, "Letter to the Editor," *Reporter*, January 28, 1965, 12.

59. "Teaching People To Hold Jobs: The 'Philadelphia Plan," *U.S. News & World Report*, January 1, 1968, 58; Community Renewal Program (City of Philadelphia), "Technical Report 13: Economic Development," December 1964, Fine Arts Library, University of Pennsylvania, 27–28.

60. Baran et al., "OIC-Philadelphia: Final Report," 62.

61. "Statement of Rev. Leon H. Sullivan," December 12, 1966, 2586–89; Herbert E. Striner, "The Opportunities Industrialization Center: A Successful Demonstration of Minority Self-Help, Training, and Education; University of Wisconsin Conference on Education and Training of Racial Minorities," May 11, 1967, GPC, Box 500-15, TUUA, 18.

62. Baran et al., "OIC-Philadelphia: Final Report," 69.

63. Ibid., 15; "Statement of Rev. Leon H. Sullivan," December 12, 1966, 2590; OIC, "Philadelphia Opportunities Industrialization Center," [1967–68], 20; Greenleigh Associates, *A Pilot Study*, 117. In 1964, Sullivan told a reporter that "I'm a militant... I always have been. I've run demonstrations and I may run them again. But right now I'm in the education business." Lees, "Self-Help in Philadelphia," 15.

64. Striner, "The Opportunities Industrialization Center: A Successful Demonstration of Minority Self-Help," 14–16; Baran et al., "OIC-Philadelphia: Final Report," 62, 69; Greenleigh Associates, *A Pilot Study*, 85,115–17; Lees, "Self-Help in Philadelphia," 16; Ben Stahl, "To: Philadelphia Area, HRDI Advisory Council Members; Subject: Summary of HRDI Activities," February 1970, JLCR, Acc. 480, Box 19, AFL-CIO HRDI 1969–70, 14.

65. Sullivan, *Build Brother Build*, 94–95; "New Hope through Self-Help," 27–28.

66. Transcript, Sullivan speech at OIC dedication, January 24, 1964, prepared from film clip by author; original clip available at http://www.philaoic.org/ (accessed December 13, 2006).

67. "Opportunities Center Graduates 20 Trainees," *PI*, May 18, 1964; "Negro Job-Training Center Graduates Its First Class," *PB*, May 18, 1964; Lees, "Self-Help in Philadelphia,"16; "New Hope Through Self-Help," 27–28.

68. Sullivan, *Build Brother Build*, 95–97; "Statement of Rev. Leon H. Sullivan," December 12, 1966, 2588; OIC National Institute, "'Helping the OICs to Help Themselves': A Final Report of the Opportunities Industrialization Centers' National Institute to the U.S. Department of Labor and the Office of Economic Opportunity," May 1970, OICAR, Acc. 688, Box 24, OIC Program Descriptions, TUUA, 34; "Tower of strength in the ghetto," 103.

69. PCCA, "Annual Report to the Ford Foundation 1963; Part I," 1963, PC-CAR, Acc. 675, Box 1, PCCA–Acty Ford Foundation Grant: Annual Report 1963, Part I, TUUA, 8–9

70. Gaeton Fonzi, "Cecil Storms In," *PM* 58 (July 1963): 23; Peter Marris and Martin Rein, *Dilemmas of Social Reform: Poverty and Community Action in the United States*, 2nd ed. (Chicago: Aldine Publishing Co., 1973), 106–7. The African-American ministerial community maintained a cautious relationship with Moore, working with him when they found his efforts positive, and "opposing him when he becomes too violent or too obviously racist" (Moore had taken a number of anti-Semitic positions). Moore could not afford a direct attack on the ministers because of their relative unity, their influence, and the efficiency of their communication networks. His relationship with Sullivan remained one of cautious rivalry. Hannah Lees, "Philadelphia, Pennsylvania: A Process of Fragmentation," *Reporter*, July 4, 1963, 19; Paul Lermack, "Cecil Moore and the Philadelphia Branch of the National Association for the Advancement of Col-

ored People: The Politics of Negro Pressure Group Organization," in Miriam Ershkowitz and Joseph Zikmund II, eds., *Black Politics in Philadelphia*, 151–52.

71. "Proposal for a Program of Community Improvement / Sponsored by the
North City Congress and the Philadelphia Council for Community Advance-
ment," January 23, 1964, in PCCA, Inc., *Annual Report to the Ford Foundation
1963; Part II*, PCCAR, Acc. 675, Box 2, PCCA-ACTY Ford Foundation Grant:
Annual Report 1963, Part II, TUUA, PCCA, "Assumptions Underlying PCCA
Programming," n.d. [1963–64], PCCAR, Acc. 675, Box 1, PCCA-AD, TUUA, 4.

72. Paul Ylvisaker to Samuel Dash, March 2, 1964, PCCAR, Acc. 675, Box
2, PCCA-ACTY Grant Letters, TUUA; Norman W. MacLeod to Samuel Dash,
March 2, 1964, PCCAR, Acc. 675, ibid.; Siegel, "Negroes to Spur Job Training in
Germantown," *PI*, November 29, 1964, 1; Sullivan, *Build Brother Build*, 96–97.

73. Alice O'Connor, "Community Action, Urban Reform, and the Fight
against Poverty," *Journal of Urban History* 22:5 (July 1996): 617.

Chapter Five

1. Jerome Cahill, "$458,000 in U.S. Aid Helps N. Phila. Group Pioneer Job
Training," *PI*, December 18, 1964, 1, 26; Bernard E. Anderson, *The Opportunities
Industrialization Centers: A Decade of Community-Based Manpower Services*, Industrial Research Unit Wharton School, University of Pennsylvania, Manpower
and Human Resources Studies, no. 6 (Philadelphia: University of Pennsylvania,
1976), 98–99; OIC, "Philadelphia Opportunities Industrialization Center: Its People, Performance and Promise," n.d. [1967], GPC, Box 865–17, TUUA, 14.

2. Lawrence O'Rourke, "Bowser Sees City Getting $6 Million," *PB*, June 22,
1965; O'Rourke, "U.S. Gives City $5.9 Million to Fight Poverty," *PB*, June 23,
1965; O'Rourke, "Poverty Unit Asks $3 Million in New Funds," *PB*, May 28,
1965; Katrina Dyke, "Where the $100 Million Went in Last 6 Years," *PB*, Au-
gust 8, 1971; Matthew J. Countryman, *Up South: Civil Rights and Black Power in
Philadelphia* (Philadelphia: University of Pennsylvania Press, 2006), 549.

3. By 1978, OIC replaced the "whole man" phrase with the more inclusive
"whole person." "Statement of Leon H. Sullivan," in Congress, House of Representatives, Select Subcommittee on Labor of the Committee on Education and Labor, *Hearings to Amend the Manpower Development and Training Act of 1962, As
Amended*, 89th Cong., 1st sess., February 19, 1965, 270; Hannah Lees, "Self-Help
in Philadelphia," *Reporter* 31:11 (December 17, 1964): 16; "New Hope Through
Self-Help," *Ebony*, May 1964, 27–36; Jerome Cahill, "$458,000 in U.S. Aid Helps
N. Phila. Group Pioneer Job Training," *PI*, December 18, 1964; OIC, "The OIC
Story: How Philadelphia Negroes established a positive self-development program
for people interested in helping themselves," n.d. [1964–65], GPC, Box 403–11,
TUUA, 6; OIC, "If Not Now—When; If Not Us—Who," n.d. [1978–79], OICAR,

Acc. 688, Box 22, Resource, Philadelphia OIC Publications, Program Descriptions, TUUA, 1.

4. Greenleigh Associates, Inc., *A Pilot Study of the Opportunities Industrialization Center, Inc. Philadelphia, Pennsylvania* (New York: Greenleigh Associates, August 1967), 13, 28–29, 51; Fletcher M. Amos, Jr., "Establishing a Feeder Program," January 22, 1969, OICAR, Acc. 688, Box 76, Establishing a Feeder Program Guidelines, TUUA, [1].

5. "Statement of Rev. Leon H. Sullivan," in Congress, Senate, Subcommittee on Executive Reorganization of the Committee on Government Operations, *Federal Role in Urban Affairs*, 89th Cong., 2nd Sess., December 12, 1966, 2578; Leon H. Sullivan, *Build Brother Build* (Philadelphia: Macrae Smith Company, 1969), 98–99.

6. Dr. Maurice A. Dawkins, "Remarks (Representing Rev. Leon H. Sullivan) at the Pre-Convention Hearing on Rights, Opportunity, and Political Power, Democratic Platform Committee, St. Louis, Missouri," June 17, 1972, OICAR, Acc. 688, Box 24, OPD Resource Center, Speeches, 1967–69, TUUA, 1; "Welcome to the Everybody Can 'Be Somebody' Spectacular" (event program), October 11, 1972, OICAR, Acc. 688, Box 34, Government Office; OIC Day . . . Program Activities, TUUA, 1.

7. Michael Baran, Flournoy A. Coles, Jr., John K. Harris, Alfred P. Parsell, and Carol E. Smith, "OIC-Philadelphia: Final Report of the SDC Task Force," February 25, 1966, GPC, Box 499–2, TUUA, 40–41, 44, 54–57; "Statement of Rev. Leon H. Sullivan," December 12, 1966, 2577; OIC, "Philadelphia Opportunities Industrialization Center," 3; Greenleigh Associates, *A Pilot Study*, 54, 57, 60–63; Herbert E. Striner, "The Opportunities Industrialization Center: A Successful Demonstration of Minority Self-Help, Training, and Education; University of Wisconsin Conference on Education and Training of Racial Minorities," May 11, 1967, GPC, Box 500–15, TUUA, 6–7; Sullivan, *Build Brother Build*, 99–105.

8. Both Roger M. and John S. eventually took jobs as drill press operators at General Electric. OIC, "'We Help Ourselves': 100 Case Studies from over 2700 OIC Alumni," December 1966, OICA, Box 566, Folder 38, Part 1, and Folder 39, Part 2, 35, 50. For lack of War on Poverty coordination, Irwin Unger, *The Best of Intentions: The Triumphs and Failures of the Great Society under Kennedy, Johnson, and Nixon* (New York: Doubleday, 1996).

9. Greenleigh Associates, *A Pilot Study*, 54–55, 57–59.

10. Baran et al., "OIC-Philadelphia: Final Report," 56–57; Amos, Jr., "Establishing a Feeder Program" [2–3].

11. Anderson, *Opportunities Industrialization Centers*, 37; O.I.C. National Institute, "Afro-American History: A Suggestive Guide of Methods and Techniques for the Instructional Use in Minority History," September 1968, OICAR, Acc. 688, Box 76, Feeder Program: Course Outlines and Procedures 1968–70, TUUA, 1–2;

OIC, "Minority History General Outline," n.d., OICAR, Acc. 688, Box 76, Feeder Program: Course Outlines and Procedures 1968–70, TUUA, 1–4.

12. O.I.C. National Institute, "Afro-American History," 1.

13. OIC, "Minority History General Outline," 1–2, 4; Baran et al., "OIC-Philadelphia: Final Report," 41, 56–57; Greenleigh Associates, *A Pilot Study*, 54, 63; Sullivan, *Build Brother Build*, 101–2.

14. OIC, "'We Help Ourselves,'" 36.

15. Baran et al., "OIC-Philadelphia: Final Report," 40–41, 56–58; Sullivan, *Build Brother Build*, 102–4; Greenleigh Associates, *A Pilot Study*, 62–63; OIC (National Institute), "Feeder Course Outlines: Social Realities," n.d., OICAR, Acc. 688, Box 76, Feeder Program-Course Outlines and Procedures 1968–70, TUUA; OIC, "How To Start a Feeder," March, 1972, OICAR, Acc. 688, Box 76, Feeder Program 3/1972, TUUA, 2.

16. Thomas J. Sugrue, *The Origins of the Urban Crisis: Race and Inequality in Postwar Detroit* (Princeton: Princeton University Press, 1996), 165–70; Gerald Horne, *Fire This Time: The Watts Uprising and the 1960s* (Charlottesville: University of Virginia Press, 1995), 319–20.

17. William Julius Wilson, *The Truly Disadvantaged: The Inner City, the Underclass, and Public Policy* (Chicago: University of Chicago Press, 1987); Wilson, *When Work Disappears: The World of the New Urban Poor* (New York: Alfred A. Knopf, 1996); Joleen Kirschenman and Kathryn M. Neckerman, "'We'd Love to Hire Them, But': The Meaning of Race For Employers," in *The Urban Underclass*, ed. Christopher Jencks and Paul E. Peterson (Washington, D.C.: Brookings Institution, 1991), 203–32.

18. OIC, "How To Start a Feeder," 2.

19. OIC, "'We Help Ourselves,'" 37.

20. OIC, "Dialogue: Who Solves the Problem of Unemployment," n.d. [1977], OICAR, Acc. 688, Box 24, OIC Program Descriptions, TUUA, 5–6; Greenleigh Associates, *A Pilot Study*, 55.

21. Greenleigh Associates, *A Pilot Study*, 54, 61.

22. The Moynihan Report actually placed greater emphasis on the employment problems of black men than on the black "matriarchy," but this perspective received little attention in the ensuing controversy. Michael B. Katz, *The Undeserving Poor: From the War on Poverty to the War on Welfare* (New York: Pantheon Books, 1989), 23–35.

23. Amos, Jr., "Establishing a Feeder Program" [3].

24. Baran et al., "OIC-Philadelphia: Final Report," 56–57; Greenleigh Associates, *A Pilot Study*, 54, 58; Sullivan, *Build Brother Build*, 105–7; Norma W. Carlson and Patricia L. Mallory, Economic Development Unit of the City of Philadelphia, "Federally Funded Manpower Development Programs in Philadelphia: An Evaluation," July 1967, GPC, Box 501–7, TUUA, 23–24.

25. OIC, "Handbook for OIC Trainees: Feeder Program," 1971–72, OICAR, Acc. 688, Box 22, Resource Center, Philadelphia OIC Publications, Program Descriptions, TUUA, 15.

26. Patrick Rael, *Black Identity and Black Protest in the Antebellum North* (Chapel Hill: University of North Carolina Press, 2002).

27. OIC, "How to Start a Feeder," 1–2. Also, Baran et al., "OIC-Philadelphia: Final Report," 4, 53; Greenleigh Associates, *A Pilot Study*, 58.

28. OIC, "'We Help Ourselves,'" 148–49.

29. Ibid., 90–94; Baran et al., "OIC-Philadelphia: Final Report," 38, 52–53; OIC, "Philadelphia Opportunities Industrialization Center," 2.

30. OIC, "'We Help Ourselves,'" 130.

31. Lyle E. Schaller, *The Churches' War on Poverty* (New York: Abingdon Press, 1967), 30–76; E. J. Dionne, Jr. and John J. Diiulio, Jr., eds, *What's God Got to Do with the American Experiment?* (Washington, D.C.: Brookings Institution Press, 2000); Dionne and Ming Hsu Chen, eds., *Sacred Places, Civic Purposes: Should Government Help Faith-Based Charity?* (Washington, D.C.: Brookings Institution Press, 2001).

32. Mayor's Anti-Poverty Program, "Congressional Delegation Meeting Agen-" da, December 29, 1964, MFC, RG 60-2.5, Box A-4489, Poverty Program, CA, 3, 9; James H. J. Tate to Joseph T. Kelley, February 3, 1965, ibid., 1; William L. Rafsky, "Memo to James H. J. Tate; Subject: Detroit Parochial Schools' Role in the Anti-Poverty Program," January 14, 1965, ibid.; Community Action Program, *OEO Community Action: Adult Education* (Washington, D.C.: Office of Economic Opportunity, July 1966), 8–9.

33. Leon H. Sullivan, "Doors Open in Philadelphia," *International Journal of Religious Education* (May 1966), 20–21, 46; *Build Brother Build*, 176–77.

34. Anderson, *Opportunities Industrialization Centers*, 22.

35. OIC, "Progress Report to the Philadelphia Anti-Poverty Action Committee," August 2 and September 3, 1965, MCF, RG 60-2.5, Box A-4489, Philadelphia Anti-Poverty Action Committee, CA; Sullivan, *Build Brother Build*, 104.

36. Anderson, *Opportunities Industrialization Centers*, 94–95; "Statement of Rev. Leon H. Sullivan," December 12, 1966, 2580.

37. Baran et al., "OIC-Philadelphia: Final Report," 31, 37; Striner, "Opportunities Industrialization Center," 3–5; Greenleigh Associates, *A Pilot Study*, 40–42, 118; Carlson and Mallory, "Federally Funded Manpower Development Programs in Philadelphia," 13–14; OIC, "How to Start a Feeder," 3–1; "Teaching People to Hold Jobs: The 'Philadelphia Plan," *U.S. News & World Report*, January 1, 1968, 59; OIC, "'We Help Ourselves,'" 68.

38. OIC, "How to Start a Feeder," 3–1.

39. OIC, "'We Help Ourselves,'" 63, 68; Striner, "Opportunities Industrialization Center," App. 2:1–2; "Statement of Rev. Leon H. Sullivan," December 12,

1966, 2578; "Tower of Strength in the Ghetto," *Business Week*, November 2, 1968, 104; Greenleigh Associates, *A Pilot Study*, 23–24, 29–33, 37, 42, 54.

40. OIC, "If Not Now—When; If Not Us—Who," 12.

41. Baran et al., "OIC-Philadelphia: Final Report," 66; The OIC National Institute, "'Helping the OICs to Help Themselves': A Final Report of the Opportunities Industrialization Centers' National Institute to the U.S. Department of Labor and the Office of Economic Opportunity," May 1970, OICAR, Acc. 688, Box 24, OIC Program Descriptions, TUUA, 32. Also, Greenleigh Associates, *A Pilot Study*, 27; Sullivan, *Build Brother Build*, 105–6; Nicholas Stroh, "Poor in Northeast Get Little Help from City's Biggest Poverty Area," *PB*, May 12, 1968.

42. Striner, "Opportunities Industrialization Center," 5, App. 2:1–2; Carlson and Mallory, "Federally Funded Manpower Development Programs in Philadelphia," 6, 17–18, 35–39; "OIC Box Score, 1964–1974," reprinted in Congress, Senate, Subcommittee on Employment, Poverty, and Migratory Labor of the Committee On Labor And Public Welfare, *Emergency Jobs and Unemployment Assistance Amendments, 1975–1976: Part 2*, 94th Cong., 2nd Sess., April 5, 1976, 120; OIC National Institute, "'Helping the OICs to Help Themselves,'" 28, 31; Greenleigh Associates, *A Pilot Study*, 4, 27–29.

43. Baran et al., "OIC-Philadelphia: Final Report," 52; "Meeting of the National OIC Executive Board of Directors" (minutes), April 23, 1969, OICA, Acc. 688, Box 1, Folder 2, TUUA, 3–4; OIC, "Program Design for Day Care Centers," May 27 and June 4, 1970, OICA, Acc. 688, Box 56, Folder 33, TUUA. For women's use of welfare in Philadelphia, Lisa Levenstein, "The Gendered Roots of Modern Urban Poverty: Poor Women and Public Institutions in Post–World War II Philadelphia" (Ph.D. diss., University of Wisconsin, 2002), 36–95.

44. Integration of the building trades had already become a volatile issue in Philadelphia. Baran et al., "OIC-Philadelphia: Final Report," 39–40; Carlson and Mallory, "Federally Funded Manpower Development Programs in Philadelphia," 17–18; Greenleigh Associates, *A Pilot Study*, 46–50, 57.

45. Striner, "Opportunities Industrialization Center," 6; Greenleigh Associates, *A Pilot Study*, 49–50, 92–94, 98–99; Carlson and Mallory, "Federally Funded Manpower Development Programs in Philadelphia," 18.

46. "Statement of Rev. Leon H. Sullivan," December 12, 1966, 2578, 2599.

47. Greenleigh Associates, *A Pilot Study*, 37; Baran et al., "OIC-Philadelphia: Final Report," 78.

48. Greenleigh Associates, *A Pilot Study*, 37–39, 92; Ewan Clague and Leo Kramer, *Manpower Policies and Programs: A Review, 1935–75* (Washington, D.C.: W. E. Upjohn Institute for Employment Research, 1976), 32–33, 38.

49. Striner, "Opportunities Industrialization Center," 12; Baran et al., "OIC-Philadelphia: Final Report," 44–47, Appendix C.

50. Sol Finestone, a farmer from nearby Bucks County, donated the five-story West Philadelphia building, requesting only an annual "cup of black coffee and a

piece of black bread" in return. OIC, "Philadelphia Opportunities Industrialization Center," 4–7; Sullivan, *Build Brother Build*, 97; Richard Siegel, "Negroes to Spur Job Training In Germantown," *PI*, November 29, 1964; Lees, "Self-Help in Philadelphia," 17; Baran et al., "OIC-Philadelphia: Final Report," 50, Appendix C; Greenleigh Associates, *A Pilot Study*, 88.

51. Ibid, 72,84–85; Lees, "Self-Help in Philadelphia," 16; Baran, et al., "OIC-Philadelphia: Final Report," 59. For primary employment of OIC's original 1964 faculty, Guian A. McKee, "Philadelphia Liberals and the Problem of Jobs, 1951–1980" (Ph.D. diss., University of California, Berkeley, 2002), 454.

52. Greenleigh Associates, *A Pilot Study*, 71–73, 84, 87, 116–17; "Business Lobbies for Ghetto Program," *Business Week*, June 28, 1969, 56–57; "Tower of Strength in the Ghetto," 103; OIC, "The OIC Story: Updating the Success Story of the Opportunities Industrialization Center, Inc.," n.d. [1970], OICAR, Acc. 688, Box 22, Resource Center, Philadelphia OIC Publications, Program Descriptions [9].

53. Greenleigh Associates, *A Pilot Study*, 69–70; Anderson, *Opportunities Industrialization Centers*, 37–40; OIC, " 'We Help Ourselves,' " 84.

54. No information was available for the remaining 12 percent of the sample. Greenleigh Associates, *A Pilot Study*, 84, 105–6; Carlson and Mallory, "Federally Funded Manpower Development Programs in Philadelphia," 32.

55. Baran et al., "OIC-Philadelphia: Final Report," 59; Striner, "Opportunities Industrialization Center," 7–8. For the specific curriculum content of a number of OIC courses, "Feeder Course Outlines," n.d., OICAR, Acc. 688, Box 76, Feeder Program, Course Outlines and Procedures, 1968–70, TUUA.

56. Siegel, "Negroes to Spur Job Training in Germantown," *PI*, November 29, 1964, 1; Greenleigh Associates, *A Pilot Study*, 73–83.

57. Greenleigh Associates, *A Pilot Study*, 74–75, 81, 83.

58. Ibid., 76, 79. The Board of Education's John F. Kennedy Center suffered from even more severe problems with inadequate facilities and outdated equipment. Carlson and Mallory, "Federally Funded Manpower Development Programs in Philadelphia," 40.

59. Ibid., 74–75, 81–83; Baran et al., "OIC-Philadelphia: Final Report," 61.

60. Greenleigh Associates, *A Pilot Study*, 80; "Statement of Rev. Leon H. Sullivan," December 12, 1966, 2584; OIC, "Labor And OIC Alliance," n.d., JLCR, Acc. 480, Box 26, Opportunities Industrialization Centers 1968, TUUA; OIC, "Apprenticeship Preparation Program," n.d. [1966], JLCR, ibid.; OIC, "Apprenticeship Opportunities," n.d. [1966], JLCR, ibid.

61. OIC, " 'We Help Ourselves,' " 66–67. On the Myrdahlian breakthrough idea, Thomas J. Sugrue, "The Tangled Roots of Affirmative Action," *American Behavioral Scientist* 41:7 (1998): 886–97.

62. " 'I Want My Men in Unions,' Rev. Sullivan Tells Builders," *PB*, May 3, 1968.

63. Herbert E. Striner, "The Opportunities Industrialization Center: A Successful Demonstration of Minority Self-Help, Training, and Education; University of Wisconsin Conference on Education and Training of Racial Minorities," May 11, 1967, GPC, Box 500–15, TUUA, 15–17.

64. Greenleigh Associates, *A Pilot Study*, 108–109; Baran et al., "OIC-Philadelphia: Final Report," 125; Department of Labor, *Public Hearing: The Philadelphia Plan, August 26–28, 1969* (Washington: Department of Labor, 1969), 62–80; OIC, "'We Help Ourselves,'" 122–23.

65. The data-set contained earnings information for only thirty-nine of the trainees; some figures were provided on an hourly basis and were converted to weekly earnings on the assumption of a forty-hour work week. OIC, "'We Help Ourselves': 100 Case Studies from over 2700 OIC Alumni," December 1966, OICA, Box 566, Folder 38, Part 1 and Folder 39, Part 2.

66. Ibid., 101–2.

67. OICA, "Job Placement Company Survey, Contract Year: 1974–75," October 1974–January 1975, and May, June, August 1975, OICA, Acc. 688, Box 57, F: 13 Philadelphia Program Statistics 1974–75, TUUA.

68. Ibid.; OIC, "'We Help Ourselves,'" 59, 84, 120–21.

69. OIC, "'We Help Ourselves,'" 46; Jill Quadagno and Catherine Forbes, "The Welfare State and the Cultural Reproduction of Gender: Making Good Girls and Boys in the Job Corps," *Social Problems* 42:2 (May 1995): 185–86.

70. Eileen Boris, "Contested Rights: The Great Society between Home and Work," in *The Great Society and the High Tide of Liberalism*, ed. Sidney M. Milkis and Jerome M. Mileur (Amherst: University of Massachusetts Press, 2005).

71. A 1972 study by the federal General Accounting Office estimated that OIC's actual trainee placement rate was approximately 47 percent of what the organization claimed. The GAO report nonetheless stated that OIC "had made some measurable progress in enrolling persons in the program, providing training and supportive services, developing jobs, and making job placements." Comptroller General of the United States, *Report to the Congress: Assessment of Operations and Management of Opportunities Industrialization Centers; B-146879* (Washington, D.C.: GAO, 1972), 1–3, 14, 52–55; also, Baran et al., "OIC-Philadelphia: Final Report," 61.

72. Baran et al., "OIC-Philadelphia: Final Report," 60–63, 123–125; Greenleigh Associates, *A Pilot Study*, 101–5.

73. Striner, "Opportunities Industrialization Center," Appendix 2, 1–2; Carlson and Mallory, "Federally Funded Manpower Development Programs in Philadelphia," 5–8; "Business Lobbies for Ghetto Program," 56; OIC, "'Moving Forward Together': Industry, Labor, Community, Government," n.d., OICAR, Acc. 688, Box 24, OPD Resource Center; Speeches; 1967–1969, TUUA, 4–5; "Statement of Rev. Leon Sullivan," in Congress, House, Subcommittee on Labor

of the Committee on Education and Labor, *Manpower Act of 1969; Hearings; Part I*, 91st Cong., 1st and 2nd sess., February 26, 1970, 382.

74. Baran et al., "OIC-Philadelphia: Final Report," 61; Greenleigh Associates, *A Pilot Study*, 107.

75. Ibid., 101–10; Anderson, *Opportunities Industrialization Centers*, 41; Thacher Longstreth, "Rewarding Efforts of a Private Agency–OIC," *Labor Law Journal* 19:8 (August 1968): 472; Sullivan, *Build Brother Build*, 124; OICA, "Building America— Together; OIC & Industry," n.d. [1971–72], OICAR, Acc. 688, Box 24, OIC Program Descriptions, TUUA, 12.

76. OIC National Institute, "'Helping the OICs to Help Themselves,'" 29.

77. OIC, "Philadelphia Opportunities Industrialization Center," 19; OIC, "The OIC Story: Updating the Success Story" [12]; Anderson, *Opportunities Industrialization Centers*, 54.

78. Charles R. Perry, Bernard E. Anderson, Richard L. Rowan, and Herbert R. Northrup, *The Impact of Government Manpower Programs: In General and on Minorities and Women*, Manpower and Human Resources Studies, no. 4, Industrial Research Unit Wharton School, University of Pennsylvania (Philadelphia: Trustees of the University of Pennsylvania, 1975), 64–72, 317–24; OIC, "'Moving Forward Together': Industry, Labor, Community, Government," n.d. [1970], OICAR, Acc. 688, Box 24, OPD Resource Center, Speeches, 1967–69, 4–5.

79. OIC National Institute, "'Helping the OICs to Help Themselves,'" 28–29; Perry et al., *The Impact of Government Manpower Programs*, 73, 317.

80. Greenleigh Associates, *A Pilot Study*, 110–11.

81. OIC National Institute, "'Helping the OICs to Help Themselves,'" 29.

82. Baran et al., "OIC-Philadelphia: Final Report," 63–65.

83. OIC, "'We Help Ourselves'": 100 Case Studies From Over 2700 OIC Alumni," 98–100.

84. "The War on Poverty: Andy Miller Moves Up," *Look*, June 13, 1967, 27–28.

85. Anderson, *Opportunities Industrialization Centers*, 77–78; Walter Isard and Thomas W. Langford, Jr., *The Impact of Viet Nam War Expenditures on the Philadelphia Economy* (Philadelphia: Regional Science Research Institute, May 1969); Perry et al., *The Impact of Government Manpower Programs*, 301–2; OIC National Institute, "'Helping the OICs to Help Themselves,'" 29.

86. Anderson, *Opportunities Industrialization Centers*, 70.

87. CAP Evaluation Team, "Memorandum to Middle Atlantic Regional Director; Subject: Findings of the Philadelphia Evaluation Team," August 30, 1966, MCF, RG 60-2.5, Box A-4527, Office of Economic Opportunity, CA, 7.

88. "Statement of Hon. Joseph S. Clark, a U.S. Senator from the State of Pennsylvania," in Senate, Subcommittee on Executive Reorganization, *Federal Role in Urban Affairs*, 89th Cong., 2nd Sess., December 12, 1966, 2572.

89. OIC, "Philadelphia Opportunities Industrialization Center," i, 12; OIC, "Building America—Together; OIC & Industry," 12; OIC, "'Moving Forward Together': Industry, Labor, Community, Government," 8; Anderson, *Opportunities Industrialization Centers*, 92; Dawkins, "Remarks (Representing Rev. Leon H. Sullivan)," 4.

90. Sherwin J. Markman, "Memorandum for the President," May 9, 1967, Ex WE 9, WHCF, Box 29, April 20–May 10, 1967, LBJ Library, 5–6. Johnson sent Markman on the secret ghetto visits because of his frustration with "all these reports from the bureaucracy and the experts." Markman described his first tour, in Chicago, as "a great eye-opener." Transcript, Sherwin J. Markman Oral History Interview I, May 21, 1969, by Dorothy Pierce McSweeney, LBJ Library, 24–33. By 1972, Sullivan had begun to speak publicly against the Vietnam War and its diversion of resources from domestic needs. Robert J. Donovan, "G.M.'s Black Director on 'Opening Doors,'" *WP* May 27, 1972.

91. "Text of President Johnson's Address at the Opportunities Industrialization Center on June 29, 1967," OICAR, Acc. 688, Box 24, OPD Resource Center, Speeches, 1967–69, TUUA; OIC Public Information Office, "The President Visits OIC," 1967, OICAR, Acc. 688, Box 24, Regional/Local OIC Newsletters, Annual Reports, and Program Descriptions, TUUA; Mike Mallowe, "Mangy Days for the Lion of Zion," *PM*, October 1973, 194–95.

92. OIC National Institute, "'Helping the OICs to Help Themselves,'" 1–24,29; OIC, "Philadelphia Opportunities Industrialization Center," 9, 19; Comptroller General, *Assessment of Operations and Management of Opportunities Industrialization Centers*, 10–12; OIC, "The OIC Story: Updating The Success Story of the Opportunities Industrialization Center, Inc.," [12, 15–16]; Sullivan, *Build Brother Build*, 111; Dawkins, "Remarks (Representing Rev. Leon H. Sullivan)," 4; Anderson, *Opportunities Industrialization Centers*, 54, 99.

93. Horne, *Fire This Time*, 319–20; OIC National Institute, "'Helping the OICs to Help Themselves,'" 9, 29.

94. Office of Economic Opportunity (OEO), *4th Annual Report: As the Seed Is Sown* (Washington, D.C.: Office of Economic Opportunity, 1969), 16; OEO, *Community Action Programs* (Washington, D.C.: Office of Economic Opportunity, April 1968), 13.

95. "OIC Goes to Africa," *Voice of Progress,* vol. 1, no. 2 (January 1970), OICAR, Acc. 688, Box 80, NPAED Voice of Progress Newsletters Nov 1969–Dec 1970, 1; David O'Reilly, "New Leader Vows to Refresh a Helping Agency," *PI*, July 18, 2000; OIC National Institute, "'Helping the OICs to Help Themselves,'" 21, 29; Anderson, *Opportunities Industrialization Centers*, 44, 67, 132.

96. OIC National Institute, "'Helping the OICs to Help Themselves,'" 25.

97. "Statement of Leon H. Sullivan," in House, Select Subcommittee on Labor, *Hearings to Amend the Manpower Development and Training Act of 1962, As Amended*, February 19, 1965, 272.

98. "Prepared Statement of Rev. Dr. Thomas J. Ritter," in Congress, House of Representatives, Select Subcommittee on Equal Opportunities of the Committee on Education and Labor, *Equal Opportunity and Full Employment: Part 3*, 94th Cong., 1st Sess., April 11, 1975, 353–54; Joint Economic Committee, Congress of the United States, *A Congressional Conference On "A Full-Employment Policy: An Examination of Its Implications,"* 94th Cong., 1st Sess., December 10, 1975, 36–38; "Statement of the Reverend Maurice Dawkins on Behalf of the Reverend Leon Sullivan," in Congress, House of Representatives, Select Subcommittee on Equal Opportunities of the Committee on Education and Labor, *Equal Opportunity and Full Employment: Part 5*, 94th Cong., 2nd Sess., March 15–16, 1976, 257–64.

99. Anderson, *Opportunities Industrialization Centers*, 97–101; PAAC, "Reply to the Office of Economic Opportunity's Memorandum of Findings of the Philadelphia Evaluation Team," November 16, 1966, MCF, RG 60-2.5, Box A-4527, Office of Economic Opportunity, CA, 22; Comptroller General, *Assessment of Operations and Management of Opportunities Industrialization Centers*, 3–7, 11–12.

100. Clague and Kramer, *Manpower Policies and Programs: A Review, 1935–75*, 32–33; Perry et al., *The Impact of Government Manpower Programs*, 12–13, 332–59; Richard D. Leone, Bernard R. Siskin, Russell E. Johannesson, and Bernard E. Anderson, *Employability Development Teams and Federal Manpower Programs: A Critical Assessment of the Philadelphia CEP's Experience* (Philadelphia: School of Business Administration, Temple University, 1972), viii, 1–7, 11–28; Anderson, *Opportunities Industrialization Centers*, 102. For the vulnerability of the War on Poverty, Office of Economic Opportunity, "The Office of Economic Opportunity During the Administration of President Lyndon B. Johnson; November 1963–January 1969; –vol. 1, Administrative History," n.d., Administrative History of the Office of Economic Opportunity, Box 1, LBJ Library, 544–607.

101. Anderson, *Opportunities Industrialization Centers*, 100–101; Comptroller General, *Assessment of Operations and Management of Opportunities Industrialization Centers*, 7–8; The OIC National Institute, "'Helping the OICs to Help Themselves,'" 25; Sherwin J. Markman, "Memorandum for the President," May 9, 1967, 3.

102. PAAC's Samuel Evans angrily responded that the federal directive undercut local autonomy. Kos Semonski, "U.S. Threatens to Halt Poverty Funds Over Cut in Sullivan Program," *PB*, September 26, 1968; "Longstreth Raps Cut in OIC Funds," *PB*, August 6, 1968; "Is Job Training Important?" *PB*, August 10, 1968.

103. Anderson, *Opportunities Industrialization Center*, 77–80, 85–87; "Statement of Hon. J. Caleb Boggs," in House, Select Subcommittee on Labor, *Manpower Act of 1969; Hearings*, February 26, 1970, 379.

104. "Statement of Rev. Leon H. Sullivan," December 12, 1966, 2586.

105. Anderson, *Opportunities Industrialization Centers*, 81–85; "Business Lobbies for Ghetto Program," *Business Week*, June 28, 1969, 56; Sullivan, *Build Brother Build*, 120–22.

106. Mallowe, "Mangy Days," 131–32, 192–95.

107. "Statement of Rev. Leon H. Sullivan," December 12, 1966, 2596–97; OIC, "Dialogue: Who Solves the Problem of Unemployment," 8.

108. Judith Stein, *The World of Marcus Garvey: Race and Class in Modern Society* (Baton Rouge: Louisiana State University Press, 1986).

109. Sar A. Levitan and Joyce K. Zickler, *The Quest for a Federal Manpower Partnership* (Cambridge, MA: Harvard University Press, 1974), 1–12; Michael J. Rich, *Federal Policymaking and the Poor: National Goals, Local Choices, and Distributional Outcomes* (Princeton: Princeton University Press, 1993), 22–30; Benjamin Kleinberg, *Urban America in Transformation: Perspectives on Urban Policy and Development* (Thousand Oaks, CA: Sage Publications, 1995), 84, 187–209; Timothy Conlan, *From New Federalism to Devolution: Twenty-Five Years of Intergovernmental Reform* (Washington, D.C.: Brookings Institution Press, 1998).

110. Kleinberg, *Urban America in Transformation*, 84, 187–209; Conlan, *From New Federalism to Devolution*, 1–76; Alice O'Connor, "Swimming Against the Tide: A Brief History of Federal Policy in Poor Communities," in William T. Dickens and Ronald F. Ferguson, eds., *Urban Problems and Community Development* (Washington, D.C.: Brookings Institution Press, 1999), 108–10.

111. Anderson, *Opportunities Industrialization Centers*, 103–4; "Business Lobbies for Ghetto program," 56.

112. Rev. Leon Sullivan and Senator Hugh Scott, "Memorandum to the President," March 22, 1973, OICAR, Acc. 688, Box 35, Government Office OIC Funding Crisis June 1973 Memos, TUUA, 1; Sullivan, *Build Brother Build*, 134–36.

113. Roger H. Davidson, *The Politics of Comprehensive Manpower Legislation* (Baltimore: Johns Hopkins University Press, 1972), 25; "Statement of Rev. Leon Sullivan," February 26, 1970, 380–406; Warren Brown, "Future of OIC Assured," *PI*, December 29, 1973; Congress, Senate, *The Employment And Manpower Act of 1970*, 91st Cong., 2nd Sess., S. 3867, Document no. 91–118, 31–34.

114. Dr. Dawkins, "Memorandum to Mr. Bradley Patterson; Subject: OIC of America Funding Crisis, July 1973," July 10, 1973, OICAR, Acc. 688, Box 35, Government Office OIC Funding Crisis June 1973 Memos, TUUA, 1; Anderson, *Opportunities Industrialization Centers*, 106–7.

115. Ibid., 49–52, 107–9; Comptroller General, *Assessment of Operations and Management of Opportunities Industrialization Centers*, 3–4, 11–13.

116. Anderson, 112–14; Marjorie Hyer, "5,000 March on Hill in Effort to Save OIC," *WP*, March 30, 1973; "Statement of the Reverend Maurice Dawkins on Behalf of the Reverend Leon Sullivan," 256.

117. Congress, Conference Committee Report, *Comprehensive Employment and Training Act of 1973*, 93rd Cong., 1st Sess., S. 1559 as amended, Reports No.

93-636 (Senate) & No. 93-737 (House), 52–53; Anderson, *Opportunities Indus-trialization Centers*, 110–14; Maurice A. Dawkins, "Remarks (Representing Rev. Leon H. Sullivan)," 2; Senator Peter H. Dominick to Peter J. Brennan, Secre-tary of Labor, July 16, 1973, OICAR, Acc. 688, Box 35, Government Office OIC Funding Crisis June 1973 Memos, TUUA; Maurice A. Dawkins, "Memorandum to Rev. Leon H. Sullivan; Subject: Major Issues Re: OIC and Decategorization by Administrative and/or Legislative Action," May 18, 1973, ibid., 1–2; Dr. Mau-rice Dawkins, "Legislative History Re: OIC in the Comprehensive Manpower and Training Act of 1973," n.d. [1974], OICAR, Acc. 688, Box 35, Government Office, Paper Presentations, 1974–76, TUUA.

118. Dr. Maurice Dawkins, "Salient Points in Comprehensive Employment and Training Act of 1973 Affecting OIC Of America," n.d. [1974], OICAR, Acc. 688, Box 35, Government Office, Paper Presentations 1974–76, TUUA; Alan Zuckerman, OICA Senior Program Analyst, "Ceta – Purpose And Prospects," n.d. [June–July 1974], OICAR, Acc. 688, Box 24, OPD Resource Center, Speeches, 1967–69, TUUA, 1–4.

119. Dr. Maurice Dawkins, "Legislative History Re: OIC in the Comprehen-sive Manpower and Training Act of 1973," 1; Congress, *Comprehensive Employ-ment and Training Act of 1973*, 6–8, 10; Dawkins, "Salient Points in Comprehensive Employment and Training Act of 1973," 2; Brown, "Future of OIC Assured"; An-derson, *Opportunities Industrialization Centers*, 115–16.

120. Elton M. Jolly, "Discussion Paper: OIC And National Employment And Training Policy," May 3, 1977, OICAR, Acc. 688, Box 22, OPD Resource Center Papers, TUUA, 2–6; Scott and Sullivan, "Memorandum to the President," March 22, 1973, 1; Anderson, *Opportunities Industrialization Centers*, 117–18,126–29.

121. Zuckerman, "CETA: Purpose and Prospects," 2–4; Jolly, "Discussion Pa-per: OIC and National Employment and Training Policy," 3; Dawkins, "Legisla-tive History Re: OIC in the Comprehensive Manpower and Training Act of 1973," 1; Anderson, *Opportunities Industrialization Centers*, 117, 128, 131.

122. Robert H. Haveman, *Direct Job Creation: Potentials and Realities* (Madi-son: Institute for Research on Poverty, University of Wisconsin–Madison, Septem-ber 1979); Clague and Kramer, *Manpower Policies and Programs*, 85–86; Franklin and Ripley, *CETA*, 45, 62–66, 104–5; Conlan, *From New Federalism to Devolution*, 166; Paul Delaney, "Job Aid Intended for Poor Is Often Spent on Others," *NYT*, September 26, 1975; "Statement of the Reverend Maurice Dawkins on Behalf of the Reverend Leon Sullivan," March 15–16, 1976.

123. Jolly, "Discussion Paper: OIC and National Employment and Training Policy," 2, 4–5; Delaney, "Job Aid Intended for Poor Is Often Spent on Others"; "Information On The OIC/CETA Relationship Collected for the Opportunities Industrialization Centers of America," reprinted in Congress, Senate, Subcommit-tee on Employment, Poverty, and Migratory Labor, *Emergency Jobs and Unem-ployment Assistance Amendments, 1975–1976: Part 2*, 94th Cong., 2nd Sess., April

5, 1976, 126; Anderson, *Opportunities Industrialization Centers*, 120–26; Dawkins, "Memorandum to Mr. Bradley Patterson," 1.

124. Zuckerman, "CETA: Purpose and Prospects," 5–6; Anderson, *Opportunities Industrialization Centers*, 83, 89.

125. Congress, Senate, Committee on Labor and Public Welfare, *Opportunities Industrialization Centers Job Creation and Training Act, 1976: Hearing Before the Subcommittee on Employment, Poverty, and Migratory Labor*, 94th Cong., 2nd Sess., May 25, 1976, 3–18, 65–83.

126. Margaret Weir, *Politics and Jobs: The Boundaries of Employment Policy in the United States* (Princeton: Princeton University Press, 1992), 131–40.

127. Joint Economic Committee, *Congressional Conference on "A Full-Employment Policy,"* 36–37; "Statement of the Reverend Maurice Dawkins on Behalf of the Reverend Leon Sullivan," 260; Thomas A. Johnson, "Congress Urged to Help Job Training," *NYT*, September 1, 1976.

128. Anderson, *Opportunities Industrialization Centers*, 117–20, 132–34; Lou Antosh, "Data on Job Placement Looks Good . . . on Paper," *PB*, November 17, 1980; OIC, "If Not Now—When; If Not Us—Who," 3; OIC, "1980 Annual Report," 1981, OICAR, Acc. 688, Box 22, Resource Center, Philadelphia OIC Publications, Annual Reports 1980, TUUA, 2; Antosh, "Firms Accused of Watching a Job-Center's Management Falter," *PB*, November 18, 1980; Antosh, "Auditors Provide Warnings, but U.S. Funds Still Pour In," *PB*, November 18, 1980.

129. Conlan, *From New Federalism To Devolution*, 1–18.

130. OIC, "Dialogue: Who Solves the Problem of Unemployment," 5–6.

Chapter Six

1. "Bridges to Human Dignity: An Address by Richard M. Nixon," broadcast on the CBS radio network Thursday, April 25, 1968 (New York: Nixon/Agnew Campaign Committee, 1968); Arthur I. Blaustein and Geoffrey Faux, *The Star-Spangled Hustle* (Garden City, NY: Doubleday & Company, Inc., 1972), 18–24; "Nixon on Racial Accommodation," *Time,* May 3, 1968, 21; "What the Candidates Would Do about 'Black Capitalism,'" *U.S. News & World Report,* September 30, 1968, 65; John McClaughry, "Black Ownership and National Politics," in William F. Haddad and G. Douglas Pugh, eds., *Black Economic Development* (Englewood Cliffs, NJ: Prentice-Hall, Inc., 1969), 38–40; John David Skrentny, *The Ironies of Affirmative Action: Politics, Culture, and Justice in America* (Chicago: University of Chicago Press, 1996), 187, 192–93; Dean J. Kotlowski, *Nixon's Civil Rights: Politics, Principle, and Policy* (Cambridge, MA: Harvard University Press, 2001), 125–33.

2. The Pittsburgh Urban League's Ronald Davenport described Nixon's black capitalism as "like a Trojan Horse without the soldiers inside." "Black Capitalism

Has a Hollow Ring," *Business Week*, August 30, 1969, 51–54; Richard S. Rosenbloom and John K. Shank, "Let's Write off MESBICs," *Harvard Business Review* 48:5 (October 1970): 90–97; Blaustein and Faux, *The Star-Spangled Hustle*.

3. Patrick J. McLaughlin, "Application to the Department of Housing and Urban Development by the Honorable James H. J. Tate, Mayor, City of Philadelphia, for a Grant to Plan a Comprehensive City Demonstration Project," March 3, 1967, GPC, Box 258–12, TUUA, 54–55; Eugene P. Foley, "The Negro Businessman: In Search of a Tradition," in Talcott Parsons and Kenneth B. Clark, eds., *The Negro American* (Boston: Houghton Mifflin Co., 1966), 555–92; Blaustein and Faux, *The Star-Spangled Hustle*, 71; U.S. Bureau of the Census, *City and County Data Book 1967* (Washington, D.C.: United States Government Printing Office, 1967).

4. Philadelphia Urban Coalition, "Declaration of Principles, Goals, and Commitments" [February 17, 1968], JLCR, Acc. 480, Box 29, Urban Coalition 1968, TUUA; "Where Negro Business Gets Credit," *Business Week*, June 8, 1968, 98–100; Susan R. Robinson, "Moving Money into Ghetto Businesses," in Federal Reserve Bank of Philadelphia, *Business Review* (October 1968): 9–12; Patricia L. Mallory, Economic Development Unit, "Review of Economic Development Unit Staff Participation with Greater Philadelphia Enterprises Development Corporation," November 1968, GPC, Box 791–4 (vol. VI), TUUA; James Crummett, "Philadelphia Urban Coalition," October 1969, GPC, Box 791-4 (vol. 4), TUUA; Kathryn L. Kindl, "Boosters of Black Business in Philadelphia," in Federal Reserve Bank of Philadelphia, *Business Review* (April 1970): 9–19; PUC, "Action' 70 (annual report)," 1971, ACWAR, Acc. 519, Box 22, Urban Coalition (1968–Feb. 1970), TUUA, 35.

5. Phyl Garland, "The Unorthodox Ministry of Leon H. Sullivan," *Ebony*, May 1971, 116.

6. *NPAED Voice of Progress*, February 1970 (p. 2) and March 1970 (p. 2), OICAR, Acc. 688, Box 80, NPAED Voice of Progress Newsletters November 1969–December 1970, TUUA, 2; Frederick E. Miller, "The Progress Movement: ZIA; A Model of Capital Formation," in *Capital Formation: Challenge for the Third Century; Selected Proceedings of the Sixth Annual Symposium of the Black Economy, 1976*, ed. Gerald F. Whittaker (Ann Arbor: University of Michigan, 1977); Leon H. Sullivan, *Build Brother Build: From Poverty to Economic Power* (Philadelphia: Macrae Smith Company, 1969), 168; "Prepared Statement of Rev. Dr. Thomas J. Ritter," in Congress, House of Representatives, Select Subcommittee on Equal Opportunities of the Committee On Education and Labor, *Equal Opportunity and Full Employment: Part 3*, 94th Cong., 1st Sess., April 11, 1975, 353–54.

7. Sullivan, *Build Brother Build*, 162; "Community Investment Cooperatives; Self Help Community Regeneration," August 1976, OICAR, Acc. 688, Box 75, OIC–Community Investment Cooperative Program Descriptions (OIC-CIC) 1968–78, TUUA, 1; OICs of America: Economic Development Division (OICA-

EDD), "Prospectus for the Future—Shares for Progress: A Community Investment Cooperative for Your City," n.d., OICAR, Acc. 688, Box 75, OIC-CIC 1968–78, TUUA, 4.

8. Garland, "The Unorthodox Ministry of Leon H. Sullivan," 120; "Community Investment Cooperatives; Self Help Community Regeneration," August 1976, 1.

9. "10-36 Plan Description, History and National Expansion Plans," n.d. [1972–73], OICAR, Acc. 688, Box 75, OIC-CIC, 1968–78, TUUA, 3–6; OICA-EDD, "The CIC ('10-36') Plan: A Community Investment Cooperative Plan for Community Self-Help, Uplift, and Individual Investment Benefit," January 1977, OICAR, Acc. 688, Box 75, A Manual for the Development of CICs January 1977, TUUA, 3–6; "The 10-36 Plan," n.d. [1968], OICAR, Acc. 688, Box 75, OIC-CIC, 1968–78, TUUA; Leon Howard Sullivan, "Building Black Economic Emancipation with $10 Building Blocks," 1969, GPC Box 555-1, TUUA, 8–9; Sullivan, *Build Brother Build*, 168–69, 173; Progress Investment Associates, Inc. (PIA), "Financial Report," March 14, 1980, OICAR, Acc. 688, Box 73, 31, TUUA, 2 and attached Consolidated Statement of Shareholders' Equity.

10. ZIA, "Preliminary Prospectus," March 31, 1971, OICAR, Acc. 688, Box 73, Contract Agreement between ZIA and the Ford Foundation 1971, TUUA, 6; "Community Investment Cooperatives; Self Help Community Regeneration," August 1976, 1; OICA-EDD, "The CIC ("10-36") Plan," 5.

11. "'Black Capitalism at Work'; What's Happening in Philadelphia: An Exclusive Interview," *U.S. News & World Report*, February 17, 1969, 63; Sullivan, "Building Black Economic Emancipation with $10 Building Blocks," 1969, 9; ZIA, "Zion Investment Associates, Inc. (ZIA), "Five Year Operating Plan 1972 Through 1976," December 9, 1971, OICAR, Acc. 688, Box 72, ZIA Board of Directors Meeting Minutes 1970–73, TUUA, 3–4; Sullivan, *Build Brother Build*, 169.

12. "10-36 Plan Description, History and National Expansion Plans," n.d., 5; OICA-EDD, "The CIC ('10-36') Plan," 3–5; ZIA, "The 10-36 Plan," n.d. [1968], 1; "Community Investment Cooperatives; Self Help Community Regeneration," 1; "Opening Doors to Opportunity," *Nation's Business*, April 1970, 49; Sullivan, *Build Brother Build*, 170.

13. Ibok Esema, "The Miracles of Reverend Leon H. Sullivan: Black Economic Development Now a Reality," *NPAED Voice Of Progress*, November 1969, OICAR, Acc. 688, Box 80, NPAED Voice of Progress Newsletters November 1969–December 1970, TUUA, 1; "Opening Doors to Opportunity," 49–50; OICs of America, Inc. Economic Development Division, "The CIC ("10-36,") Plan," 6–7; Sullivan, *Build Brother Build*, 170.

14. Philadelphia Redevelopment Authority, *Annual Report, 1964* (Philadelphia: City of Philadelphia, 1965), 24–25; Philadelphia Redevelopment Authority, *Annual Report, 1968* (Philadelphia: City of Philadelphia, 1969), 26–27.

15. "'Black Capitalism at Work,'" 64; Esema, "Progress Plaza—Philadelphia," *NPAED Voice of Progress*, November 1969, OICAR, Acc. 688, Box 80, NPAED

Voice of Progress Newsletters November 1969–December 1970, TUUA, 4; "Opening Doors to Opportunity," 51–52.

16. These contracts required supplementary rent payments of between 1.5 and 5 percent of gross revenues above base-lines that ranged between $250,000 and $3.5 million. "'Black Capitalism at Work,'" 64; ZIA, "Preliminary Prospectus," March 31, 1971, 15–16.

17. "'Black Capitalism at Work,'" 64; "Opening Doors to Opportunity," 51–52; Esema, "The Miracles of Reverend Leon H. Sullivan" and "Progress Plaza—Philadelphia"; ZIA, "Preliminary Prospectus," March 31, 1971, 18.

18. Ibid., 4; ZIA, "Five Year Operating Plan 1972 through 1976," December 9, 1971, OICAR, Acc. 688, Box 72, ZIA Board of Directors Meeting Minutes 1970–73, TUUA, 3.

19. ZIA, "Preliminary Prospectus," March 31, 1971, 16; ZIA and Zion Non-Profit Charitable Trust (ZNPCT), "Seventh Annual Report; Year Ended December 31, 1972," 1973, OICAR, Acc. 688, Box 72, ZIA Annual Reports, 1971–72, 1975, TUUA, 4–5; Frederick E. Miller, "Memorandum to the Members of the ZIA Board of Directors; Subject: Operations Status Report," May 16, 1973, OICAR, Acc. 688, Box 72, ZIA Board of Directors Meeting Agendas 1972–73, TUUA, 1–2.

20. Progress Aerospace Enterprises Inc./Progress Products Company, "Progress Parade: The Newsletter of America's Finest Black-Owned, Black Managed Manufacturing Facility," Summer 1974, OICAR, Acc. 688, Box 74, ZIA–Progress Aerospace Enterprises (PAE) Publications, TUUA, 1–2; ZIA, "Memorandum to the Members of the ZIA Board of Directors; Subject: Review of Operations and Progress Report," September 17, 1975, OICAR, Acc. 688, Box 73, ZIA—Review of Operations and Progress Report, TUUA, 13–14; ZIA, "Annual Report 1975: People Make Progress, Progress Makes Products," 1976, OICAR, Acc. 688, Box 72, Zion Investment Associates Annual Reports, 1971–72, 1975, TUUA, 3; Miller, "The Progress Movement: ZIA: A Model of Capital Formation," 287; OICA-EDD, "Prospectus for the Future: Shares for Progress: A Community Investment Cooperative for Your City," n.d., 2.

21. Ford Foundation, *Minorities in Business: Ford Foundation Assistance, 1965–1975* (New York: Ford Foundation, 1976), 19–20, 23–24; "NPAED Organization Chart," *NPAED Voice of Progress*, November 1969, 2; ZIA, "1971 Annual Report," 1972, OICAR, Acc. 688, Box 72, ZIA Annual Reports, 1971–72, 1975, TUUA, 8; ZIA and ZNPCT, "Seventh Annual Report: Year Ended December 31, 1972," ibid., 12, 29; "Third Phase of OEO-PMED Training Begins Jan. 15," and "Location of NPAED Affiliates and Economic Developers," *NPAED Voice of Progress*, January 1970, 2; "Who Is Who in the Progress Movement," *NPAED Voice of Progress*, February 1970, 2; "NPAED Creates Four Regions," and "PDS," *NPAED Voice of Progress*, March 1970, 1–3; "Incorporation of PAED," *NPAED Voice of Progress*, December 1970, 4 (all *Voice of Progress* issues in OICAR, Acc. 688, Box 80, NPAED Voice of Progress Newsletters November 1969–December

1970, TUUA); ZIA, "Preliminary Prospectus," March 31, 1971, 24–25; "Opening Doors to Opportunity," 52.

22. "'Black Capitalism' at Work," 64.

23. "Opening Doors to Opportunity," 52; PAE, "No Small Business: The PAE Story; as It Appeared in: Challenge General Electric Company Missile and Space Division," Fall 1968, OICAR, Acc. 688, Box 74, ZIA–Progress Aerospace Enterprises (PAE) Publications, TUUA.

24. "Black Church Launches Space Factory," *Ebony*, November 1968, 42; "Black Business in Aerospace," *NPAED Voice of Progress*, January 1970, 4; "Opening Doors to Opportunity," 52; PAE, "No Small Business: The PAE Story; As It Appeared in Challenge General Electric Company Missile and Space Division," Fall 1968; "'Black Capitalism' at Work," 64.

25. "Black Church Launches Space Factory," November 1968, 44; "Black Business in Aerospace," January 1970, 4; "Opening Doors to Opportunity," 52.

26. PAE, "No Small Business: The PAE Story," Fall 1968, 1; "Black Business in Aerospace," January 1970, 4; PAE, "A New Dimension in Aerospace Excellence," n.d. [1972–73], OICAR, Acc. 688, Box 74, ZIA–Progress Aerospace Enterprises (PAE) Publications, TUUA, 1–2; "Opening Doors to Opportunity," 52; "Black Church Launches Space Factory," November 1968, 44; Congress, Senate, Committee on Labor And Public Welfare, *Opportunities Industrialization Centers Job Creation and Training Act, 1976: Hearing Before the Subcommittee on Employment, Poverty, and Migratory Labor*, 94th Cong., 2nd Sess., May 25, 1976, 60.

27. "'Black Capitalism' at Work," 64; OICA-EDD, "The CIC ('10–36') Plan," 6.

28. "'Black Capitalism' at Work," 64; Sullivan, *Build Brother Build*, 172–73; "Opening Doors to Opportunity," 52.

29. "From 16 Workers at Start PGM Co. Producing Over 4000 Garments a Week; New Clothes From PGM," *NPAED Voice of Progress*, February 1970, 4; "Opening Doors to Opportunity," 52.

30. "10-36 Plan Description, History and National Expansion Plans [untitled]," n.d. [March 1973], 8; Ford Foundation, *Minorities in Business*, 23.

31. "Rev. Sullivan Opens the First Our Markets," *NPAED Voice of Progress*, March 1970, 1; ZIA, "Minutes from the Board of Directors' Meeting," February 11, 1970, OICAR, Acc. 688, Box 72, ZIA Board of Directors Meeting Minutes 1970–73, TUUA, 2–3; ZIA, "Preliminary Prospectus," March 31, 1971, 19–20; ZIA, "Five Year Operating Plan 1972 through 1976," December 9, 1971, 9–10.

32. ZIA, "Preliminary Prospectus," March 31, 1971, 20–21; ZIA, "Five Year Operating Plan 1972 through 1976," December 9, 1971, 8–9; "Zion Burns . . . but Sullivan Builds On," *NPAED Voice of Progress*, December 1970, 1–2; ZIA, Board Of Directors' Meeting Minutes, October 12, 1971, OICAR, Acc. 688, Box 72, ZIA Board of Directors Meeting Minutes 1970–73, TUUA, 4–5.

33. Robert Halpern, *Rebuilding the Inner City: A History of Neighborhood Initiatives to Address Poverty in the United States* (New York: Columbia University

Press, 1995), 127–48; Sara Stoutland, "Community Development Corporations: Mission, Strategy, and Accomplishments," in *Urban Problems and Community Development,* ed. William T. Dickens and Ronald F. Ferguson (Washington, D.C.: Brookings Institution Press, 1999).

34. Robert O. Self, *American Babylon: Race and the Struggle for Postwar Oakland* (Princeton, NJ: Princeton University Press, 2003), 191–98, 233–42.

35. Sullivan's appointment was the direct result of Ralph Nader's Project for Corporate Responsibility, which had lobbied for increased minority hiring and environmental responsibility from the automaker. Leonard Sloane, "Negro in G.M. Board Ready for Challenge; Minister Stresses Role of Private Enterprise," *New York Times,* January 5, 1971, 35, 38; "A Black for G.M.'s Board," *Time,* January 18, 1971, 72.

36. Leon H. Sullivan, *Moving Mountains: The Principles and Purposes of Leon Sullivan* (Valley Forge, PA: Judson Press, 1998).

37. "A New Kind of Corporate Director," *Business Week,* May 20, 1972, 101; "The Black on GM's Board," *Time,* September 6, 1976, 55. OIC's international growth may be traced in the manuscript collection Opportunities Industrialization Centers International Records, Acc. 689, TUUA. For criticism of the Sullivan Principles, "Principles," *New Yorker,* December 22, 1980, 25–26; Manning Marable, *How Capitalism Underdeveloped Black America: Problems in Race, Political Economy, and Society* (Cambridge, MA: South End Press, 2000), 179–80.

38. Ditzen, "Dreams of Black Capitalism become Nightmarish Failures," *PB,* November 20, 1980, A1, A10.

39. ZIA, "Preliminary Prospectus," March 31, 1971, 18; William V. Downes to Philadelphia Apparel Producers Association; Re: Progress Garment Mfg., November 13, 1970, OICAR, Acc. 688, Box 75, CIC Correspondence William V. Downes 10-36 Plan Nat'l CIC Coordinator, TUUA.

40. Progress Garment Manufacturing Company, "Monthly Report: General Operations," June 5, 1971, 1–2, and October 1971, 1, both in OICAR, Acc. 688, Box 74, Progress Garment Manufacturing Co. Monthly Reports 1971, TUUA; ZIA, Board of Directors' Meeting Minutes, October 12, 1971, 3; PAE, "Progress Report of Progress Products Company," July 31, 1972, OICAR, Acc. 688, Box 74, ZIA–Progress Products Company: Progress Report 1972, TUUA, 1–2.

41. ZIA, "Five Year Operating Plan 1972 through 1976," December 9, 1971, 7–8, 12; Lucas, Tucker & Co., CPA, "ZIA and Subsidiaries Summary Findings," December 1971, OICAR, Acc. 688, Box 73, ZIA Long Range Projections 1972–1977, TUUA, 2; ZIA, "1971 Annual Report," 6; ZIA and ZNPCT, "Seventh Annual Report; Year Ended December 31, 1972," 1973, 5–6.

42. ZIA, "1971 Annual Report," 6; PAE, "A New Dimension in Aerospace Excellence," n.d. [1972–73], 1–6; "Introduction: Progress Aerospace Enterprises, Inc.," July 24, 1973, OICAR, Acc. 688, Box 74, ZIA–Progress Aerospace Enterprises (PAE) Industrial Park Open House, TUUA, 1–2.

43. "Zion Expands Plant Facilities," in Progress Aerospace Enterprises Inc. / Progress Products Company, *Progress Parade: The Newsletter of America's Finest Black-Owned, Black Managed Manufacturing Facility*, vol. I, no. 1, Summer 1973, OICAR, Acc. 688, Box 74, ZIA–Progress Aerospace Enterprises (PAE) Publications, TUUA, 4; ZIA and ZNPCT, "Seventh Annual Report; Year Ended December 31, 1972," 1973, 5.

44. Miller, "Memorandum to the Members of the ZIA Board of Directors; Subject: Operations Status Report," May 16, 1973, 3–4; "Surviving in a Risky Market," *Business Week*, October 18, 1976, 58.

45. ZIA and ZNPCT, "Seventh Annual Report; Year Ended December 31, 1972," 1973, 5; Miller, "Memorandum to the Members of the ZIA Board of Directors; Subject: Operations Status Report," May 16, 1973, 3.

46. ZIA, Board of Directors' Meeting Minutes, January 12, 1972, OICAR, Acc. 688, Box 72, ZIA Board of Directors Meeting Minutes 1970–1973, TUUA, 4–5; ZIA & ZNPCT, "Seventh Annual Report; Year Ended December 31, 1972," 1973, 7.

47. ZIA, "Minutes from the Board of Directors' Meeting," February 11, 1970, 4; Lucas, Tucker & Co., CPA, "ZIA and Subsidiaries Summary Findings," December 1971, 1; ZIA and ZNPCT, "Seventh Annual Report; Year Ended December 31, 1972," 1973, 4, 7.

48. "Surviving in a Risky Market," 58.

49. ZIA, "Preliminary Prospectus," March 31, 1971; ZIA, Board Of Directors' Meeting Minutes, October 12, 1971, 1–4; ZIA, Board Of Directors' Meeting Minutes, January 12, 1972, 2–3; ZIA, "Historical Description and Scope of the 10–36 Plan," n.d. [March 1973], OICAR, Acc. 688, Box 75, OIC-CIC 1968–1978, TUUA 2–4; PIA, "Financial Report," March 14, 1980, 1.

50. ZIA, "Preliminary Prospectus," March 31, 1971, 7–8; Miller, "The Progress Movement: ZIA—A Model of Capital Formation," 278–80.

51. ZIA and ZNPCT, "Seventh Annual Report; Year Ended December 31, 1972," 1973, 6–8.

52. ZIA, Board of Directors' Meeting Minutes, October 12, 1971, 4.

53. ZIA, "1971 Annual Report," 4–5, 7–8.

54. Ibid., 4.

55. ZIA and ZNPCT, "Seventh Annual Report; Year Ended December 31, 1972," 1973, 2–7; Miller, "Memorandum to the Members of the ZIA Board of Directors; Subject: Operations Status Report," May 16, 1973, 1. ZIA, "Memorandum to the Members of the ZIA Board of Directors; Subject: Review of Operations and Progress Report," September 17, 1975, 15.

56. Miller, "The Progress Movement: ZIA—A Model of Capital Formation," 281–82; "Miller named ZIA President," *Progress Parade: The Newsletter of America's Finest Black-Owned, Black Managed Manufacturing Facility*, Summer 1973, 1, 3; Miller, "Memorandum to the Members of the ZIA Board of Directors;

Subject: Operations Status Report," May 16, 1973, 3–4; ZIA, "Minutes from the Board of Directors' Meeting," February 11, 1970, 1; "Surviving in a Risky Market," 58; Mike Mallowe, "Mangy Days for the Lion of Zion," *PM*, October 1973, 196–97.

57. ZIA and ZNPCT, "Seventh Annual Report; Year Ended December 31, 1972," 1973, 7; "Surviving in a Risky Market," 58; Ditzen, "Dreams of Black Capitalism become Nightmarish Failures," A10.

58. Miller, "Memorandum to the Members of the ZIA Board of Directors; Subject: Operations Status Report," May 16, 1973, 2–4; "PPC Produces GM Auto Cables," *Progress Parade: The Newsletter of America's Finest Black-Owned, Black Managed Manufacturing Facility*, Summer 1973, 3.

59. "NASA Awards PAE Contract," *Progress Parade: The Newsletter Of America's Finest Black-Owned, Black Managed Manufacturing Facility*, Summer 1973, 1; Miller, "The Progress Movement: ZIA: A Model of Capital Formation," 283; "ZIA New Business Efforts Pay off Again," *Progress Parade: The Newsletter of America's Finest Black-Owned, Black Managed Manufacturing Facility*, Summer 1974, 1–2; Miller, "Memorandum to the Members of the ZIA Board of Directors; Subject: Operations Status Report," May 16, 1973, 3–4.

60. ZIA, "Memorandum to the Members of the ZIA Board of Directors; Subject: Review of Operations and Progress Report," September 17, 1975, 3–4; Miller, "The Progress Movement: ZIA: A Model of Capital Formation," 287; "Surviving in a Risky Market," 58.

61. Ditzen, "Dreams of Black Capitalism Become Nightmarish Failures," A10.

62. Miller, "The Progress Movement: ZIA: A Model of Capital Formation," 282; ZIA, "Annual Report 1975; People Make Progress, Progress Makes Products," 1976, TUUA, 13.

63. "PPC Gears Up for Banner Year; Business Added, Production Areas Now More Efficient," *Progress Parade: The Newsletter of America's Finest Black-Owned, Black Managed Manufacturing Facility*, Fall 1977, 1–2; Miller, "The Progress Movement: ZIA: A Model of Capital Formation," 285, 287.

64. "PAE Wins $2.45 Million Lock Production Contract," 1, 4, and "New Business Acquisition Rate For 1977 is Best in Company History," 3, both in *Progress Parade: The Newsletter of America's Finest Black-Owned, Black Managed Manufacturing Facility*, Fall 1977; ZIA, "Annual Report 1975; People Make Progress, Progress Makes Products," 1976, TUUA, 2; Miller, "The Progress Movement: ZIA: A Model of Capital Formation," 282.

65. George Konstandt, Arawak Consulting Corporation, "Business Evaluation Summary; Progress Investment Associates, Inc. 100-07-037," September 16, 1980, OICAR, Acc. 688, Box 73, Folder 26, TUUA, 2–3, App. 4 and 5. ZIA changed its name to Progress Investment Associates in 1977; to avoid confusion, the original name is used in the text.

66. Leon Sullivan served on the board of both Girard Bank (the main creditor) and the Pennsylvania Saving Fund Society. PIA, "Financial Report," March 14, 1980, 2–3; "Surviving in a Risky Market," 58; "The Rev. Leon H. Sullivan: He Gets No Pay from OIC," *PB*, November 16, 1980.

67. Konstandt, "Business Evaluation Summary; Progress Investment Associates, Inc.," 3–4; Ditzen, "Dreams of Black Capitalism Become Nightmarish Failures," A1, A10; Progress Investment Associates, Inc., Meeting of the Board of Directors Minutes, June 17, 1980, OICAR, Acc. 688, Box 73, 2, TUUA, 1.

68. In a desperate attempt to keep ZIA operating, Leon Sullivan raised $200,000 from such local corporate supporters as Scott Paper, Rohm & Haas, and Campbell's Soup. In some cases, executives from these companies donated money personally. Sullivan contributed $10,000. PIA, "Meeting of the Board of Directors Minutes," June 17, July 23, August 19, September 16, October 21, 1980, OICAR, Acc. 688, Box 73, 2, TUUA, 1–2, 2–4, 1–3, 2–4, 2–4, resp.; Ditzen, "Dreams of Black Capitalism Become Nightmarish Failures," A1, A10.

69. PIA, Meeting of the Board of Directors Minutes, December 16, 1980, February 17, March 17, May 19, October 20, 1981, July 22, 1982, OICAR, Acc. 688, Box 73, 2, TUUA, 2–4, 2–5, 2–4, 3–4, 2–3, 1–2, resp.

70. PIA, Meeting of the Board of Directors Minutes, September 15, 1981, February 16, March 16, May 18, July 22, 1982, OICAR, Acc. 688, Box 73, 2, TUUA, 2, 2–4, 2–3, 1–3, 1–4; PIA, "PIA Board Meeting Management Report," September 21, 1982, OICAR, Acc. 688, Box 73, 2, TUUA, 1–2.

71. Vincent Thompson, "Sullivan Celebrates 'a Dream Fulfilled,'" *PT*, August 24, 1993; Barnes, "Super Fresh Deal in Works for New Buyer, Store Remains Closed," *PT*, October 6, 1998; Ayana Jones, "City to Get 3 New Supermarkets," *PT*, October 3, 2006; Vernon Clark, "Shopping Center's Rebirth in N. Phila.," *PI*, April 7, 2007; Robert Hightower, "Progress Plaza Revitalization Unfolds," *PT*, April 20, 2007.

72. "OIC Owes $435,000 in Withholding Taxes, Gets IRS Extension," *PB*, April 30, 1969; Orrin Evans, "Nixon Promises to Support OIC, Now $1 Million in Debt," *PB*, May 22, 1969.

73. L. Stuart Ditzen, "Agency Owes $420,000 in Back Taxes to Phila.," *PB*, November 18, 1980; Ditzen, "Ritter: We Were Missionaries," *PB*, November 19, 1980; Antosh, "Auditors Provide Warnings, but U.S. Funds Still Pour In," *PB*, November 18, 1980; Antosh and Ditzen, "A Giant Jobs Program Flounders," *PB*, November 16, 1980.

74. Charles McNamara, "The Power Crisis: In a City with a Lame Duck Mayor and a Tired Establishment, Who's Running the Store?" *PM*, November 1971, 144.

75. Antosh and Ditzen, "A Giant Jobs Program Flounders," *PB*, November 16, 1980; OIC, "1980 Annual Report," 16; OIC National Institute, "'Helping the

OICs to Help Themselves': A Final Report of the Opportunities Industrialization Centers' National Institute to the U.S. Department of Labor and the Office of Economic Opportunity," May 1970, OICAR, Acc. 688, Box 24, OIC Program Descriptions, TUUA, 29.

76. Antosh, "Data on Job Placement Looks Good . . . on Paper," Antosh, "Auditors Provide Warnings, but U.S. Funds Still Pour In," and "Feds Make Blunt Demand: Rent Too High, Pay It Back," PB, November 18, 1980; Gunter David, "OIC Gets a Big Bill from U.S.; Labor Dept. Orders $1,720,728 Returned," PB, April 19, 1981.

77. Antosh and Ditzen, "A Giant Jobs Program Flounders"; Claude Lewis, "Story Concerning OIC Is One That Had to Be Told," PB, November 19, 1980; Philip Lentz, "Rev. Sullivan: Bulletin's 'Not Going to Trample on Me!'" PB, November 17, 1980; Kendall Wilson, "Sullivan Vows to Fight Charges against OIC," PT, November 18, 1980; Wilson, "Sullivan Cools Talk of Bulletin Boycott," PT, November 25, 1980; "Leaders Rip Bulletin OIC Stories," PB, November 25, 1980; Bob Perkins, "He's in Rev. Sullivan's Corner," editorial, PT, November 25, 1980; John T. Acton, "There Was No Thievery," PB, November 26, 1980; Mamie J. Fains, "Unjust Attack on OIC," PB, November 28, 1980.

78. Elmer Smith and Michael E. Ruane, "Sullivan: Let's Fix OIC Ills; He Rejects Demands to March on Bulletin," PB, November 24, 1980; Gunter David and Lou Antosh, "Seek Help and Reorganize OIC, Phila. Businessmen Tell Sullivan," PB, November 25, 1980; David, "28 OIC Groups Not Doing Job, Panel Reports," PB, March 22, 1981; David, "OIC Gets a Big Bill from U.S.; Labor Dept. Orders $1,720,728 Returned."

79. O'Reilly, "New Leader Vows to Refresh a Helping Agency," PI, July 18, 2000. For urban policy retrenchment, O'Connor, "Swimming against the Tide," 113–15. For a 1998 list of "active and developing" OIC centers, Leon H. Sullivan, Moving Mountains: The Principles and Purposes of Leon Sullivan (Valley Forge, PA: Judson Press, 1998), 292–93.

80. In its original OIC form, CET had close ties to the United Farmworkers campaigns of the 1960s and 1970s; it still focuses primarily on the Chicano population. Harrison and Weiss, Workforce Development Networks: Community-Based Organizations and Regional Alliances (Thousand Oaks, CA: Sage Publications, Inc., 1998), 50–70; Harrison with Weiss and Jon Gant, Building Bridges: Community Development Corporations and the World of Employment Training: A Report to the Ford Foundation (New York: Ford Foundation, 1995), 19–20.

81. Avis Vidal, "CDCs as Agents of Neighborhood Change: The State of the Art," in W. Dennis Keating, Norman Krumholz, and Philip Star, eds., Revitalizing Urban Neighborhoods (Lawrence, KS: University of Kansas Press, 1996); Dickens and Ferguson, eds., Urban Problems and Community Development; Alexander von Hoffman, House by House, Block by Block: The Rebirth of America's Urban Neighborhoods (New York: Oxford University Press, 2003).

Chapter Seven

1. Martin Herman, "U.S. Orders Quota Plan Here for Negroes in Building Jobs," *PB*, June 27, 1969. For the revised plan, Arthur A. Fletcher, "Memorandum to Heads of All Agencies," June 27, 1969, in Joseph F. Fulton, *Equal Employment Opportunity in the Construction Industry: The Philadelphia Plan, with Related Documents* (Washington, D.C.: Library of Congress, Legislative Reference Service, 1970), 9–11, A. 11–25.

2. Bernard McCormick, "The Hour of the Hard Hat," *PM*, November 1970, 81, 192.

3. In 1964, the Commission on Human Relations (CHR) found that 65 percent of the construction workers employed at the site of the city's new Municipal Services Building were black, but that almost all worked as unskilled laborers. Joseph B. Meranze, "Negro Employment in the Construction Industry," Herbert R. Northrup and Richard L. Rowan, eds., *The Negro and Employment Opportunity: Problems and Practices* (Ann Arbor: Bureau of Industrial Relations, Graduate School of Business Administration, University of Michigan, 1967), 204–5; "Jim Crow's Sweetheart Contract," *PM*, February 1963; Matthew J. Countryman, *Up South: Civil Rights and Black Power in Philadelphia* (Philadelphia: University of Pennsylvania Press, 2006), 64–65, 130–32; Thomas J. Sugrue, "Affirmative Action from Below: Civil Rights, the Building Trades, and the Politics of Racial Equality in the Urban North, 1945–1969," *Journal of American History* 91:1 (June 2004): 155–59.

4. Jim Crow's Sweetheart Contract," *PM*, February 1963; Countryman, *Up South*, 130–32; Sugrue, "Affirmative Action from Below," 159–60.

5. Countryman, *Up South*, 132–48; Hannah Lees, "Philadelphia, Pennsylvania," *Reporter*, July 4, 1963, 20; Gaeton Fonzi, "Cecil Storms In!!!," *PM*, July 1963, 22–23.

6. Countryman, "*Up South*, 144–54, 164–71.

7. John Skrentny, *The Ironies of Affirmative Action: Politics, Culture, and Justice in America* (Chicago: University of Chicago Press, 1996), 133–39; Hugh Davis Graham, *The Civil Rights Era: Origins and Development of National Policy 1960–1972* (New York: Oxford University Press, 1990), 95–99, 125–62, 282; Sugrue, "Affirmative Action from Below," 160–70.

8. "Commencement Address at Howard University: 'To Fulfill These Rights,' June 4, 1965," *Public Papers of the Presidents of theUnited States: Lyndon B. Johnson, 1965* (Washington, D.C.: GPO, 1966) 2:636.

9. Graham, *Civil Rights Era*, 184–89, 284–88; Skrentny, *Ironies of Affirmative Action*, 133–39.

10. "To: All Members of the Philadelphia Executive Board; From: Warren P. Phelan; Subject: Philadelphia Pre-Award Plan Starting Date," October 27, 1967, FCR, Acc. 626, Box 34, 1-Philadelphia Plan, 1967–70, 1973–76, TUUA, 11;

Graham, *Civil Rights Era*, 278–90; Thomas J. Sugrue, "The Tangled Roots of Affirmative Action," *American Behavioral Scientist* 41:7 (April 1998): 886–97.

11. "To: All Members of the Philadelphia Executive Board," October 27, 1967, 2, 6; Graham, *The Civil Rights Era*, 287–90.

12. "To: All Members of the Philadelphia Executive Board," October 27, 1967, cover letter, 5–6; Nicholas Stroh, "U.S. to Require Builders to Hire Negroes," *PB*, October 26, 1967.

13. Martin Herman, "U.S. Clears Drexel Project after Accord on Negro Jobs," *PB*, 26 April 1968; "Negro Hiring Issue Settled at Institute," *PB*, May 2, 1968.

14. Martin Herman, "Engineers Union Raps U.S. Decree, Says It Has Sought Negro Members," *PB*, April 28, 1968; Department of Labor (hereafter DOL), *Public Hearing: The Philadelphia Plan, August 26–28, 1969* (Washington: Department of Labor, 1969), 165–66, 189.

15. Martin Herman, "Agreement is Reached on Hiring of Negroes for Highway Plan," *PB*, August 1, 1968.

16. "Extra Negroes to be Added on Mint Job," *PB*, April 30, 1968; Martin Herman, "2 of 11 Negroes Qualify for Jobs at Mint; Union Protests 'Union Busting," *PB*, May 3, 1968.

17. Martin Herman, "3 of 11 Negroes Pass Tests for Mint Jobs," *PB*, May 3, 1968.

18. Herman, "2 of 11 Negroes Qualify for Jobs at Mint."

19. Ibid.; "25 Electricians Quit Mint Job Over Negroes," *PB*, May 7, 1968.

20. Martin Herman, "Building Unions Vote to Take More Negroes," *PB*, 2 May 1968; Herman, "Engineers Union Raps U.S. Decree; "Extra Negroes to be Added on Mint Job";

21. DOL, *Public Hearing*, 260–61.

22. "Union Charges 3 Whites Were Denied Mint Jobs," *PB*, May 7, 1968; Martin Herman, "2 Negro Electricians Contest Firing from Mint Job," *PB*, June 7, 1968.

23. Orrin Evans, "'End Poverty,' Abernathy Demands Here," *PB*, May 15, 1968.

24. William Forsythe, "U.S. to Dedicate Mint on Mall This Week," *PB*, September 15, 1968.

25. Graham, *The Civil Rights Era*, 293–97.

26. Douglas Bedell, "'Philadelphia Plan Beginning to Work," *PB*, September 24, 1968.

27. "Philadelphia Plan Topping Hiring Goals, Labor Agency Says," *WSJ*, September 11, 1970; CEJO, "For Immediate Release: CEJO Calls Federal 'Minority Hiring' Report False," October 16, 1970, FCR, Acc. 626, Box 34, 6-Press Releases, 1969–70, 73, 75, TUUA; DOL, *Public Hearing*, 185–86.

28. Herman, "Building Unions Vote to Take More Negroes," *PB*, May 2, 1968.

29. Kos Semonski, "Trade Unions Agree on Plan of Recruitment," *PB*, May 8, 1968; "Promising Job Project Begins," *PB*, May 12, 1968.

30. Martin Herman, "Unions Pick 65 Negro Apprentices in 8 Months," *PB*, April 27, 1969.

31. "Don't Miss This Big Opportunity," *PT*, January 7, 1969; Herman, "Unions Pick 65 Negro Apprentices in 8 Months"; DOL, *Public Hearing*, 17.

32. CHR, "City Administration's Philadelphia Plan," FCR, Acc. 626, Box 34, 1-Philadelphia Plan, 1967–70, 1973–76, TUUA, 1; CHR, *From This Day Forward,* 1968–69 annual report (Philadelphia: City of Philadelphia, 1969), 12; Richard J. Levin, CHR memo to School Board members and administrators, August 1, 1968, FCR, Acc. 626, Box 34, 1-Philadelphia Plan, 1967–70, 1973–76, TUUA; "The Two Philadelphia Plans," *PB*, August 17, 1968.

33. CHR, "City Administration's Philadelphia Plan," 1.

34. "The 'Two Philadelphia Plans,'" *PB*, August 17, 1968.

35. CHR, *From This Day Forward*, 12.

36. Brother Daniel Bernian to Bishop Willard D. Pendleton, October 18, 1968, FCR, Acc. 626, Box 34, 1-Philadelphia Plan, 1967–70, 1973–76, TUUA; Gaylord P. Harnwell to Brother Bernian, November 5, 1968, ibid.; Clarence Farmer to Maurice Fagan, August 6, 1968, ibid.

37. Orrin Evans, "Urban League Here Finds 'Encouraging Aspects' in Race Relations in 1968," *PB*, January 3, 1969; DOL, *Public Hearing*, 84.

38. Bedell, "'Philadelphia Plan Beginning to Work"; Katrina Dyke, "Dilworth Renews Pledge to Adopt Phila. Plan," *PB*, July 23, 1968; John Gillespie, "Bias Agency Prods Schools; Dilworth Calls Rules Vague," *PB*, August 13, 1968; "For Immediate Release: Community Groups Boycott the 'Philadelphia Plan' Hearings," September 13, 1968, FCR, Acc. 626, Box 34, 1-Philadelphia Plan, 1967–70, 1973–76, TUUA; "Shedd Cancels Hearing on Hiring Plan," *PB*, September 15, 1968; Gillespie, "1,200 Storm Hearing to Protest Proposal for Busing White Pupils from Northeast," *PB*, September 19, 1968.

39. "Don't Miss This Big Opportunity," *PT*, 7 January 1969; "Operating Engineers Seek Apprentices," *PT*, January 28, 1969; John Brantley Wilder, "Shedd Gives Second Jim Crow Union the Heave-Ho Treatment," *PT*, March 8, 1969; Wilder, "Detail Methods Unions Use to Bypass Negroes," *PT*, March 22, 1969; "Where to Go for Jobs As Apprentices," *PT*, March 8, 1969; "Union Opens Door to Black Youth," *PT*, June 3, 1969; Wilder, "Apprenticeship Programs Opened to Negroes by Two Craft Unions," *PT*, June 28, 1969.

40. "School System Is Urged to Support Men Seeking Recognition for Union," *PT*, September 6, 1969; Lawrence Geller, "A. B. Dick Strikers March on City Hall," *PT*, September 16, 1969.

41. Ibid.; "A. B. Dick Company Off 'List'," *PT*, September 20, 1969.

42. Lawrence Geller, "Non-Bias Pact Agreed to by Dick Company," *PT*, October 11, 1969.

43. Urban Coalition, "Emergency Convocation: The Urban Coalition; Washington, D.C., the Shoreham Hotel," September 24, 1967, JLCR, Acc. 480, Box 29, Urban Coalition 1968, TUUA; Robert B. Semple, Jr., "Coalition Urges U.S. Act to Spur Jobs in the Cities," *New York Times*, August 25, 1967, 1; Marjorie Hunter, "Senate Unit Votes $2.8-Billion Plan for Ghetto Jobs," *New York Times*, August 30, 1967, 1.

44. Philadelphia Urban Coalition (Urban Coalition), "Declaration of Principles, Goals, and Commitments" [February 17, 1968], JLCR, Acc. 480, Box 29, Urban Coalition 1968, TUUA; Alfred Klimcke, "Urban 'Coalition' of 200 Tours City Poverty Pockets," *PI*, February 16, 1968; Klimcke, "Help for Needy Is Pledged by Civic Leaders," *PI*, February 16, 1968; Urban Coalition, "Board of Directors," n.d., JLCR, Acc. 480, Box 29, Urban Coalition 1970–71, TUUA; Charles W. Bowser to Messrs. Herman C. Wrice and Robert O. Fickes and All Members of All Task Forces, July 8, 1968, JLCR, Acc. 480, Box 29, Urban Coalition 1968, TUUA; Urban Coalition, "Action '70 (annual report)," 1971, ACWAR, Acc. 519, Box 22, Urban Coalition (1968–February 1970), TUUA, 35.

45. Richard L. Olanoff, Walter H. Powell, Thomas J. Ritter, and James Kelch to Alex Wollod, February 29, 1968, JLCR, Acc. 480, Box 29, Urban Coalition 1968, TUUA (and attached lists); Urban Coalition, "Board of Directors Meeting Minutes," March 12, 1970, ACWAR, Acc. 519, Box 22, Urban Coalition (March 1970–May 1970), TUUA, 3; Urban Coalition, "Action 70 (annual report)," 30–33; Urban Coalition, "Board of Director's Meeting; Exhibit E: Report on Task Forces," September 17, 1970, ACWAR, Acc. 519, Box 22, Urban Coalition September 1970–December 1970, TUUA, 1.

46. Urban Coalition, "Summary of Manpower Task Force Workshop," February 16, 1968, JLCR, Acc. 480, Box 29, Urban Coalition 1968, TUUA; Alex Wollod to Richard L. Olanoff, March 4, 1968, JLCR, ibid.; Philadelphia Urban Coalition, "Statement of Principles, Goals and Commitments of the Philadelphia Urban Coalition," July 8, 1968, JLCR, ibid., 2.

47. Urban Coalition, "Action 70 (annual report)," 3–4; James Crummett, "Philadelphia Urban Coalition," October 1969, GPC, Box 791-4 (vol. 4), TUUA, 5–6; Urban Coalition, "Board of Directors Meeting Minutes," January 12, 1970, ACWAR, Acc. 519, Box 22, Urban Coalition (1968–February 1970), TUUA, 3–4; "Model Cities Minority Contractors Assistance Program Revolving Loan Fund; Loans Outstanding," June 10, 1970, ACWAR, Acc. 519, Box 22, Urban Coalition (June 1970–August 1970), TUUA.

48. Urban Coalition, "News Release," August 17, 1970, ACWAR, Acc. 519, Box 22, Sec.-Treas.Phila. Urban Coalition (June 1970–August 1970), TUUA, 1–5; Urban Coalition, "Action 70 (annual report)," 3–4. The Action Construction Team included volunteers "from business, finance and industry, government, education and urban affairs." Urban Coalition, "News Release," July 5, 1970, ACWAR, Acc. 519, Box 22, Sec.-Treas. Phila. Urban Coalition (June

1970–August 1970), TUUA, 1–2; Crummett, "Philadelphia Urban Coalition," 7.

49. Urban Coalition, "News Release," April 18, 1972, FCR, Acc. 626, Box 33, F 19: PFC-CEJO-P / A Manpower Policy 1971–74, TUUA, 1–7.

50. Urban Coalition, "Board of Directors Meeting Minutes," January 12, 1970, 4; Urban Coalition, "Board of Directors Meeting Minutes," June 11, 1970, ACWAR, Acc. 519, Box 22, Urban Coalition June 1970–August 1970, TUUA, 5; Urban Coalition, "Board of Directors Meeting Minutes," September 17, 1970, 2, "Exhibit C," 1, "Exhibit F," 1; Urban Coalition, "News Release," May 3, 1970, ACWAR, Acc. 519, Box 22, Sec.-Treas. Phila. Urban Coalition (March 1970–May 1970), TUUA; Urban Coalition, "Action 70 (annual report)," 5, 16, 22; Crummett, "Philadelphia Urban Coalition," 6.

51. Urban Coalition, "Board of Director's Meeting; Exhibit E: Report on Task Forces," September 17, 1970, 2; Joseph Harvey, Urban Coalition Manpower Task Force Chairman to James C. McConnon, SEPTA Chairman, October 9, 1970, ACWAR, Acc. 519, Box 22, Sec.-Treas. Phila. Urban Coalition (Sept. 1970–Dec. 1970), TUUA; Urban Coalition, "News Release," October 12, 1970, ibid., 1–2; Urban Coalition, "Executive Committee Meeting Minutes," March 23, 1970, ACWAR, Acc. 519, Box 22, Urban Coalition March–May 1970, TUUA, 6–7; Urban Coalition, "Board of Directors Meeting Minutes," June 11, 1970, 8; Urban Coalition, "News Release," August 5, 1970, ACWAR, ibid.; "Help Wanted, Needed," editorial, *PI*, August 5, 1970.

52. Arthur A. Fletcher and John L. Wilks, "Order to: Heads of All Agencies," September 23, 1969, in Fulton, *Equal Employment Opportunity*, 9–11, A. 26–49.

53. "The Philadelphia Plan: Half a Loaf at Least," *WP*, January 14, 1970; Graham, *Civil Rights Era*, 326–29; "Elmer Staats to Labor Secretary," August 5, 1969, in Fulton, *Equal Employment Opportunity*, 12–20, A. 50–66.

54. Ibid., and "John Mitchell to Labor Secretary," September 22, 1969, in Fulton, *Equal Employment Opportunity*, A. 67–86.

55. "Clarence Farmer to Elmer Staats," June 11, 1969, quoted in Graham, 540; also, 330. "8 Groups Plan to Test Action on Phila. Plan," *PI*, March 28, 1969; Skrentny, *Ironies of Affirmative Action*, 195–204; "'Philadelphia Plan' is Back in Business, Thanks to the Efforts of Bowser, Burress and Farmer," *PT*, June 14, 1969.

56. "Democratic Coalition Urged U.S. to Enforce Equal Job Program Here," *PT*, September 2, 1969; Lawrence Rutter and Marjorie Satinsky, "The Rise and Fall of the Liberal Establishment," *PM*, September 1970, 76, 115; Matthew J. Countryman, "'From Protest to Politics'": Community Control and Black Independent Politics in Philadelphia, 1965–1984," *Journal of Urban History* 32:6 (September 2006): 813–61.

57. Ben Stahl, "To: James De. Boyle; Re: The 'Philadelphia Plan,'" July 7, 1969, JLCR, Acc. 480, Box 19, AFL-CIO HRDI 1969–1970; Ben Stahl to James De. Boyle, "Philadelphia Plan," July 15, 1969, ibid.

58. CEJO, "For Immediate Release," September 12, 1969, FCR, Acc. 626, Box 34, 5-Press Releases, 1948–50, 1964–65, 1969, TUUA; "Building Trades Offered Plan on Minority Jobs," *PI*, September 13, 1969.

59. Ben Stahl to H. Louis Evert, September 16, 1969, JLCR, Acc. 480, Box 19, AFL-CIO HRDI 1969–70.

60. DOL, *Public Hearing*, 120, 277.

61. Ibid., 250, 253–54; Ben Stahl, "To: Local Union Officials; Subject: Support of Summer Hiring Program for Needy School Youth," May 1, 1969, JLCR, Acc. 480, Box 19, AFL-CIO HRDI 1969–70, 2.

62. DOL, *Public Hearing*, 258–59.

63. Ibid., 65,79.

64. Ibid., 168–69, 174.

65. Ibid., 180–81.

66. Ibid., 285.

67. Ibid., 166, 188, 285.

68. Annelise Orleck, *Storming Caesar's Palace: How Black Mothers Fought Their Own War on Poverty* (Boston: Beacon Press, 2006); Felicia Kornbluh, *The Battle for Welfare Rights: Politics and Poverty in Modern America* (Philadelphia: University of Pennsylvania Press, 2007).

69. Damon Stetson, "Negro Groups Step up Militancy in Drive to Join Building Unions," *NYT*, August 28, 1969; Seth King, "Whites in Chicago Disrupt Hearing," *NYT*, September 26, 1969.

70. Robert Maynard, "Unions' Job Policies Defended by Meany," *WP*, September 25, 1969; "Union Leader Raps Fair Job Plan as Unfair," *PT*, September 23, 1969; George Meany, *Labor and the Philadelphia Plan* (Washington, D.C.: AFL-CIO, 1970).

71. John Herbers, "Gains Are Made in Federal Drive for Negro Hiring," *NYT*, January 25, 1970.

72. Donald Janson, "Labor Department Welcomes Contractor's Suit Testing Legality of Philadelphia Plan," *NYT*, January 8, 1970.

73. Office of the City Representative, "News Release," January 30, 1970, FCR, Acc. 626, Box 34, 2-Philadelphia Plan, 1967–70, 1973–76, TUUA; Martin Herman, "O'Neill Quits Building Trade Council Post," *PB*, November 21, 1968.

74. Donald Janson, "U.S. Judge Upholds Controversial Philadelphia Plan to Increase Hiring of Minorities in Building Industry," *NYT*, March 15, 1970; Janson, "Minority Hiring Upheld by Court," *NYT*, April 24, 1971; "Legality of Philadelphia Plan Is Upheld by Circuit Court," *PT*, May 4, 1971; Fred Graham, "High Court Lets Hiring Plan Stand," *NYT*, October 13, 1971.

75. USCCR, *Federal Civil Rights Enforcement Effort: A Report of the United States Commission on Civil Rights 1971* (Washington, D.C.: GPO, 1971), 64–65; "Schultz Warns 18 Cities to End Bias in Building Jobs," *NYT*, February 10, 1970; "Schultz Orders a 'Washington Plan' for Minorities," *WP*, June 2, 1970; Byron

Calamie, "Labor Department Setting Up Unit to Spur Local Solutions to Construction Job Bias," *WSJ*, July 6, 1970.

76. "Philadelphia Plan Fails Its Early Tests," *NYT*, May 3, 1970; Paul Delaney, "Nixon Plan for Negro Jobs in Construction Is Lagging," *NYT*, July 20, 1970. For OFCC's early compliance procedures, John L. Wilks, "Memorandum to: All Contract Compliance Officers; Subject: Implementation of the Revised Philadelphia Plan (Philadelphia 5–County Area), March 4, 1970, FCR, Acc. 626, Box 34, 2-Philadelphia Plan, 1967–70, 1973–76, TUUA.

77. "U.S. Group Here Checks on Phila. Plan Compliance," *PB*, August 25, 1970; "Contractors Top Goals of Phila. Plan," *PB*, September 11, 1970; CEJO, "For Immediate Release: CEJO Calls Federal 'Minority Hiring' Report False," FCR, Acc. 626, Box 34, 6-Press Releases, 1969–70, 73, 75, TUUA.

78. Ben Stahl to William Becker, October 21, 1970, JLCR, Acc. 480, Box 19, AFL-CIO HRDI 1969–1970.

79. "Philadelphia Plan Fails Its Early Tests," *NYT*, May 3, 1970.

80. USCCR, *Federal Civil Rights Enforcement Effort*, 67; "HUD and HEW Move against Contractors over Minority Hiring," *WSJ*, July 10, 1970; "U.S. Will Terminate a Contract for Failure to Hire Negroes," *NYT*, August 20, 1970; "Penna. Contractors Barred, No 'Minority' Men Hired," *PB*, September 18, 1971.

81. William C. Gutman and H. Louis Evert to Peter J. Brennan, October 12, 1973, FCR, Acc. 626, Box 34, 1-Philadelphia Plan, 1967–70, 1973–76, TUUA.

82. It had already been applied in the mandatory Washington Plan. DOL, "Extension of Philadelphia Plan to Cover Private Construction Announced," February 19, 1971, FCR, Acc. 626, Box 34, 1-Philadelphia Plan, 1967–70, 1973–76, TUUA; "Urban Coalition gets $648,000 to Train And Place 180 Construction Tradesmen," *PT*, February 20, 1971; Ben Stahl, "To: Philadelphia Area HRDI Advisory Council Members; Subject: Report of Activities in Greater Philadelphia," February 1971, JLCR, Acc. 480, Box 19, AFL-CIO HRDI 1971–1972, 3; Gutman and Evert to Brennan, October 12, 1973, 1.

83. DOL, Untitled News Release, December 28, 1973, FCR, Acc. 626, Box 34, 1-Philadelphia Plan, 1967–70, 1973–76, TUUA; Gutman and Evert to Brennan, October 12, 1973.

84. DOL, Untitled News Release, December 28, 1973, FCR, Acc. 626, Box 34, 1-Philadelphia Plan, 1967–70, 1973–76, TUUA.

85. "232 Area Firms Charged with Racial Bias," *PT*, April 14, 1973.

86. DOL, *Public Hearing*, 84–85.

87. Ibid., 282

88. Stahl to Evert, September 16, 1969, 2.

89. DOL, *Public Hearing*, 352.

90. Ben Stahl, "To: Philadelphia Area HRDI Advisory Council Members; Subject: Report of Activities," June and July 1970, JLC, Acc. 480, Box 19, AFL-CIO HRDI 1969–1970, 3; Stahl, "To: Philadelphia Area HRDI Advisory Council

Members; Subject: Report of Activities—in Greater Philadelphia," August 1970, JLC, Acc. 480, Box 19, AFL-CIO HRDI 1969–1970, 1.

91. Ben Stahl, HRDI, AFL-CIO, "Report of Activities—October 1971" [November 1971], JLC, Acc. 480, Box 19, AFL-CIO HRDI 1971–1972, 1.

Chapter Eight

1. S. A. Paolantonio, *Frank Rizzo: The Last Big Man in Big City America* (Philadelphia: Camino Books, Inc, 1993), 85–104; Conrad Weiler, *Philadelphia: Neighborhood, Authority, and the Urban Crisis* (New York: Praeger Publishers, 1974), 192–205.

2. The GPM initially supported Rizzo's tactics as Police Commissioner; their opposition to Tate rested on political and fiscal considerations. Many of the liberal reformers, however, opposed the new police commissioner from the beginning. Carolyn Adams et al., *Philadelphia: Neighborhoods, Division, and Conflict in a Postindustrial City* (Philadelphia: Temple University Press, 1991), 126–27, 140–41; Adams, *The Politics of Capital Investment: the Case of Philadelphia* (Albany: State University of New York Press, 1988), 47–49.

3. Charles McNamara, "The Power Crisis," *PM*, November 1971, 92; Lou Antosh and Peter H. Binzen, "Business Leadership Fractured; Once-Powerful GPM Turns Flabby," in *Philadelphia in the Seventies: A Climate for Growth or Decay? A Bulletin Team Effort 5-Week Study* (reprint of *Philadelphia Bulletin* series), October 1972, GPC 648-10, TUUA.

4. U.S. Department of Commerce, Bureau of the Census, *City and County Data Books* [1967 and 1972] (Washington, D.C.: United States Government Printing Office, 1967, 1972); Adams et al., *Philadelphia*, 27.

5. Walter D'Alessio, interviewed by Walter M. Phillips, June 7, 1977, transcript, POHP, Box 3, 12.

6. James H. J. Tate to John P. Bracken, Esq., February 18, 1970, DC-IDPF, RG 64.18, Box A-5193, PIDC, CA; Tate to Harry S. Galfand, February 18, 1970, DC-IDPF, ibid.

7. David G. Davis, "Memo to S. Harry Galfand; New Directions For PIDC," February 25, 1970, DC-IDPF, RG 64.18, Box A-5193, PIDC, CA, cover sheet, 1–5, and notes; Davis, "Memo to S. Harry Galfand; New Directions For PIDC," February 26, 1970, DC-IDPF, ibid.

8. John P. Bracken to James H. J. Tate, February 20, 1970, MCF, RG 60-2.5, Box PRSC 42,702, Phila. Industrial Development Corp., CA.

9. The difference between Philadelphia and other areas was actually not particularly large, with 58 percent of the regional labor force in services, compared to 62.5 percent in the nation's seven other largest metropolitan areas. Economic Research Associates (ERA), "A Program for Developing the Service Sector in Philadelphia: Prepared for the Philadelphia Industrial Development Corpora-

tion," July 1970, MCF, RG 60-2.5, Box PRSC 42,702, Philadelphia Industrial Development Corporation, CA, i–ii; Bracken to Tate, February 20, 1970; Davis, "Memo to S. Harry Galfand," February 25, 1970 [i].

10. They also suggested that the corporation seek changes in state industrial assistance laws to permit low-interest financing for service sector projects. ERA, "A Program for Developing the Service Sector in Philadelphia," i–v, 20–21.

11. Desmond Ryan, "PIDC to Aid Growth of Service Industries," *PI*, February 18, 1971; Office of the Mayor, "News Release: Remarks by Mayor James H. J. Tate, PIDC Luncheon, Bellevue-Stratford Hotel," February 17, 1971, DC-BSF, RG 64.18, Box A-5197, PIDC 1970–74, CA, 2.

12. Douglas D. Gill, "City Will Woo Service Industries as PIDC Program Gets Underway," *PB*, February 24, 1971.

13. PIDC, *Annual Reports*, 1971–76, GPMR, Acc. 294, 296, 307, 311, Box 6A, Garment Industry Development, 1973, TUUA; PIDC, "Minutes of the Meeting of the Board of Directors of the Philadelphia Industrial Development Corporation," June 15, 1971, MCF, RG 60-2.5, Box A-3837, Philadelphia Industrial Development Corp., CA.

14. PIDC, "Minutes of the Meeting of the Board of Directors," June 15, 1971, 2; PIDC, "Minutes of the Meeting of the Board of Directors of the Philadelphia Industrial Development Corporation; Commercial Development, Pollution Control Equipment," PIDC fact sheets, October 19, 1971, MCF, RG 60-2.5, Box A-3837, Philadelphia Industrial Development Corp., CA; PIDC, *Annual Reports*, 1971–76; PIDC, "25th Anniversary Annual Report; 1983," Free Library of Philadelphia, Government Documents Collection, Cities P53–1320.

15. Between 1972 and 1982, Philadelphia lost 1,030 manufacturing firms and experienced a decline in total manufacturing jobs from 202,600 to 125,000. Similar percentage drops occurred in the smaller retail and wholesale sectors. Only the services sector saw an increase in employment (66,623 to 85,619) despite a drop in the number of establishments from 12,694 to 7,352. U.S. Department of Commerce, Bureau of the Census, *City and County Data Books, 1972, 1982* (Washington, D.C.: United States Government Printing Office, 1972, 1983). Overall employment in the city fell from 936,800 in 1969 to 805,900 in 1980 (up from a low of 790,300 in 1977). Carolyn Teich Adams, "The Flight of Jobs and Capital: Prospects for Grassroots Action," in John C. Raines, Lenora E. Berson, and David McI. Grace, eds., *Community and Capital in Conflict: Plant Closings and Job Loss* (Philadelphia: Temple University Press, 1982), 4; Adams et al., *Philadelphia*, 38–48.

16. PIDC, "Analysis of Real Property Transactions Financed through PIDC," n.d. [1975], GPPR, Acc. 612, Box 12, PIDC Annual Report (1973–76), TUUA, 14; PIDC, *Annual Reports*, 1972–76, GPMR, Acc. 294, 296, 307, 311, Box 6A, Garment Industry Development, 1973, TUUA; PIDC, "25th Anniversary Annual Report; 1983," 6.

17. Robert B. Semple, "Signing of Model Cities Bill Ends Long Struggle to Keep It Alive," *NYT*, November 4, 1964, 1; Charles M. Haar, *Between the Idea And the Reality: A Study in the Origin, Fate and Legacy of the Model Cities Program* (Boston: Little, Brown and Company, 1975); Nelson Lichtenstein, *The Most Dangerous Man in Detroit: Walter Reuther and the Fate of American Labor* (New York: Basic Books, 1995), 402–3; Irving Bernstein, *Guns or Butter: The Presidency of Lyndon Johnson* (New York: Oxford University Press, 1996), 458–60; Alice O'Connor, "Swimming against the Tide: A Brief History of Federal Policy in Poor Communities," in William T. Dickens and Ronald F. Ferguson, eds., *Urban Problems and Community Development* (Washington, D.C.: Brookings Institution Press, 1999), 104–5.

18. Bernstein, *Guns or Butter*, 464–68; O'Connor, "Swimming against the Tide," 105.

19. Committee on Citizen Participation, "Minutes," January 30, 1967, reprinted in Patrick J. McLaughlin, "Application to the Department of Housing and Urban Development by the Honorable James H. J. Tate, Mayor, City of Philadelphia, for a Grant to Plan a Comprehensive City Demonstration Project," March 3, 1967, GPC, Box 258-12, TUUA, IV:13; Erasmus Kloman, "Citizen Participation in the Philadelphia Model Cities Program: Retrospect and Prospect," *Public Administration Review* 32, special issue (September 1972): 402–3.

20. "The View from City Hall," *Public Administration Review* 32, special issue (September 1972): 390–91; Semple, "Signing of Model Cities Bill Ends Long Struggle."

21. Economic Advisory Council (EAC), "Minutes," November 23, 1966, KRPP, Acc. 202, Box 4, EAC, TUUA, 4; EAC, "Minutes," January 3, 1967, ibid., 2; "The View from City Hall," 391; Kos Semonski, "Tate Picks 2 to Direct Bid for Funds to Fight Blight," *PB*, January 13, 1967.

22. North City Area Wide Council (AWC), "Maximum Feasible Manipulation (as told to Sherry R. Arnstein)," *Public Administration Review* 32, special issue (September 1972): 378–79; "The View from City Hall," 390–391; Committee on Citizen Participation, "Minutes," January 30, 1967 and February 2, 1967, reprinted in McLaughlin, "Application to the Department of Housing and Urban Development," March 3, 1967, IV:12–15; Economic Advisory Council, "Minutes," November 23, 1966, KRPP, Acc. 202, Box 4, EAC, TUUA, 3.

23. McLaughlin, "Application to the Department of Housing and Urban Development," March 3, 1967, II:29, 34–36,43; "The View from City Hall," 391.

24. McLaughlin, "Application to the Department Of Housing and Urban Development," March 3, 1967, II:45–47.

25. Ibid., V:8,10; The Area-Wide Council for Participation in the Model Cities Program, "General Meeting, Minutes," March 16, 1967, ULR, URB 16/V, Box 24, 86, TUUA; Robert McMullin, "Subject: Model Cities Planning in Philadelphia," March 10, 1967, ibid.

26. McLaughlin, "Application to the Department of Housing and Urban Development," March 3, 1967, I:17, V:1–13; Kos Semonski, "15 Named to Oversee Model Cities Program," *PB*, February 9, 1967.

27. Economic Advisory Council, "Minutes," January 3, 1967, 2–3.

28. McLaughlin, "Application to the Department of Housing and Urban Development," March 3, 1967, I:7; City of Philadelphia, *Community Renewal Program: Major Policies and Proposals* (Philadelphia: City of Philadelphia, February 1967), 1.

29. McLaughlin, "Application to the Department of Housing and Urban Development," March 3, 1967, I:8–12, II:53–54; EAC, "Minutes," November 23, 1966 (2–4), January 3, 1967 (3), and April 24, 1967 (3), KRPP, Acc. 202, Box 4, EAC, TUUA. Members of the advisory council later publicly criticized the program for not adopting an exclusive focus on jobs. "Poor Must Be Given 'Real Power' in Programs for Betterment, Philadelphia Studies Assert," *PB*, May 21, 1967.

30. McLaughlin, "Application to the Department of Housing and Urban Development," March 3, 1967, I:11–12, III J:7–16.

31. Paul F. Levy, "Planning Fund for N. Phila. Cut Is Cut in Half; U.S. Agency Finds Scope of Rebuilding Project Too Large," *PB*, April 21, 1967; Francis M. Lordan, "'Model City' Aid Cut Denied," *PB*, April 22, 1967; Lordan, "Area Council Fights Change in Model City Plan," *PB*, May 9, 1967; AWC, "Maximum Feasible Manipulation," 380–81; "The View from City Hall," 392.

32. "Phila. to Get $178,000 for 'Model Cities,'" *PB*, November 16, 1967; AWC, "Maximum Feasible Manipulation," 380–81; "The View from City Hall," 392–93.

33. Accounts of the number injured and arrested varied. Matthew Countryman, *Up South: Civil Rights and Black Power in Philadelphia* (Philadelphia: University of Pennsylvania Press, 2006), 223–30; Paolantonio, *Frank Rizzo*, 91–94; AWC, "Maximum Feasible Manipulation," 380–81; "The View from City Hall," 392–93.

34. Kos Semonski, "Mayor Plans Inquiry into Student Protest," *PB*, November 23, 1967; Paolantonio, *Frank Rizzo*, 87–94; Countryman, *Up South*, 240–41.

35. Semonski, "Mayor Plans Inquiry into Student Protest"; AWC, "Maximum Feasible Manipulation," 380–81; "The View from City Hall," 392–93; Countryman, *Up South*, 303–4; Mike Mallowe, "The $75 Million Misunderstanding," *PM*, February 1973, 174.

36. Nicholas W. Stroh, "Model Cities Unit Pledges Attack on 'Unrest in N. Phila.,'" *PB*, December 8, 1967; "Sign Contract or Else, City Tells Meek," *PB*, December 13, 1967; "$21,000-a-Month Budget Sought from City 2d Time by Model Cities Council," *PI*, December 20, 1967; Jack Smyth, "Restoration of Model City Funds Sought," *PB*, December 27, 1967; AWC, "Maximum Feasible Manipulation," 381–82; "The View from City Hall," 393–94.

37. "Lawyer Named Director of Model Cities," *PB*, June 20, 1968; "The View from City Hall," 393–96; AWC, "Maximum Feasible Manipulation," 382–84; Countryman, *Up South*, 304–5.

38. AWC, "Maximum Feasible Manipulation," 384; "The View from City Hall," 396.

39. The Economic Development Unit (EDU) Advisory Council had discussed the community corporation concept as early as fall 1966. EAC, "Minutes," January 3, 1967, 2; "Maximum Feasible Manipulation," 385; "The View from City Hall," 395–97; Countryman, *Up South,* 305–6.

40. Bedell, "Ghetto Needs Entrepreneurs," *PI,* January 12, 1969; "Maximum Feasible Manipulation," 385; Oberman, "A Proposal for Economic Development Submitted to the Model Cities Administration of Philadelphia," October 1969, GPC, Box 791-4 (vol. 4), TUUA.

41. Oberman, "A Proposal for Economic Development Submitted to the Model Cities Administration of Philadelphia," 8–37.

42. AWC, "Maximum Feasible Manipulation," 385; Oberman, "A Proposal for Economic Development Submitted to the Model Cities Administration of Philadelphia," 8–17; Bedell, "Ghetto Needs Entrepreneurs."

43. O'Connor, "Swimming against the Tide," 108–10; "The View from City Hall," 397–98; Kloman, "Citizen Participation in the Philadelphia Model Cities Program," 405–6.

44. Kendall Wilson, "Goldie Watson, City's First Black Deputy Mayor," *PT,* June 3, 1994; "5 Teachers Suspended," *NYT,* February 20, 1954; "Teacher Case Declined," *NYT,* December 6, 1960; Mallowe, "The $75 Million Misunderstanding," 74; Countryman, Up South, 35–44.

45. "The View from City Hall," 397–400; AWC, "Maximum Feasible Manipulation," 385–86.

46. "The View from City Hall," 400; Kloman, "Citizen Participation in the Philadelphia Model Cities Program," 407.

47. The city appealed the decision to the U.S. Supreme Court, which refused to hear the case. Kloman, "Citizen Participation in the Philadelphia Model Cities Program," 400–402, 407–8; Mallowe, "The $75 Million Misunderstanding," 72–74, 175; "The View from City Hall," 399–402.

48. City of Philadelphia, "Philadelphia Model Cities Program Handbook: The Plan Is You!" n.d. [April 1973], GPC, Box 597-1, 7.

49. Mallowe, "The $75 Million Misunderstanding," 76–77, 177–79. For summaries of the economic program's operation up to 1972, Walter D'Alessio, interviewed by Walter M. Phillips, June 7, 1977, transcript, POHP, Box 3, TUUA, 13; Office of the City Controller , "Model Cities Economic Development Project," December 11, 1972, MCF, RG 60-2.5, Box A-3621, CA, 7.

50. D'Alessio, interviewed by Phillips, 13–14; Walter D'Alessio, "Memo to: Alec Bastos; Subject: Possible Projects for the Expenditure of Model Cities Economic Development," May 7, 1973, MCF, RG 60-2.6, Box A-3426, PIDC, CA; PIDC, News Release, November 1974, GPPR, Acc. 612, Box 12, Folder: PIDC

Correspondence, TUUA, 1–2. For Gola's additional charges and the federal action, see Mallowe, "The $75 Million Misunderstanding," 74–76.

51. Joseph Oberman, "A Proposal for Economic Development Submitted to the Model Cities Administration of Philadelphia," 32–34; PIDC, "Minutes of the Executive Committee Meeting of the Philadelphia Industrial Development Corporation," April 13, 1971, MCF, RG 60-2.5, Box A-3837, Philadelphia Industrial Development Corp., CA, 3.

52. D'Alessio, interviewed by Phillips, 13–14. Also, Walter D'Alessio, "Memo to: Alec Bastos; Subject: Possible Projects for the Expenditure of Model Cities Economic Development," May 7, 1973, MCF, RG 60-2.6, Box A-3426, PIDC, CA; D'Alessio to Goldie Watson, Director, Model Cities Administration, August 1, 1973, MCF, ibid.; PIDC, "Proposed Industrial Development Projects of Direct Benefit to Residents of Model Cities," August 1, 1973, MCF, ibid.

53. For PIDC's twenty-four transactions in the Model Cities area between 1965 and 1970, Robert H. Lurcott, "Memo to Jan Vegas; Subject: Economic Development Section of Workable Program Submission [draft materials, table 6 & appendix 23]," October 7, 1971, DC-IDPF, RG 64.18, Box A-5198, Planning Commission, CA.

54. "$7.5 Million Mill Planned on Spring Garden St.," PB, January 10, 1974; Peter H. Binzen, "A $7.5 Million Bet on Philadelphia; Knitting Company Decides to Stay in Town," PB, January 10, 1974; Daniel F. O'Leary, "PIDC Deal Makes Room for 2,500 Jobs; Merck Building Converted for Lease to Industries," PB, June 30, 1963.

55. Walter D'Alessio to Donald Cutler, May 29, 1973, MCF, RG 60-2.6, Box A-3426, PIDC, CA, 1–2; D'Alessio to Watson, August 1, 1973; PIDC, "Proposed Industrial Development Projects of Direct Benefit to Residents of Model Cities," August 1, 1973, MCF, ibid.; D'Alessio, "Memo to: Alec Bastos," May 7, 1973, 2; PIDC, News Release, November 1974, GPPR, Acc. 612, Box 12, PIDC Correspondence, TUUA, 2; D'Alessio, interviewed by Phillips, 15; PIDC, "1973 Annual Report," GPMR, Acc. 294, 296, 307, 311, Box 6A, Garment Industry Development, 1973, TUUA, 2.

56. Harold A. Barker, "Memo to: Philip Carroll and Anthony Zecca; Subject: PIDC Executive Committee Meeting of August 7, 1973," August 8, 1973, MCF, RG 60-2.6, Box A-3426, PIDC, CA; "$7.5 Million Mill Planned on Spring Garden St.," PB, January 10, 1974; PIDC, News Release, November 1974. Quotation from: Binzen, "A $7.5 Million Bet on Philadelphia," PB, January 10, 1974.

57. Bob Schwabach, "Knitting Mill Paints Its Walls to Say 'We Care,'" PI, February 20, 1975.

58. In 1992, Phillips–Van Heusen moved Somerset's production to Puerto Rico. Faced with a steep drop in business, the company sought to lower its costs by consolidating operations and cutting labor costs. A union leader remarked that

"even if we agreed to give up 50 percent of wages, it wouldn't have been enough to offset the loss of business and customers." After Somerset closed, the Red Cross moved its Philadelphia blood processing operations into the building. Raymond A. Berens, "Apparel Tenants Buy 9-Story Building for Garment Center," *PB*, November 24, 1974; John T. Gillespie, "Firm Flouts a Trend, Eyes Expansion in City; 100 More Jobs Seen at Somerset Mills," *PB*, April 25, 1977; Tawn Nhan, "The Local Apparel Industry Unravels," *PI*, May 4, 1992; Julia C. Martinez, "The Red Cross, Urban Pioneer: Spring Garden Street Awaits a Transfusion," *PI*, September 20, 1992.

59. Pamela Haines, "Clothing and Textiles: The Departure of an Industry," in Raines et al., eds., *Community and Capital in Conflict*, 211–19; Edward B. Shils, "Philadelphia's Apparel Industry: A Digest of the Findings and Recommendations of the Industry Study," May 1966, GPC, Box 518-12, TUUA, 3–11, 15–21; "City's Apparel and Textile Industry Clings to Hope of Better Days Ahead," *Focus: Philadelphia's Independent Business Newsweekly*, September 8, 1971, GPMR, Acc. 294, 296, 307, 311, Box 6A, Apparel Industry, 1971, TUUA, 1, 12; Shils to William L. Rafsky, October 21, 1971, GPMR, Acc. 294, 296, 307, 311, Box 6A, ibid.; Rafsky, "Memo to: Files; Subject: November 18 Meeting Re. Apparel Industry," November 24, 1971, GPMR, ibid.; "The Garment Industry in Philadelphia: Why We Need It; How We Improve It: A Challenge for the 70s," n.d., [1973], GPMR, Acc. 294, 296, 307, 311, Box 6A, Garment Industry Development, 1973, TUUA, 1–2; [Joseph Egan, James Mahoney, and James Martin], "Proposal for a Comprehensive Program of Assistance to the Garment Industry and Garment Employment Trades for Philadelphia," ibid., 1–4.

60. In a 1966 survey of 304 firms, Edward Shils determined that 88.8 percent of apparel industry workers lived within the city limits and that African Americans constituted 50 percent of the workforce. Shils, "Philadelphia's Apparel Industry," 15–23; [Egan, Mahoney, and Martin], "Proposal for a Comprehensive Program of Assistance," 1, 3; "A Proposal for a GPM Action Project," September 22, 1970, GPMR, Acc. 294, 296, 307, 311, Box 6A, Apparel Industry, 1971, TUUA. For the employment statistics, U.S. Bureau of the Census, *Census of Manufacturers, 1967 Vol. III, Area Statistics, Part 2, Pennsylvania* (Washington, D.C.: U.S. Government Printing Office, 1971), 39–38; U.S. Bureau of the Census, *Census of Manufacturers, 1972, Vol. III, Area Statistics, Part 2, Pennsylvania* (Washington, D.C.: U.S. Government Printing Office, 1976), 39–38; Carmen Theresa Whalen, *from Puerto Rico to Philadelphia: Puerto Rican Workers and Postwar Economies* (Philadelphia: Temple University Press, 2001), 142–52.

61. Shils, "Philadelphia's Apparel Industry," 4–5, 8–14; PIDC, ["A Proposal for a Garment Center at … "], 1967, RG 60-2.5, Box A-4566, Phila. Industrial Development Corp., CA; William Zucker, "Memorandum on Philadelphia's Apparel Industry," n.d. [1971], GPMR, Acc. 294, 296, 307, 311, Box 6A, Apparel Industry, 1971, TUUA, 1; Shils to Rafsky, October 21, 1971.

62. Zucker, "Memorandum on Philadelphia's Apparel Industry," n.d. [1971], 3; [Egan, Mahoney, and Martin], "Proposal for a Comprehensive Program of Assistance," 1, 3, 7–8; "The Garment Industry in Philadelphia," n.d., [1973], 3–6; James Martin to Stephen S. Gardner, May 1, 1973, GPMR, Acc. 294, 296, 307, 311, Box 6A, Garment Industry Development, 1973; Russell Byers, "Memorandum to: GPM Executive Committee; Subject: Garment Industry Proposal," May 8, 1973, GPMR, ibid.; "Confirmed Membership of the Philadelphia Garment Industry Board as of June 26, 1973," GPMR, ibid.; City of Philadelphia, Office of the Mayor, "News Release: Remarks by Mayor Frank L. Rizzo; Garment Industry Center," June 28, 1973, GPMR, ibid.; PIDC, "1973 Annual Report" (unpaginated, Special Projects section); Shils to Rafsky, October 21, 1971, 2.

63. Office of the Mayor, "News Release: Remarks by Mayor Frank L. Rizzo; Garment Industry Center," June 28, 1973, 2; City of Philadelphia, Office of the Mayor, "News Release: Remarks by Mayor Frank L. Rizzo; Garment Square Day," September 18, 1973, GPMR, Acc. 294, 296, 307, 311, Box 6A, Garment Industry Development, 1973; PIDC, "News Release," November 1974, 2–3; [Egan, Mahoney, and Martin], "Proposal for a Comprehensive Program of Assistance," 5–6; "The Garment Industry in Philadelphia," n.d. [1973], 3–5; PIDC, "Annual Report 1975," POHP, Box 3, Walter D'Alessio, TUUA, 12–13.

64. Walter D'Alessio, "Memorandum to: The Worriers; Subject: Community Development Block Grant Program—Economic Development," April 13, 1976, GPPR, Acc. 307, 311, 382 (December 1975–October 1977), Box 7, Philadelphia Industrial Development Corporation (PIDC), TUUA, 1–2; PIDC, "Model Cities Land Development Program," and "City Wide Land Development Program," n.d. [attached to April 13, 1976 D'Alessio memo], GPPR, ibid.; City of Philadelphia, "The Housing and Community Development Act of 1974," Development News, October–November 1974, GPC Box 585–13, TUUA, 1–3; Greater Philadelphia Partnership, "Philadelphia's Community Development Block Grant Program: Its Past and Future," March 1977, GPC 451–3, TUUA, 9–17, 73–74.

65. PIDC, Annual Reports, 1983, 1986, 1988, Free Library of Philadelphia, Government Documents Collection, Cities P53-1320; PIDC, Annual Report, 1988, 13.

66. Andrew Feffer, "The Land Belongs to the People: Reframing Urban Protest in Post-Sixties Philadelphia," in The World the Sixties Made: Politics and Culture in Recent America, ed. Van Gosse and Richard Moser (Philadelphia: Temple University Press, 2003), 67–99.

67. Paolantonio, Frank Rizzo, 190–97, 202–9, 238; Luce and Summers, Local Fiscal Issues in the Philadelphia Metropolitan Area, 98–107; Adams, The Politics of Capital Investment, 49–52; Adams et al., Philadelphia, 132, 140–43.

68. Luce and Anita A. Summers, Local Fiscal Issues in the Philadelphia Metropolitan Area, 106, 112–13, 127–29; Pennsylvania Economy League—Eastern Division (PEL), Factbook on the Philadelphia Economy 1995 (Philadelphia: Pennsylvania Economy League, November 1995), iii, 1–11, 21–24; Paolantonio, Rizzo,

203–4, 237–40; Carolyn Teich Adams, *The Constrained City*, the Integrative Paper Series of Philadelphia: Past, Present and Future, Paper 3 (Philadelphia: School of Public and Urban Policy, University of Pennsylvania, 1982), 1–2; William P. Hankowsky, "The Philadelphia Center for Health Care Sciences," *Economic Development Review* 9:4 (Fall 1991): 74–75; U.S. Department of Commerce, Bureau of the Census, *City and County Data Books 1972 and 1983* (Washington, DC: United States Government Printing Office, 1972, 1983).

69. Memo to Steve Gardner, n.d. [1973], GPMR, Acc. 294, 296, 307, 311, Box 6A, Garment Industry Development, 1973, TUUA, 2–3; [Egan, Mahoney, and Martin], "Proposal for a Comprehensive Program of Assistance," 9.

70. U.S. Bureau of the Census, *Census of Manufacturers, 1982 Vol. III, Area Statistics, Part 2, Pennsylvania* (Washington, D.C.: U.S. Government Printing Office, 1985), PA-90; U.S. Census Bureau, *1997 Economic Census; Manufacturing; Geographic Area Series: Pennsylvania* (Washington, D.C.: U.S. Census Bureau, 2000), 111.

71. Nhan, "Local Apparel Industry Unravels"; Don Russell, "Unions Mark Labor Day Despite Bad Times," *PDN*, September 3, 2002.

Conclusion

1. Sam Bass Warner, "If All the World Were Philadelphia: A Scaffolding for Urban History, 1774–1930," *American Historical Review* 74:1 (October 1968): 26–43.

2. Robert O. Self, *American Babylon: Race and the Struggle for Postwar Oakland* (Princeton, NJ: Princeton University Press, 2003); Mike Davis, *City of Quartz: Excavating the Future in Los Angeles* (New York: Verso Press, 1990); Becky M. Nicolaides, *My Blue Heaven: Life and Politics in the Working Class Suburbs of Los Angeles, 1920–1965* (Chicago: University of Chicago Press, 2002); Thomas J. Sugrue, *The Origins of the Urban Crisis: Race and Inequality in Postwar Detroit* (Princeton, NJ: Princeton University Press, 1996); June Manning Thomas, *Redevelopment and Race: Planning a Finer City in Postwar Detroit* (Baltimore: Johns Hopkins University Press, 1997); Arnold R. Hirsch, *Making the Second Ghetto: Race and Housing in Chicago, 1940–1960* (New York: Cambridge University Press, 1983); Amanda I. Seligman, *Block by Block: Neighborhoods and Public Policy on Chicago's West Side* (Chicago: University of Chicago Press, 2005); John F. Bauman, *Public Housing, Race, and Renewal: Urban Planning in Philadelphia, 1920–1974* (Philadelphia: Temple University Press, 1987); James Wolfinger, *Philadelphia Divided: Race and Politics in the City of Brotherly Love* (Chapel Hill: University of North Carolina Press, 2007).

3. Sara Stoutland, "Community Development Corporations: Mission, Strategy, and Accomplishments" in *Urban Problems and Community Development*, ed. William T. Dickens and Ronald F. Ferguson (Washington, D.C.: Brookings

Institution Press, 1999); Martha Biondi, *To Stand and Fight: The Struggle for Civil Rights in Postwar New York City* (Cambridge: Harvard University Press, 2003); Joshua B. Freeman, *Working Class New York: Life and Labor Since World War II* (New York: New Press, 2000), 145–50.

4. Matthew D. Lassiter, *The Silent Majority: Suburban Politics in the Sunbelt South* (Princeton: Princeton University Press, 2005).

Index

(Page Numbers in *italics* refer to illustrations.)